Henry Eyster Jacobs

The Lutheran Commentary

Vol. I.

Henry Eyster Jacobs

The Lutheran Commentary
Vol. I.

ISBN/EAN: 9783337103637

Printed in Europe, USA, Canada, Australia, Japan

Cover: Foto ©Lupo / pixelio.de

More available books at **www.hansebooks.com**

THE LUTHERAN COMMENTARY

A PLAIN EXPOSITION OF THE

Holy Scriptures of the New Testament

BY

SCHOLARS OF THE LUTHERAN CHURCH IN AMERICA

EDITED BY

HENRY EYSTER JACOBS

VOL. I.

New York
The Christian Literature Co.
MDCCCXCV

ANNOTATIONS

ON THE

GOSPEL ACCORDING TO ST. MATTHEW

BY

CHARLES F. SCHAEFFER, D.D.

Formerly Professor of Theology, in Capital University, Columbus, O., and in the Theological Seminary of the General Synod, Gettysburg, Pa.; and Chairman of the Theological Faculty in the Lutheran Theological Seminary, Philadelphia, Pa.

PART I.—MATTHEW I.—XV.

New York
The Christian Literature Co.
MDCCCXCV

COPYRIGHT, 1895,
BY
THE CHRISTIAN LITERATURE CO.

INTRODUCTION TO THE LUTHERAN COMMENTARY.

THE Lutheran Commentary owes its name, as well as its suggestion, to the enterprising firm that publishes it. A demand has been found for a plain and unequivocal exposition of the New Testament, which, while not indifferent to the advances made in scholarly criticism, may be depended upon for its loyalty to the faith of Gospel, as that faith was taught by the Lutheran Church in the century of Reformation. Mere negations soon tire. The critical spirit reacts upon itself; and the specious hypotheses offered as substitutes for the teachings of the old faith, soon fall victims to the very weapons which they direct against Christianity. The exhibits of exegetical processes that present no results, but are accumulated as contributions to the history of the exposition of the Bible, are not without value. But they must constantly yield in importance to those works that aim simply at attaining and conveying the meaning of God's Word. We demand expositors having positive convictions concerning that which they expound, and who express these convictions with directness and point. The Bible is not to be commented upon as a literary curiosity, or to be made the groundwork for the display of ingenuity in the application of learning to literary criticism. It is to be reverently used, and prayerfully expounded, as the revelation of an All-wise and All-holy God to sinful and erring mortals, who, without the enlightening influences of the Holy Spirit, are incapable of understanding a single sentence found within its pages.

If the term "Lutheran" applied mainly to a particular ecclesiastical organization, its use here would be objectionable. But as the name of a specific form of Christian life, referring, within the intellectual sphere, to a particular type of Christian doctrine, and within the sphere of exposition, to a particular mode of treating God's Word, it can certainly be employed without any reflection upon those who are not in the communion of the Lutheran Church. The object is not to bring into prominence the matters in doctrine and exposition that are distinctive of this Church; but at the same time not to avoid any statement or interpretation because such is distinctive of Lutheranism. Lutheran exposition is with us that of concrete Evangelical Christianity, including all the features of distinctive Lutheranism, and proportioned according to the standards of Lutheranism. This necessarily implies the grateful use and recognition of much in other expositors that does not claim to be Lutheran. For such is the Lutheran conception of the Church and Christianity itself, as not to be determined by external boundaries, but, as "the communion of saints," to underlie and pass beyond the limits of all ecclesiastical organizations, imparting to all the children of God, however scattered, a share in each other's labors, and each other's confession.

The name "Lutheran" ought always, in the sphere of scholarship, to designate first of all devotion to exegetical study. Luther and his associates, as theologians, were above all else exegetes. Whatever other theological learning they possessed was made entirely subservient to their calling as expounders of both the letter and spirit of the Holy Scriptures. Book by book, chapter by chapter, verse by verse, Luther expounded the Holy Scripture to his students at Wittenberg. Melanchthon's *Loci* grew out of his introduction to his lectures on Romans. Even with this great dogmatician of the Reformation period of the Lutheran Church, his system was only formulated as an aid to elucidate frequently recurring terms in the New Testament. Lutheran Theology of the Sixteenth Century is preponderantly exegetical. From Luther to Chemnitz inclusive, the greatest care is taken to keep within the bounds of the very statements of Holy Scripture, and not to draw inferences, even with apparent logical consistency, where the Scriptures are silent. Chemnitz's *Loci*, the greatest Lutheran treatise on Systematic Theology of the Sixteenth Century, may be called according to the terminology of to-day, a Biblical Theology.'

The decline of Lutheranism began, as Dogmatical Theology gradually encroached upon the domain of exegesis, and the strength of teachers was expended more upon the elaboration of systems than upon fresh and living contact with the Word of God. The work of the great masters of the Seventeenth Century is not to be disparaged. The dogmatician has, as well as the exegete, his calling in the kingdom of God. The results attained by one generation, if they are to be permanently preserved, must be gathered and classified by the generation that follows. But a twofold error resulted. On the topics, that were treated by their predecessors, they were too much content to abide by the results already attained, instead of pressing forward in the same line of exegetical treatment. On those topics which had not entered into elaborate discussion during the time of their fathers, they resorted too much, in order to complete the system and give it a symmetrical development, to the material found in the scholastics of the Middle Ages. For this entire tendency, the divines who composed the Confessions of the Lutheran Church, from the Catechisms to the Formula of Concord inclusive, were not responsible.

The Lutheran Church was saved, however, from the full consequences of the later development by two circumstances. One was the expository mode of preaching that prevailed, based generally upon the pericopes of the Church Year. That this mode is capable of abuse from the temptation afforded by a vast mass of material made ready for the homiletical purposes of the preacher, is undoubtedly true. Any mode of preaching, that is not accompanied by constantly fresh study of the Holy Scriptures, and the stimulus of new discoveries, on the part of the preacher, of riches hitherto hidden from him in the Divine Word, must become lifeless and mechanical. Nevertheless where the pericopes are followed, or other lessons from the Scriptures are explained according to an established order, the mind of the people is brought in a peculiar way, to the sources of spiritual life.

Another compensation was the numerous and rich popular expositions of Scripture, found in the massive Bibles of the two centuries succeeding the Reformation. Commend, as we may, the Bible without note or comment, the importance of notes and comments to introduce the reader into its meaning cannot be questioned. It was for this reason, that, while Rationalism might prevail at the Universities and do much damage among the clergy, the homes of the people were, in large degree, proof against its attacks, and furnished a second generation of theologians and pastors, who repudiated the unscriptural theories of their immediate predecessors.

A great impulse has been given in late years to the study

of the Bible. That the movement has not been in all respects a wholesome or a reverent one, cannot be denied. Certain systems of philosophy, the testimony of the Christian experience of individuals, the contents of the experience in the entire community, known as the invisible Church or fellowship of believers, etc., have successively been constituted the standards according to which to interpret both the Old and the New Testament. The statement of the Formula of Concord that the Holy Scriptures are to be the sole touch-stone according to which all teachers and doctrines are to be judged has been completely reversed. One class of interpreters start out with the assumption of the impossibility of the miraculous, and assort the material of each Biblical book in such a way as to exclude all its supernatural elements. Another class, admitting the supernatural element, denies the authority of the passages of Scriptures that state occurrences that cannot be verified by the experience of Christians or of the Church of to-day.

Certainly the very error against which the Reformation was a protest, is involved in this controversy. The modern Negative Criticism is Romanism over again, only adorned with a new name, and wearing a new disguise. Both elevate human authority above the word of God as taught in Holy Scripture. Perhaps the greatest peril to Modern Christianity lies in the threatened union of these closely allied, but apparently antagonistic forces, viz. the Rationalism of extreme ecclesiasticism, which exalts polity above doctrine, with the Rationalism of extreme radicalism, which exalts reason above Revelation. The Mediæval system, against which the reaction, known as Lutheranism, arose, was the result of the application of the philosophy of Aristotle to the truths of Christianity. While the ostensible aim was only to clothe the material of Christianity with the form of Aristotelianism, to cast its rich substance into the molds of the thoughts of the Stagirite, the process was often reversed, and the material became that of Aristotle, while only the form of Christianity was retained. So in later days, new systems of philosophy have arisen that have treated Christianity and the Holy Scriptures, precisely as they were treated by the scholastics. Theological schools that seem to be antagonistic to each other, are thus found to differ, not within the sphere of Theology, but only within that of Philosophy. A Church Union among them should not be difficult, since they all alike agree in subordinating the Holy Scriptures to reason. What the end will be no one can tell.

But the experience of the Church in past ages testifies that the ultimate effect of skepticism, is that God's people are driven anew to the study of the Scriptures, and that rich results follow by their use of the material accumulated and the weapons used even by their opponents. Every item of truth discovered by even the most relentless foe of Christianity, in so far as it is actually truth, only advances the cause for whose discomfiture it was intended. The more the world rages, the closer they cleave to the simple word of their Master.

There is a place for the extensive scientific discussion of Holy Scripture, which subjects the assumptions of the most advanced critics to thorough criticism. There is also a place for the positive exhibition of results and principles, independently of the review of the battle that may be raging around them. This Commentary belongs to the latter class. While the scope and mode of exposition necessarily varies with the individual writer, the general aim is to mediate between the more popular and the strictly scientific exposition.

The opening volumes on Matthew, prepared before this

series was projected, had a more popular end in view. Its scope also is somewhat more extensive than the scheme of the Commentary provided. But so thorough is its treatment, that, even though it may be regarded at first sight as not entirely up to date, we are sure that the general verdict will be one of most sincere gratitude that such an exposition was at hand. It has undoubtedly merits which will gain for it a very high rank among Commentaries in the English language upon St. Matthew. The author with his characteristic painstaking accuracy had mastered the literature of the subject down to the period at which he wrote. Nor can we find in more recent literature any substantial additions to what he has given. Many more recent discussions, notwithstanding their pretensions, do little more than run around a circle, one generation of scholars completely undoing the work of their immediate predecessors. It is remarkable how thoroughly the judgment of Dr. Schaeffer has anticipated not only the changes in translation made by the Revised Version, but also the results attained by most recent scholars.

Charles Frederick Schaeffer was the youngest member of a distinguished family of Lutheran clergymen. The son of Rev. F. D. Schaeffer, D. D., Pastor in Philadelphia, he was born in Germantown, Sept. 3d, 1807. His three brothers were prominent Lutheran pastors. A graduate of the University of Pennsylvania, after completing his theological studies in Philadelphia, he served pastorates at Carlisle, Pa.; Hagerstown, Md.; Lancaster, O.; Red Hook, N. Y., and Easton, Pa. He was Professor of Theology first at Columbus, O. (1840–5), Gettysburg, Pa. (1855-64), and Philadelphia (1864–79). In the Lutheran Seminary in Philadelphia, he was Chairman of the Faculty from its organization until his death, Nov. 23d. 1879. He represented the strictly conservative type of Lutheran

Theology, and was one of the most earnest advocates of a strict adherence to all the Confessions of the Lutheran Church.

As an author, he is known to scholars outside of his own Church by his translation of Kurtz's Sacred History, long used as a text-book in many Theological Seminaries in this country, and his translation, with additions, of Lechler's Commentary on Acts in the Lange series. The minuteness and comprehensiveness of his scholarship are sufficiently attested by the latter volume, which justly can be claimed to be one of the best of that most valuable set of Commentaries, his additions raising it immeasurably above the Edinburgh translation of the same volume. No one has combined more successfully the very best methods of the experienced and conscientious pastor with those of the scholarly theologian and accomplished teacher. There is an absence of all speculation that is not directed to some practical end. In the class-room, as well as in the pulpit, he knew how to apply the words of Holy Scripture in the most searching manner.

Throughout the entire exposition of St. Matthew, the qualities appear, of which one who knew him most intimately (the late Dr. B. M. Schmucker) has said:

"He was a born teacher. All the peculiarities of his mind, and all the habits of his life, united to make him excel in this office. The minute accuracy, even in the least matters, which his nature required, made him both exact and exacting as a teacher. Nothing was trivial, no generalities would satisfy, precise knowledge and accurate statement were absolutely necessary with him. The enthusiasm too with which he entered into every study was contagious, and communicated itself to his students. Above all, his convictions of truth were so absolute; all doubts had been overcome and the assurance of faith was perfect. He could not rest satisfied with uncertainty. He must thoroughly and exhaustively examine the subject, and it was only thus that his convictions were attained, but, when attained, they were immovable."

This Commentary was completed shortly before Dr. Schaeffer's removal from Gettysburg to Philadelphia. Its publication was delayed probably by the diversion of his time and energy to his labors upon Lechler. While the copy was complete for the printer's hands, it was found that considerable condensation was necessary to bring the material within the space allowed in this series. This work was performed, with a reverent hand, by the author's son-in-law, Rev. Reuben Hill, D. D., Financial Secretary of the Theological Seminary at Mt. Airy. The condensation has been made chiefly by the omission of the practical inferences that close each chapter.

It is understood that the interpretation throughout the entire series are those of the individual authors. It would be remarkable if important divergences in this series would not become manifest in the interpretation of passages, as well as in the mode of treatment. The editor assumes no other responsibility than that of a general superintendence of the entire work. The details are left to each contributor.

The text used throughout the entire series is that of the Revised Version, as this obviates as a rule, the necessity of referring to defects in the Authorized Version, which would otherwise be frequent.

In the gracious Providence of God, this Commentary may become a means of affording the scattered Lutheran Church of America another bond of union, and contributing to a better understanding of the manner in which representatives, of its various sections teach God's Word. If this large and rapidly growing communion in America is ever to be externally united, it must first be united in its convictions as to the meaning of Holy Scripture. There will be one fold and one Shepherd, only as the sheep all hear the One Shepherd's voice and follow it.

May God bless this Lutheran Commentary to this end.

HENRY E. JACOBS.

LUTHERAN THEOLOGICAL SEMINARY.

MT. AIRY, PHILADELPHIA, *March 2nd*, 1895.

Since the above was written and, while this volume was being set up, Rev. Reuben Hill, D.D. (born July 22nd, 1826), who was seeing it through the press, was suddenly called away, after an illness of a few hours, on Sunday, March 3rd, 1895. One hundred and fifty-one pages of the proof had passed through his hands. It had been a delightful task for him, during his last months to be employed upon this interesting work. The same conscientious fidelity that characterized his labors in other spheres is manifest in the care with which this revision was made. His name will ever be held in the highest esteem by the people of the important parishes which he filled at Gettysburg, Pa., Hagerstown, Md., Pittsburgh, Pa., Rhinebeck and Rochester, N. Y., and Allentown, Pa. His chief monument, however, is found at Mount Airy in the grounds and buildings of the Theological Seminary. The location was chosen by his wise foresight, the new building erected under his direction and according to his plans, and the means for it were collected largely through his efforts. It was fitting, therefore, that, as a diligent student of the New Testament throughout his entire life, he should close it with this contribution to the exposition of the Holy Scriptures. Both the author and the reviser rest now from their labors; their work will follow them.

Long after the hand that writes has crumbled to dust, the witness to Christ that has been spoken through the pen of the writer, will continue its work upon earth, in fruit, bearing seed, that will again yield a harvest, as a germ for other harvests, that are yet to come.

H. E. J.

March, 5th 1895.

Google

PREFACE

THE author of the present work has, as a leading purpose in preparing it, steadily kept in view the intimate connection existing between the Old and the New Testaments; the latter, according to a remark once made by one of the Reformers of the Church in the Sixteenth Century, is the best interpreter of the former. As the Gospel according to St. Matthew exhibits this connection with great fulness, the references, in the following Annotations, to the Books of the Old Testament, will be found to be very numerous. After a pastoral experience of nearly thirty years, which furnished the author with numerous opportunities for instructing young persons in divine truth, and after an experience of several years in aiding in the work of preparing students of theology for the ministry, his early conviction of the importance of combining the Old Testament with the New in unfolding the treasures of the latter, has been fully established. The former presents in its numerous predictions the rich blossoms of devout hope, expanding with increasing beauty, until the abundant and wholesome fruit is furnished in the latter, which reveals the promised Messiah in all the glory of His divine power and love.

The author has conscientiously endeavored to exhibit the true sense of every portion of the text, without directly controverting adverse views; it was his object, not to engage in unprofitable discussion, but, as far as his means and opportunities extended, both to exhibit divine truth as taught on the sacred page, and also to honor the Redeemer. He has, in accordance with principles that are now well established and universally adopted in practice, availed himself of all the sources of information which the labors of other interpreters and of theological writers generally, have vendered accessible to him.

The author is largely indebted to the many able Commentaries on the Scriptures in general, and on the Gospel of St. Matthew in particular, which have already been presented to the Church; he has, in accordance with the common practice, inserted in his own words much valuable matter which others had collected, without mentioning the source in every case, believing that the present general acknowledgment will be deemed sufficient. The Commentaries, Notes or Explanations of the following authors have been regularly consulted:—*A. Barnes; J. J. Owens; M. W. Jacobus; J. A. Alexander* (Notes on Mark); *J. Macknight* (Harmony); *G. Campbell* (Four Gospels); *S. T. Bloomfield* (Notes); *H. Alford; Luther's* Works; *Olshausen; De Wette; H. A. W. Meyer; J. P. Lange;* (Bibelwerk); *Stier* (Reden Jesu); *Gerlach; Ebrard* (Kritik); *Lisco* (Parabeln); *Tholuck* (Bergpredigt); *Beausobre* (Rem. Historiques, etc.); *Jean Le Clerc* (Remarques); *Lightfoot* (Horæ Hebr.); *Grotius* (Annotationes); *Bengel* (Gnomon); *Kuinoel,* and others. Valuable contributions have also been made to the present work by the following:—*Trench* (Parables, Miracles); *Robinson* (Biblical Researches, etc., 3 vols.); *Karl von Raumer* (Palœstina); *K. F. Kiel* (Archæologie); *Herzog's* Real-Encyklopœdie; *Winer* (Realwoerterbuch); *Zeller's* Bibl. Woerterbuch, etc. Numerous other publications, such as the *Englishman's Greek Concordance; Coleman's* Text

Book and Atlas; *Josephus; Prideaux;* various Commentaries on the Old Testament: the Harmonies of *Griesbach* (Synopsis), *Newcome* and *Robinson;* early and recent works on New Testament Philology, etc., have been more or less frequently consulted during the progress of the work, and have rendered important aid.

Google

INTRODUCTION.

§ 1. Matthew, the writer of the present Gospel, first appears in history as a publican, and was originally named Levi (see the annotation to ch. 9, ver. 9). Of his early history no details have been preserved. Neither his labors as an apostle after the ascension of Christ, nor the circumstances under which he died, are recorded on the pages of authentic history.

§ 2. The Church-historian Eusebius remarks, on the authority of Papias, who lived soon after the apostles (Book III., ch. 24, ch. 39), that after Matthew had proclaimed the Gospel to his countrymen in Hebrew (or the dialect of Palestine), and when he was on the point of going to other nations, he committed the Gospel to writing in the same language, in order to supply the want of his presence by his writings. No ancient writer, however, whose works are extant, alleges that he saw this Hebrew [Aramaic] Gospel; it may have been a brief composition which soon afterwards disappeared, when Matthew prepared the present *Greek* narrative. His later experience of the rapid diffusion of Gospel truth among the vast numbers of those who spoke the Greek language, no doubt furnished him with a sufficient reason for giving to the Church a translation of his own work, or, more probably, a new and original history or Gospel in Greek. This production of his pen is the only one which we now possess. He was guided in the preparation of his Gospel by the same Holy Spirit who taught him when he proclaimed Gospel truth orally (Luke 12 : 11, 12); hence the present writing is an inspired work; containing pure and unmixed truth, taught by the unerring Spirit of God.

§ 3. The year in which Matthew wrote this Gospel is not known with precision. The words of the Lord recorded in ch. 24, ver. 15, compared with Matthew's own incidental remark in 27:8 and in 28:15, indicate, however, that while this Gospel was written before the actual destruction of Jerusalem, A. D. 70, a considerable period of time had elapsed since the ascension of the Saviour, A. D. 33; it was composed possibly in A. D. 60, but not later than A. D. 69, or rather A. D. 66, when the Jewish War commenced.

§ 4. The title, prefixed by a later hand (except, as it is said, the single word " Gospel ") is: " The Gospel according to St. Matthew." The word "Gospel," equivalent to " good tidings" (see ann. to 4 : 23, C.), is descriptive of the whole spirit of the narrative; the latter communicates the joyful intelligence to our fallen race that "the Son of man is come to seek and to save that which was lost " (Luke 19: 10). The phrase: "according to " simply indicates that the glorious truths and facts which are here revealed, are indeed in perfect harmony with those which the other three Gospels present, but that they are selected by Matthew from the vast amount of materials before him (John 21 : 25), arranged as a complete whole, and illustrated with a *special object* in view. This object—the exhibition of the evidence that Jesus Christ is the true Messiah promised by the prophets—is illustrated below, ch. 1 : 1, A. The word *Saint*, of which " St." is the abbreviation, simply means *holy*, and was applied already in the days of the apostles to prophets and to believers generally (see below, ann. to 27: 52, 53, B.). The early Church, adopting the practice of the apostles, applied the title, first, to the Evangelists and Apostles themselves, and then, to eminent martyrs. The word, subsequently, was often misapplied, and, after the rise of Popery, was given so indiscriminately, and, indeed, unwisely, that while it is sanctioned as a fitting epithet in itself by the apostolic usage, its employment has been almost entirely discontinued by many Protestants.

§ 5. Matthew adopts the following order of subjects in his narrative:—(I.) The early history of Christ, ch. 1, 2. (II.) John the Baptist, ch. 3. (III.) The temptation of Christ, ch. 4: 1-11. (IV.) The Lord's labors in Galilee—discourses and miracles—His conflicts with the Pharisees and others—premonitions of His sufferings and the glory that should follow, ch. 4: 12; 18: 35. (V.) The journey to Jerusalem, 19: 1; 20: 34. (VI.) Entrance into the city, and subsequent events, 21: 1; 23: 39. (VII.) Final discourses addressed to the disciples, ch. 24, 25. (VIII.) The ufferings and death of Christ, ch. 26, 27. (IX.) His ressurrection, and the commission given to the apostles. The other three evangelists, while they also begin with the earliest events in the life of Christ, and also close with an account of His death, have adopted other modes of arranging the intermediate matter which they present; each one appears to have chosen subjects either specially adapted to the wants of a particular class of readers, or else corresponding to the special purpose for which they record the life of Christ; the precise order in which different discourses, miracles, etc., are presented is then of no importance. The contents of the four Gospels, accordingly, cannot be arranged in four columns in such a manner that the same passage in one will correspond in location and contents precisely with the other three. If we take two different biographies of even a mere human being, for instance, of Luther or Washington, while the history of the birth and of the death of the individual will occupy similar places, the details in the body of the two books respectively, will be found to vary both in the general selection, and in the particular order and mode of expressing them, while both works may substantially coincide, and in no case contradict each other. The distinguished British divine, Newcome, remarks: "The evangelists are more intent on representing the substance of what is spoken, than the words of the speaker; they neglect accurate order in the details of particular incidents, though they pursue a good general method; detached and distant events are sometimes joined together on account of a sameness in the scene, the persons, the cause or the consequences; in such concise histories as the Gospels, transitions are often made from one fact to another, without any intimation that important matters intervened." (Newcome's Harmony of the Four Evangelists; preface, p. 1.)

ABBREVIATIONS, REFERENCES AND SIGNS

USED IN THIS VOLUME.

O. T. or *Old Test.* and *N. T.* respectively, indicate the Old and the New Testaments.

    ch. . . . . . . chapter.
    ver. . . . . . verse.
    ann. . . . . . annotation.
    art. . . . . . . article.
    lit. . . . . . . literally.
    transl. . . . . translated.
    comp. . . . compare, that is, the book, chapter and verse mentioned.

f. or ff, the verse or verses *following* the one specified.

e. g. (Latin, *exempli gratiâ*) for example, for instance.

A. B. C. etc. prefixed to clauses of verses, in the annotations, are designed both to distinguish the particular word or words explained, and also to facilitate the reference to any particular place, and that avoid repetition.

— This sign represents the two words: *that is*, or, *equivalent to*.

§ This sign marks sections or divisions of extended annotations, etc., and is designed for convenient reference.

: The colon (:) placed *after the number of a chapter* indicates that the next numeral or figure designates the *verse*. When two or more chapters are quoted from the same book, and at the same time, they are separated by a semicolon (;).

Google

CHAPTER I.

Verse 1. *The book of the generation of Jesus Christ, the son of David, the son of Abraham.*

A. The Book of the Generation. As it was the special object of Matthew to furnish Christians of Jewish birth with the evidence that our Saviour is the Messiah to whom Moses and the prophets refer (Luke 24:27; John 1:45), he commences his Gospel by connecting it with the records of the Old Testament. The numerous quotations from the latter show that it was the writer's intention to exhibit the fulfilment in Christ of a long series of predictions. Genealogical tables appear to have been the original source of Jewish historical composition. These family records often combined strictly genealogical matter with historical narratives. According to this view of the origin and subsequent use of the phrase, the first verse in Matthew is not merely the title of the genealogical table which immediately follows, but also of the whole Gospel, the main design of which is to demonstrate the truth of the statement in ver. 1, that Jesus Christ is the "son of David," in the sense explained below.—" In this first verse Matthew indicates, as in a Preface, that it is his purpose to write of Jesus Christ, the son of David, the son of Abraham. Behold, O man, thou art a sinner, and the penalty which thou deservest is death. But God has had mercy on thee, and sent a Saviour to thee, even as He promised unto Abraham and David. Have thou faith, rejoice and thank God for His mercy; behold the book of the generation of Jesus Christ is before thee, wherein it is written, for thy instruction and consolation, that the promises made of old, were all fulfilled in Jesus Christ."—(LUTHER.)—**B. Jesus Christ.** The signification of this name is: *Jehovah is the Saviour.* He who was " the Desire of all nations," Hagg. 2 : 7, is emphatically called the SAVIOUR of the world, 1 Tim. 1 : 15; 1 John 2 : 2, for He saves the soul of every believer from eternal death.—Many proper names of the Jews included those usually given to God; this practice appears to have been observed by the Jews in a spirit of reverence and devotion. Moses called one of his sons *Eleazer— God is my help*, Exod. 18 : 4; *Jeremiah* signifies *he whom Jehovah exalts; Elnathan* (2 K. 24 : 8) in Hebrew, like the Greek *Theodore* and *Dorothy*, signifies *gift of God.* The blessed Saviour "took part of flesh and blood," and was "found in fashion as a man," Phil. 2 : 8; he also assumed a name which common mortals had previously borne. "I am meek and lowly in heart," Matt. 11 : 29. The name CHRIST was not originally a proper name. The corresponding Hebrew word *Messiah*, in the sense of the *Anointed One*, was given in reference to their consecration, as an official title, to *priests* (Ex. 28 : 41; Lev. 4 : 3, 5; 8 : 12). In 1 Sam. 2 : 10; Ps. 18 : 50, *King* and *Anointed* occur as equivalent terms. The spiritual import of the act of anointing is specially indicated in Isai. 61 : 1, which passage prophetically describes the Redeemer, Luke 4 : 17-21. The inspired prophets taught the Jews that they should be delivered from all the evils which they suffered, by a descendant of David, whom they described as a *prophet, priest* and *king.* At a later period, all these offices, as combined in the Person of the Saviour, were summarily expressed in the one Hebrew word Messiah, Dan. 9 : 25, 26. In John 4 : 25, 26, the

Lord announces that he is the Messiah. The Hebrew word was then translated into Greek, in which language it assumed the form of *Christ*, John 1:41; 7:41; the Greek name was finally transferred, without material change, to the Latin and other languages. It was originally added to the name of Jesus in order to designate His comprehensive office, as when He is called "*the* Christ," in Matt. 16:20; 26:63, frequently in the Gospels of Mark, Luke and John, and particularly in the Acts, as 2:36; 9;22. It was soon, however, employed in the Church after the manner of a proper name, as the Lord Himself once used it, John 17:3.

The various names which the Son of God receives in the N. T. are all highly significant and instructive, as they present His Person and His Work to the devout mind in all their different aspects. He is our Prophet or Teacher, Matt. 11:29, and Example, 1 Pet. 2:21; our High Priest, who offered up Himself as a sacrifice, Heb. 7:25-27; our King, Matt. 21:5; Heb. 1:8; 2 Pet. 1:11. He is the Good Shepherd, John 10:11. He will hereafter appear as our Judge, Matt. 16:27; Acts 10:42.

C. The Son of David. The Jews occasionally used the word *son* to designate a grandson, 2 Sam. 19:24, or even a remote descendant, Joel 2:28; thus in ver. 20 below, Joseph the descendant of David, is called his *son*. The Scriptures of the O. T. frequently (2 Sam. 7:12, 13; Ps. 132:11; Isai. 9:7; 11:1; Jerem. 23:5) represent the Messiah as a son—descendant of the great King David. In the sense of *Messiah*, the name is given to Christ in Matt. 9:27; 12:23; 20:30; 21:9; 22:42; Luke 1:32; John 7:42; Acts 2:30. Matthew, therefore, after furnishing the genealogy which contained the proof of Christ's regular descent from David, proceeds to demonstrate in the succeeding chapters, by the exhibition of the discourses and acts of the Lord, that He was also *the Christ*, the Messiah of whose coming the prophets had spoken.—D. **The Son of Abraham.** Jesus Christ is also the son or descendant of Abraham. Matthew intends by this clause to imply, not that David was a son of Abraham, which fact all well knew, nor simply that Christ was, according to the flesh, a Jew, a descendant of Abraham through David, but that He was *that* seed in which, according to the divine promise (Gen. 22 : 18), all the nations of the earth should be blessed (Gal. 3 : 16). The Gospel of Matt., as a whole, contains the explanation of the manner in which the divine promise made to Abraham was fulfilled by the atonement of Christ. The blessings granted in consequence of Abraham's faith (Gal. 3 : 9), prevailed over the curse pronounced after the fall (Gen. ch. 3). " Where sin abounded, etc.," Gal. 5 : 20.

² Abraham begat Isaac; and Isaac begat Jacob; and Jacob begat Judah and his brethren;

A. Preliminary Observation. Another genealogy is found in Luke 3 : 23–38, which, as it is usually and satisfactorily explained, exhibits the *natural* descent of Jesus through Mary His mother. The annotations which follow here refer exclusively to the names presented in the present Gospel. These names are usually regarded as those of the ancestors of Joseph, through whom the *legal* descent or succession of Christ, or His legal right to the kingdom, is exhibited.

The double genealogy of Christ, as well as the obscurity in which some of the names are involved, may be illustrated in general by the following case : In Numb. 32 : 39–41, Deut. 3 : 14, 15, Jair is called the son of Machir, of the tribe of Manasseh, in the territory of which his family inheritance accordingly lay. Nevertheless the same Jair, according to another genealogy in 1 Chron. 2: 3, 4, 5, 9, 21, 22, 24, is a descendant of Judah, through his father, who is here called Hezron. It appears from the statement of this chapter, however, that Hezron, the paternal grandfather of Jair, belonged to the tribe of Judah, and that the inheritance of his first children also lay in that tribe; at a later period of his life, he took a second wife, Abiah, a daughter of Machir, who belonged to the tribe of Manasseh, Numb. 27: 1. His first son by this marriage was Segub, the father of Jair. Ashur, his second son by this marriage, who was a posthumous son (1 Chron. 2: 24, born shortly after his father's death), received his inheritance in Judah, to which his father belonged, and is counted among Judah's descendants in 1 Chron. 4: 5. But Ashur's older brother Jair, the first son and heir by the second marriage, although a descendant of Judah also, was inscribed in the genealogical table of his mother and his maternal grandfather Machir, and reckoned as a son of Manasseh, in whose tribe he received his inheritance. An arrangement somewhat analogous to Jacob's claim on Joseph's first two sons (see Gen. 48: 5, 6) was contemplated by the *Levirate* law (*levir*—a husband's brother, a brother-in-law) found in Deut. 25: 5, 6, 10, and illustrated in Ruth 4: 5, with which compare Mt. 22: 24, A. below. In such cases the first-born son after this marriage was regarded as the son and heir of the deceased or first husband. In Ezra 2: 61, the children of the priest Hakkoz (1 Chron. 24: 10) or Koz (Neh. 3: 4) are called after their maternal ancestor, "the children of Barzillai." Now, as Luke wrote his Gospel for Christians who had originally been Gentiles, and who were unacquainted with the legal institutes of the Jews, he sets forth Christ's descent from David according to the flesh (Rom. 1: 3; Acts 13: 23), or His real descent through Mary His mother, who was a descendant of David through his son Nathan (Luke 3: 31; 2 Sam. 5: 14), while Joseph descended from Solomon; he continues the record until he reaches the first man. But as Matt. wrote for Jewish Christians (on which account he begins with Abraham, whose ancestors were well known to every Jew), it was indispensable that he should furnish the evidence that Jesus was the true heir and successor of David according to the laws of Moses. Now, by the Jewish laws of inheritance, Christ, as the adopted and acknowledged son of Joseph, was a descendant of David through his son Solomon (Matt. 1: 6), and, in a legal point of view, all the rights and dignities of Joseph were transferred to Christ. Christ was, in reality, the son of Mary only, and not of Joseph; He had no earthly father, but was the Son of God, Luke 1: 35. When Joseph is occasionally represented as His father, as in Matt. 13: 55, he was merely reputed or *supposed* to be His father, Luke 3: 23. The angel of the Lord at an early period revealed the divine will to Joseph (Matt. 1: 19–25), who obeyed it at once by taking Mary as his wife, by adopting Jesus as his son, and, in strict conformity to the law, by publicly recognizing Him as his heir or son. Luke's genealogy accordingly refers to the parentage or true descent of Christ, Matthew's to his legal inheritance of the rights of Joseph. The latter, therefore, omits the word *begat* in ver. 16, as Joseph was not the real or true, but only the legal father of Christ, who was miraculously born of Mary; the latter was a daughter of Heli (Luke 3: 23), who accordingly appears as the father-in-law of Joseph.—B. **Abr. begat Isaac**—was the father of Isaac, Gen. 21: 2, 3.—C. **Jacob**, Gen. ch. 25.—D. Judah, Gen. 29: 35.—E. **His Brethren**, Gen. 35: 23–26. They are the twelve patriarchs, Acts 7: 8, the founders of the twelve tribes of Israel, to whom the promises pertained, Acts 26: 7; Rom. 9: 4, 5; Hebr. 11: 13. But Judah, the fourth son of Jacob, was declared to be the ancestor of Christ, Gen 49: 10; Hebr. 7: 14.

³ And Judah begat Perez and Zerah of Tamar; and Perez begat Hezron; and Hezron begat Ram;
⁴ And Ram begat Aminadab; and Aminadab begat Nashon; and Nashon begat Salmon;
⁵ And Salmon begat Boaz of Rahab; and Boaz begat Obed of Ruth; and Obed begat Jesse;
⁶ And Jesse begat David the king; and David begat Solomon of her *that had been the wife* of Uriah.

A. **David**, Ruth 4: 22; 1 Sam. 17: 12; 1 Chron. 2: 15.—B. **The King**—*that* David who is mentioned in ver. 1, the first member of the family who ascended the throne, in fulfilment of the promise made to Abraham: "Kings shall come out of thee," Gen. 17: 6; 35: 11—and afterwards, a type of Christ, whom he prefigured; see Jer. 30: 9; 33: 15; Ezek. 34: 23; 37: 24; Hos. 3: 5; Amos 9: 11.—C. **And David**; he constitutes the fourteenth (ver. 17) and last of the first series of ancestors mentioned by Matt., or the patriarchs, Acts 2: 29; the next group of fourteen consists of kings.—D. **Solomon**, 2 Sam. 12: 24.—E. **The wife of Uriah.** Uriah the Hittite, one of David's "mighty men," 2 Sam. 23: 39, was killed at the siege of Rabbah, 2 Sam. 11: 17. Four females are mentioned in the preceding portion of the genealogy: Thamar, Rahab, Ruth and Bathsheba. Ruth exhibits many beautiful traits of character; still, she belonged originally to a heathenish people. The other three females were guilty of grievous sins. Nevertheless, these females are direct ancestresses of the Saviour after the flesh, while three others, Sarah, Rebekah (Rebecca) and Leah, are not mentioned. "Matthew greatly encourages and comforts the humble, penitent sinner, by giving prominence to the fact that the Saviour was not ashamed to reckon great sinners among His ancestors."—LUTHER.

⁷ And Solomon begat Rehoboam; and Rehoboam begat Abijah; and Abijah begat Asa;
⁸ And Asa begat Jehoshaphat; and Jehoshaphat begat Joram; and Joram begat Uzziah.

A. Uzziah. Between Joram and Uzziah, the great-great-grandson of the former, the three following names are omitted: (1) *Ahaziah*, the son of Joram, 2 K. 8: 24; 1 Chr. 3; 11; 2 Chr. 22: 1, also called Azariah, 2 Chr. 22: 6, and originally Jehoahaz, 2 Chr. 21: 17; this king died in Megiddo, 2 K. 9: 27. (2) *Joash*, the son of Azariah, 1 Chron. 3 : 11; he succeeded to the throne after the usurpation of Athaliah, 2 K. ch. 11; 2 Chr. ch. 23. The name of Joash assumes the form of Jehoash in 2 K. 12: 1. (3) *Amaziah*, the son of Joash, 2 K. 12: 21; 1 Chr. 3: 12; 2 Chr. 24 : 27. This king was the father of Uzziah, 2 Chr. 26 : 1, and Azariah, 1 Chr. 4 : 12.—The omission of these three names, which were well known to Matthew, has been variously explained. (It is not an unusual circumstance to omit names in such lists. Thus Ezra, when exhibiting his own descent from Aaron, abbreviates by omitting at least six generations which are introduced in 1 Chr. 6 : 3–15, as compared with Ezra 7 : 1–5). The personal character of the kings omitted by Matt., did not entitle them to reverence, and as he had arranged 14 names in the first series, he perhaps omitted these three names here, for the purpose of presenting the same number in the second; it was always easy to supply them from the Scriptural records. The list is sufficiently complete without them, as the main object of the genealogy —the historic proof of the royal descent of Christ according to the Mosaic law—was still attained.

⁹ And Uzziah begat Jotham; and Jotham begat Ahaz; and Ahaz begat Hezekiah;
¹⁰ And Hezekiah begat Manasseh; and Manasseh begat Amon; and Amon begat Josiah;
¹¹ And Josiah begat Jechoniah and his brethren, at the time of the carrying away to Babylon:

A. Jechoniah. Josiah was succeeded by his son Jehoahaz (2 K. 23: 30, 31; 2 Chr. 36: 1), who was dethroned by the king of Egypt, after a reign of only three months. He was succeeded by his brother Eliakim, who received the name of Jehoiakim; the latter was succeeded by his own son Jehoiachin (2 K. 24: 6) or Jeconiah. He is the fourteenth of the second series of ancestors. Matt. has here abbreviated the list by simply saying: "Josiah begat Jechoniah and his brethren,"—B. **His brethren,** 1 Chr. 3: 15-17. *Brethren* is a word often used by the Jews to designate *kinsmen* in general. Members of the same tribe are called "brethren," Numb. 8: 26; 2 Sam. 19: 12, or of the same nation, Judg. 14: 3, or of kindred nations, Numb. 20: 14. Lot, the nephew of Abraham, Gen. 11: 31, is called his brother, Gen. 13: 8; 14: 12, 14, 16: the word occurs in its widest sense in Gen. 9: 5; 19: 7. See annot. to 13: 55, C.—C. **At the time**—of the Babylonish Captivity, which commenced during the reign of Nebuchadnezzar. It began after the death of Josiah (2 K. 22: 20), about the year B. C. 606. —D. **Babylon.** It is not the city of Babylon itself, but the country then called Babylonia, of which empire Babylon was the principal city.

¹². And after the carrying away to Babylon, Jechoniah begat Shealtiel; and Shealtiel begat Zerubbabel;

A. Shealtiel is the first of the third group of ancestors. These are no longer kings, but are gradually lost to public view; nevertheless, they are the lineal descendants of the kings mentioned above. Shealtiel was a grandson of Jeconiah; his father, Assir (1 Chron. 3 : 17) died as a captive in obscurity, without power or name (2 K. 24: 12; 25 : 27-30).—**B. Zerubbabel** (Ezr. 2 : 2; Neh. 12 ; 47 ; Hagg. 1 : 1 ; Zech. 4: 6) was the son of Pedaiah (1 Chr. 3 : 19); the latter was a younger brother of Shealtiel (1 Chr. 3 : 17, 18), who either complied with the Levirate law in Deut. 25 : 5, 6, (See 1: 2, A. above), or else adopted his nephew Zerubbabel as his own son after the early death of Pedaiah, and made him the heir of his dignities; for Zerubbabel is called "the prince of Judah," and "the son of Shealtiel," in Ezr. 5 : 2; Hagg. 1 : 1. He conducted the captives on their return to their country, Ezr. 2 : 2. His numerous descendants, some of whom are mentioned in 1 Chr. 3 : 19-24, appear to have been unknown to fame. The power and wealth of ancestors cannot always secure their descendants from poverty and an obscure condition, while the children of the poor and lowly often acquire the highest distinction.

¹³⁻¹⁵ And Zerubbabel begat Abiud; and Abiud begat Eliakim; and Eliakim begat Azor; And Azor begat Sadoc; and Sadoc begat Achim; and Achim begat Eliud; And Eliud begat Eleazar; and Eleazar begat Matthan; and Matthan begat Jacob;

The nine names which occur in these three verses are not mentioned in the O. T. The obscure position of these several successive generations of a family which had declined, afforded no opportunity for introducing their names on the pages of the O. T. At this point accordingly, at which various lines of descent diverge, forming new branches of the genealogical tree, Matthew simply presents the names of several of the direct legal ancestors of Christ. They all appear to have occupied situations in private life. It was sufficient that kings *had*, according to the divine promise (Gen. 17 : 6 ; 35 :

11) proceeded from Abraham, as ancestors of Christ. A line of obscure men now follows, terminating with Joseph, an equally obscure man.

¹⁶And Jacob begat Joseph the husband of Mary, of whom was born Jesus, who is called Christ.

A. Joseph. Of his personal history we possess no reliable account, except the few facts furnished in the Gospels. He appears to have been a poor man; for the sacrifice which he and Mary offered at the presentation of the child Jesus in the temple (Luke 2 : 22-24) consisted of the second kind mentioned in Lev. 12: 8, which they alone brought, whose pecuniary means did not allow them to purchase even a lamb for the occasion. He probably died before the Saviour commenced His public ministry. He is not mentioned when Mary appears, e. g. John 2 : 1 ; Mat. 12 : 46. The omission of his name in Matt. 13: 55, when the people refer to him as one that had been a carpenter, while they mention Mary's name, seems to indicate that he was no longer personally known to them; the passages in which the name occurs (Luke 4 : 22; John 6 : 42), do not state that he was then alive. The circumstance that the Lord, at His crucifixion, entrusts Mary to the care of John (John 19 : 25-27) with whom she found a home seems to imply very clearly that she was then a widow

B. Mary—The Virgin. Her name coincides with that of Miriam, the sister of Moses (Exod. 15 : 20), whose name in its Greek form is Maria, and in its abbreviated English form, Mary. She was, according to the most satisfactory interpretation of the passage in Luke 3 : 23, a daughter of a descendant of David named Heli, who became by this marriage the father-in-law of Joseph. The angel who visited Mary speaks of David as the father of her son (Luke 1 : 32), clearly referring to her own descent from King David. She was poor and unknown in the world, but was rich in faith, and highly favored of the Lord; she was blessed among women by becoming the mother of the Lord (Luke 1 : 28, 43). Humble before God and truly devout, thoughtful (L. 2 : 19, 33, 51) and unassuming (Acts 1 : 14), she exhibits all the gentleness, the purity, and the love and fear of God, which are the highest ornaments of the female character. Nevertheless— "the Scriptures have given us no account of the birth of Mary, and have related very few facts belonging to her history, in order that we might not assign undue importance to her. Mary, and all others that believe, are saved from their sins by Christ alone." LUTHER.—**C. Of whom was Christ.** See 1 : 1, B. "We are all under sin (Rom. 3 : 9), and, indeed, born in it (Ps. 51 : 5); we are therefore by nature the children of wrath (Eph. 2 : 3). Christ alone, who was born of the virgin, was without sin (John 8 : 46 : 2 Cor. 46 : 21 : Heb. 4 : 15; 7 : 26; 1 Pet. 1 : 19; 2 : 22; 1 John 3 : 5). Through Him we are to be born again, and by his Holiness we are to be cleansed."—LUTHER.

¹⁷ So all the generations from Abraham unto David are fourteen generations; and from David unto the carrying away to Babylon fourteen generations; and from the carrying away to Babylon unto the Christ fourteen generations.

Fourteen generations. The third group of ancestors, like the two former, consists of fourteen members; here the family of David is exhibited in its decay. Different arrangements of the entire series of names have been proposed. If Jechoniah, ver. 11, is counted, like David, ver. 6, once only as above, and Shealtiel commences the third series, Joseph is only the twelfth in the last group. The name of Jesus Himself, as the last of the whole line, naturally constitutes the fourteenth, for as the words " to David " assign to Him the fourteenth place in the first series, so the words " unto the Christ " assign the same place to Him in the third. The *thirteenth* name can be no other than that of Mary. It was not, indeed, usual to insert female names in the Jewish genealogies; but there were exceptions to the rule. Joab, the distinguished general of David, was his nephew, the son of Zeruiah, David's sister, 2 Sam. 2 : 13 ; 19 : 22 ; 1 Chr. 2 : 15, 16. He is uniformly mentioned as " the son of Zeruiah " (2 Sam. 3 : 39; 8 : 16; 16 : 10; 1 Chr. 11 : 6; 18 : 15; 26 : 28; 27 : 24), while his father's name is withheld. In his family register, Zeruiah, his mother, must have necessarily occupied the place of one of the links in the whole chain of descent. In the present case, Matthew designs to furnish the legal descent of Christ (See above, ver. 2, A.); he accordingly introduces the name of Joseph, the twelfth. But as Mary was alone the true parent of Jesus according to the flesh, to whose son Joseph only transmitted his legal rights, she is mentioned as the representative of the thirteenth generation. The words " of whom," ver. 16, in which the singular number is used in the original, distinctly and expressly excludes Joseph.

¹⁸ Now the birth of Jesus Christ was on this wise; when his mother Mary had been betrothed to Joseph, before they came together, she was found with child of the Holy Ghost.

A. The birth . . . this wise—the circumstances which preceded and attended it, were the following. Comp. Luke ch. 1 and ch. 2.—**B. Betrothed.** The ceremony of betrothal was very solemn; it took place before witnesses. After the espousals, the bride often remained for some time in her father's family, until the man to whom she was affianced came to claim her, Deut. 20 : 7; Judg. 14 : 7, 8. During the period intervening between the betrothal and the actual marriage ceremonies, the parties were regarded as bound together by ties as solemn and inviolable as those which unite man and wife; hence the bride who became unfaithful during this period, was punished with death, Deut. 22 : 23, 24.—C. **She was found.** Neither the public in general, nor even Joseph in particular, had at first received a revelation such as was made to Mary in Luke 1 : 35.—D. **The Holy Ghost.** The words *Spirit* (Latin) and *Ghost* (Anglo-Saxon, German *Geist*) are the same in meaning. In Luke 1 : 35 the angel informs the Virgin Mary that through the Holy Ghost she shall become the mother of a son, who, not having an earthly father, shall be called the Son of God. He is called the Only-begotten of the Father (John 1 : 14, 18 ; 3 : 16, 18) or God's " own son " Rom 8 : 32. Hence, as he had no earthly father, being " conceived of the Holy Ghost " (ver. 20), He was sinless (ver. 16, C.) and free from Original Sin, which clings to all who are " born of the flesh " (John 3 : 6).

¹⁹. And Joseph her husband, being a righteous *man*, and not willing to make her a public example, was minded to put her away privily.

A. **Her husband**—betrothed as her future husband; comp. Deut. 22 : 23; Rev. 21 : 2.—B. **A righteous man.** The word righteous in the Jewish or legal sense described the character of those who, like Simeon (Luke 2 : 25), Joseph of Arimathea (Lu. 23 : 50) and others, strictly and conscientiously observed the laws of Moses; thus the word may indicate in general *freedom from any fault, innocence*, as in ch. 27 : 19, 24. As Mary had not communicated to Joseph the divine interposition related in Lu. 1 : 26 ff., he supposed that she had committed a gross sin ; as a conscientious man he dreaded the divine displeasure if he should conduct her to his home as an honored wife. In the Gospel sense, the word righteous describes the character of those who, being justified by faith in Christ, have received pardon and found acceptance with God; comp. Rom. 1:17.—**C. Not willing . . . privily.** His genuine kindness of heart inclined him to waive the right of accusing her publicly, and to refrain from exposing her to such a disgrace, ver. 18, B.; it was possible for him, as a devout man, to obey the letter of the law by "putting her away" or repudiating or dismissing her with a bill of divorcement (Deut. 24:1) *privily* (privately), without publicly assigning the cause.

²⁰ But when he thought on these things, behold an angel of the Lord appeared unto him in a dream, saying, Joseph, thou son of David, fear not to take unto thee Mary thy wife: for that which is conceived in her is of the Holy Ghost.

A. But when . . . . things. Even this measure, which Joseph's conscience taught him to adopt, he refrained from carrying precipitately into effect. That justice to which others are entitled, requires us to withhold our censure, and especially to refrain from a public accusation, until we have sufficient reason to believe that they are worthy of condemnation. **B.—Behold.** In Matt. and Luke, this word occurs far more frequently than in Mark and John. It usually precedes the mention of a fact or truth of special importance, and is equivalent to *lo,* (2:9, B.).—**C. A dream.** Such dreams, in which the Lord communicated His will, are mentioned on various occasions. But the Lord also solemnly warns "against them that prophesy false dreams." Jer. 23:32; 29:8. In our day, neither such prophetic dreams, nor messengers from the other world, are sent by the Lord, inasmuch as we have not only "Moses and the prophets" (Luke 16:29), but also the perfect and complete lessons taught by

Christ and His inspired apostles, (For the dream of Pilate's wife, see 27 : 19 C.).—D. **Thou son of David** (see ver. 1, C). The scriptural genealogies appear to contain only uninteresting names; but the present case illustrates the high importance of the object for which they are inserted; they constitute one of the proofs of the right of Christ to the title of *Son of David.*—E. **Mary thy wife**—who was espoused to thee as thy future wife (see ver. 19, A.). —F. **Conceived .... Holy Ghost.** The angel not only restored the character of Mary in the mind of Joseph to its original purity, but also revealed the wonderful event which almighty power had ordered, namely, that Mary should be the mother of a son who would have no earthly father.

²¹ And she shall bring forth a son, and thou shalt call his name JESUS: for it is he that shall save his people from their sins.

A. **Thou .... Jesus**; see 1 : 1 B.—B. **For it is he .... sins.** The deep import of the name of Jesus is here set forth; He comes to His people as *Jehovah their Saviour.* He *saves* them from their sins in a twofold sense: first, He takes away by His atoning work the guilt and punishment of sin (Isai. ch. 53; John 1 : 29; 1 John 1 : 7); then, He also renews and sanctifies believers (Tit. 3 : 5), and imparts His grace so bountifully that they no longer love sin (1 John 3 : 5, 9) but are dead to it (Rom. 6 : 2, 11), are restored to communion with God, and "made meet to be partakers of the inheritance of the saints in light," Col. 1 : 12; 3 : 24. **His people**; the people of God, in the Jewish sense, are the children of Abraham, the Jews, Deut. 14 : 2; in the wider, Gospel sense, all true believers, bought and redeemed with the blood of Christ (1 Pet. 1 : 18, 19), are the people of God (Rom. 9 : 25; Tit. 2 : 14; Hebr. 4 : 9, 10, comp. with

Exod. 19 : 6 ; Hos. 2 : 23), the spiritual children of Abraham. " Know ye therefore, etc." Gal. 3 : 7.

²² Now all this is come to pass, that it might be fulfilled which was spoken by the Lord through the prophet, saying.

A. That it might be fulfilled. (Here Matt. resumes the narrative in his own words.) This phrase, which indicates, in general, a divine intention, frequently occurs in Matt., e. g., 2 : 15, 23 ; 4 : 14 ; 8 : 17 ; 12 : 17 ; 13 : 35 ; 21 : 4 ; 26 : 56 ; 27 : 35, and several times in John. It differs from another : *then was* (or, *is*) *fulfilled*, which occurs in Matt. 2 : 17 ; 13 : 14 ; 27 : 9, inasmuch as it *seems* to imply that the event necessarily occurred, because it had been foretold, as if the origin or cause of the event lay in the prediction ; the latter phrase obviously states the mere fact that a prophecy *was* really fulfilled. (Comp. Ann. to 26 : 31 D.) Now the words : *that*, or, *so that, in order that the prophecy might be fulfilled*, mean neither simply : *it was fulfilled*, nor, on the other hand, *that*, because a certain prophecy was once written, *therefore*, such prophecy, as an independent and operating cause, required the event to follow as its necessary effect. The phrase may be presented in the following light :—The Omniscient and Almighty God had devised the plan of salvation through Christ with all its blessings, before " the foundation of the world," 1 Pet. 1 : 20 ; Eph. 1 : 4 ; 3 : 11 ; 2 Tim. 1 : 9. At different successive periods (Heb. 1 : 1) He announced this gracious purpose to His people through the prophets. In the order of time, according to man's imperfect conception of the thoughts of God, this plan of salvation was first devised in the divine mind, 1 Pet. 1 : 20 ; afterwards, the world was created, and occupied by the human race, and the predictions respecting the events embraced in that divine plan of salvation were then made.

Now as God's plan was necessarily to be carried into effect, it follows that any prophecy which was founded on that divine, fixed purpose must also necessarily be fulfilled, not primarily because a prophecy announcing it stood on record, but because God had previously determined to cause or to permit the event to occur. Hence the phrase: *that it might be fulfilled* is equivalent to: *inasmuch as it was certain that such a predicted event would occur.* There are cases again in which this established phrase occurs, where the quotation from the O. T. is a prophecy not so much of events that God Himself desires and orders, as of those the occurrence of which, for wise and just reasons, He permits, or which occur in consequence of men's ignorance, sinfulness, etc.; see, for instance, ch. 13: 35. In such cases the sense of the phrase is:—so that, in consequence of man's sinfulness, the event occurred, in accordance with the prediction, which itself proceeded from God's foreknowledge alike of His own future course and of the course which men, in the exercise of their liberty, would adopt.—**B. The prophet.**—Isai. 7: 14. Matthew assumes that his readers (1 : 1, A.) were so familiar with the writings of the O. T., and particularly with those which referred to the Messiah, that he omits even the prophet's name. Isaiah uttered this prediction more than 700 years before the event occurred.

²³. Behold, the virgin shall be with child, and shall bring forth a son, and they shall call his name Immanuel, which is, being interpreted, God with us.

A. Behold . . . . son. The allied armies of the king of Syria and the king of Israel besieged Jerusalem. Ahaz, the king of Judah, in place of trusting to the arm of God, entreated the heathen king of Assyria to save him from these enemies, 2 Kings 16 : 5–7. Even when divine mercy afforded him a new opportunity to show a penitent spirit, he turned away with pretended humility, but with evident scorn and unbelief, from the Lord's messenger, the prophet; Isai. 7: 10-12. The latter, after referring in ver. 13 to the king's irreverent rejection of the offered sign, is guided by the inspiration of the Divine Spirit to reveal the following glorious truth:—that the God of David whom Ahaz now discarded as unable to afford him relief, would at a future time give to the world a far more wonderful sign of His power and willingness to save than Ahaz, or, indeed, than any other human being could have imagined, as the prophet himself elsewhere (Isai. 64:4) remarks. The sign, as the prophet, looking away from the scenes of his own age, proceeds in ver. 14 to say, shall be this: "A virgin shall conceive and bear a son," that is, a son shall be born of a virgin and shall have no earthly father. To this child the prophet, in a succeeding chapter (9:6), gives the names "Wonderful, Counsellor, The Mighty God, The Everlasting Father, The Prince of Peace." That this child is Jesus Christ, is proved by the introductory words of the chapter, ver. 1 and 2, which are distinctly applied to Christ by Matt. ch. 4 : 14-15. The original Hebrew and the original Greek in the present 23d verse, both prefix the article and say: *the* virgin shall, etc.; the prophet looking "in Spirit" (22 : 43) to that distant future event, sees the Virgin Mary as *that one* of her whole sex who was to be so "blessed among women," Luke 1:28:42; he seems to say emphatically: *the* virgin specially chosen by the Lord for that purpose shall, etc. This virgin's son is therefore by no means the son of the prophet's wife, mentioned in Isai. 7 : 16 ; 8 : 3, 4, who bears an entirely different name, but is that "Immanuel" to whom, as to the Lord over all, the prophet declares in ch. 8:8 that the breadth of the land belongs.—B. **Immanuel;** translated literally, is: *with us (is) God.* The Saviour bears this name in view of the fact that while He is "God" (Rom. 9:5), He was also "made flesh and dwelt among us" (John 1:14). Hence in Christ two natures, the divine and the human, were inseparably united in one Person (11:27, B.). The name is full of encouragement to the believer's soul. When Christ is with us, God is with us (Col. 2:9); unseen by mortal eyes, He is ever present with His believing people in the fulness of His love.

²⁴ And Joseph arose from his sleep and did as the angel of the Lord commanded him, and took unto him his wife;

²⁵ And knew her not till she had brought forth a son: and he called his name JESUS.

A. **Son**—Mary's son, not Joseph's.
B. **Jesus.** See above, ver. 1, B.

CHAPTER II.

¹ Now when Jesus was born in Bethlehem of Judæa in the days of Herod, the king, behold, wise men from the east came to Jerusalem.

    A. Was born—as related in Lu. ch. 2.—**B. Bethlehem.** This town (now called by the Arabs *Beit Laham*) is mentioned in Judg. 17: 7, and belonged to the tribe of Judah. At an earlier period it had been called Ephrath, Gen. 35: 19. It was a fortified place in the reign of Rehoboam (2 Chron. 11: 5, 6), but never became a large city, and in the time of Christ was a mere *village*, John 7: 42. It was six miles south of Jerusalem. It was the birthplace of David, 1 Sam. 16: 1; 17: 12;—the words **of Judæa** ("of Judah," ver. 6) are added in order to distinguish it from another Bethlehem belonging to the tribe of Zebulon, Josh. 19: 10,15.—**C. In the days**—during the reign; the precise time is not specified; it was very near the end of Herod's reign. The events related in this chapter occurred after the visit of the shepherds and the presentation of Christ in the temple as related in Luke ch. 2. Mary and the child had returned to Bethlehem, and then received the visit of the wise men; on their return from Egypt, they retired to Nazareth, Luke 2: 39.—**D. Herod the king.** After Hyrcanus II., the last of the Maccabees or Asmonæan princes, had been thrust from his office, Herod (the son of Antipater, an Idumæan, who had been appointed Procurator of Judæa by Cæsar, B. C. 47) was constituted king of Judæa by the Romans. He was a **crafty,** ambitious and cruel ruler (2: 3, A). He died soon after the birth of Christ of a loathsome malady, which caused his body to putrefy before life was extinct. His sons who bear the same name and are prominent in history, are usually distinguished by an additional appellation. Among them are the following: (1) *Aristobulus*, a son of Mariamne, the grand-daughter of Hyrcanus; he was the father of Herod Agrippa I., Acts 12: 1, 20, and of Herodias, Mark 6: 17; (for Herodias, see 14: 3, B.). This Agrippa, was the father of Herod Agrippa II. and Berenice, mentioned in Acts 25 : 13, and of Drusilla, Acts 24: 24. (2) *Philip*, the first husband of Herodias, is mentioned in Matt. 14: 3; Mark 6: 17, (see below, 14: 3, B.). His mother, one of Herod's ten wives, and a daughter of Simon the highpriest, also bore the name of Mariamne. (3) *Archelaus;* (see 2: 22, A.). (4) *Herod Antipas;* (see 2: 22, C.). He is called Herod the *Tetrarch* (14: 1, B.) of Galilee, in Luke 3 : 1, and is also mentioned in Matt. 14: 1–12; Mark 8: 15; Luke 8: 3; 13: 31; 23: 7. The mother of these two sons, Archelaus and Antipas, was Malthace, a Samaritan woman. (5) *Philip* (who is to be carefully distinguished from his halfbrother Philip, No. 2, above) was tetrarch of Batanæa, Gaulonitis and Ituræa. He is mentioned in Luke 3: 1, and was the son of Cleopatra of Jerusalem. (Herod had also named two others of his sons *Antipater*.)—E. **Wise men.** In the Greek they are called *Magoi*. The *Magians* or Persian priests and learned men as well as those of the Chaldeans, Medes, etc., originally received this name as an official title. The word occurs in Jerem. 39: 3, 13, where *Rab-mag* signifies the *Chief Magian* or prince of the order of the Magi (For the first syllable see below, 23 : 7, B.). The original Magi constituted a class of men of the highest distinction, whose cultivated minds and superior intelligence invested them with great power and influence.

In Persia they not only conducted the religious rites of the people, and cultivated science with success (Astronomy, Medicine, etc.), but also belonged to the council of the king. We possess, however, no reliable knowledge of the names, rank or number of the "wise men" here mentioned, in the present passage. Later traditions, besides inventing names for them respectively, referred Ps. 72 : 10, 11 ; Isai. 49: 7 ; 60 : 3 to them specially, without a firm historical basis, and termed them "the three kings." The circumstance that they were heathens or Gentiles, and that at this early period they are directed by Providence to worship the new-born king, is an indication of the gracious purpose of God to call the heathen nations into the Church of Christ. It is a conjecture of Luther that the pupils of Daniel transmitted to their descendants the divine knowledge which he imparted to them, and that the "wise men" may have originally through such a medium in the Providence of God received an impulse by which they were conducted to a still more complete knowledge of the way of salvation through Christ.—F. **From the east**—oriental travellers, men from a region not specially named (as in Job 1 : 3), but lying east of Palestine. A general belief appears to have prevailed at this period, probably orginating in the expectations entertained by the dispersed Jews respecting the Messiah, that an eminent personage would appear in Judæa, whose vast power and influence would be widely felt. This historical fact is well attested. —G. **To Jerusalem.** (For *Jerusalem*, see below, 4 : 5, C.) "Why did not the star that afterwards guided them to the very house which they sought, conduct them at once to Bethlehem ? Why could they obtain no precise information until an appeal was made to the Scriptures, as in ver. 5 ? Doubtless this course of events is designed to teach us to value the Holy Scriptures as our unerring light and guide, to adhere faithfully to them, to desire no human opinions, no visions, no intercourse with spirits, but to listen solely to God when He speaks to us in His Word.—Others may ask: Where is Aristotle? Where is the Pope? Where is human reason? What do *men* teach? But let us rather ask: Where is Christ? What does the Bible teach concerning Him?"—LUTHER.

² Saying, Where is he that is born King of the Jews? for we saw his star in the east, and are come to worship him.

A. Where is .... Jews? The statement of the wise men that a royal child, a king of the Jews, had been born at that time in Judæa, and the proof of the fact which they adduce, namely, the appearance of a peculiar star, indicate that the Lord had conveyed information to them in a manner which removed all doubts of its accuracy. —**B. His star.**—the star which indicated His birth. The studies of the Magi specially included astronomy or observations of the heavenly bodies, and hence they would readily distinguish a new star, or an appearance which resembled a star, from those objects with the sight of which they were familiar. It is remarkable that a star and a sceptre, the emblem of royalty, are mentioned in Balaam's prediction (Numb. 24 : 17), and that the Saviour, when speaking of His second coming, of which one of the signs is the falling of the stars, adds: "then shall appear the sign of the Son of man in heaven," Matt. 24 : 29, 30). A star seems to have been the symbol of the expected Messiah. A new light appeared in the heavens at the birth of the Saviour; at His death "there was darkness over all the earth .... and the sun was darkened," Lu. 23 : 44, 45. While all the angels of God worship Him (Hebr. 1 : 6), even the visible heavens thus acknowledge

His power and dominion.—C. **In the east;** the words of the translation could be appropriately transposed and stand thus: *We have* [while dwelling] *in the east, seen His star,* for it originally appeared in the direction of Palestine, before they commenced their journey, as their words imply; it therefore occupied a western position in reference to their country, which was east of Palestine, ver. 1. The language in ver. 10, "when they saw the star, etc.," and the circumstance that it now guided them to the house of Mary, seem to imply that after its first appearance in the east, it disappeared from their view. Hence they naturally proceeded to Jerusalem, the chief city, where they hoped to obtain further information; the star reappeared after they had seen Herod, and they "rejoiced" that in their great perplexity the heavenly light again became their guide.—D. **To worship Him.** According to the customs of the east, the subjects of a monarch kneeled or prostrated themselves before him (ver. 11 "fell down"), and inferiors rendered similar homage to those who were of high rank, or whom they desired to honor, as in Gen. 19 : 1 ; 37 : 7, 8; 42 : 6. In such a sense the word *worship* occurs in Matt. 8 : 2 ; 9: 18; 18 : 26. Thus, also, the old English phrase: *Your Worship,* is simply a title of honor given to certain magistrates, etc. But the same word is also used to designate specially the adoration of God. If the Magi did not know that Christ was both God and man, the word would bear the former sense. But as they visit the child by special direction from heaven, they may have come to pay divine honors to Him. Indeed, as one king did not prostrate himself before another, and yet Herod says (ver. 8) that he too would "worship" the child, the word in his conversation with the men must have referred to divine honors. The Magi find a child apparently in very humble circumstances, and nevertheless they regard their mission as successful (ver. 11); they must have been enabled to recognize the divinity of Christ even at that early period. The genealogy in ch. 1 shows that the Jews could claim Jesus Christ as their own Saviour; the visit of the wise men, the first worshippers of Jesus, shows that by the gracious will of God, the Gentiles also, even unto the end of the earth, shall find light and salvation in Him (Isai. 49: 6) as their divine King (Rev. 11: 15).

³ And when Herod the king heard it he was troubled, and all Jerusalem with him.

A. Herod. . . . troubled. In order to secure himself on the throne (2: 1, D.), he had already cruelly put to death all who seemed to possess any hereditary claims to it. He was accordingly startled by the tidings that a new competitor had been born, and the tyrant immediately determined to discover and murder the latter.—**B. And all Jerusalem.** The people of Jerusalem were greatly excited. The partisans of Herod dreaded the fall of their chief; others, possibly, apprehended new sanguinary edicts of Herod and serious political convulsions.

⁴ And gathering together all the chief priests and scribes of the people, he inquired of them where the Christ should be born.

A. Chief priests and scribes. These chief priests were doubtless the heads of the 24 courses of priests; the scribes were men versed in the Scriptures, sometimes called doctors, or teachers of the law; they were members of the Supreme Council or Sanhedrin mentioned in 5: 22.—**B. He inquired . . . . born**—in what place, according to the Jewish faith, founded on the sacred writings, the Christ would be born. Herod rightly interprets the language of the wise men: *King of the Jews* as equivalent to *Christ* or Messiah; Matt. 21:5. But the heart of this evil king was as destitute of the love and fear of God, as it was of an experimental knowledge of the precious promises of God's word. He now causes the Scriptures to be searched in order to facilitate the commission of a new crime. "Here are three very different kinds of believers: we have, first, the chief priests and scribes; they know the Scriptures, profess to believe them, and nevertheless do not receive the promised Saviour in faith. We have, secondly, Herod and his party: they also believe the Scriptures, as their earnestness in this case shows; nevertheless, they wickedly attempt to resist the will of God and scorn His grace. We have, thirdly, the wise men, who possess only a limited knowledge, but who follow the light which they receive, and forsake their country and their homes in order to seek Christ. *They* believe the Scriptures, for they obey in a devout and humble spirit. Those who seek Christ alone, Christ in His divine power and grace, are guided like these inquirers until they find Him."—LUTHER.

⁵ And they said unto him, In Bethlehem of Judæa: for thus it is written by the prophet,

A. In Bethlehem; for *Bethlehem*, see ver. 1, B. We have here an illustration of the deep interest with which the Jews at that period consulted the writings of the prophets, as far as these contained predictions respecting the Messiah. These men promptly and accurately answer the king's question; compare John 7:42.—**B. The prophet**—Micah 5:2. They repeat substantially the words of the prophet. He lived in the age of Hezekiah and his immediate predecessors (Mic. 1:1), more than 700 years before the Christian era. He describes Bethlehem as an unimportant place (ver. 1, B. above). After the captivity only 123 persons returned who claimed that spot as the home of their fathers; Ezr. 2: 21.—**It is written**; see 21: 42, B.

⁶ And thou Bethlehem, land of Judah, art in no wise least among the princes of Judah: for out of thee shall come forth a Governor, which shall be shepherd of my people Israel.

A. Thou Bethlehem; this striking figure of speech, according to which any inanimate object, city, etc., is addressed like a living person, often occurs where powerful emotions control the speaker or writer; it is common in the language of the prophets (e.g. 2 Sam. 1: 21; 1 Kings 13: 2; Hos. 10: 8, comp. with Luke 23: 30), and is employed by the Saviour, Matt. 23: 37, A.—**B. Land of Judah;** see ver. 1, B.—**C. Art in no wise .... of Judah,** the prophet had said: "Although thou be little among the thousands of Judah," alluding to the practice of arranging entire tribes in smaller divisions, among which were those severally termed *thousands*, Num. 1: 16; 10: 4; Josh. 22: 21, 30; the heads or leaders who respectively represented a whole division, are here styled princes. (Thus, in ancient times certain districts or divisions of a county in England were styled *hundreds*.)—**D. A governor**—a ruler, prince; the scribes give the substance of the prophet's words. Bethlehem held an inferior rank with respect to political influence and military resources, but its greatness arose from the fact that the Saviour of the world should proceed from it.—**E. That shall .... people.** The scribes had given Herod the required answer by referring to the prophet Micah; they omit several of the succeeding clauses which contrast the eternal reign of Christ with the transitory reign of David, but refer to an additional statement of the prophet (5: 4) by adding the words: "which shall be shepherd of my people." The Lord Jesus is frequently described by

the prophets as a shepherd (Isai. 40: 11; Ezek. 34: 23) and assumes the name Himself (John 10: 11 ff.). "We are his people, and the sheep of his pasture," Ps. 100: 3.—
F. **Israel;** see 8: 10, C. Here *Israel*, in a spiritual sense, denotes true believers, Matt. 8: 11; Rom. 2: 28, 29; 9: 6; Gal. 6: 16. "Bethlehem was itself a very insignificant town; if the Lord had desired earthly splendor, He would have selected some magnificent city like Jerusalem or Rome. He puts to shame the foolish pride and vanity of men."—LUTHER.

⁷ Then Herod privily called the wise men, and learned of them carefully what time the star appeared.

A. **Privily** (—*secretly*, as in 1 : 19, C.) . . . . **men.** The suspicious and artful tyrant, anxious to allay the public excitement, holds a private interview with the strangers, doubtless desiring them to refrain from divulging the facts. Herod was conscious that his title to the throne had been obtained by violence and fraud; he therefore dreads the light, John 3: 19, 20.—B. **Learned . . . . appeared;** he desired to know the precise time (see ver. 16) when they had first seen the star in their own country, supposing that its first appearance coincided with the hour or day in which the child was born; he could thus the more easily identify and destroy him. As he did not afterwards see the men, he appears to have conjectured that the child was now somewhat more than a year old, and in order to assure himself of its death, he gave orders to spare the life of no male child in Bethlehem that was not older than two years.

⁸ And he sent them to Bethlehem, and said, Go and search out carefully concerning the young child; and when ye have found *him*, bring me word that I also may come and worship him.

A. **Go, and, etc.** The wise men needed no admonition to make the most careful inquiries; it would have been sufficient for Herod to furnish them with the information which they sought, but his eagerness to destroy the child prompted him to give these superfluous instructions.—B. **Bring me . . . . . worship him.** Herod disguised his cruel purpose so artfully that he completely deceived the wise men; the divine warning (ver. 12) exposed his dissimulation and wickedness. Deceitfulness does sometimes seem to secure greater advantages than candor and honesty; but the eye of God observes it. Even when it does not meet with a disappointment such as Herod experienced, the Lord abhors it (Ps. 5: 6), and " who can stand before His indignation?" (Nahum 1 : 6).

⁹ And they, having heard the king, went their way; and lo, the star, which they saw in the east, went before them, till it came and stood over where the young child was.

A. They went their way, proceeded, without suspecting the real design of Herod, to Bethlehem. They had no previous knowledge of the house and family of the child, but they believed that the same God who had so far guided their steps, would not now desert them.— **Lo, the star . . . . east.** Matthew does not expressly say that the star had disappeared, and now re-appeared as they approached Bethlehem; the language, however, which he employs here, seems to lead to such a conclusion (see ver. 10, A.). Stars that are very bright have been occasionally visible to the naked eye during the day: this star was, therefore, very bright if they travelled by day. But, possibly, Herod dismissed them by night in order that their departure might escape prying eyes; in that case, a feeble light in the heavens might be visible. Some peculiarity certainly attended the appearance of this star, for they at once recognized it as the one which they had seen in their own country.—C. **Went before them,**—was not stationary as it, possibly, seemed to be when they saw it in their own country, but now began to move, indicating the precise road which they should take. —**Came and stood over**—the house mentioned in ver. 11. The star, if it was at a great elevation previously, must have now taken a lower position (see 2 : 2, B.), and diffused its light over a particular spot for a short time; **it stood**—it ceased to move onward, before it finally disappeared. These visible movements of the star render the divine agency of God in the whole event even now visible to the eye of faith.

¹⁰. And when they saw the star, they rejoiced with exceeding great joy.

Rejoiced . . . . joy (literally *rejoiced a great joy*). Such expressions frequently occur in the Hebrew language, and are not unusual in other languages; they are always highly emphatic; the expression in this case indicates a very high degree of joy. The trial of the faith of the wise men had been severe. They had been disappointed in many respects: they found that the Jewish people knew nothing of the great event which had brought them from a distant country, and their tidings seemed to inspire fear rather than joy. The star had also disappeared (ver. 9, B.), and doubts and fears may have disturbed their minds. Nevertheless, the words of the prophet gave them new consolation, and the reappearance of the heavenly light produced indescribable rapture in their souls. Let the sorrowing and distressed soul never yield to despondence, but lean on the divine word, 2 Peter 1 : 19. The star of promise will re-appear in God's own time to those who persevere in faith and prayer. The holy Scriptures are a lamp, etc., Ps. 119 : 105 ; those who walk in that light will never fall; John 8 : 12.

¹¹ And they came into the house, and saw the young child with Mary his mother; and they fell down and worshipped him: and opening their treasures, they offered unto him gifts, gold, and frankincense and myrrh.

A. **The house**—where the family had taken their abode, and, consequently, not the spot where the manger was.—B. **Saw . . . . mother.** They speak of a "king" whose birth had been announced to them by a sign from heaven—they seek one whom they desire to *worship*. What do they now see? A poor family, a mother and a child, possibly in a shepherd's hut (Luke 2 : 8-17), or another shelter corresponding to their limited means (1 : 16, A.). Can this child be the *King* of the Jews?— "The wise men do not allow themselves to be discouraged by the suggestions of human reason; they depend on the light which heaven gave, and are supported by the words of the inspired prophet; thence they derive comfort and peace (Matthew 16 : 17). They find a guide, not in erring reason, but in the star and the prophet."—LUTHER.—C. **Fell down and worshipped him** —prostrated themselves (ver. 2, D.) in deep humility and "did reverence" (2 Sam. 9 : 6), according to the oriental mode. They proceed as if they saw, not a child of poverty, but a mighty king, surrounded by all the attributes of power. It is evident that God had granted much knowledge and grace to them; they seem to discern the true character of the Saviour, although the external appearances are so humble.—D. **Opening their treasures**—not the precious articles or contents, but the several receptacles in which these had been placed, as the word seems also to be used in 13 : 52.—E. **Offered unto him;** they address themselves, not to Joseph nor even to Mary, who is not entitled to special homage, but directly and exclusively to Him who alone is to be honored and adored; to Him they render homage and offer **gifts.** According to oriental customs, those who appeared before a king, or man of superior rank, presented such costly gifts (Gen. 43 : 11; 1 Sam. 10 : 27).

When the Queen of Sheba visited Solomon, and brought gifts which it suited a person of her high rank to bestow on a great monarch, she produced, in addition to precious stones, precisely such gifts as the child Jesus here receives—gold and spices (1 Kings 10: 10). That child Jesus is, however, the Son of God, the God-Man, and entitled to divine worship (John 5 : 23). To Him the devout Stephen, the first Christian martyr, who was "full of the Holy Ghost and wisdom," of "faith and power" (Acts 6 : 3, 5, 8), like so many dying believers since his day, in holy joy and peace, addressed his last prayer. (Acts 7 : 59).—F. **Gold and frankincense.** Gold is the most valuable and longest known of all the metals (Gen. 2: 11, 12). Frankincense is a gum of a pale yellow color, of a bitter taste, but emitting a very agreeable perfume when placed on burning coals. It is obtained in drops or small pieces from certain trees in the east, in the bark of which incisions are made in the hottest season of the year, when it exudes most freely. It was much used in the service of the tabernacle and temple (Exod. 30 : 34 ; Luke 1 : 10).—G. **Myrrh** is the gum of a large shrub growing in Arabia and Ethiopia. It was much used in embalming the dead (John 19 : 39). Both it and frankincense were believed to possess certain valuable medicinal qualities. Their value was so great, that it was deemed an honor even for a king to receive them as voluntary offerings and gifts. These gifts of the wise men, whose great wealth is indicated by their ability to present such costly articles, were designed to express their sentiments of humility and reverence in the presence of the King, who was the Son of God (Luke 1 : 35). "The gifts of the wise men were intended, in the Providence of God, to supply the wants of this poor family, to which the Saviour, in His human nature, belonged ; thus they were really a contribution to the Kingdom of God. It is our duty to consecrate a part of our property, all of which is the Lord's (Ps. 24: 1; 1 Cor. 4: 7; 10: 26), to the same cause, so that while, on the one hand, the poor may be relieved, on the other hand pastors and teachers may be sustained in their labors, and, in general, men may be sent forth to preach the Gospel (Rom. 10: 14, 15). Such contributions are especially necessary, in order that young men, who seem to be suited for the work, may be trained for the ministry, so that our descendants may also have well qualified pastors and teachers, even as it is wise to raise young fruit trees for the purpose of supplying the place of those that are decayed, and of generally increasing the supply of wholesome fruit."—LUTHER.

[12] And being warned of God in a dream that they should not return to Herod, they departed into their own country another way.

A. **Warned . . . dream.** The Greek word translated *warned* indicates in such a connection a revelation of the divine will; it is translated, according to the connection in which it stands, *revealed*, in Luke 2 : 26, and warned in Hebr. 8 : 5; 12 : 25. As the word also indicates generally *a divine answer*, it perhaps implies that the wise men had specially besought God to guide them mercifully on their return. Believers consult the divine will at every step which they take.—B. **That they should not, etc.** Herod expected to counteract the divine purpose, but the prophet says : " Take counsel together, and it shall come to nought, etc.," Isai. 8 : 10. **Another way** —road, which did not lead through Jerusalem.

[13] Now when they were departed, behold, an angel of the Lord appeareth to Joseph in a dream, saying, Arise, and take the young child and his mother, and flee into Egypt, and be thou there, until I tell thee ; for Herod will seek the young child to destroy him.

A. **When they were departed.** Leaving rich treasures behind, of special value in view of the hasty journey to Egypt.—B. **Arise, etc.** The numerous Jews who then resided in Egypt were not molested on account of their religion. Such a journey might require, according to the most probable estimate, not more than five or six days, even when women and children performed it. "Arise," required prompt obedience, and Joseph accordingly departed at once, without waiting till morning (ver. 14).—C. **Egypt** is very frequently mentioned in the O. T. Its Hebrew name is *Mizraim* (in Gen. 13 : 10; 15 : 18 ; 45 : 20 and elsewhere), which originally belonged to a son of Ham (Gen. 10: 6, 13) and still exists in the modern Arabic name *Misr*. In the time of Abraham as well as of Moses, Zoan (Num. 13 : 22 ; Ps. 78 : 12, 43 ; Isai. 19 : 11 ; 30 : 4), on an eastern branch of the Nile, was the seat of government (see 26 : 2, B., § 5). —D. **Until**; see ver. 19, 20.—E. **For Herod, etc.** The most secret thoughts of men are known to God ; Ps 139 : 4; 1 Cor. 4 : 5 ; Hebr. 4 : 13.

[14] And he arose, and took the young child and his mother by night, and departed into Egypt.

By night; the utmost secrecy appears to have been observed by Joseph, lest Herod should cause him to be pursued.

[15] And was there until the death of Herod: that it might be fulfilled which was spoken by the Lord through the prophet, saying, Out of Egypt did I call my son.

Out of Egypt, etc. The words of the prophet are : "When Israel was a child, then I loved him, and called my son out of Egypt." Hosea 11 : 1. The people of Israel are here viewed as a distinct nation descended from the same progenitor; they are then, as a whole, represented as a single individual. "Thus saith the

Lord, Israel is my son, etc.," Exod. 22: 23. It is in allusion to this language and the occasion on which it was employed that God, when He afterwards speaks by the prophet of His ancient acts of mercy, employs the terms here quoted by Matthew. It was through divine love that He called forth Israel His son from Egypt (Deut. 4; 37); now, the same love watched over Him who was in a special sense His son—His *only*-begotten Son (John 3: 16).

¹⁶ Then Herod, when he saw that he was mocked of the wise men, was exceeding wroth, and sent forth, and slew all the male children that were in Bethlehem, and in all the borders thereof, from two years old and under, according to the time which he had carefully learned of the wise men.

A. **Saw that he was mocked**; the Greek word here, and uniformly elsewhere (20: 19; 27: 29) translated *mock*, describes derisive, contemptuous or insulting treatment of a person. Although the wise men simply obeyed the divine command by avoiding a second visit to Herod, he heard of their departure with great anger, and probably applied this word himself to their conduct, as insulting to him.—B. **Wroth**, an old English word, which, like *exasperated*, is more emphatic than the word angry (18: 34, A.), but is no longer as commonly used.—C. **Sent forth and slew**. The sanguinary Herod, who scorned the grace of God, could not govern his wicked passions; he foolishly supposed that he would secure the death of the new-born King, by giving orders to the executioners to spare the life of no little child in that region which corresponded to his description of it.—D. **All the male children .... borders thereof**. This act of the ungodly tryant, who at another time slew two of his own children, was quite consistent with his cruel character.— E. **From two years, etc.** See ver. 7, B.

¹⁷ Then was fulfilled that which was spoken by Jeremiah the prophet, saying,

¹⁸ A voice was heard in Ramah, weeping, and great mourning, Rachel weeping for her children; and she would not be comforted, because they are not.

A. Ramah . . . . Rachel. Ramah (the modern *er-Ram*), a city originally belonging to the tribe of Benjamin (Josh. 18:25), six miles north of Jerusalem, was afterwards attached to the northern kingdom of Israel or the Ten Tribes, 1 Kings 15:17; 2 Chron. 16:1; Jer. 40:1. The descendants of Benjamin returned to it after the Captivity, Nehem. 7:30; 11:31, 33. Rachel, the wife of Jacob, was buried in the vicinity of Bethlehem (Gen. 35:19, 20; 48:7), and her sepulchre in the border of Benjamin was a well-known spot in the days of Samuel (1 Sam. 10:2); it is now called by the Arabs *Kubbet Râhil*—Rachel's tomb. Her memory, as one of those that "did build the house of Israel" (Ruth 4:11), was always held in reverence. Hence Ramah may represent, by an easy figure of speech, the region which furnished Rachel with a grave. The prophet Jeremiah had been commissioned to deliver very gracious promises of the Lord respecting the restoration of Israel to Palestine after the close of the Babylonish Captivity, which commenced during his ministry. Thus, in ch. 31:1-14, tender words of consolation are spoken by him to his distressed countrymen. Then, by way of application, he produces in the next verse (the one here quoted by Matthew) an instance of the national calamities, and in the succeeding verses shows the great consolation which the divine promises afford under the painful circumstances of the times. Ramah was the station where the captives were collected, who were to be carried to Babylon; hence Jeremiah himself was conducted to the spot, ch. 40:1. When the train of captives, consisting of Benjamites, Ephraimites, etc., that is, children of Rachel, commenced their mournful march, all wept bitterly. Now as Jacob's name often represents collectively his descendants (e. g. Num. 24: 17, 19; Deut. 33: 10; Ps. 14: 7), so here the weeping Rachel is introduced as the representative of her weeping descendants. But at the same time the prophet obviously intends also to employ a striking figure of speech, similar to one already occurring above, ver. 6, and also in Isai. 52: 1, 2, where Jerusalem, the holy city, is addressed as a living person, and invited to put on her beautiful garments, etc. So here, amid loud expressions of grief which the prophet hears on every side, he identifies Rachel with her descendants, and exhibits her as weeping and lamenting. But now, six centuries after the prophet's day, Matthew informs us that an additional and a deeper meaning lay in these words; they refer also to another calamity which would cause Rachel's sons and daughters to weep anew. She seems to be called forth from her grave by the lamentations of the parents of the murdered children—again she weeps bitterly and refuses to be comforted; her children are torn from the parental embrace and cruelly robbed, not now of their liberty but of their lives.—**B. They are not**—have disappeared, are dead; comp. Gen. 42: 13, 36.

¹⁹⁻²¹ But when Herod was dead, behold, an angel of the Lord appeareth in a dream to Joseph in Egypt,—Saying, Arise, and take the young child and his mother, and go into the land of Israel: for they are dead that sought the young child's life. And he arose, and took the young child and his mother, and came into the land of Israel.

A. After the death of Herod, an angel again appeared to Joseph in a dream, in fulfilment of the promise in ver. 13. It is not known how long the latter remained in Egypt with the mother and child, as the interval between the birth of Christ and the death of Herod, although not of long duration (probably less than a year), cannot now be defined with entire precision.—B. **Land of Israel.** This name designates the territory originally occupied by the twelve tribes of Israel; see 1 Sam. 13:19.

²² But when he heard that Archelaus was reigning over Judæa in the room of his father Herod, he was afraid to go thither; and being warned of God in a dream, he withdrew into the parts of Galilee.

A. **Archelaus**—one of the sons of Herod. After Herod's death the emperor Augustus divided his dominions among three of the sons. The portion assigned to Archelaus (who received the title of *ethnarch*, which was inferior in dignity to that of *king*) consisted of Judæa, Idumæa and Samaria, or the southern portion of the original kingdom. As he was known to be suspicious and cruel like his father, Joseph was "afraid to go thither," namely, to Bethlehem, which lay in Judæa. Several years after the birth of Christ, Archelaus was deposed by the emperor, and Judæa together with Samaria was ultimately annexed to the Roman province of Syria, and governed by Roman officers; of these one was Pilate, 27:2, B.— B. **Galilee.** Herod Antipas, who now ruled here, a superstitious, artful and unprincipled man (Luke 13:32), was, nevertheless, less cruel than his brother Archelaus; the influence of the chief priests and Pharisees, whom Joseph had reason to dread, was, besides, far less powerful in Galilee than in Judæa. The phrase **parts of Galilee** seems to indicate that Joseph did not immediately find a permanent home; according to ver. 23, he afterwards established himself in Nazareth, in Lower Galilee.

²³ And came and dwelt in a city called Nazareth: that it might be fulfilled which was spoken by the prophets, that he should be called a Nazarene.

A. **Nazareth.** This small town had previously been

the place of residence of Joseph and Mary, at least temporarily, Luke 2:4, although Joseph's family originally belonged to Bethlehem, Luke 2 : 3, 4. The angel who announced the birth of Christ to Mary, found her in Nazareth, Luke 1 : 26, 27. In this place the Lord continued to reside permanently until He commenced His public ministry (Luke 4: 16-24; Matt. 13 : 53-58), and hence He acquired the name of " Jesus of Nazareth" (Matt. 21: 11; 26: 71; John 19 : 19; Acts 10: 38), that is, Jesus the Nazarene.—B. **By the prophets.** Matthew does not specify a particular prophet, but mentions those of the O. T. collectively, so that we may expect not so much a particular passage quoted in the words of any prophet, as rather, some truth or fact derived from the general tenor of their language.—C. **He . . . . Nazarene.** These words, in accordance with the foregoing annotation, do not constitute a particular verse or passage in the O. T. The Nazarenes or inhabitants of Nazareth and the Galileans in general, were regarded by the stricter classes of the Jews with a certain degree of contempt; see John 1 : 46; 7 : 52. Hence the appellation " Nazarene" became a term of reproach. Now the prophets had foretold that the Messiah should encounter shame and reproach, Ps. 22 : 6-8 ; Isai. 53 : 2-12. The phrase " to be called " is often equivalent simply to the words "to be," as in Matt. 5 : 19, or "to be appointed or constituted," as in Heb. 5 : 4. In this sense, Christ *was* one that is scorned, or, was constituted " a reproach of men," Ps. 22 : 6. The words of Matthew are accordingly to be thus understood : Even as the prophets foretold that the Messiah should be treated with scorn, so it also came to pass; He was contemptuously called by His enemies Jesus of Nazareth, and He suffered the shame of the cross.

CHAPTER III.

¹ And in those days cometh John the Baptist, preaching in the wilderness of Judæa.

A. In those days. Between the events related at the close of the preceding chapter and those which now follow, nearly thirty years intervene (Luke 3 : 23). Matt. at once proceeds to the history of the public ministry of the Lord, without relating the events of the intermediate years. The phrase **in those days,** in its close connection with the last words of the preceding verse, may possibly refer to that whole period of Christ's humiliation (Phil. 2 : 6–8), during which He was regarded as a Nazarene (2 : 23), that is, was "despised and rejected of men" (Isai. 53 : 3), namely, in "the days of His flesh" (Hebr. 5 : 7). Then "Jesus was not yet glorified" (John 7 : 39), or, had not yet finished His atoning work (John 13 : 31) and ascended to heaven (Phil. 2 : 8–11 ; Luke 24 : 26 ; Hebr. 2 : 9).—**B. John the Baptist.** For his early history (see Luke ch. 1); the circumstances attending his death are described in Matt. 14 : 3–12. The epithet **the Baptist,** or, *the Baptizer* (as he is called in the original in Mark 6 : 14, given to him also by Josephus, Antiq. 18. 5. 1.), is derived from the circumstance that he introduced and practised a religious rite of a peculiar character, directly referring to the Saviour's work, and entirely distinct from the washing with water frequently mentioned by Moses (Exod. 29 : 4; 40 : 12; Lev. 14 : 7; Num. 8 : 7, and comp. Hebr. 9: 10). The epithet *Baptist* also serves to distinguish him from many other Jews who bore the same name (signifying *whom Jehovah bestows*). John's Baptism was readily understood to be a religious rite, corresponding in some measure to the washings just mentioned, but its precise import was not at first apparent. It differed from the washings or ablutions commanded in the Law, in being "a baptism of repentance for the remission of sins" (Luke 3 : 3), which character and power these ablutions did not possess. There is no satisfactory evidence that proselytes who were received by the Jews were baptized as well as circumcised, as early as the days of John, or indeed before the destruction of the city of Jerusalem. *After* that event, when the sacrifices had ceased, the Jews appear to have substituted a species of baptism of the proselytes whom they received. The passages Luke 3 : 3 and John 1 : 33 seem to teach that John's Baptism with water had been then first introduced when he received his divine commission. It referred in its spiritual import to the cleansing of the heart mentioned in Jer. 4 : 14; Isai. 1 : 16. Now that cleansing and renewing of the heart could be effected by Christ alone, not by human works (Jer. 2 : 22). The circumstances under which this remarkable man appears, his secluded life in the wilderness until God sent him forth to preach (Luke 1 : 80; 3 : 2), his vigorous self-denial, his earnest and even vehement appeals to his hearers, etc., are readily explained by the peculiar office which God had assigned to him. According to the law found in Num. ch. 6, concerning Nazarites (by whom are to be understood persons who were secluded, separated or withdrawn from the ordinary habits of social life for a specified period), these individuals, like the officiating priests (Lev. 10 : 9), drank no wine, refrained from cutting their hair, etc. The whole institution (named from a

Hebrew word indicating *separation, restraint, abstinence*), was designed to render special honor to God, and deepen the religious feelings of the Jews. It is an image of the spiritual consecration of the Christian to God (Rom. 12: 1). Some were devoted by their parents to the life of a Nazarite from their birth, of which custom Samson (Judges 13: 5) and the prophet Samuel (1 Sam. 1: 11) are instances. John was invested with the same character by the angel who foretold his birth (Luke 1: 15). This circumstance naturally tended to produce in him, even from childhood, a certain gravity and austereness of character (see Matt. 11: 7, 8). John knew, moreover, as it appears from John 1: 23, that an office had been assigned by the Lord to him alone, of all mortals, even before his birth, which was loftier and more solemn than that of any prophet who went before him (Matt. 11: 9, 11), namely that of being the immediate forerunner or herald of the Messiah, as the ancient prophets had predicted (Isai. 40: 3; Mal. 3: 1; 4: 5; Matt. 11: 10; 17: 12, 13; Luke 1: 17). These circumstances produced contemplative habits in him, a deep feeling of his responsibility, a consciousness of his own insufficiency, and a firm purpose to be faithful to God who had called him, and to consecrate his whole life to the great work which had been assigned to him.—
C. **Preaching;** the word used in the original was primarily applied to the act of a herald or other person who published or publicly proclaimed important tidings (see Mark 1: 45; 13: 10; Luke 12: 3); it almost uniformly signifies in the N. Test. the act of announcing, making publicly known, or teaching the Gospel of Jesus Christ. Luke (3: 2) specifies that John had received a regular call; "the word of God came" unto him, as to other prophets whom God sent forth (e. g. Jer. 1: 2; Ezek. 1: 3; 6: 1). As he was, moreover, a member of the order

of Jewish priests, that is, a descendant of Aaron (Luke 1 : 5, 62, 63; Exod. 28 : 1; Num. 16 : 40), no Jew questioned his authority to assume the functions of a priest, namely, to teach and to perform religious rites. Only a portion or the substance of John's preaching is recorded in the N. T. (Luke 3 : 18).—D. **Wilderness of Judæa.** This was a wild and rocky region east of Jerusalem, extending from the Jordan in a southern direction along the western shore of the Dead Sea. It is already mentioned in Judg. 1 : 16. The words *desert* and *wilderness*, usually employed to designate tracts that are destitute of vegetation, were sometimes applied not to barren wastes but to uninhabited regions which were not entirely destitute of the means of subsistence, but which afforded pasture for cattle, even if not suited for tillage. Thus the "desert place" mentioned in Mark 6 : 35, 39, abounded in "green grass" (comp. Ps. 65 : 12). This wilderness contained several cities at an early period (Josh. 15 : 61, 62 : Judges 1 : 16). It was also in this wilderness that Josephus, the Jewish historian, spent three years with his teacher Banus, "having no other food than that which grew of its own accord" (Life, § 2). It is hence apparent that the locusts and bees, which, according to ver. 4, furnished John with food, could easily exist there in large numbers. In Isai. 7 : 22, the abundance of honey is described as a feature of a desolate country.

* Saying, Repent ye: for the kingdom of heaven is at hand.

A. **Repent ye.** "John's preaching was intended to teach the Jews that their descent from Abraham could not secure them from deserved punishment, that they were all under sin, (Rom. 3 : 9), that neither circumcision nor any works of the law would avail anything or justify the sinner (Gal. 2 : 16; 6 : 15), and that the law gave a knowledge of sin (Rom. 3 : 20; 7 : 7), but could not give peace to the conscience (Hebr. 9 : 9; 10 : 1), as it could not take away sins (Hebr. 10 : 11). Therefore he baptized the people unto repentance, and directed them to Christ, through whom alone remission of sins and peace with God could be obtained."—LUTHER. John begins his preaching with a loud call to repentance, like the Saviour (Mark. 1 : 15) and the apostles (Mark. 6 : 12; Luke 24 : 47; Acts 2 : 38; 3 : 19; see also Rev. 2 : 5, 16). *Repentance* is often explained to be "a change of mind"; but this phrase does not fully give the Gospel sense of the word. Passages like 2 Tim. 2 : 25; Acts 8 : 22; 2 Cor. 7 : 10; Luke 13 : 3, with many others, teach the following lessons:—the duty of repentance is imposed on all men (Acts 17 : 30), inasmuch as all are by nature sinners (Eph. 2 : 3); they are required to learn and understand the greatness of their guilt and danger; this knowledge is accompanied by deep feeling, namely, sorrow for sin and grief, produced by the revelation of God's displeasure. Then, the sinner to whom the divine message is addressed, and who is at the same time made acquainted with God's gracious plan of salvation through Christ, is led by his awakened conscience and distressed heart to seek the offered means of salvation, that is, to come to Christ. This deep, heartfelt conviction of sin, and this desire for pardon through the atonement of Christ, as the only means of salvation, constitute essentially Gospel repentance. It is evident that the basis of the whole change is *faith*, in varying degrees of clearness and power; indeed, the remark is true that there can be no genuine repentance which is unconnected with a hope for the remission of sins as announced by John (Luke 3 : 3), that is, which is not accompanied by faith. While the sinner believes that the danger exists, he also believes that he may escape if he chooses God's appointed way. This faith becomes more and more clear, until by the aid of the divine Spirit, who is in truth the author of this whole work of grace in the soul, it assumes distinctly the character of faith in the crucified Redeemer. The result which this faith produces, as it gradually advances in depth and efficacy, is the actual, cordial return of the sinner to God, and his consecration to the Redeemer's service. Strictly speaking, therefore, Repentance implies sorrow for sin and faith in Jesus Christ, and is wrought by the Spirit through the means of grace.—B. **The kingdom of heaven:** see Excursus I. The kingdom here mentioned, which is not of this world (John 18: 36), is described in Dan. 7: 13, 14, as the Messiah's kingdom.—The motive which is assigned by John for performing the duty claims attention. He seems to say: The grace of God is first offered; He loved us first, while we were yet enemies (1 John 4:19; Rom. 5:8, 10). Now let such divine compassion and goodness lead you to repentance (Rom. 2: 4). Your repentance will not render you deserving of the kingdom of heaven—you will not thereby *earn* it, but it will fit you to enter it, after divine pity has brought it near to you. The glory and honor of man's salvation belong exclusively to Christ.—C. **At hand**, literally, *has come near* (as in Rom. 13: 12), alluding to the approaching public appearance of the Saviour, who shortly afterwards commenced His public ministry.

³ For this is he that was spoken of by Isaiah the prophet, saying, The voice of one crying in the wilderness, Make ye ready the way of the Lord, make his paths straight.

A. For this . . . prophet=Isaiah, who lived seven centuries before John. Matt., who relates many events which fulfil predictions of the O. Test., here informs his readers that John the Baptist is the individual crying in

the wilderness, to whom Isaiah refers in ch. 40 : 3–5. The same explanation is given both by John himself in his answer to the deputation sent to him by the leaders of the Jews (John 1 : 19–24), and also by Christ (Matt. 11 : 10). Matt. furnishes only a portion of the passage, with the whole of which his Jewish readers were familiar; Luke quotes it more fully in 3 : 4–6, for the sake of his gentile readers. Isaiah had previously announced the national afflictions which were approaching, and which would result in that awful catastrophe, the Babylonish Captivity, ch. 39 : 6. He is then commanded to comfort the distressed people by the promise of a gracious deliverance. Now that divine grace which pardons sin is revealed in its highest glory, not when it merely restores liberty and temporal prosperity to impoverished exiles and oppressed bond-servants, but when it bestows the gift of eternal life through Jesus Christ (Rom. 6 : 23) on sinful mortals, " who, through fear of death, were all their lifetime subject to bondage " (Hebr. 2 : 15). The true consolation, as administered by the prophet, accordingly consists in a prediction of the appearance of the Messiah, the saviour of the world, whose coming the voice of John proclaimed. This is the general sense of the prophecy.
—B. **The voice . . . wilderness**—the voice of one *is heard*, crying, etc. The prophet, with the same minuteness with which the parting of the Saviour's garments under the cross is elsewhere predicted (Ps. 22 : 18; Matt. 27 : 35), here points to the wilderness (see above, ver. 1, D), from which the voice of John proceeds.—C. **Prepare . . straight**. It was the custom of oriental monarchs, when they travelled with a large retinue or army, to send forward pioneers who levelled and repaired the roads. The prophet refers to this practice not simply as an illustration of the facilities which God would afford the cap-

tives for returning to the land of their fathers, but preeminently as an illustration of the special duties of John, the harbinger of Christ. John's office required him to preach the duty of repentance, to awaken a desire after God, to bear testimony to Christ as the Saviour of the world (John 1 : 26–36), and thus prepare the way for Christ's own ministrations. "Make straight in the desert," says the prophet, the substance of whose words Matt. quotes, "a highway for our God." Jesus, the Messiah, whose approach is proclaimed by the prophet, is called by him the LORD, that is, JEHOVAH, as it is in the original Hebrew, and "our God."

⁴ Now John himself had his raiment of camel's hair, and a leathern girdle about his loins ; and his food was locusts and wild honey.

A. **Raiment . . . hair.** John exhibits a striking resemblance to Elijah, not only in his character (Mal. 4 : 5 ; Matt. 11 : 14; 17 : 12, 13), but also in his very appearance, (2 Kings 1 : 8). The **camel**, as it is well known, is one of the most useful of the domestic animals of the Arabs and other oriental nations (see below, 19 : 24, B. and 23 : 24, B.). A coarse cloth was made of its long and shaggy **hair**, which was much used for tent coverings, etc.; it often constituted the clothing of the poor. Such a "rough garment" (Hebr. *mantle of hair*), the opposite of "soft clothing," worn by those who are in kings' houses (11 : 8), appears to have been customarily worn by the ancient Jewish prophets, Zech. 13 : 4.—B. **A leathern girdle.** The girdle was a necessary part of the dress of the ancients; it attached the tunic or undergarment (John 21 : 7; Acts 12 : 8) to the body, and secured the purse in which money was carried (Matt. 10 : 9). It was concealed by the upper garment, mantle or cloak, which was a loose garment thrown around the person. The girdles of the rich were made of more costly materials than leather, and were richly embroidered.—C. **Locusts and wild honey** (see ver. 1, D. above). The facts are here mentioned as illustrations of the austere life which John led, and which the Jews afterwards maliciously compared with that of the Saviour, who conformed to the ordinary mode of living (Matt. 11 : 18, 19). **Locusts** are flying insects of various species. Some of them were very large, and were allowed by the laws of Moses to be eaten (Lev. 11 : 22). Modern travellers relate that poor persons in the East still eat them, after removing the wings and legs, and boiling or roasting them with salt. Wild bees readily found nourishment in that wilderness, and deposited their **honey** in trees and clefts of the rocks. The abundance of wild honey in ancient Palestine is well known (Exod. 3 : 8; Judg. 14 : 8; 1 Sam. 14 : 25, 26; Jer. 41 : 8; Ps. 81 : 16). Such honey, and not the gum of a tree (treehoney), appears to have been meant.

⁵ Then went out unto him Jerusalem, and all Judæa, and all the region round about Jordan.

A. **Went ... Judæa** (see 2 : 3, B.). It is obvious that the preaching of John made a deep impression on the public mind. Matthew implies here that large numbers, or the people generally, not only from the city of Jerusalem, but also from all other parts of the country, came to him. We do not learn from the Gospel that all those whom John baptized, received Christ in faith, when he appeared in public. An interest in religion may seem at times to prevail very extensively, while many who appear to be moved by devout feeling fail to receive Christ sincerely in faith, or, as in John 6 : 66, "go back," and return to the world and sin. Every one has here abundant cause to examine his own spiritual

4

state, as each one must answer to God for himself and not for others.—B. **Jordan.** This river, the only important stream in Palestine, is originally formed by three streamlets or springs in the extreme north (not far from Cæsarea Philippi, 16 : 13, B.), the Banias, the Dan and the Hasbany; after passing through lake Merom (Joshua 11 : 5), it still follows a southerly course, flows through the sea of Galilee, and finally empties into the Dead Sea. The distance between the Sea of Galilee and the Dead Sea is 60 miles, but in this distance the Jordan, in consequence of its numerous windings, runs a course of 200 miles.

⁶ And they were baptized of him in the river Jordan, confessing their sins.

A. **Were baptized of** (by) **him.** The baptism of John was "from heaven" (Matt. 21 : 25), that is, God sent or commissioned him to baptize, John 1 : 6, 33. It was, as John himself shows (ver. 11, below), not a sacrament like Christian baptism (see 19 : 14 and 20 : 22 C.), which was instituted by the Saviour as "the washing of regeneration, and renewing of the Holy Ghost" (Tit. 3 : 5); hence the latter was administered to the disciples whom Paul found in Ephesus, and who had previously received John's baptism (Acts 19: 1–5). It did not impart grace itself, but it directed men to Him by whom "grace and truth came" (John 1 : 17). It was thus a religious rite of deep import: "it was a baptism of repentance for the remission of sins," according to Mark 1 : 4; Acts 13 : 24. The preaching of John convinced his hearers of their sinfulness and guilt, and led them to inquire: "What shall we do?" (Luke 3 : 10, 14). When they felt the need of divine mercy, John announced that the "Lamb of God, which taketh away the sin of the world," was already standing among them, John 1 : 26–29.

His baptism, accordingly, made Jesus "manifest to Israel" (John 1 : 31), and conducted the people in faith to Him (Acts 19 : 4). In this sense he turned many of the children of Israel to the Lord their God, as the angel had said (Luke 1 : 16).—**B. In Jordan.** John preached and baptized at various places during his ministry, at Bethabara, or beyond the Jordan (John 1 : 28), and elsewhere, evidently selecting at all times a spot which afforded a supply of water for his own wants, and for those of the multitudes that came to him. Thus we find him on one occasion in "Enon near to Salim, because there was much water there" (John 3 : 23), or, as the original says, "many waters," that is, many springs or fountains. The *Greek* word here translated *in*, resembles, in the variety of its meanings in the N. Test., the corresponding *Hebrew* word. In 1 Sam. 29 : 1, it is translated, "by a fountain;" in Ezek. 10 : 15, "by the river." Thus, too, the tower mentioned in Luke 13 : 4, stood *at* or *by* or *near* Siloam, which was a pool of water (Nehem. 3 : 15; John 9 : 7), and not actually *in* the water. Again, the same word here translated "*in* the Jordan" is rendered in Rom. 8 : 34 and Hebr. 1 : 3, respectively, "*at—on* the right hand," in the sense of proximity or nearness. It is sometimes translated *with*, as (Gen. 32 : 10), "*with* my staff" (Hebr.), Matthew 26 : 52, "*with* the sword" (Greek), or *by*, as "*by* the hand" (Acts 7 : 35). Sometimes *among, through, for,* etc. These passages show that the sense here can be: he baptized *at* or *near* the Jordan. As the Scriptures never say that John immersed any persons, it is probable that he baptized according to the mode which is observed when Christian baptism is rightly administered, that is, by sprinkling or pouring (aspersion or affusion). This mode was doubtless employed in reference to certain purificatory rites enjoined by the law, and performed by sprinkling (see Lev. 14: 7, 27; Numb. 8:7; 19:13; Hebr. 9:13). In allusion to this legal mode of cleansing, the prophets refer to the cleansing of man from sin, which is accomplished by Christ. Hence we read: "so shall he sprinkle," etc. (Isai. 52:15); "then will I sprinkle," etc. (Ezek. 36:25, 26); thus, too, we read in Hebr. 10:22, of "hearts *sprinkled* from an evil conscience." This profound spiritual meaning of the religious rite of sprinkling, as setting forth the cleansing of the sinner through the Saviour's blood, is sustained by passages like Hebr. 12:24; 1 Pet. 1: 2. The sanctifying influence of Christ is set forth in the usual mode of administering baptism (see 20: 22, C.). This mode also corresponds to another description of it in the Bible: the *pouring out* of the Spirit, predicted by Joel (ch. 2: 28), and described in Acts 2: 1-21, is called by John, in allusion to the visible part of the rite, a baptism with the Holy Ghost (Matt. 3:11). Immersion or dipping in water is never mentioned in the N. Test. as a Christian or religious rite. Indeed, the opinion that the application of water to the whole body, as in immersion, is necessary for religious purposes, is discountenanced by the Lord Jesus as an error, John 13: 9, 10. (For Rom. 6:4, which has often been supposed to refer to immersion, see below, 27 : 60, B.)—**C. Confessing their sins.** (See above, annot. A.) The nature of the confession which the people made is not specified; it may have consisted in a general acknowledgment of their sinfulness (see Levit. 26:40; Ps. 32: 5; Luke 19: 8; Acts 19: 18; 1 John 1: 9). External religious rites (Isai. 1: 11-20), prayer, alms-giving (Matt. 6:1-8), or religious professions (Matt. 7: 21, 22), are, as our Lord teaches, of no avail, without true repentance and faith in the heart (Isai. 57:15; 66: 2; Luke 18:9-14). A **sin** is any transgression of the law of God (1 John 3 : 4) in thought or feeling, in word or deed.

⁷ But when he saw many of the Pharisees and Sadducees coming to his baptism, he said unto them, Ye offspring of vipers, who hath warned you to flee from the wrath to come?

A. Coming to his baptism. The severe rebuke which John administers to them, expresses his well-founded conviction of their insincerity. Their corrupt hearts impelled them to seek notoriety by the practice of external religious acts; the reverence with which John was generally regarded (Luke 3 : 15; Matt. 21 : 26), led them to fear that their character for piety would suffer, if they treated him with disdain. But afterwards, when he refused to receive them in their continued impenitent state (Matt. 21 : 32), they withdrew; they would not humble themselves before God and repent of their sins (Luke 7: 30).—**B. Ye offspring of vipers**—ye deceitful and wicked people, who boast that ye are Abraham's children! (*offspring.*) This language is addressed by John and the Saviour to Pharisees and Sadducees, who exceeded all others in hypocrisy and malice (Matt. 12 : 34; 23 : 33); the words, which unveil their own hearts to them, are designed to rouse them from their false security (Jerem. 6 : 14). Various poisonous reptiles, the serpent, viper, cockatrice, adder, asp, etc., are mentioned in the Scriptures, Gen. 49: 17; Isai. 11 ꞏ 8; 14 : 29; 59 : 5; Ps. 58 : 4; 140 : 3; Acts 28 : 3; Rom. 3 : 13; they usually serve as images of deceitfulness and malevolence, or represent any injurious or deadly influence. In the most favorable sense, the serpent (as a general name) was proverbially known as an emblem of caution, prudence or wisdom (Matt. 10 : 16, C.). The serpent which beguiled Eve (2 Cor. 11 : 3; Gen. ch. 3) was the means of introducing sin and death into the world (John 8 : 44; Rev.

20:2). The wicked, in whom, according to Paul, the evil spirit worketh (Eph. 2:2), who obey Satan and are governed by his counsels, are termed the offspring or children of the serpent or the devil (Matt. 13:38; Acts 13:10).—C. **Who hath warned ... to come ?** The **wrath** here mentioned (called "the wrath to come," or, the approaching wrath, in 1 Thess. 1:10) is the judgment which will overtake the wicked (see ver. 10 and ver. 12 below). The displeasure with which God beholds all sin, and the eternal punishment which He has reserved for it (Matt. 25:41; 2 Thess. 1:7-9; 2 Pet. 2:17) and which He will inflict, are, in their combination, called His wrath (Ps. 79:6; Mic. 7:9; Rom. 1;18; 5:9; Eph. 2:3). None can effectually flee from it (that is, be delivered from it), who do not repent and believe in Christ (John 3:36); He alone can deliver us from the wrath to come (1 Thess. 1:10). The word **warned** here, as in Acts 20:35, occurs in the sense of *show, instruct* or *notify*. John's meaning then is: Has any one ever been authorized to tell you that you can be delivered from divine punishment by mere outward acts, without a renewal of the heart? If you are sincere in seeking this baptism of repentance, produce the proof by beginning a new life, as the fruit of your professed humility, love and faith.

⁸ Bring forth therefore fruit worthy of repentance :

A. **Bring ... fruit.** This figure of speech, by which a man and his conduct, as influenced by the state of his heart, are respectively compared to a tree and its fruits, often occurs (Ps. 1:3: Jer. 17:8; Matt. 7:16-20; 21:43; Rom. 11:17). These fruits are called *works* in Acts 26:20. The works which John demands in Luke 3:10-14 must consequently be viewed in their intimate connection with the repentance and faith, of which they are the result and evidence. They are wrought by the

Holy Spirit (Gal. 5:22; Eph. 5:9); if they proceed from any other source, such as ostentation, a mere sense of decorum, etc., they are of no value in the eyes of God (Isai. 1:11-18).—B. **Worthy.** John means: If you desire to escape, and allege that you are sincere, *then* furnish the proof.—C. **Repentance** (see above, ver. 2, A.).

⁹ And think not to say within yourselves, We have Abraham to our father: for I say unto you, that God is able of these stones to raise up children unto Abraham.

A. **Think not . . . yourselves**—do not secretly entertain the thought or belief, etc. (comp. Matt. 9:21; Luke 7:49); the phrase is derived from the Hebrew: " to say in the heart" (Ps. 10:6; 14:1).—B. **Abraham** (see Gen. ch. 11:27; 25:8). With him God made a covenant, and he was the founder of the Jewish nation; to him the promises were given (Gal. 3:16); he is the " father of all them that believe" (Rom. 4:11). The Jews supposed that, independently of their own personal faith and obedience, their mere descent from Abraham after the flesh imparted his righteousness to them, and entitled them alone to the blessings of the Messiah's kingdom, to the exclusion of the entire Gentile or heathen world (John 8:39). These vain thoughts, which are here reproved, and so often exposed by Christ, are afterwards combated by Paul, Rom. ch. 4; ch. 9; Gal. 5:6; Heb. ch. 7; ch. 11. The rich man mentioned in the parable is not relieved from the torment which he suffered, by his " father Abraham" (Luke 16:24).—C. **These stones**—the pebbles lying near the banks of the river, or the stones and rocks of the desert, which no one valued. The reasoning of John may be thus expressed : Ye descendants of Abraham suppose that ye are necessary to God, or that the terms of the covenant made with the fathers relieve you from its obligations, while they bind God!

But I tell you that the Almighty God, who "lightly esteems them that despise Him" (1 Sam. 2 : 30), can always accomplish His purposes without depending on your aid. Even as He originally formed men of the dust of the ground (Gen. 2 : 7), so His infinite power could, if He so desired, now convert these stones, which His hand created, into fit instruments for fulfilling all His promises to Abraham, independently of you. Indeed, the Gentiles or heathen, whom the Jews abhorred as vile and unclean, and who were not descendants of Abraham according to the flesh, were afterwards by faith made the children of Abraham (Rom. ch. 11 ; Gal. 3 : 7, 14), and to this circumstance the Lord refers in Matt. 8: 11, 12 ; Luke 4: 25 ; 20: 16 ; and see above 4 : 15, 16. On another occasion, when the hardness of heart of the Jews is rebuked, there is also a reference to the "stones" on the ground, (Luke 19 : 40).

¹⁰ And even now is the axe laid unto the root of the trees: every tree, therefore, that bringeth not forth good fruit is hewn down, and cast into the fire.

A. **The axe . . . trees**=the signs of the approaching divine judgment are already visible (see Isai. 10: 33, 34 ; Jerem. 46: 22, 23). John possibly alludes to the words: "Behold, I will send you Elijah the prophet before the coming of the great and dreadful day of the Lord" (Mal. 4: 5); he intends to say that God's chastisements of the impenitent will not linger long (comp. 2 Pet. 2: 3). The destruction of Jerusalem occurred in less than forty years afterwards. John's words strikingly correspond here to the Saviour's parable of the barren fig-tree (Luke 13: 6–9). "Seek ye the Lord while," etc. (Isai. 55 : 6), "walk while, etc." (John 12 : 35). "The Gospel was offered to the Jews; it was rejected, and now they are left without any other resource. Paul carried it to Greece and Asia Minor, but the impostor Mohammed now dwells there; he carried it to Rome, but now they have only the Pope there. 'Hold fast that which thou hast, that no man take thy crown' (Rev. 3 : 11)."—LUTHER. **B. Hewn down ... fire.** The act of casting an object into the fire for the express purpose of destroying it, is here, as the language of Scripture elsewhere shows (2 Kings 19: 17, 18; Jer. 36: 23; Ps. 140: 10; John 15: 6; Hebr. 6: 8) an image of that utter destruction which awaits the guilty (comp. 7: 19).—**Every tree —** every sinner who remains impenitent.

¹¹ I indeed baptize you with water unto repentance: but he that cometh after me is mightier than I, whose shoes I am not worthy to bear: he shall baptize you with the Holy Ghost and *with* fire:

A. I indeed ... repentance. (see above, ver. 2, A. and ver. 6, A.).—According to Luke 3 : 15, 16 and Acts 13 : 25, John appears to have repeated these words on a later occasion. He designs here to show the vast difference between the power of his baptism and that of the baptism which the Lord Jesus instituted, and also implies that He who would come after him would possess the power of executing judgment. The evangelist John reports additional remarks of the Baptist in ch. 1 ; ch. 3 : 27 ff.—**Unto repentance —** your submission to the rite is equivalent to a penitent confession of your sins.—**B. Mightier than I**=greater in power, higher in rank.—**C. Shoes**; the shoes mentioned here and in ch. 10: 10 are probably, as the word (*=what is bound under*) indicates, the sandals named in Mark 6 : 9; Acts 12 : 8; they consisted merely of soles made of leather or wood, and were fastened to the foot by means of strings which are called *latchets* (Gen. 14: 23; Isai. 5: 27); the word may, however, designate any covering of the feet. The common kind of shoes, on account of their inferior value, are mentioned in Amos 2: 6; 8: 6, as images of objects which are only lightly esteemed. The shoe was regarded as an unclean object in a chamber or holy place, Exod. 3 : 5; Josh. 5 : 15; hence the Jewish priests probably ministered at the altar with bare feet, after washing in the laver of brass (Exod. 30 : 18–21 ; 40 : 30–32). The duty of bearing, tying and untying such unclean articles, like the other menial service of stooping and washing the feet of another person, was usually assigned to the meanest of the slaves; it was a much more humble service than that which Elisha performed for Elijah, viz. pouring water on his hands (2 Kings 3 : 11). Paul alludes to this meaning of the words of John, when he contrasts him in Acts 13 : 25 with the Son of God.—D. **With the Holy Ghost and with fire.** The Baptism with the Spirit of God, in its most striking form, and to which John primarily referred, as we learn from the Saviour's words in Acts 1 : 5, occurred fifty days after the resurrection of Christ (see Acts 2 : 1–4), " cloven tongues like as of fire." With Acts 2 : 16–21 compare Joel 2 : 28–32. The *fire* here mentioned by John is not the " unquenchable fire," to which he refers in ver. 12, where it is an image of rejection and punishment, as in ver. 10, and 2 Thess. 1 : 8, but is added for the purpose of more particularly describing the effect or *power* (Act 1 : 8) of the Baptism of the Holy Ghost. It is hence omitted altogether in the abbreviated narrative in Mark 1˚: 8, where the baptism alone is mentioned. The same object may serve to illustrate opposite things, according to the different aspects in which it is presented. Thus, in Job 30 : 5, the thief represents those whose character is vile and odious; but in Rev. 3 : 3, the thief illustrates the sudden and unexpected coming of the Lord Himself. So, too, the refiner's fire mentioned in the prophetic passage referring to John and the Lord (Mal. 3 : 2, 3) is an image of purification, as in Zech. 13 : 9; Isai. 6 : 6, 7 ; 1 Pet. 1 : 7 ; and, in Isai. 4 : 4, the " spirit of burning " takes away filth. The **fire** in the present passage is, in the same manner, intimately connected with the Holy Ghost, and on this account also the preposition translated *with* is not repeated in the original before the word *fire*. This **fire** is an illustration of the cleansing, purifying, sanctifying influences of the Holy Ghost as exercised in holy Baptism. This explanation agrees with the words in Tit. 3 : 5, where regeneration and the renewing of the Holy Ghost are described as the effects of Baptism. See also John 3 : 5, where the second birth or regeneration is declared to be effected by water or baptism and the Holy Ghost. In the present case, John's inferior baptism with water is compared with the Lord's renovating and life-giving Baptism with fire — the influences of the Holy Spirit.

[12] Whose fan is in his hand, and he will thoroughly cleanse his threshing-floor ; and he will gather his wheat into the garner, but the chaff he will burn up with unquenchable fire.

Fan—floor—garner, etc. The **floor** was an elevated, open spot on the grain-field (Judg. 6 : 37), where the ground had been previously beaten or pressed, until the whole surface was hard and even. On this floor the sheaves were spread out and threshed by being simply beaten (Ruth 2 : 17), or by means of wheels (Isai. 28 : 27, 28) which passed over them, or else the grain was trodden out by cattle, asses, etc. (Hos. 10 : 11). After the grain had been sufficiently threshed, it was taken up from the threshing-floor (Ruth 3 : 2; 2 Sam. 24 : 18–22) and thrown against the wind (Jer. 4 : 11) by means of a winnowing shovel or **fan** (Isai. 30 : 24 ; 41 : 16), in order that the chaff might be separated from the grain and blown away (Ps. 1 : 4); thus the "floor," that is, *the grain lying on it*, was thoroughly cleansed. The wheat was then stored in the **garner**, the **chaff** and particles of straw were regarded as an encumbrance, and were frequently burned (Isai. 5 : 24) at once, or used as fuel. The term **unquenchable fire** (see Mark 9: 44, 46, 48) is taken from Isai. 66 : 24, but also alludes to Mal. 4: 1. It is called by the Lord "everlasting fire" (Matt. 25 : 41); it describes the awful doom of the wicked, whose punishment will be eternal.

¹³ Then cometh Jesus from Galilee to the Jordan unto John, to be baptized of him.

A. Then—near the close of the period of John's ministration, Acts 13 : 25.—**B. From Galilee to Jordan**=from Galilee in the north (Nazareth, Mark 1 : 9) to Judæa in the south, and specially to that point near the river where John was at that time preaching and baptizing.—**C. Unto John to be baptized of him.** The purpose for which the Saviour, who was without sin, and therefore needed no repentance, nevertheless received the baptism of John, which, in the case of all others was "unto repentance," ver. 11, is not fully explained by the remark that He was simply baptized like others, even as He was, like others, circumcised. His baptism, which must be considered in its intimate connection with the divine manifestations, the voice of the Father and the visible descent of the Holy Spirit, constituted His divine inauguration, or consecration, when viewed in His human nature; it was the commencement of His public ministry, of which the divine acknowledgment now occurs. The most striking feature of His baptism was the anointing with the Holy Spirit which He then received (Isai. 61 : 1–3; Luke 4: 18), and which so wonderfully distinguished His baptism from that of others. They confessed their sins; He, on the contrary, received a special attestation from heaven of His holy and divine nature. Further, He became our substitute, that is, performed and suffered all that divine justice demanded of fallen man, Isai. ch. 53; 1 Peter 2:

24; 3: 18; Rom. 8: 3; 2 Cor. 5: 21. Now, in order to fulfil the duties required of such a substitute and to bear our sins, the Son, who was God from all eternity, assumed our human nature, according to Hebr. 2: 14. In His human nature He was " made under the law ".(Gal. 4: 4, 5) that He might fulfil the law perfectly in our place, according to Rom. 5: 19, and thus acquire that " righteousness" mentioned in Deut. 6: 25, which no man had yet attained (Rom. 9: 31). Hence, all the requirements of the law, or the ordinances of God, were observed by Him in the spirit, as well as according to the letter. He was circumcised (Luke 2: 21); He regularly engaged in the worship of God in the synagogue (Luke 4: 16); He observed the festivals (John 7: 10; 10: 22, 23; 13: 1, 2, etc.), and, while He performed these external duties, He also fulfilled the whole law in a spirit of obedience, love and faith. Such *perfect* obedience in the spirit and in the life, constituted His "righteousness," and it is imputed to us by faith, Rom. 4: 24 ; see ver. 15, A. Now, John's baptism was of divine origin (see above, ver. 6, A.), although it was, like the Mosaic law, only temporary in its character ; as such a divine ordinance, like circumcision, the reception of it, or submission to it, was a part of that "righteousness," of which Christ was to be a perfect example in every respect, 1 Peter, 2: 21. By being baptized of John, he accordingly " fulfilled all righteousness," that is, obeyed every individual command of God, even when such command, like that of receiving John's baptism, was not contained in the laws of Moses. If Christ received baptism like the people, this sameness of the act does not imply that He was unclean as they were. When Moses sanctified Aaron, he sprinkled blood on him (Lev. 8: 30). But the priest sprinkled blood also upon the mercy-seat (Lev. 16: 14, 15), which itself was most holy, for God appeared in the cloud resting upon it, Lev. 16 : 2. So John sprinkled the unclean people, but, as a priest, he also sprinkled Jesus, "whom God hath set forth," says Paul (Rom. 3 : 25), "to be a propitiation," that is, a "mercy-seat," as the same Greek word is rendered in Hebr. 9 : 5. Thus in the case of the people, John's baptism was "unto repentance;" in the case of Christ it was, as in Aaron's case (Lev. ch. 8), His consecration as our high priest.

¹⁴ But John would have hindered him, saying, I have need to be baptized of thee, and comest thou to me?

A. **Would have hindered**;—at first declined to baptize him—B. **I have . . . . thou to me?** John, like all others, needed a Saviour ; the sense of his words may be thus expressed :—I am, like all the Jews, a sinner by nature (Eph. 2 : 3); I have need of the regenerating and sanctifying influences of the Holy Ghost wherewith thou wilt baptize men (John 1 : 33). But *Thou* art from above, the Son of God (John 1 : 34 ; 3 : 31); Thou takest away the sin of the world (John 1 : 29); Thou art the Messiah (John 3 : 28). Why then dost Thou come to one so unworthy as I am (John 1 : 27)? Thou who hast power to cleanse others from sin, needest not my baptism of repentance. John's hesitation proceeded partly from his deep humility in the presence of his Lord, and partly from the circumstance that the precise purpose of the Lord had not yet been fully revealed to him.

¹⁵ But Jesus answering said unto him, Suffer it now : for thus it becometh us to fulfil all righteousness. Then he suffereth him.

A. **Suffer . . . now**=refrain now from making objections ; thou shalt know all hereafter. These are the first words of Jesus on record which He pronounced on commencing His public ministry. The work which He designed to perform was truly a "fulfilling of all righteousness"; by it He became *the Lord our Righteousness*, which is the name given to Him in Jer. 23 : 6 ; comp. 1 Cor. 1 : 30 with 2 Cor. 5 : 21.—B. **For thus . . . . righteousness** (see above, ver. 13, B.).—This fulfilling of all righteousness was performed by the Lord alone ; when He says : "*thus* it becometh *us*," He associated John with Himself simply as the instrument appropriately employed by Him in the work. The Lord does not, like the Jews, make a confession of sins, neither does He, like John, say : " I have need, etc.," but "it becometh," that is, it is fitting or suitable to My atoning work. In the same sense the word *become* is used in Hebr. 2 : 10 ; 7 : 26.—**Righteousness** in a *legal* sense (1 : 19, B.) depends on a conscientious fulfilment of the laws of God. John's baptism was a divine appointment (ver. 1, above); the Saviour, by subjecting Himself to it and thus recognizing the holy mission of John, honored God when He honored God's messenger and God's appointment, For *righteousness* in the *Gospel* sense, see 5 : 6, B.—**C. Then he suffereth him**—yielded, and baptized Jesus. John understood his duty, even if he did not understand perfectly the Saviour's motives, and he promptly obeyed. So Abraham obeyed when God commanded him to offer Isaac (Gen. ch. 22). The Christian never asks : Is my reason capable of understanding it? He only asks : Has God spoken? " Blessed are they that have not seen, and yet have believed." John 20 : 29.

¹⁶ And Jesus, when he was baptized, went up straightway from the water : and, lo, the heavens were opened unto him, and he saw the Spirit of God descending as a dove, and coming upon him.

A. Straightway=immediately after the baptism.— **B. From the water.** Matt. means to say, that the baptism had been performed at the river where John could readily obtain water for his numerous baptisms, and that the Saviour immediately afterwards withdrew from the valley of the river; comp. "led up" in 4:1, B.—**C. The heavens were opened.** In the tabernacle and the temple (Exod. 26:31-33; 2 Chron. 3:14), a curtain or vail concealed the most holy place, which none but the high priest entered, "the Holy Ghost thus signifying, that the way into the holiest of all was not yet made manifest, etc.," Hebr. 9:8. That vail was rent in twain when Christ expired on the cross (Matt. 27:51, and comp. Hebr. 10:19, 20). The opening of the heavens at this baptism, and the rending of the vail at the crucifixion, teach us that now Christ has given all men free access to the Father, Eph. 2:18.—In Mark 1:10 a word is used in the original for "opened," which is translated *rent, rend,* in Matt. 27:51; John 19:24, and *divided* in Acts 14:4; comp. also Isai. 64:1. The language of the text, including the words "unto him," imply that the brightness and glory of heaven were at that moment revealed to Jesus specially, reminding us of the vision of the "glory of God" afterwards granted to Stephen, Acts 7:55; comp. Ezek. 1:1. The nature and extent of these wonderful exhibitions of the glories of heaven, like the revelation granted to Paul, of which he speaks in 2 Cor. 12:2-4, we are not now permitted to understand fully; hence the facts alone are mentioned.—**D. He saw**—*Jesus* saw it; see Mark 1:10; He had been engaged in prayer, when the event occurred, Luke 3:21. The heavens are still open whenever believing prayer is offered. Through Christ we now have "a new and living way—into the holiest" (Hebr. 10:19, 20; Eph. 3:12), and He will open Paradise to the believer.—**E. Spirit of God**=the Holy Ghost; 1:18 D.—**F. Descending as a dove.** The same Spirit evermore descends invisibly, and imparts His grace, when the Holy Baptism which the Saviour instituted is administered. John also saw the appearance (John 1 : 32)—"descending in a bodily shape," Luke 3 : 22. Hence a visible manifestation of the Holy Spirit, doubtless very brilliant, was made. The easy, gentle hovering, or the rapid movement of the Spirit also seems to be here implied. The dove (whose flight was proverbially rapid, Ps. 55 : 6) was an emblem among oriental nations of purity, innocence or harmlessness (Matt. 10: 16), and of faithful love. " The dove is the most gentle of all birds; this heavenly sign teaches us that our Father in heaven, for Christ's sake, through the grace of the Holy Spirit, designs to deal very gently with His children, and to exhibit all the tenderness of His love to them through the Son."—LUTHER. As the dove first announced to Noah that the waters of the destroying deluge had abated (Gen. 8 : 11), so this dove announces that now salvation is come into the world.—**C. Coming upon him.** The same Spirit, afterwards poured out on the day of Pentecost, "sat upon " each of the disciples, Acts 2 : 3. The Spirit that here comes upon the Saviour ever afterwards " abode upon Him," John 1 : 32; He was " full of the Holy Ghost," Luke 4 : 1; comp. John 3 : 34, 35 ; Isai. 61 : 1.

¹⁷ And lo, a voice out of the heavens, saying, This is my beloved Son, in whom I am well pleased.

A. A voice. This voice of God the Father was heard on other occasions, Matt. 17 ; 5 ; John 12 : 28.—**B. This is my beloved, etc.** (For *Son of God*, see 8 : 29, C.) The same words were repeated at the Transfiguration with an important addition: "hear ye him," Matt. 17: 5. The two passages, Ps. 2 : 7 and Isai. 42 : 1, both of which are predictions of the Messiah (for the latter in particular, see below 12 : 18), contain the words now uttered by the Father. Jesus is here declared, with great solemnity, to be the *Son* of God, both in His human (Luke 1 : 35), and in His divine (John 1 : 1, 14, 18) nature. The name was understood both by Christ Himself and by many Jews to designate one whose nature was divine, and who was equal with the Father, as it clearly appears from John 5: 18; 10: 33, 36; the terms "beloved," and "well pleased" (that is, "in whom my soul delighteth" (Isai. 42: 1), which are here very emphatic, could not be so applied to any mere creature, and really refer to His holy and divine nature, Col. 2: 9; John 10: 30. "For unto which, etc.," Hebr. 1 : 5. See also Ps. 110: 1, 4; Matt. 22 : 44; Hebr. 5: 5, 6; 7: 17.—" Here the Almighty God is the preacher; His sermon is: This is My beloved, etc. The angels listen in silence, look into these things with wonder (1 Pet. 1 : 12), and adore. Christ, the Beloved, is the sole theme of this sermon (1 Cor. 1 : 23; 2 : 2; Phil. 3: 7, 8). This voice is very different from that voice which was once heard from Sinai, and which made even Moses fear and quake. (See Hebr. 12: 18–24 and Exod. ch. 19.) In conclusion, nothing is found here save that divine love which comforts the soul. The Father seemed to say: Look, all the ends of the earth (Isai. 45: 22) on Him whom John has now baptized: I love Him so well, I am so well pleased in Him, that I will pardon, I will love, I will save all whom He presents to Me; He, and He alone, My only-begotten Son, is the appointed Saviour of the world (Hebr. 3: 2; John 14: 6; Acts 4: 12; 1 Cor. 3: 11; 1 John 2: 1; 1 Tim. 2 : 5).—But who is able to fathom the words of this voice?"—LUTHER. The three Persons of the Holy Trinity (28 : 19, F.) are here revealed, the Father who speaks, the Son to whom this public testimony is given, and the Spirit who descends upon Him in a visible form. In such a solemn manner the Saviour of the world commences His public ministry.—" From this baptism of

Christ, the holy sacrament of Baptism, which He Himself gave, derives new light and glory. Shall we deride the holy ordinance and say that it is nothing but water? Yet the Saviour was also baptized with water. But—it is objected—the three persons of the Holy Trinity were present there!—And are they not still present when the divinely appointed sacrament is administered? Has the Saviour who loved little children, took them in His arms, and blessed them, now ceased to love them? And shall the gift of Baptism with all its blessings be now denied to them? Again: Is this holy ordinance a mere ceremony, a shadow, a mockery—or is it designed to convey rich blessings to the soul? But can those blessings be bestowed on the thoughtless and impenitent? The Saviour says: 'He that believeth and is baptized, etc.,' Mark 16: 16. Unless we observe our baptismal covenant in faith, we convert our baptism, which was designed to be a blessing to the soul, into a loss."—LUTHER.

CHAPTER IV.

¹ Then was Jesus led up of the Spirit into the wilderness to be tempted of the devil.

A. Then—" immediately " (Mark 1 : 12) after his Baptism.—**B. Led up of** (=by) **the Spirit**—the Holy Ghost. This action of the Spirit is called in Mark 1 : 12 a *driving* or *putting forth* or *out*, as the same word is rendered in John 10 : 4. Jesus did not unnecessarily expose Himself to temptation, but found it in the path of duty. The wilderness lay higher than the valley of the Jordan.— **C. Into the wilderness**—either the wilderness mentioned in 3 : 1, or the one near Jericho, to which there is a reference in Josh. 16: 1. A steep lime-stone mountain on the north of the plains of Jericho (2 Kings 25: 5) is called in the traditions of the region *Quarantania*, in allusion to the Lord's fast of forty days. During the Saviour's state of humiliation (Phil. 2: 7, 8), He endured all the trials and sorrows to which we are exposed, in order that the view of His patient endurance, and of His victory, might comfort our hearts and strengthen our faith (see Hebr. 2 : 18 ; 4 : 15). " From this history we learn that every baptized Christian belongs to the host which is marshalled against Satan ; if the Adversary assaulted Christ, he will not spare Christ's people. The Saviour's example teaches us the mode in which we should resist the devil—it is faith in God and His word. The Christian, besides, continually prays that the kingdom of God may come unto him, and that he may not fall into temptation.

God is faithful to His promise: " Resist, etc. ! " (James 4 : 7).—LUTHER.—**D. To be tempted**—*that he might be tempted*; " for in that, etc." (Hebr. 2 : 18). The expression *to tempt* sometimes means simply *to try, prove, put to the test*, etc., as in John 6: 6 (transl. " prove "), 2 Cor. 13 : 5, (" examine "); see 22 : 35, B. But it is more frequently used in an unfavorable sense indicating the intention *to lay a snare*, as in 22 : 18, B.; see also 16 : 1. C.; it is then equivalent, as in the present case, to the phrase: *to solicit with an evil design*, or *incite to an evil act*, as in 1 Thess. 3 : 5 ; Gal. 6 : 1 ; Jam. 1 : 13. The connection in which the word occurs usually determines its special meaning. The event here recorded occurred in accordance with wise and gracious purposes of God referring to the Saviour's redeeming work. The original victory of Satan, " the tempter " (1 Thess. 3 : 5), coincided with the fall of man: the defeat of Satan coincides with the beginning of Christ's work of redemption. The first Adam yielded to Satan's temptation and fell ; then " sin entered into the world, and death by sin ; " " by one man's offense death reigned by one," and " judgment came upon all men to condemnation" (Rom. 5 : 12, 17, 18). If man was to be delivered from the power of death (Hebr. 2 : 14), it was necessary, as a part of the work of redemption, that the " last Adam " should be " a quickening (—life-giving) spirit " (1 Cor. 15 : 45). Now if the Saviour should wrest Satan's victory from him, by resisting his most powerful temptations, and, by other deeds, complete the work of man's emancipation from sin and death, which both proceeded from Satan, then men could be made "alive from the dead " (Rom. 6: 13), that is, they who were " dead in sins " could be " quickened " (—made alive) with Christ (Eph. 2 : 5), and " live with Him " (Rom. 6: 8). Hence the Saviour was sent " in

the likeness of sinful flesh" (Rom. 8 : 3), and took part of flesh and blood (Hebr. 2 : 14). In His human nature, Christ was capable of yielding to temptation, but was also able to overcome Satan. The temptation of Christ and His victory, therefore, constitute the appropriate commencement of His great work of restoring fallen man.
—E. **Of** (=by) **the devil.** This Greek word originally signifies a *slanderer* or *false accuser*, and, in the plural number, is so translated in 1 Tim. 3 : 11 ; 2 Tim. 3 : 3. As such a calumniator is governed by hostile sentiments, the word, in the sense of *enemy* or *adversary* (Matt. 13 : 39), was specially applied to the great Enemy of God and man, as in John 8 : 44 ; 1 Pet. 5 : 8. The Hebrew word *Satan* (1 Chron. 21 : 1), which signifies in general an enemy or adversary (so translated in 1 Sam. 29 : 4; 1 Kings 5 : 4), became specially the proper name of this great Adversary (Rev. 20 : 2). It occurs in the parallel passage, Mark 1 : 13, as well as in ver. 10, below. He is the prince of the evil spirits or fallen angels (2 Pet. 2 : 4; Jude, ver. 6; Eph. 6 : 12; Matt. 25 : 41); the latter are called in the Greek *demons* (daimon, daimonion), which word is also translated *devils*, as in Matt. 7 : 22; 8 : 31; 9 : 33. This enemy of the human race, who effected the fall of man through the instrumentality of the serpent (Gen. ch. 3 ; 2 Cor. 11 : 3), comes forward in the present case, with the vain hope of gaining another victory. The tempter feared that his destroyer (Luke 4 : 34; 1 John 3 : 8) stood before him; his purpose in these repeated attempts to induce the Lord to perform unholy acts will possibly appear in a clearer light when we reflect that he had not forgotten the divine words: "the woman's seed (=a descendant of Eve) shall bruise thy head" (Gen. 3 : 15)=shall rescue man from thy power. This conquerer of Satan was Christ (Hebr. 2 : 14); the

tempter now designs to ascertain the fact, and, if possible, defeat the divine purpose by occasioning the Lord's own fall. The temptation of Christ immediately succeeded the glorious manifestation of God described in 3 : 16, 17. Immediately after Paul had been "caught up into Paradise," he was buffeted by "a thorn in the flesh, the messenger of Satan" (2 Cor. 12 : 4, 7). Similar trials, succeeding remarkable manifestations of divine grace, are recorded in the religious experience of Luther and other believers. The Christian is involved anew in contests with Satan, lest he should "be exalted above measure." Paul describes his experience in 2 Cor. 12 : 7-10, and in it many believers recognize their own. Satan always attempts to interfere with the operations of the Divine Spirit. But "in the time of trouble, etc." (Ps. 27 : 5).

² And when he had fasted forty days and forty nights, he afterward hungered.

A. Fasted—abstained, without injury, from food of every kind (Luke 4: 2), and also from water, which was the strictest mode of fasting, as in Esth. 4: 16. In this case, as in those of Moses and Elijah, the fast was miraculously sustained, that is, protracted by the divine interposition beyond the ordinary limits of human endurance; see 6 : 16 A.—**B. Forty ... nights.** When the Lord was transfigured on the mountain (Matt. 17 : 1-8), Moses, through whom the law was given, and Elijah, whose life was devoted to the great work of restoring the observance of the law and the worship of Jehovah, appeared to Him. Both of these eminent men had, at eventful periods of their lives, observed a fast of the same length of time, Exod. 24: 18; 34: 28, and Deut. 9: 9; 1 Kings 19: 8.—**C. He .... hungered.** It was only after the expiration of the forty days that the Lord became conscious of the want of food, Luke 4: 2; at this precise point of time His struggle with the tempter begins. The account in Mark 1: 13 agrees with this statement; it simply presents the two facts, first, that He passed forty days in the wilderness, and, secondly, that He was tempted by Satan. Since Christ possessed a human, as well as a divine nature, He was capable of experiencing hunger; see 8 : 24, B. That a very powerful temptation here meets Him, will be apparent when we reflect that He is now exposed to all the pangs which hunger can occasion —pangs, so severe, that they have often driven shipwrecked mariners, captives, etc., to acts of frenzy.

³ And the tempter came and said unto him, If thou art the Son of God, command that these stones become bread.

A. The tempter ... said, If, etc. The apostle John perhaps referred to this three-fold temptation proceeding from the "prince of this world" (John 12: 31) when he wrote the words: "All that is in the world, the lust of the flesh, and the lust of the eyes, and the pride of life, is not of the Father, but is of the world," 1 John 2: 16. I. "The lust of the flesh." To this class belong all those temptations which connect themselves originally with bodily affections, and which occasion impatience and discontent, or which lead to gluttony, intemperance, licentiousness, etc. Satan connected his first temptation with the Saviour's sense of hunger. II. "The lust of the eyes." The temptations of this class are apparently less gross, but they still more insidiously assail us than those of the former; they lead to acts which receive the various names of ambition, covetousness (Col. 3 : 5), avarice, etc. Satan connected his second temptation, according to the order in Luke (the third in Matt.), with the power and pleasures supposed to be derived from the possession of earthly treasures. III. "The pride of life." The temptations of this class easily connect themselves with the pride and vanity which control every unregenerate heart; they ultimately lead to all those crimes and sins which are committed in consequence of the indulgence of human pride and of the passions engendered by it. Satan connected his third temptation with the proposition that the Lord should dazzle the multitude by His superior powers, and thus gratify His supposed pride by the acquisition of honor and fame. To the three classes of temptations here exhibited, all those precisely correspond which the same tempter employed in the case of Eve, Gen. ch. 3. I. "The woman saw that the tree was good for food"—the lust of the flesh. II. "It was pleasant to the eyes"—the lust of the eyes. III. "Ye shall be as gods, etc.," ver. 5, 6—the pride of life. The language of the tempter may be thus paraphrased: Thou hungerest and hast no food; and yet, at Thy baptism, a voice from heaven said of Thee: "This is My beloved Son." If that was really the voice of God, and if Thou art the Son of God, then exercise Thy divine power at once for the purpose of satisfying Thy human wants; convert the stones lying around Thee into bread. We have no information concerning the visible form which the tempter here assumed, and mere conjectures, as, whether he appeared as a man, or an angel, etc., are of little value. That he was visibly present is implied by the whole tenor of the narrative.—**B. Bread;** the plural in the original (see 26: 26, B.), corresponding to the plural "stones," indicates that the meaning strictly is: *loaves* of bread.

⁴ But he answered and said, it is written, Man shall not live by bread alone, but by every word that proceedeth out of the mouth of God.

It is written, Man, etc. The proposal of the tempter seemed to be reasonable and harmless; nevertheless it was treacherous and malignant, for it covertly implied that the Father had forgotten His Son, and would allow Him to perish from hunger. The tempter availed himself of a bodily want of the Lord as the means of awakening impatience and distrust of God in Him. The Saviour does not commence an argument with him, but finds an answer in Deut. 8 : 3. The sense is as follows :—When the people of Israel apprehended that they would perish from hunger (Exod. 16: 3, 15), God supplied them miraculously (or, by His creative *word:* Let there be— Gen. ch. 1) with manna, a species of food which had never been seen before. By this unexpected supply He taught them that He could sustain their lives independently of the ordinary means of subsistence. Thus—the Lord says—My life does not necessarily depend on the eating of bread; the same creative " word " of God, the " breath of His mouth," by which the heavens were made (Ps. 33 : 6), can preserve My life and supply My necessary wants.

⁵ Then the devil taketh him into the holy city; and he set him on the pinnacle of the temple,

A. Then. Luke arranges this temptation as the third, according to a certain gradation in the locality, namely, the wilderness, the mountain, and, lastly, the temple in the city. Since the three temptations of Christ occurred in a comparatively short time, and are distinct from each other, the order in which they are related does not affect the meaning of the text.—**B. Taketh him**; see 20: 17, A. Luke says, 4: 9, " brought "=*led* him. The original word in Matt. here translated " taketh " is applied (as in ch. 17 : 1 ; 20 : 17 ; 26 : 37 ; 27 : 27) to the act of a person who invites, directs or requires another to accompany him. Balak " brought " Balaam to the top of Pisgah, Numb. 23: 14. Still it would be a phrase liable to misconception, if we should say that the Lord proceeded thither "at the suggestion of Satan." The first verse of the chapter shows that He was really led by the Divine Spirit, of whose holy purpose Satan was doubtless ignorant. Peter refers to another instance in which iniquity seemed to rule and to accomplish its own purposes, while in reality at the same time the overruling Providence of God fulfilled exalted divine purposes (see Acts 2 : 23.)—C. **The holy city** (as in 27 : 53)—Jerusalem, Luke 4 : 9. It received this name on account of the holy temple situated within its walls (Isai. 48 : 2 ; 52 : 1 ; Nehem. 11 : 1, 18), "the place which God chose to put His name there," Deut. 12 : 5, 14 ; Ps. 122. Christ calls it, in Matt. 5 : 35, "the city of the great King"; it is still called *The Holy* (*el-kuds*), by the Arabs (see 24 : 15, B.). Some identify it with Salem (— peace, Hebr. 7 : 2), the city of Melchizedek (Gen. 14 : 18), to which the words in Ps. 76 : 2 appear to refer. It was a distinguished and royal city in the days of Joshua (Josh. 10 : 1), when it was called Jebusi (Josh. 18 : 16, 28) and held by the Jebusites (Josh. 15 : 8, 63 ; 18 ; 28 ; Judg. 1 : 21) ; it was finally seized and occupied permanently by David, 2 Sam. 5 : 6–9.—D. **Setteth him.** An act is often said to have been performed by one who simply desires or directs it to be done. So Solomon says : "*I* have built an house," 2 Chron. 6 : 2.—E. **The pinnacle of the temple**—the summit of the temple. The word here translated *temple* (*hieron*), comprehended not only the sacred edifice itself (called *naos*, Matt. 23 : 16, 35 ; 27 : 5), from which the people were at all times excluded, but also all the external courts which inclosed that edifice (see Matt. 21 : 12, A.). The pinnacle or apex here mentioned was probably the highest part of the roof either of Herod's royal portico on the south side (Josephus, Ant. 15, 11, 5), or of Solomon's porch (John 10 : 23) on the east side (Jos. Ant. 20, 9, 7). From the summit of each of these structures, which were raised to a vast height, there was a perpendicular descent to the bottom of a deep valley beneath.

⁶ And saith unto him, If thou art the Son of God, cast thyself down: for it is written, He shall give his angels charge concerning thee: and on their hands they shall bear thee up, lest haply thou dash thy foot against a stone.

A. **Saith unto him . . . He shall, etc.** The passage quoted by the tempter is Ps. 91 : 11, 12 ; the whole psalm is intended to comfort the people of God by the assurance that they shall always enjoy God's protecting care. In the words here quoted, every believer receives the divine assurance that while his ways are those which God appoints, the holy angels (Ps. 34: 7 ; Hebr. 1 : 14) shall be commissioned to avert all real injuries, and render his path through life easy and safe, Prov. 3 : 23. But the tempter thus perverts the passage : If such a promise is made to the ordinary believer,—says he,—much more must Thou claim its fulfilment, as, at Thy baptism (3 : 17), Thou wast declared to be the Son of God.—He omits the clause : " in thy ways," which confines the fulfilment of the promise to those who walk in the path of duty. The temptation consists in the effort to persuade the Lord to commit the rash and unnecessary act of casting Himself from the pinnacle.—B. **It is written.** The tempter repeats the words of the Lord in ver. 4 ; he seems to say : Since You profess to be guided by the Scriptures, You have here divine authority to do the act which I propose. Those who consciously and deliberately pervert the true sense of the Scriptures, are hence guilty of a truly Satanic act.

⁷ Jesus said unto him, Again it is written, Thou shalt not tempt the Lord thy God.

Jesus said etc. The passage quoted by the Saviour

occurs in Deut. 6: 16, where Moses refers to the events described in Exod. 17: 1-7. At a place afterwards called Massah (—Temptation), the water failed; the people would not believe that God could supply them with water in that desert region, and when Moses expostulated, they said: "Is the Lord among us, or not?" These words imply that they doubted the truth and power of God; they proposed to test the point whether God was able to provide for them (see Ps. 78 : 15-22, 41; Hebr. 3 : 8, 9). Hence, *to tempt God* is equivalent to the phrase: *to distrust God*, or to test His power presumptuously, or with secret unbelief.

⁸ Again, the devil taketh him unto an exceeding high mountain, and sheweth him all the kingdoms of the world, and the glory of them;

A. Taketh him (see ver. 5, B.).—**B. Mountain**—one of the many lofty mountains of the country.—**C. Sheweth . . . world.** As the earth is not a plain, even the most elevated spot on its surface would not afford to a spectator on one side of it, a view of the opposite side. Hence the words, "sheweth him all," do not mean that the tempter literally pointed to each kingdom of the whole world, as if all were visible; they are simply equivalent to the one word *describe;* Paul "shewed" the Corinthians a more excellent way (1 Cor. 12: 31), by describing (ch. 13) the nature and influence of Christian love; the Greek word is the same in both places (comp. also Matt. 16: 21; Acts 10: 28). The statement of Luke (4: 5) that this *shewing* occurred in "a moment of time" indicates the act of pointing to objects generally, lying beyond the distant horizon.—D. **The glory of them**—described the splendor of remote cities, the distant cultivated lands teeming with wealth, the military resources and political power of the various kingdoms then known to exist, etc. —" these things," ver. 9. The whole description of this earthly power and magnificence was intended to dazzle, and to awaken ambition and cupidity in the soul of the Lord.

⁹ And he said unto him, All these things will I give thee, if thou wilt fall down and worship me.

A. All . . give thee. Luke furnishes the explanation which the tempter added: "for that is delivered unto me; and to whomsoever I will, I give it." Satan had usurped power in the world by introducing sin and death; the unregenerate sinner now yields to the influences of Satan and is a servant of sin, Rom. 6: 12–17. Hence Satan is styled the "prince of this world" (John 12: 31; 14: 30; 16: 11), the "god of this world" (2 Cor. 4: 4), and, with his angels (Matt. 25: 41), a "ruler of the darkness of this world" (Eph. 6: 11, 12).—Satan, the *liar* and *father of lies* (John 8: 44), falsely asserts that the deadly influence which he wields, and which he acquired by lies and malevolence (Gen. 3), was "delivered" to him, and speaks as if he were the rightful Lord of all. The Saviour knew all the sorrows which He would be called to endure (Hebr. 12: 2) in executing the Father's plan of salvation (Rom. 3: 25); the tempter proposes an easier method, if He simply desires to be the ruler of men. We are often tempted to rebel against the divine will, according to which we must "through much tribulation enter into the kingdom of God" (Acts 14: 22). Satan claims in this case a power which belongs to God alone.—**B. If thou . . . . worship me.** The Greek word translated *worship* does, it is true, sometimes designate simply the homage which was rendered to an oriental king, but is also applied to the act of *adoring the Supreme Being* (see 2: 2, D.). The answer of the Lord shows that Satan used the word in the latter sense. Such is indeed the result in the case of all impenitent sinners; by withholding their homage and love from the true God, and loving the world, they declare themselves to be the servants of Satan and sin, Matt. 6: 24; Rom. 6: 12–18; James 4: 4. —" Satan does not always find it necessary to offer such costly bribes as in the present instance. Many a soul is led away from the path of duty by the Satanic offer of a dollar, or a house and lot, or an article of apparel, or a dance, or a drink, or a game of chance, etc."—BESSER.

[10] Then saith Jesus unto him, Get thee hence, Satan; for it is written, Thou shalt worship the Lord thy God, and him only shalt thou serve.

A. Get . . . Satan. The Lord Jesus here adopts a course very different from that which Eve pursued, Gen. 3: 1–6. She listened to the tempter, reflected on the probable truth of his statements, and, by harboring such thoughts, practically disobeyed the divine injunction, Gen. 2: 17. The Saviour teaches us by His example to cultivate constantly a sense of God's presence, power and grace, and to resist and dismiss every evil suggestion instantly.—**B. It is written . . . serve;** it is thus written in substance in Deut. 6: 13; 10: 20, and especially in the First Commandment: "I am, etc.; thou shalt have no other gods before me." Exod. 20: 2, 3; Deut. 5: 6, 7. The Lord adds the explanatory word: "him *only*," thus fixing the true meaning of the commandment, excluding every other object of adoration.

[11] Then the devil leaveth him, and, behold, angels came and ministered unto him.

A. Leaveth him—"for a season," Luke 4: 13. The present attempt of Satan is completely defeated; his subsequent efforts appear in the persecution of the Lord by the Jews, whom he prompted (Luke 22: 53), and the treachery of Judas (Luke 22: 3; John 13: 27). "The Lord, who is mighty in battle (Ps. 24: 8), engaged in this conflict not for His own sake but for mine, that I might receive a lesson of faith, and learn for my encouragement that the Saviour's victory is my own by faith (1 John, 5: 4). Be not dismayed when thou art tempted. The Holy Spirit does not permit thee to pass thy time in indolence, but suffers temptations to approach thee that the trial of thy 'faith might be found unto praise and honor and glory at the appearing of Jesus Christ' (1 Peter 1 : 7), and that God's strength may be made perfect in thy weakness (2 Cor. 12 : 9). Look to Christ; 'be not afraid, only believe' (Mark 5 : 36). See how the serpent's head is here bruised, and learn to trust thy heavenly friend."— LUTHER.—B. **Angels . . . . unto him.** The worship of the Lord Jesus by the angels is mentioned in Hebr. 1 : 6. They *ministered*—rendered services by supplying the food which He needed. The same word—*minister*—in the general sense of providing for the wants of any one, occurs in Matt. 8 : 15 ; 25 : 44 ; 27 : 55. Doubtless the ministrations of these angels were also designed to afford the Redeemer spiritual strength and joy after His severe but successful struggle. When the Lord was in an agony, an angel strengthened him, Luke 22 : 43.

¹²Now when he heard that John was delivered up, he withdrew into Galilee;

A. **John . . . . delivered up.** Matthew has here omitted several events which occurred between the Lord's temptation and His departure into Galilee; they are related in John 1 : 43—4 : 42 ; various journeys were performed by the Lord during this interval, John 2 : 1, 12, 13, etc. Matthew presents the history of John in ch. 14 : 3 ff.—B. **He withdrew,**—probably from some point in Judæa or Samaria, where he was when he received the tidings concerning John. Herod Antipas, who slew John, was at this time the tetrarch or ruler of Galilee (Luke 3 :

1; 23: 7; see Matt. 2: 1, D. and 2: 22, C.); hence the Lord, by entering Galilee, did not flee from Herod, but rather approached nearer to Tiberias, his place of residence, in order to spread the light of the Gospel (ver. 16) in that benighted region, from which John was now withdrawn.

¹³ And leaving Nazareth, he came and dwelt in Capernaum, which is by the sea, in the borders of Zebulun and Naphtali.

A. **Leaving Nazareth** (for which see 2: 23, A.)—not remaining long in it on this occasion, possibly in consequence of the occurrences related in Luke 4: 16–31.—
B. **Capernaum**—a town in Galilee on the Sea of Tiberias (Sea of Galilee, John 6: 1, also called Lake of Gennesaret, Luke 5: 1), at some distance from the point where the Jordan empties into this sea. It lay in the **borders** of Zebulun and Naphtali—near the line separating the ancient territories of these two tribes, in the "land of Gennesaret" (14: 34). Its precise site is not yet fully determined, but its situation on the north-western side of the lake is generally admitted. It is not mentioned in the Old Test. It was the usual abode of the Saviour (Matt. 4: 13), and is hence called "his own city" (9: 1); possibly Mary resided there (John 2: 17); there He taught on the Sabbath days (Luke 4: 31), and performed numerous miracles (see below, ch. 8; ch. 9; ch. 11: 23). Capernaum was situated on the main route leading from Damascus to Akko and Tyre, and also furnished quarters for a Roman garrison at the period when the miracle related in 8: 5, ff. was performed.

¹⁴ That it might be fulfilled which was spoken by Isaiah the prophet, saying,

See 1: 22, A.—The evangelist here calls attention to the fulfilment of another divine prediction, containing a promise of spiritual blessings.

15, 16. The land of Zebulun, and the land of Naphtali, toward the sea, beyond Jordan, Galilee of the Gentiles;—The people which sat in darkness saw a great light; and to them which sat in the region and shadow of death, to them did light spring up.

A. **The land of** etc. Matt. quotes Isai. 9: 1, 2, in an abbreviated form, with a few unimportant variations in the phraseology. The territories originally assigned to these two tribes (Josh. 19: 10, 32) lay on the western side of the Sea of Galilee. The phrase **toward the sea** designated the western or maritime district, while the additional words, **beyond Jordan**, indicate that the people dwelling beyond, or on the eastern side of the sea and the river, shall also share in the blessings diffused by the Saviour's presence. In the time of Christ, the whole of North Palestine, including the territory of the tribes just mentioned (2 Kings 15: 29), was called Galilee. The northern part of this region, sometimes called Upper Galilee, was termed Galilee of the Gentiles (=heathens, pagans), because many heathen inhabitants, Phenicians, Syrians, etc., were intermingled with the Jewish population.—B. The prophet, after alluding in ch. 8: 19–22 to the grievous sins of the inhabitants of North Palestine, and to the political and spiritual evils in which they were involved, as the punishment of their impiety, is next directed by the Divine Spirit (9: 1), to announce that after all these calamities, the divine mercy which shall be granted to them, will be proportionably great; their "darkness," or the period of affliction and hopelessness, shall pass away, and "light" or knowledge and joy shall succeed, in consequence of the appearance of Christ in the world; "for unto us a child is born . . . Prince of Peace," Isai. 9: 6.—C. **Shadow of death.** This phrase (occurring in Job 3: 5; 10: 21; 28: 3; 34: 22; 38: 17; Ps. 23: 4; 44: 19; 107: 10) indicates, as an examination of these passages shows, an intense darkness, such as that which covered the abode of the dead, alarming in its character, and a cause or sign of ruin or death; in the passage before us, it figuratively describes, with increased significance, the state called *spiritual death*, Eph. 2 : 1. While the whole human race, represented by those who dwelt in the region here specified, was surrounded by this *deadly darkness*, that is, exposed to the fatal influences of religious ignorance, destitute of the means of obtaining pardon and salvation, and in "the way that leadeth to destruction" (Matt. 7 : 13), the Lord Jesus, the "light of the world" (1 John 1 : 4, 5, 8, 9; 8 : 12; 9 : 5), came to seek and save the lost (see Luke 1 : 78, 79); He arose as the "Sun of righteousness with healing in his wings," Mal. 4 : 2.

¹⁷. From that time began Jesus to preach, and to say, Repent ye; for the kingdom of heaven is at hand.

From that time, etc.—after taking up His abode in Capernaum, ver. 13. A new period in the public ministry of the Lord commences here (comp. Luke 4 : 14, 15; John 4 : 43–45). Matt. gives the substance of the discourses of the Lord, which confirmed the teaching of John the Baptist, Matt. 3 : 2. Nevertheless, new lessons were also taught, the Lord added, as we learn further from Mark 1 : 14, 15, that *the time was fulfilled*, namely, the design of the old covenant (—"to bring us unto Christ," Gal. 3 : 24), was now fulfilled, and the New Covenant was to be established by the Messiah, who now appeared (Luke 1 : 68) in the "fulness of the time" (Gal. 4 : 4), agreeably to the decision of divine wisdom; He also added: "believe the Gospel." He here requires faith in Himself as the author of the Gospel, and consequently claims more than John was authorized to ask.—For the terms: **Repent** and **kingdom of heaven**, see annotations to ch. 3 : 2.

¹⁸. And walking by the sea of Galilee, he saw two brethren, Simon who is called Peter, and Andrew his brother, casting a net into the sea; for they were fishers.

A. **Simon .... brother.** The name of their father was Jonas. The family appears to have originally resided in Bethsaida, a town situated on the Sea of Galilee, not far from Capernaum; in the latter place Peter afterwards established himself, Matt. 8 : 5, 14. He occupied a very prominent position in the four Gospels; his labors are partially described in the Acts of the Apostles, and he is the author of the two Epistles in the New Test. which bear his name. His brother Andrew, originally a disciple of John the Baptist (John 1 : 35, 40), afterwards also became one of the twelve apostles, but is less frequently mentioned (see 10 : 2-4).—B. **Fishers.** The Sea of Galilee abounded in fishes (John 21 : 11). The occupation of fishers was humble and laborious. The Saviour chose His disciples not from the ranks of the wealthy and learned (1 Cor. 1 : 26), but from the humbler classes, in order that the success of the Gospel might not be ascribed to the power and wisdom of man, 2 Cor. 4 : 7 ; 1 Cor. 1 : 28, 29 ; 2 : 5.

¹⁹ And he saith unto them, Come ye after me, and I will make you fishers of men.

A. **Come ye after me, and, etc.** Peter and Andrew had previously obtained a knowledge of Christ (John 1 : 35-42), and knew that He was the Messiah. The command which He now issues, implies, as in the case of Matthew (Matt. 9 : 9), that they shall henceforth devote their whole time to His service as disciples. The power of the command, and the prompt obedience of both Simon and Andrew, are fully explained by the circumstances related in Luke 5 : 3-10. Christ speaks with authority; He addresses a similar command to all men (as in Matt. 19:

21, E.), in a general sense, teaching that we are bound to render prompt obedience, not outwardly alone, but also with all the heart, and to consecrate our life and strength to His service alone.—C. **Fishers of men**—My agents in transferring men from the world into the kingdom of heaven, as into a net (13: 47). The Saviour's language evidently alludes to their previous occupation; He informs them that while they should exhibit similar industry and zeal in their new calling, the object for which they labored would be far more exalted. They should reach *men*—intelligent and immortal beings, by the word of the Gospel, and conduct them to Christ.—The Saviour often applied present circumstances and events, as images of spiritual things, e. g. Matt. 12: 50; 18: 2; John 4: 10.

[20] And they straightway left the nets, and followed him.

Straightway—immediately. They obey promptly and unconditionally, teaching us by their example that it is our duty to be governed in all our thoughts and actions by the divine will alone.

[21] And going on from thence, he saw other two brethren, James *the son* of Zebedee, and John his brother, in the boat with Zebedee their father, mending their nets; and he called them.

James . . . John his brother. James, the son of Zebedee, whose death is mentioned in Acts 12: 2, is to be carefully distinguished from another James, the son of Alpheus (10: 3), called in Mark 15: 40 James *the less*, or, the younger.—There are, according to some interpreters, *two*, according to others, *three* persons of the name of James, who are mentioned in the New Testament. The first is this James, the son of Zebedee (see 20: 20, B.); the second is James the son of Alpheus (=Klopas, see below, 13: 55, C.), and Mary (Matt. 27: 56). Both are enumerated in Matt. 10: 2, 3, among the twelve disciples. The third, according to the interpretation of some writers, is James, the brother of Joses (Matt. 13: 55); but it is more probable that he is identical with the second James. He is called "the Lord's brother," in Gal. 1: 19, and is there evidently regarded as one of the Twelve. We may then assume that he became a believer at an early period, while his brethren did not originally believe (John 7: 5), but became believers at the period of the death or resurrection of Christ, according to Acts 1: 14. He is the James mentioned in Acts 12: 17; 15: 13; 21: 18; 1 Cor. 15: 7; Gal. 2: 12. He is sometimes called James *the Just*, and is doubtless also the author of the *Epistle of James*.— John, the brother of James, was the author of the fourth Gospel and of the three Epistles bearing his name in the New Test.

²² And they straightway left the boat and their father, and followed him.

Straightway . . followed. Their father appears to have cheerfully consented to their withdrawal from his service; the mother's well-known devotion to the Saviour (Matt. 27: 56) demonstrates that she, too, willingly consecrated her sons to their new and holy calling. The divine blessing is abundantly bestowed on parents who, like the mother of Samuel the prophet (1 Sam. 1: 28), "lend" their children to the Lord, and aid them in consecrating their life and strength to the work of preaching the Gospel.

²³ And Jesus went about in all Galilee, teaching in their synagogues, and preaching the Gospel of the kingdom, and healing all manner of disease and all manner of sickness among the people.

A. Jesus went about=doing good (Acts 10: 38).—**B. Synagogues**=places of worship. The various labors of the Lord here described bear a close analogy to those mentioned in Luke 4: 18, as quoted from Isai. 61: 1, 2.—**C. Gospel of the kingdom**=the glad tidings that the kingdom of God was at hand (ver. 17), that the Messiah had appeared, and that whosoever believed in Him should be saved (see 24: 14, C.).—The word **Gospel** is formed from two Anglo-Saxon words: *god*—good, and *spell*—word, speech, tidings; the whole term signifies *good tidings*. In place of this word, old English writers sometimes used the Greek word itself in the forms of *Evangel, Evangely*.

[24] And the report of him went forth into all Syria: and they brought unto him all that were sick, holden with divers diseases and torments, possessed with devils, and epileptic, and palsied; and he healed them.

A. Syria. This somewhat indefinite geographical name was given to a large extent of country in Asia, lying between Palestine, the Mediterranean, Mount Taurus and the Tigris, thus including Mesopotamia. The whole, or large portions of the territory, belonged in different ages, according to the progress of wars and conquests, to the Assyrians, the Chaldees or Babylonians, the Persians and the Macedonians. At the Christian era, and consequently in the New Test., Syria appears as a Roman province of greatly reduced dimensions, sometimes including, under the same governor (called a Proconsul), the neighboring land of Palestine, and, at other times, in so far discriminated from it, that the latter had a governor or Procurator distinct from the Syrian proconsul. The ancient Syrian language, a branch of the Aramæan, was in a great degree supplanted by the Greek, which continued to be spoken till the country was occupied by the Arabs.—**B. Torments**—local diseases attended with acute pains; the original word, here equivalent to a *tormenting malady*, is applied in Luke 16: 23 to the pains of hell.—**Divers**—various, manifold. — **C. Possessed with devils,** see Excursus II.—**D. He healed them**—all were restored to health and happiness by the grace and power of Christ. "Earth has no sorrows that heav'n cannot heal."

²⁵ And there followed him great multitudes from Galilee, and Decapolis, and Jerusalem, and Judæa, and *from* beyond Jordan.

A. Followed .... multitudes, as in 12:15; 19:2; 20:29. Many were, doubtless, deeply impressed by the power of His words, as in Matt. 7:28; 8:1; others were influenced by impure or selfish motives, as in John 6:26, or by idle curiosity, and, at a somewhat later period, by hostile purposes, as in Luke 20:20.—**B. Decapolis.** This name (signifying *Ten Cities*) was given to a region lying principally east of the Jordan and south of the Sea of Galilee, Scythopolis alone (the ancient Bethshean, Josh. 17:11, now called Beisân, near the northern boundary of Samaria) being west of the river; among the ten cities were Gadara and Pella. The inhabitants were chiefly heathens. The combination here of all these names is equivalent to the phrase: "from all parts of the country."—**C. Beyond Jordan**—the country east of the river, the northern part of Peræa, between the rivers Jabbok and Arnon.

CHAPTER V.

Preliminary Observation. The following discourse of the Lord, usually termed the *Sermon on the Mount*, and extending through three chapters in Matt. appears in an abbreviated form in Luke 6 : 20-49. That both evangelists furnish the same discourse is proved, first, by the similarity of the arrangement of the materials in both cases; secondly, by both the introductory words (blessings, usually called the *Beatitudes*, from the Latin, or *Makarisms*, from the Greek), and also by the conclusion (the houses exposed to the flood); thirdly, by the reference to the Lord's entrance into Capernaum, immediately after the delivery of the Sermon, and the healing of the centurion's servant, Matt. 8 : 5 ; Luke 7 : 1, 2.—It is believed by many that the Sermon was delivered long after the occurrence of the Temptation described in the preceding chapter, inasmuch as various passages, like 5 : 17 ; 7 : 21, seem to indicate that the Lord had already attracted much attention as a teacher, and been repeatedly assailed and persecuted. Dr. Robinson, in his *Harmony of the four Gospels in English*, arranges, immediately after the history of the Temptation, the whole of the first three chapters of John; Matt. 4 : 12; 14: 3-5 ; John, ch. 4; portions of Luke, ch. 4; ch. 5 ; ch. 6 : 1-19; portions of Matt. ch. 8 ; ch. 9; the whole of John, ch. 5 ; Matt. 12: 1-21 ; 10: 2-4. He supposes that only after all the occurrences mentioned in these passages, the Lord delivered this Sermon. Such an arrangement, which assumes that a considerable period of time intervened between Matt.

4:22 and 5:1, may be readily admitted, in view of two considerations: first, that the events related in the last three verses of Matt. ch. 4, must have extended over a considerable period of time, and, secondly, that the events occurring between the first public appearance of Christ and His *passion* (ann. to 26:1) are of the same importance to us, whether they are or are not related in precisely the same order in which they originally occurred. Matt. seems to arrange the matter which he furnishes, rather according to certain classes of subjects, than the mere external chronological order. Thus the Lord's words: "The very works that I do, bear witness of me, etc." (John 5:36), are illustrated in ch. 8 and ch. 9, which present various miracles as witnesses of His divine mission and power. The hostility of the Pharisees is shown in several cases in the portion now occurring as ch. 12. The next chapter (see Prel. Obs. to ch. 13) consists almost entirely of parables; it is evidently intended to illustrate the Lord's method of teaching by parables. Again, His mode of answering difficult questions is illustrated by several cases in ch. 19. Another portion of the Gospel describes the Lord's manner of speaking of the Pharisees (see 21:45).—Soon after the journey of the Israelites commenced, God delivered the Law from Mount Sinai (Exod. 19:11); so too, as the Saviour had delivered the Gospel, which is the fulfilment of the Law and the prophets (5:17) from a mount at a period not very remote from His first public appearance, Matt. at once proceeds to furnish this summary of the Christian faith and practice. Luke wrote his Gospel for believers of Gentile origin, and hence does not presuppose on their part an extensive knowledge of the Old Test.; Matt. on the contrary, who writes for Jewish Christians, abounds in references to the writings of the prophets.

¹ And seeing the multitudes, he went up into the mountain; and when he had sat down, his disciples came unto him.

A. And seeing; the original Greek word (de) translated *and* is here simply a general or introductory word, used at the commencement of a new paragraph or division, and is equivalent to *but* or *now* or *further:* the sense is: On a certain occasion, the Lord seeing a multitude, etc.—
B. The multitudes—which had been attracted by the fame or current reports concerning Him.—**C. The mountain;** the one on which, according to Luke 6: 12, He had spent the previous night in prayer. After the completion of His private devotions, He appointed twelve of the whole number of His usual attendants as His twelve apostles, Luke 6: 13. He then descended from that elevated spot, stood in the plain, and healed the sick, Luke. 6: 17-19. The pressure of the multitude induced Him to resume His former elevated position, whence He addressed the people; the plain mentioned by Luke is to be conceived as a plateau or level mountain summit. The locality and name of this mountain, which could not have been far distant from Capernaum (8 : 5), are not now certainly known.—**D. His disciples;** here the word (signifying *learners*, 11 : 29, B.), designates, as in Luke 6: 13; Matt. 8 : 21 ; John 6: 66, all His attendants, besides the twelve ; to the latter the name was only afterwards exclusively appropriated. The hearers constituted a miscellaneous audience (7 : 28 ; see ann. to 8 : 19, C.).

² And he opened his mouth, and taught them, saying,

A. Opened his mouth—an oriental phrase (Job 3 : 1 ; 32 : 20; Dan. 10: 16), often implying that a very weighty message is to be delivered (Acts 8: 35 ; 10: 34), or that the speaker fearlessly declares the whole truth, 2 Cor. 6: 11 ; Eph. 6: 19.—"Let the preachers of the Gospel not be afraid of men, but faithfully and boldly deliver their message; let them not be blind and ignorant, like 'dumb dogs' (Isai. 56: 10); let them 'not shun to declare all the counsel of God,' Acts 20: 27."—LUTHER.

³ Blessed are the poor in spirit: for theirs is the kingdom of heaven.

A. In the verses which open the discourse, the Lord mentions various features that essentially belong to the Christian character, and, at the same time, exhibit the spirit of His Gospel, as contradistinguished from the form of religion prevailing among the Jews of His day.—**B. Blessed**—*happy*, as the same word is rendered in John 13: 17. It is sometimes applied even to God, 1 Tim. 1: 11; 6: 15. The Hebrew word to which it corresponds, and which occurs in Ps. 1: 1, describes the state of him whose course is prosperous, whose condition is marked by safety, abundance, felicity, etc. Here it specially implies that the favor of God is the only source of true happiness;— **C. Poor in spirit.** Temporal poverty is so far from being an absolute evil, that it often proves to be a blessing (see James 2: 5); it is not subject to the temptations which proceed from wealth, Mark 10: 24; 1 Tim. 6: 17. But the words "in spirit" show that in this passage *spiritual* poverty is meant, precisely as Paul was "pressed in the spirit," and Apollos was "fervent in the spirit," Acts 18: 5, 25. Still, the meaning cannot be that those are blessed who are destitute of spiritual treasures, such as faith and love. The opposite word *rich* in Luke 1: 53; 6: 24, and especially Rev. 3: 17, plainly designates those who think that they "have need of nothing," who are well satisfied with their condition, and hence have no desire for spiritual treasures. Thus the word *poor* in this passage refers to those who *are conscious* of their spiritual poverty, who are of a contrite and humble spirit (Isai. 57: 15; 66: 2; Ps. 34: 18), and who desire to become "rich in faith" (James 2: 5; see also 2 Cor. 6: 10; 8: 9). They are *blessed*—rendered happy by the Gospel (Isai. 61 : 1 ; Luke 4 : 18), which guides them to heaven.—D. **For . . . heaven;** the explanation is furnished by Paul: "Godliness is profitable, etc." 1 Tim. 4: 8. The **kingdom of heaven** with all its blessings here on earth, the favor of God, peace and joy, and with all its glories in the eternal world, *is* theirs—its possession is sure to them ; the believer *hath* everlasting life, John 6: 47.

⁴ Blessed are they that mourn ; for they shall be comforted.

A. They that mourn. These are mentioned in Isai. 61 : 1–3, the passage which the Lord applies to Himself in Luke 4 : 18–21 (see also Isai. 57 : 15, 18). Devout men of old mourned over the calamities of the people of Israel, which the promised Messiah had not yet come to remove; but they found comfort in the promise that he should appear, Isai. 40: 1–5. Thus, the devout Simeon waited until "the consolation of Israel" (Luke 2 : 25) should really come.—The humble sinner still mourns over his spiritual misery ; when his "godly sorrow worketh repentance to salvation " (2 Cor. 7 : 10), he shall be comforted, or find joy and peace in believing (Rom. 15 : 13). —" Wilt thou understand what this mourning and this comfort mean? Become a believer, a true Christian, and thou wilt understand it all."—LUTHER.—**B. Comforted.** The poor and humble sinner, who puts his trust in Christ, shall find comfort in this life already, amid his many trials (2 Cor. 1 : 4; 2 Thess. 2 : 16, 17), but his highest comfort and peace will be found hereafter in the heavenly kingdom, 2 Cor. 4 : 17, 18.

⁵ Blessed are the meek ; for they shall inherit the earth.

A. The meek; the Lord refers to the words in Ps. 37 : 11. In that psalm the godly and the wicked are contrasted. One feature of the character of the former is *meekness*, by which term (see 21 : 5, D.) a lowly or humble mind is indicated, as in Matt. 11 : 29; Eph. 4: 2, the opposite of a spirit of envy and strife, James 3 : 13, 14; Rom. 12 : 19. This devout frame of mind is produced in the penitent and believing sinner by a deep sense of his unworthiness before God, and of his many sins which caused Him to *mourn*. It is exemplified in the Prodigal Son, Luke 15 : 21.—**B. They shall inherit the earth**—they shall not lose, but gain. The "first commandment with promise" (Eph. 6: 2) secures to children who honor their parents a long life "upon the land, etc.," Exod. 20 : 12. In this happy land the Israelites found liberty and every other temporal blessing. Hence it served as an image of all the blessings, whether temporal or spiritual, which God bestows (see Ps. 37 : 3, 9, 11, 22, 29; Isai. 60: 21). In accordance with this view, the "rest" which the Israelites found in the land of Canaan, is represented in Hebr. 4 : 1–9, as an image of the *rest* which awaits believers in heaven. "To inherit the earth" (Ps. 25 : 13), or, strictly speaking, the *land* of promise (Hebr. 11 : 9), is therefore equivalent to the phrase, to receive fulness of joy and peace from God (see 1 Tim. 4; 8, and comp. 25 : 34, C.). To the meek the Lord elsewhere (11 : 29) promises rest for their souls. The sense is: The true disciples receive the kingdom (Luke 12 : 32); they are sanctified by the Holy Spirit and made "kings and priests unto God" (Rev. 1 : 6) or invested with a holy and royal (kingly) priesthood in this life already (1 Pet. 2 : 5, 9). When they shall be glorified in heaven (Phil. 3 : 21 ; Rom. 8 : 30) and behold the Saviour's glory (John 17 : 24), they shall be "glad with exceeding joy" (1 Pet. 4 : 13), and live and reign with Christ forever, enjoying all the happiness and glory of heaven, 2 Tim. 2 : 12; Rom. 5 : 17; 8 : 17. Thus they inherit the heavenly land, the "land of pure delight, where saints immortal reign."

⁶ Blessed are they that hunger and thirst after righteousness: for they shall be filled.

A. Hunger and thirst after. The bodily sensations of hunger and thirst, as images of strong desires of the soul, frequently occur in the Scriptures; Ps. 42 : 2; Isai. 41 : 17; 49 : 10; 55 : 1; 65 : 13; Amos 8 : 11; John 6 : 35. The Saviour satisfies the soul with the bread and water of life (John 4 : 10, 14; 6 : 35).—**B. Righteousness.** Paul distinguishes in Phil. 3 : 9 two kinds of righteousness: first, human righteousness, or that external rectitude which the Jews sought after by the strict observance of the laws of Moses—the righteousness of the scribes and Pharisees, mentioned below, ver. 20, and 23 : 23–28; Luke 18 : 9; secondly, *that* " righteousness which is of God by faith," and which, in Rom. 1 : 17; 3 : 21, 22, is called the " righteousness of God "—that which alone avails before Him, and He alone bestows. It is that state of the believer to which he attains through the imputation of the merits of Christ (Rom. 4 : 5–8; 8 : 1–4; 1 John 2 : 2; Gal. 4 : 4, 5; Hebr. 10 : 4–14; Isai., ch. 53). For an illustration, see Phil. 3 : 8–14. The believer will be " delivered from the body of this death " (Rom. 7 : 24) in a future state, and be clothed with perfect righteousness (2 Pet. 3 : 13. See above 1 : 19, B.; 3 : 15, B.).—**C. They . . . . filled**—the wants or desires of their hearts shall be fully satisfied by Him whose Spirit produced such hunger and thirst. The believer is justified and delivered from guilt and punishment by his Saviour (Rom. 3 : 24; 5 : 9); his conscience finds peace through the atonement of Christ (Rom. 5 : 1); his painful sense of guilt (his *hunger* and *thirst*) is relieved (Col. 1 : 19–22), and he gives a reason of the hope that is in him (1 Pet. 3 : 15) by gratefully repeating the words of Paul: " There is therefore now no condemnation, etc." (Rom. 8 : 1).

⁷ Blessed are the merciful: for they shall obtain mercy.

A. Merciful—compassionate (like the Saviour, to whom the same term is applied in Hebr. 2: 17), somewhat in the sense of *tender-hearted* (Eph. 4: 32), or sympathizing and prompt in relieving, as illustrated in Jam. 2: 13-16. The exhibition of such a feeling, in a genuine form, cannot occur, unless those sentiments to which the foregoing verses allude, have previously taken possession of the soul. Faith is first wrought by divine grace—faith in Christ, as the only and the all-sufficient Saviour of sinners. This faith, which is the true source of genuine love, "worketh by love" (Gal. 5: 6). Love, "the fruit of the Spirit" (Gal. 5: 22), regards God as its first great object (Matt. 22: 37, 38); He first loved us (1 John 4: 19) and showed us mercy. The heart, now purified by faith (Acts 15: 9), and filled with gratitude and love to Christ, becomes the temple of the spirit of Christ, which is the spirit of love—of love to man. Hence the believer loves all men, friends and strangers, benefactors and enemies. At this period of his religious life he becomes *merciful* in heart as well as in outward appearance, and receives in all its fullness the blessing mentioned in the text.—**B. They . . . mercy** (Ps. 18: 25). The whole work of Christ's redeeming love is styled *mercy* in Luke 1: 72. The mercy of God is seen in all His acts—in every temporal and in every spiritual gift bestowed in this life. Its loftiest exhibition will occur on the day of judgment, when the merciful, whose life of faith and love is described in Matt. 25: 34-40, shall be invited to enter the joy of their Lord.

⁸ Blessed are the pure in heart: for they shall see God.

A. The pure in heart (comp. Ps. 24: 3, 4). He alone that is pure or clean shall approach the divine presence. Those who were legally unclean or defiled were removed from the camp, and could not approach the place of worship (Lev. 5 : 2 ; 13 : 46; Numb. 5 : 2 ; 12 : 14). The legal mode of cleansing was an image of the spiritual cleansing effected by the atonement of Christ (Hebr. 9 : 9–14). Sin is represented in the Scriptures as having made man spiritually filthy or unclean (Job 15 : 16; Ps. 14 : 3 ; 1 Thess. 4 : 7; 2 Pet. 2 : 10). Those who by faith (Acts 15 : 9) obtain forgiveness through Christ (Zech. 13 : 1 ; 1 John 1 : 7) and are renewed and sanctified by the Spirit of God (2 Thess. 2 : 13; 1 Cor. 6 : 11; Titus 3 : 5) attain to a state of purity. A clean heart is the gift of God (Ps. 51 : 10). Inasmuch as the word *heart* (see 13 : 19, B.) in Scripture often comprehends the whole moral nature of man (that is, the understanding, the emotions, the will and the conscience), the pure in heart are those who are pure in all these respects.—B. **They shall see God.** It was anciently regarded in oriental countries as the highest honor and happiness which an individual could receive, when he was permitted to enter the royal palace and see the king's face; comp. Esther 1 : 14; Prov. 2 : 29; 1 Kings 10 : 8, and especially 2 Kings 25 : 19, where the five men mentioned were among those who, according to the Hebrew as translated in the margin, "saw the king's face." This access to the presence of an earthly monarch is now employed in the New Test. as an image of the honor and felicity which the redeemed will enjoy in heaven in the presence of God (see Hebr. 12 : 14 ; 1 Cor. 13 : 12 ; 1 John 3 : 2 ; Rev. 22 : 4). Of this inexpressible happiness (Ps. 73 : 1) the believer enjoys a foretaste on earth already, when he experiences in his heart the power of the grace of God (2 Cor. 3 : 18).

⁹ Blessed are the peacemakers: for they shall be called the sons of God.

A. **Peacemakers.** The natural man is the enemy of God (Rom. 5 : 10; 8 : 7; Col. 1 : 21). He is reconciled to God through the atoning work of Christ and the influences of the Divine Spirit. This peace between God and man, which Christ established on the cross (Eph. 2: 12-19), proceeded originally from the love of God, whom Paul, therefore, continually calls the God of peace (e. g. Rom. 15:33; 16:20), and for whose grace and peace he continually prays at the commencement of every epistle. This peace which the penitent and justified believer enjoys (Rom. 5:1), is solely the work of Christ, who is styled in Isai. 9:6: "The Prince of Peace," as He brought peace to the earth (Luke 2:14). Now peace or the love of peace is a fruit (Gal. 5:22) of that Spirit of Christ which all believers possess (Rom. 8:9); it is one proof, among others, that Christ dwells in them. They are "counsellors of peace" (Prov. 12:20)—not only peaceful themselves, but also authors of peace, like their Master, the great Peacemaker (Col. 1:20). This disinterested and continued desire to secure and maintain peace and love is one of the evidences that they are "new creatures" (2 Cor. 5:17), precisely as active kindness to orphans and widows, and purity of life, are mentioned in James 1:27, not as constituting the whole of pure and undefiled religion, but as illustrations and evidences of it.—B. **They shall be called**—*they shall be*. The phrase *to be called* or *named* sometimes signifies *to be constituted* or *regarded* (Matt. 5:9, 19; 21:13; 1 Cor. 15:9); it designates the possession of an elevated office or character, or it is the honorable recognition of such possession (see below, ver. 19, and Luke 1:76; Rom. 9:26; Eph. 1:21).—C. **The sons of God**—who is the God of peace (Rom. 15:33), and love (2 Cor. 12:11), and whose image peacemakers accordingly bear. Through Christ believers receive the adoption of sons (Gal. 4: 5-7). Paul remarks, in allusion to the future glory of the children of God: "If children, then heirs, etc." (Rom.

8 : 17). Believers are "now the sons of God" (1 John 3 : 1, 2).

¹⁰ Blessed are they that have been persecuted for righteousness' sake: for theirs is the kingdom of heaven.

A. Persecuted ... sake=harassed or afflicted unjustly by the enemies of the Gospel, on account of their confession of the Christian faith, and their faithful and unwavering adherence in spirit and life to the divine commands (2 Tim. 3 : 12). These words are strikingly explained and applied in 1 Pet. 3 : 14, 17 ; 4 : 1, 12–16, 19. —**B. For theirs is, etc.**=Their fidelity proves that they already live in communion with God, and the fulness of peace and joy will be their portion in the eternal world ; to them the promise in verse 3, is renewed. The true believer is poor in spirit, humble and feeble in himself, but the weapons of his warfare are mighty through God (2 Cor. 10 : 4); he can " do all things through Christ which (who) strengtheneth " him (Phil. 4 : 13). " This is the victory, etc." (1 John 5 : 4).

¹¹ Blessed are ye, when *men* shall reproach you, and persecute you, and say all manner of evil against you falsely, for my sake.

A. Reproach ... persecute. The former word specially refers to the malignant *language* (comp. Matt. 11 : 19; 27 : 39–44; John 8 : 48 ; 1 Pet. 2 : 23), the latter to the malignant *acts* of enemies, as in Acts 8 : 1 ; 11 : 19 ; 1 Cor. 4 : 12.—**B. Say all ... evil**=Heaping up reproachful and slanderous words, representing every good trait in a false and repulsive form, as the words *slander* and *evil report* are used in Numb. 14 : 36, 37.—**C. Falsely.** Peter applies the divine promises (1 Pet. 2 : 20 ; 3 : 16) to those only who "do well, and suffer for it," and whose adversaries " falsely accuse " them.—**D. For my sake** (comp. Matt. 10 : 22 ; 19 : 29 ; 24 : 9)—not because ye committed unlawful acts, but because ye have professed your faith in Me and conscientiously obey the precepts of my religion.

¹² Rejoice, and be exceeding glad: for great is your reward in heaven: for so persecuted they the prophets which were before you.

A. **Rejoice ... glad.** The first term, *rejoice*, in the original, is the one usually employed to designate an internal delight which the soul experiences; the second, *be exceeding glad* (—exult), like a similar term which Luke employs (6: 23, *leap for joy*), indicates a degree of joy so high that the emotion cannot be repressed, but exhibits itself outwardly.—B. **For great ... heaven.** The Lord does not mean that God contracts a debt in the case of His faithful servants; on the contrary, His words in Luke 17: 10 declare that even the most zealous and devout Christians are nothing more than "unprofitable servants." So, too, Paul shows in Rom. 4: 4 ff., that a *reward*, in the sense of payment for services rendered, is inconsistent with the doctrine of God's grace. The figurative term, *reward*, here designates the fruits or results of a certain course of action, according to the righteous appointment of God, a reward of grace; so, too, unrighteousness receives its reward or recompense (2 Pet. 2: 13), that is, it leads to consequences which correspond to its true character (comp. Rom. 2: 6–10; 2 Cor. 5: 10; Hebr. 11: 6).—C. **For so persecuted ... you.** For the persecutions of the prophets see Acts 7: 52; 1 Thess. 2: 15; Hebr. 11: 32 ff.; Jam. 5: 10; 1 Kings 18: 4; 19: 14; 2 Chron. 24: 21; Jer. 20: 2, 8; Dan. 6: 16. The Lord mentions two sources of the joy of His persecuted followers; the former is found in the eternal rest of the redeemed in heaven; the latter is the assurance which they derive from their afflictions for righteousness' sake, that they really belong to the people of God, such as the prophets and righteous men of old, whose fidelity to God attracted the hatred of the world. The strength and comfort which this promise of the Lord afterwards gave the apostles may be seen in Acts 5 : 29, 41 ; Rom. 5 : 3.

¹³ Ye are the salt of the earth; but if the salt have lost its savour, wherewith shall it be salted? it is thenceforth good for nothing, but to be cast out and trodden under foot of men.

Ye . . . salt of the earth, etc. Salt has been employed from the earliest ages for the two-fold purpose of seasoning certain articles of food (see 16 : 23, D.), and of preserving them from putrefaction. It hence served as an image expressive of many moral and religious thoughts. When, for instance, two parties in the east made a covenant, each of them swallowed a few grains of salt, to indicate that they would inviolably maintain their obligations. A "covenant of salt" (Numb. 18 : 19 ; 2 Chron. 13 : 5) is hence one that is to be faithfully observed by the contracting parties. As an image of purity and of continued fidelity to God, a portion of it was added to every meat-offering required by the laws of Moses (Lev. 2 : 13 ; Ezek. 43 : 24; Mark 9 : 49). It was employed by the oriental nations as an emblem of friendship; the modern Arabs still profess to regard him as an ally, with whom they have "eaten salt." When Paul directs that the conversation of believers should "be seasoned with salt" (Col. 4 ; 6), he not only alludes to the improved flavor which salt conveys to articles of food, but also implies that the subjects of discourse should be free from that corruption, against which salt (used as a figure for a heavenly spirit) is a protection. As Elisha healed the unwholesome water of Jericho, when he mingled salt with it (2 Kings 2 : 21), so the first teachers of the Gospel are appointed to cleanse men, and call them into that "glorious church, which should be holy and without blemish" (Eph. 5 : 27).

The Saviour now also alludes to the circumstance that the salt employed by the Jews was often mixed with other ingredients, which, when the whole was dissolved, destroyed its virtue. The sense then is:—If you, the agents through whom the Gospel is communicated, are unfaithful, and resemble salt that has lost its power to season and to preserve (its saltness, Mark 9: 50) by admixture with unclean ingredients, you will lose the promised great reward in heaven; and, further, even as men would cast away that worthless salt, so will God deal with you. The cause of the stern judgment pronounced on the unfaithful lies in the grievous injury which they inflict; if they destroy the purifying influences of the Gospel, what other mode of healing men can be found? If *their* light is extinguished, "how great is that darkness" (Matt. 6: 23); they have then the form of godliness, but deny its power (2 Tim. 3: 5).—**Wherewith . . . salted**—how should the earth be redeemed, if those who are entrusted with the Gospel are unfaithful to their trust? "The salt also loses its savour when the preaching of the word ceases, when men are no longer admonished and warned, when they are not taught to discern their misery and helplessness, nor called to repentance, when they are permitted to regard themselves as righteous and to depend on their own imaginary holiness, and when in this manner the pure doctrine concerning faith disappears, and Christ is set aside."—LUTHER.

¹⁴ Ye are the light of the world. A city set on a hill cannot be hid.

A. Ye . . . world. In its highest sense, this title—*light of the world*—belongs to Christ alone (Isai. 49:6; John 1:9; 8:12; 9:5; 12:35-46). The world, on the other hand, is "darkness" (John 1:5; Eph. 6:12). The disciples of Christ, on whom His light shines, who receive the saving truth from Him (Eph. 1:18), and live by faith, now reflect the light which they have received (Eph. 3 : 8, 9), and thus become "children of light" (2 Thess. 5 : 5), or "lights (*luminaries*) in the world" (Phil. 2 : 15; they are themselves a "light in the Lord" (Eph. 5 : 8), guiding others in the way of life and peace.—B. **A city . . . hill.** The sense is: Those who are truly the people of God can be readily distinguished from the people of the world, not only by their superior knowledge of divine things, but also by their holy walk and conversation (ver. 16 below, and comp. Isai. 2 : 2).

[15] Neither do *men* light a lamp and put it under the bushel, but on the stand; and it shineth unto all that are in the house.

A. Neither. This word (as in 6 : 26, "they sow *not, neither*") refers to the word *not* ("can *not*") in ver. 14, and the whole may be thus understood: *Neither* can a city, etc., *nor* do men, etc.—**B. Bushel**—a Roman measure called *modius*, for things dry, such as grain, etc., containing nearly one peck: it was an article which, on account of the many uses to which it could be applied, was very generally found in private houses. It was customary to place this vessel over lamps burning in a chamber that was temporarily unoccupied.—**C. It giveth light, etc.** The sense is: The light of the Gospel is designed, not to be hidden or neglected, but to shine before men, that they may know whither they go (John 12 : 35), and ascertain the path that leads to heaven.

[16] Even so let your light shine before men, that they may see your good works, and glorify your Father which is in heaven.

Even so . . . light (in like manner as an uncovered and brightly burning candle) **shine before men**—not for the purpose of display, through spiritual pride (which is forbidden, 6 : 1, 5, 6, 17). The words are explained in 1 Pet. 2 : 12: the faith and holy life of God's **people** glorify the author of their spiritual life. The phrase. **that they may see—and glorify,** is a Hebrew mode of expressing a cause and its effect, which modern languages do by means of a participle, thus: *that, on seeing—they may glorify.* The sense is: Let no persecutions, no temptations whatever, prevent you from living in strict accordance with the Gospel. Let your religious principles be so strictly avowed and maintained in your conduct, that the honor and glory resulting from your new life may be ascribed by all who witness it, to its proper source, to your religious faith which God gave, and to the power of that grace by which *you are what you are* (1 Cor. 15 : 10 ; Eph. 2 : 10).

¹⁷ Think not that I came to destroy the law or the prophets: I came not to destroy, but to fulfil.

A. Think not—because I am not one of the scribes and do not repeat their lessons, but proclaim truths never heard before.—**B. To destroy**—to abrogate, subvert, or, *set at nought* (comp. the same word in Acts 5 : 38), by teaching an opposite system of faith. The child is not destroyed but brought to a more perfect state when it at last appears as the full-grown man—the old covenant passes over into one that is still better (Hebr. 8 : 6).— **C. Law . . . prophets.** This is the phrase by which the whole collection of the sacred writings was frequently designated; *the law* specially denoted the Five Books of Moses, *the prophets* then comprehended the remainder of the O. T. (Matt. 22 : 40; Luke 16 : 16; 24 : 27; John 1 : 45 ; Acts 28 : 23; Rom. 3 : 21). All these writings constituted the first or old covenant, containing commands, doctrines, types and prophecies, and were designed to prepare the way for the coming of Christ (Gal. 3 : 24).—**D. To fulfil**—*to fill out, make complete,* as the same original word signifies in John 15 : 11 ("might be full"), 2 Cor. 10 : 6. The old covenant, which had only "a shadow of good things to come" (Hebr. 10 : 1) was not intended to be permanent, but to be succeeded by the "very image" and substance of the things foreshadowed in it; "God having provided some better thing for us" (Hebr. 11 : 40; see Jer. 31 : 31-34), as explained in Hebr. 8 : 7-13; 10 : 16, 17. Hence "the law and the prophets were until John: since that time the kingdom of God is preached" (Luke 16 : 16). The holy law gave men a knowledge of sin (Rom. 7 : 7), but it "made nothing perfect" (Hebr. 7 : 19; 9 : 9). It contained commandments which none perfectly obeyed, and set forth blessings which were unattainable under it (Rom., ch. 2 and 10 : 5). Throughout the whole of the O. T. Christ is foreshadowed as the "mediator of a better covenant, which was established upon better promises" (Hebr. 8 : 6). By His appearance on earth, and by His whole mediatorial work, he fulfilled all the purposes to which the law and the prophets referred (Luke 24 : 44); thus, He did not reject it, but established it (Rom. 3 : 31), by completing the gracious plan of salvation for which the old covenant prepared the way. So, when two parties make a contract, and both comply with its terms, they have strictly *fulfilled*, not *destroyed* it.

[18] For verily I say unto you, Till heaven and earth pass away one jot or one tittle shall in no wise pass away from the law till all things be accomplished.

A. Verily. The original word, which occurs more than thirty times in Matt., and elsewhere very frequently, is *Amen*. It does not occur in the Acts; it is very frequently found in the Epistles and the Revelation. It is a Hebrew word, indicating *firmness, fidelity*, and is equivalent to *surely, certainly;* it is so used by the Saviour, giving peculiar emphasis to the remark which it introduces. As the concluding word of a prayer, it is equivalent to an ejaculation expressive of the desire that the prayer may be answered.—B. **I say.** The ancient prophets introduced their messages with the words: *Thus saith the Lord.* But when the Lord Himself speaks, He begins, as here and elsewhere; I SAY,—**heaven and earth**—the whole visible creation, as in Gen. 1:1.—C. **Pass away**—disappear, cease to be, perish, as in 2 Cor. 5:17; 2 Pet. 3:10; Hebr. 1:11; James 1:10; see below, 24:35.—D. **Jot . . . tittle.** The former word represents the letter *jod*, the smallest letter of the Hebrew alphabet, and is used proverbially to designate the minutest part of anything. A *tittle* (in the original *a horn*, figuratively, for a *point* or extremity) designates any dot, point, little curve, corner or mark which distinguishes one Hebrew letter from another of a somewhat similar form, and was applied to any object which was very small. Thus the small lower curve of the English printer's letter **b** is the tittle which distinguishes that letter from **h**. The dot of the letter **i** is also an obvious illustration. These words represent portions of the divine law which seem to the thoughtless to be insignificant, but which are as essentially parts of it as those which are admitted to be of the highest moment.—E. **The law,** here—the old covenant, as contradistinguished from the new covenant or the Gospel.—F. **Till all etc.** Since heaven and earth are appointed to pass away (2 Pet. 3:10), the Saviour intends to declare emphatically that all *shall* be really fulfilled, before the end of the world arrives.—G. **All,**—all things promised or predicted respecting the Messiah and His kingdom, such as the evangelization of the whole world, the prosperity and glory of the Church of Christ, etc. (Isai. 40:8; 1 Pet. 1:24, 25).—H. **Be fulfilled**—accomplished, completed. The Lord here clearly establishes the divine inspiration and authority of the

O. T., and, consequently, the strict accuracy of its historical, as well as of all its other portions.

¹⁹ Whosoever therefore shall break one of these least commandments, and shall teach men so, shall be called least in the kingdom of heaven: but whosoever shall do and teach them, he shall be called great in the kingdom of heaven.

A. Least commandments The Pharisees, who regarded the letter of the law alone, distinguished between the great and the minor commandments of God; this course only embarrassed humble believers, as illustrated in Matt. 22 : 36. All the commands of God are entitled to the same reverence and obedience (see James 2 : 10, 11). The Lord here applied this principle by referring to the *spirit* of obedience as distinct from a mere formal observance of the letter; no religious duties are so unimportant that they may be neglected without sin. Hence the *least* commandment only seems to the carnal eye to be the least.—**B. Least . . . great.** The *least* are those who are "unskilful in the word of righteousness" (Hebr. 5 : 12, 13), or are "babes in Christ" (1 Cor. 3 : 1; 1 Pet. 2 : 2; Rom. 2 : 20). He who has, on the contrary, made progress in the Christian life, as the power and depth of his faith advance, and has become an intelligent and experienced Christian, is a "perfect man" (Eph. 4 : 13; 1 Cor. 14 : 20). The Pharisees therefore, even when they were honest in professing their belief that some commandments were less important than others, proved by such ignorance that they were the *least* or most unfit of all to belong to the Messiah's kingdom.—**C. Great, etc.** —he shall be regarded as having reached the period of manhood or adult age in his religious life. He alone is competent to be a teacher of religion in the Church (Hebr. 5 : 12), either by his example or by direct instruction, who *does* and *teaches* all the divine commandments, as alike holy and necessary to be obeyed with sincerity and zeal.

²⁰ For I say unto you, That except your righteousness shall exceed *the righteousness* of the scribes and Pharisees, ye shall in no wise enter into the kingdom of heaven.

A. Righteousness of the Pharisees. (see ver. 6, B.). This Pharisaic righteousness is illustrated by the Lord in Luke 18 : 11, 12, where the Pharisee, a strictly *moral* man, performs apparently an act of worship and devotion—he prays. But he shows no sense of sin, no humility; spiritual pride, arising from the observance of the mere letter of the law, fills his heart to the exclusion of all humble faith and love; holiness of *heart* he regards as one of the *least* commandments. Hence his supposed righteousness was only a name, and had no reality (comp. Rom. 10 : 3).—**B. Your . . . exceed**=your righteousness, founded on an enlightened and living faith, which receives *all* God's commandments as truth (Ps. 119 : 151), and which leads to the pardon of your sins; it must *exceed*=*be more abundant*, as the word occurs in Phil. 1 : 26, or, *be better*, *excel*, as in 1 Cor, 8 : 8, or be of a purer character. " The Pharisees were right in attaching high importance to a moral life, but they were wrong in supposing that their moral life rendered them meritorious in the eyes of God, and in forgetting that God desires first of all a new and clean heart.—LUTHER.—**C. In no wise, etc.** Nominal Christians may easily continue to be members of the Church *on earth;* the emphatic words: *in no wise* (=*by no means, not at all*), indicate that the *kingdom of heaven* here means " the kingdom prepared for—the blessed—from the foundation of the world." (Matt. 25 : 34).

²¹ Ye have heard that it was said to them of old time, Thou shalt not kill; and whosoever shall kill shall be in danger of the judgment:

A. This verse and those which follow contain illustrations of the spurious righteousness of the Pharisees.— **B. Ye have heard**—in the synagogue, when the scribes and Pharisees (23 : 2) read portions of the laws of Moses (John 12 : 34 ; Acts 15 : 21 ; Rom. 2 : 13), and then made their comments. **To hear,** as in Eph. 1 : 13, often means *to listen to public instructions.*—**C. That it was said**—by the oldest teachers from whom the traditions or established interpretations of the divine word, current in the days of Christ, were said to be derived (see 15 : 2, B.). The Lord does not mean the teaching of Moses himself, but the erroneous mode of interpreting his words. The phrase: **I say,** indicates that the Lord's doctrine is the opposite of that which was taught by the false Jewish interpreters who lived after the age of Moses.—**D. By them . . . not kill**—said *by* * (not *to*) the ancients, by the rabbins or doctors (—teachers) of the laws of Moses, of earlier ages, also called *elders* (Matt. 15 : 2 ; Mark 7 : 3, 5) and *fathers* (Gal. 1 : 14). The interpretations of Scripture by the ancient teachers were regarded as of equal authority with the inspired word itself. Indeed, some of the Jews impiously compared the written word to water, but the traditions to wine. These interpretations, handed down by successive generations and gradually acquiring the authority of precedents, constituted in the time of Christ, the body of "the traditions of the elders."—**Thou shalt not kill** (Exod. 20 : 13). The trivial and shallow mode of interpretation adopted by the scribes, regarded the letter of the law alone. Thus they taught that this commandment prohibited merely the act of killing a person, but did not condemn the wish of the heart for the death of

---

* While the Author has, almost invariably, anticipated the changes made in the Revised Version, with many of the ablest commentators, he here prefers the A. V. Editor.

another. Such a mode of explaining the Scriptures, which allowed all the uncleanness of the heart to remain (Matt. 23 : 27), is here rejected by the Lord. The Christian and inspired interpretation of the commandment here quoted is found in 1 John 3 : 15.—E. **And whosoever ... judgment.** This clause furnishes a specimen of the prevalent Pharisaic mode of interpretation.—**Shall ... danger of**—amenable to, subject to be called to account by.— The **judgment** here mentioned was an inferior or local court of justice established in every town or village (see Deut. 16 : 18); a higher tribunal is mentioned in Deut. 17 : 8, 9; 19 : 16–18. The judges in the former case were probably not twenty-three in number, as the rabbins relate, but only seven, according to Josephus, Antiq. 4. 8. 14. There was, however, a tribunal, established not long before the Christian era, subordinate to the Great Council or Sanhedrin (see next verse), and consisting of twenty-three members. The Pharisaic reference of the crime of murder to an inferior tribunal, implied that they maintained the dangerous opinion that murder was not one of the most heinous crimes which could be committed.

[22] But I say unto you, That every one who is angry with his brother shall be in danger of the judgment: and whosoever shall say to his brother, Raca, shall be in danger of the council: and whosoever shall say, Thou fool, shall be in danger of the hell of fire.

A. **But I say**—in opposition to the erroneous interpretation of the scribes. *Love* is the spirit of the divine law (Matt. 22 : 37–40; Rom. 13 : 8–10). *Thou shalt not kill* does not mean simply : Thou shalt not take the life of another, but also, Thou shalt love; for "whosoever hateth his brother is a murderer" (1 John 3 : 15). The Lord refers to three tribunals; first, the *judgment* mentioned in the foregoing verse; secondly, the *council*

(SANHEDRIN), which was of a higher rank and authorized to inflict higher punishments than the former; and, lastly, the tribunal of God Himself, who "is able to destroy both soul and body in hell" (Matt. 10 : 28). He also shows that there is a gradation in impiety, which, in its fully developed form, is a total want of a sincere and perfect love to God and man. On the day of judgment, God "will render to every man according to his deeds" (Rom. 2 : 6); the punishments in the eternal world will correspond in degree to the degree in which the offender's heart in this life lacked a holy love.—**B. Angry . . . brother.** The apostle's words (in Eph. 4 : 31, 32; 1 Cor. ch. 13) plainly show that the anger or wrath here mentioned is totally at variance with a Christian spirit; the explanatory words below (ver. 44) further teach that no cause can exist which would justify hate or a revengeful feeling towards a "brother."—**C. Danger . . . judgment** (see ver. 21, E.). The sense is: Such an offender shall suffer a corresponding punishment in the eternal world; the inferior earthly tribunal is an image of the divine tribunal. Anger and hatred, even when confined to the heart, render man guilty in the eyes of God.—**D. Raca** This Hebrew word, translated *vain* in Judges 9: 4; 2 Sam. 6 : 20; 2 Chron. 13 : 7, and common among the Jews as a term of reproach, does not, as the connection of these passages abundantly shows, signify merely *empty, empty-headed or brainless*, but empty or destitute of all sound religious principle. The opposite term is *wisdom*, which occurs in the sense of true *godliness* (Deut. 4 : 5, 6; Ps. 111 : 10; Prov. 1 : 7). The use of the term indicates very bitter feelings, and is a violation of the law of love: "charity (Christian love) suffereth long, and is kind—beareth, believeth, hopeth, endureth all things" (1 Cor. 13 : 4, 7). That holy feeling does not allow the imputation to another of a character so destitute of honor and principle as the word *Raca* implies.—E. **The council.** This tribunal could inflict more severe punishments than the lower courts; hence it is an image of the increased severity with which the Lord will hereafter deal with those whose anger so far controls them that, in a malevolent spirit, they address reproachful words to a fellow-man.—H. **Thou fool.** The original word (*moros*), the use of which is represented as a very grievous offence, is, nevertheless, repeatedly employed by the Saviour and the apostles (Matt. 7 : 26; 23 : 17; 25 : 2: 1 Cor. 3 : 18), in whom unerring wisdom spoke, and who were not controlled by unholy sentiments in uttering it. Since the general sense of the word seems to differ but little from that of *Raca*, the reason for which its use is still more impious, must be sought in the intensity of the feeling of hatred which prompts the use of it. He who is angry with his brother proceeds at length to that degree of impiety, that all love in the soul becomes extinct; he now entertains feelings of the utmost contempt and abhorrence, and he takes pleasure in the thought that his brother is an ungodly man, worthy of God's curse. He says to him: *Thou fool*, in the sense of *impious*, as Asaph applies the term to the blasphemer (Ps. 74 : 18, 22), David to the atheist (Ps. 14 : 1; 53 : 1), and God Himself to the grievous sin of Achan (Josh. 7 : 15); he seems to triumph in the thought that his brother will perish. The sin consists in the circumstance that he harbors such deadly hate in his soul; he has the tongue which is "set on fire of hell" (James 3 : 6). Thereby he himself incurs the divine wrath, and casts away all the mercy of Christ" (2 Cor. 6 : 14, 15).—G. **Hell of fire.** In the original it is: *geenna*. The valley of the son of Hinnom (Josh. 15 : 8; 18 : 16; Nehem. 11 : 30; Jer. 19 : 2) was situated on the south or south-west side of the city of Jerusalem; the Arabs still call it Wady Jehennam. In this valley, which was once distinguished for its beauty and fertility, the idolatrous Israelites of a former age sacrificed their children to the god Molech (2 Chron. 28 : 3; 33 : 6; Jer. 7 : 31). King Josiah, who desired to extirpate idolatry, defiled the whole valley by causing dead bodies to be cast there (2 Kings 23 : 10, 14). It then became, according to ancient Jewish accounts, a place of deposit for the bodies of dead animals and all manner of filth. Its vicinity to the city rendered it necessary to maintain constant fires there for the purpose of destroying the accumulated mass of filth, and purifying the atmosphere. The Hebrew name of "the valley of Hinnom" (Ge-Hinnom, Josh. 15 : 8), expressed with Greek letters, assumed the form of Geenna. The whole character of the valley rendered the region a fit image of the condition of the ungodly, and of the place of their eternal punishment; its name was accordingly transferred to the latter in the sense of *hell* (Matt. 10 : 28; 18 : 9; 23 : 15, 33; James 3 : 6). Earthly tribunals and punishments were employed in the former two cases by the Lord as images of future punishments; here, where He designs to express the most extreme misery of the sinner, He finds in the sentence of no earthly tribunal an adequate representative of it, and He therefore dispenses with all images.

^{23,24} If therefore thou art offering thy gift at the altar, and there rememberest that thy brother has aught against thee, leave there thy gift before the altar, and go thy way; first be reconciled to thy brother, and then come and offer thy gift.

A. **Therefore.** Even the worship of God is an unmeaning and useless act when the "heart is not right in the sight of God" (Acts 8 : 21; see Isai. 1 : 10–20). Even as it is at all times a duty to worship God, so it is at all times a solemn duty to seek a reconciliation with those who believe that they have been aggrieved by us.—**B. Gift ... altar** — when thou dost bring an offering, and intendest to engage in an act of worship. The "gift" is any offering or sacrifice brought to the priest and laid by him on the altar. For **altar**, see 23 : 18, A.—**C. There rememberest.** Self-examination is indispensable as a part of all acceptable worship of God.—**D. Thy brother** — thy fellow-man, who is a creature of that God who made thee (Mal. 2 : 10).—**E. Hath aught ... thee**—has any complaint or charge to bring against thee, either a real or an imaginary grievance, as the phrase occurs in Mark 11 : 25 ; Acts 24 : 19.—**F. Leave, etc.**—omit the useless outward act, which cannot please God until thy worship proceeds from a pure heart (Ps. 24 : 3, 4).—**G. First be reconciled.** The sense is: Whether the interruption of peace and love was occasioned by thy act or by that of thy fellow-man, "if it be possible" (Rom. 12 : 18), first be reconciled=let peace be restored. The Lord shows (Matt. 18 : 15-17) that the believer is not accountable for the conduct and feelings of irreconcilable enemies. The disciples peacefully partook of the Holy Supper which He instituted (Matt. 26 : 26-29), although many enemies were near, for He forgave and loved them (Luke 23 : 34). —**H. Then come**—with a loving spirit (see Isai. 33 : 15, 16; Eph. 4 : 31, 32).

25, 26 Agree with thine adversary quickly, whiles thou art with him in the way; lest haply the adversary deliver thee to the judge, and the judge deliver thee to the officer, and thou be cast into prison. Verily I say unto thee, Thou shalt by no means come out thence, till thou have paid the last farthing.

A. These words contain the application of the preceding declarations. The Lord selects a case occurring in the ordinary transactions of men, a civil process, as an illustration of the lot of those who fail to keep the divine law of love.—B. **Adversary—judge—officer— prison.** All these figurative terms are taken from the forms of ancient judicial proceedings. The *adversary* (accuser) in a court of justice can subject the other party to imprisonment until the latter pays the whole claim, if he is not satisfied *in the way*, namely, before the trial commences. The *judge* directs the appropriate *officer* to collect the debt or fine, or else imprison the debtor (see below, 18 : 30). The *last farthing* is a proverbial phrase, implying that no mercy or remission of any part of the sentence can be expected after the trial has been held.—C. **Thou shalt by no means, etc.** As the debtor will receive no mercy, if he does not satisfy the creditor before the trial, so he who violates the law of love, and who is not restored to peace with God *in his way* to the grave and eternity, shall never obtain life eternal ; for after this life has passed, and the day of judgment has come, the season of repentance is gone forever (see Eccl. 9 : 10, and comp. 18 : 34, C. for an illustration).

²⁷ Ye have heard that it was said, Thou shalt not commit adultery:

A. **Ye ...** (see ver. 21).—B. **Thou ... adultery** (Ex. 20: 14). Here, too, as in ver. 21, the Lord refers to the loose mode of interpretation which was prevalent in His day ; the commandments of God were supposed to refer only to outward actions and not to the heart, from which all evil acts really proceed (Matt. 15 : 19). When the whole passage, ver. 27–32, is read in connection, it appears that the Lord designs to rebuke the levity and sinful contempt with which the tie of marriage, as originally instituted by the Creator (Gen. 1 : 27, 28 ; 2 : 21–24 ; Mark 10 : 2–9), was regarded by the Jews; He traces the evils which prevailed in this respect, to the unholy feelings of the heart, which perverted the words of the commandment here quoted.

⁲⁸ But I say unto you, That every one that looketh on a woman to lust after her, hath committed adultery with her already in his heart.

A. Every one ... her. The Lord requires that every unholy emotion, unchaste thought or forbidden desire which arises in the soul should be instantly suppressed, by divine aid; to cherish an evil thought, on the other hand, or, like Eve (Gen. 3 : 6), to listen to the tempter's pleading rather than to obey the divine command at once and absolutely, is itself already a sin.—**B. Hath ... heart**—the all-seeing eye of God (Hebr. 4 : 13) marks the unholy thoughts and purposes of the heart; these defile the sinner in His sight even before the outward acts are committed (see especially Col. 3 : 5, 6).

²⁹, ³⁰ And if thy right eye causeth thee to stumble, pluck it out, and cast it from thee: for it is profitable for thee that one of thy members should perish, and not thy whole body be cast into hell. And if thy right hand causeth thee to stumble, cut it off, and cast it from thee: for it is profitable for thee that one of thy members should perish, and not thy whole body go into hell.

A. What course shall we adopt when we are powerfully tempted to entertain evil thoughts or commit evil acts? The answer of the text is illustrated by the words of Paul : " If ye through the Spirit do mortify (—deaden, put to death) the deeds of the body, ye shall live " (Rom. 8 : 13).—**B. Right eye ... right hand**—the more highly valued of the two eyes and hands (1 Sam. 11 : 2 ; Zech. 11 : 17 ; Ps. 137 : 5), here employed as an image of the most powerful and dangerous temptations. Men yield through the medium of the *hand* or the body generally, that is, the eye represents the temptation, the hand, the yielding to it. Thus Eve *saw* the forbidden fruit, and then *took* it with her hand (Gen. 3 : 6).—**C. Causeth thee to stumble**—to furnish an occasion for sinning. The original word (from which the English word *scandal* is derived) was originally applied to a trap or snare of any kind (or specially to that part of a trap on which the bait is placed, and which, when touched by an animal, occasions its fall and capture), and then to any object which causes an unwary person to stumble. It is applied in the N. T. to spiritual things, designating any cause that may interrupt the believer in his Christian course, or that has a tendency to turn him from the path of duty and cause him to fall into sin (see 13 : 57, A.).—**D. Pluck it out . . . cut it off**—overcome and extirpate the unholy feeling by divine aid (see Rom. 8 : 13). The language is not to be literally understood, any more than the English phrase: *to cast in the teeth* of a person, which in Matt. 27 : 44 simply means *to revile*. The Lord refers to man's existence, first, in this present world; secondly, in the eternal world. (For the word "hell" (geenna), see ver. 22, G. It here signifies, as there, the abode of those who suffer eternal punishment.) The sense of the two verses is: If thou art even very strongly tempted, insomuch that self-denial will be as painful to thee (see 19 : 21, B.) as the plucking out of an eye or the cutting off of a hand would be to thy body, nevertheless it is profitable (=better for thee, in view of the future judgment) to endure that temporary pain, rather than to yield to the evil thought or temptation, and, for thy sin, lose thy soul (Matt. 16 : 26), and suffer eternal pain (comp. Matt. 18 : 8, 9).

[31] It was said also, Whosoever shall put away his wife, let him give her a writing of divorcement:

A. After the Lord had pronounced the foregoing impressive words respecting sins of the heart committed against the spirit of the divine law on adultery, He completed His remarks on the general subject in ver. 31, 32.— **B. It hath been said.** The Lord refers to a common perversion of the divine law in Deut. 24 : 1, 2. That law did not by any means advise, much less prescribe, divorces, but merely tolerated an ancient custom of the people introduced before the age of Moses; the abolition of it was temporarily deferred in consequence of the rude character of the Jews, and their dullness in appreciating such elevated principles as are revealed in the Gospel (19 : 8; Mark 10 : 5 ; Gal. 3 : 19). Of this dullness the prophets often complained (Ezek. 3 : 7 ; Isai. ch. 1). The Saviour now abolishes the whole system as it existed among the Jews, and prescribes an unalterable law for the Christian Church in place of the licentious and pernicious rules of the Jewish teachers (see 19 : 3, C.)—C. **Writing of divorcement**—bill of divorce (Isai. 50 : 1 ; Jer. 3 : 8); It was a document or written statement given to the repudiated wife for her benefit, in which the husband released her from all obligation to live with him, and pledged himself never to reclaim her as his wife, if she should marry another (Josephus, Antiq. 4, 8, 23).

³² But I say unto you, That every one that putteth away his wife, saving for the cause of fornication, maketh her an adulteress : and whosoever shall marry her when she is put away committeth adultery.

A. **Putteth away**—*divorce.* The same word is translated in the latter part of this verse (in the passive voice) "her that is divorced." The declaration is repeated below, 19 : 9.—B. **Saving** (—except) **for, etc.** The Lord absolutely forbids all divorces, except in the single instance of unfaithfulness to the marriage vows ; in such a case, the offending party has already dissolved the marriage-tie virtually by criminal conduct. Hence the innocent party may, in this case alone, after a legal divorce, marry again before the death of the offending party.— C. **Causeth, etc.** The sense is: Even if men tolerate such practices, yet, in the eyes of God the Judge, the crime of adultery is committed by the marriage of a person divorced for any cause except adultery.

³³ Again, ye have heard that it was said to them of old time, Thou shalt not forswear thyself, but shalt perform unto the Lord thine oaths :

A. Again—*further*. The Lord shows by other instances the spirit of His religion as contrasted with that of the corrupt teachers in His day (He resumes the subject below, 23 : 16, which see). Their whole system respecting oaths, for instance, was a perversion of the teachings of the O. T. In the whole passage, ver. 33-37, the Lord refers to the abuse of a religious principle, and not to oaths which have a proper sanction (see below, ver. 34, B.). So, too, the words : *Thou shalt not kill* (ver. 21 D.), do not refer, as indeed the language of Paul shows in Rom. 13 : 3, 4, to " rulers," but only to the private individual. Hence God commands (Exod. 21 : 12) that the unauthorized act of putting a man to death, shall be punished by inflicting death on the murderer.—**B. Forswear**—*swear falsely*, commit perjury (Exod. 20 : 7 ; Levit. 19 : 12 ; Numb. 30 : 2).—**C. But shalt perform, etc.** One of the false interpretations of the scribes consisted in the combination of passages of the O. Test. between which no connection really existed. It appears from these words of Christ that with the passage in Lev. 19 : 12, which is an independent law, the rabbins connected Numb. 30 : 2 and Deut. 23 : 21. But these two passages refer to voluntary vows, which were not required as a part of the duties of religion (Deut. 23 : 22). The Lord takes occasion here to give rules on the general subject of " swearing."

[34] But I say unto you, Swear not at all ; neither by the heaven ; for it is the throne of God.

A. Swear. To swear or take an oath, in the lawful form of the act, is, to declare or promise something, and, for the purpose of showing the sincerity of the declaration or promise, to make a direct appeal to God as the witness and final judge (Deut. 6 : 13). It is, therefore, a religious act, in which the presence, power, truth and justice of God are distinctly set forth and confessed. That this direct appeal to God, whose vengeance is invoked, if the oath be wantonly broken or evaded, constitutes the very essence or being of an oath, is evident from the fact that the oath of an atheist is regarded as an unmeaning act; he does not believe that it binds him. The scribes and Pharisees were fully aware that a direct oath was binding, and hence proposed various expedients by which the solemnity and the obligation of an oath could be evaded. They held that an oath in which the name of God did not expressly occur was not binding. They substituted, accordingly, for the name of God the names of various objects (*heaven, earth, etc.*), and thus exhibited levity and impiety in an aggravated form. The Lord, who desires to set forth the true nature of a lawful oath, exposes in the following words the sophistry and dangerous influence of the Jewish theory.—**B. Not at all.** The original word translated *at all* (holos), signifies *wholly* or *altogether* (comp. 1 Cor. 15 : 29). It is often an emphatic term, and refers to an entire class of objects, actions, etc., viewed as a whole, while it admits that exceptional cases may exist. Its force is here directed against the corrupt practices by which an oath was supposed to be capable of being evaded, and it further prohibits us to use any words (lies, prevarications, etc.) which we would fear to employ if we were under an oath. The exception naturally consists of that class of oaths which has a legal or divine sanction. Under the old covenant oaths were required (Exod. 22 : 11 ; Deut. 6 : 13 ; 10 : 20), and constituted religious acts (Isai. 19 : 18 ; 65 : 16 ; Ps. 63 : 11); God swears by Himself (Gen. 22 : 16 ; Hebr. 6: 13, 14 ; Luke 1 : 73). Under the new covenant similar appeals to God occur (Rom. 1 : 9 ; 2 Cor. 1 : 23 ; Gal. 1 : 20 ; Phil. 1 : 8 ;

Thess. 2 : 5); Christ Himself recognizes the validity of the oath (see below 26 : 63, C.). The Lord forbids here all irreverent appeals to God in ordinary conversation, all mockery of the forms of an oath, all attempts to delude others by hypocritical appeals to the invisible God. Judicial oaths (in a court of justice), when properly administered and taken, are as little here forbidden, as capital punishments are forbidden by the words: " Thou shalt not kill " (see ver. 33, A.). " Let no one swear, unless he is authorized by the word of God to do so."—LUTHER.—C. **By the heaven, etc.** The Lord refers to Isai. 66 : 1. The language here implies that heaven is holy and regarded with reverence, only because God dwells there, that is, manifests all His glory there (see Matt. 23 : 22.) The Lord shows that such an oath, far from being "nothing" (—not binding, Matt. 23 : 18), as the scribes taught, is really a solemn oath.

[35] Nor by the earth ; for it is the footstool of his feet : nor by Jerusalem; for it is the city of the great king.

A. **Footstool.** The sense is: If the scribes swear by the earth, they select it professedly as a representative of the divine power, presence and glory ; in such a case, the oath is either a mockery or a valid oath. It was not alleged by the scribes that such an oath was a mere mockery; the Lord hence declares that, by their own confession, it was a valid oath.—B. **Jerusalem.** Such an oath is not reverential and allowable ; if it is meant to be an evasion, it can only be a mockery ; if Jerusalem is selected because it is the "city of the great king," Jehovah (Ps. 48 : 2; 46 : 4, 5), then the oath is indeed binding, but the form proceeds from an irreverent spirit.

[36] Neither shalt thou swear by thy head, for thou canst not make one hair white or black.

Swear by thy head. This expression perhaps signifies

that the person taking the oath was willing to pledge his life for the truth of his words. The evasion here consisted both in avoiding a direct reference to God, whose witnessing alone constitutes an oath, and also in the assumption that a person could pledge his life at his own will, while in reality his life belonged to God. The Saviour shows the folly of this form of an oath, independently of its impiety, by referring to the simple fact that man has no absolute right or control as to his own life.

37 But let your speech be, Yea, yea; Nay, nay: and whatsoever is more than these is of the evil *one*.

A. (see James 5 : 12). The apostle James, after forbidding oaths of all kinds, as described above, adds, according to the sense of the passage: Let your words be strictly true; when you say: Yea (=yes), do so sincerely, etc. Such appears to be the sense in the present verse. —**B. Yea** (=yes), **etc.** Remember that God is present, and that He hears and judges your language; hence, always speak the truth in uprightness, whether you affirm (" yea ") or deny (" nay ") anything.—**C. For whatsoever . . . evil one.** The Lord declares that the devil is a liar (John 8 : 44), and adds: Whatsoever in your words exceeds the bounds of truth, or implies irreverence towards God, comes from the *Evil* One (1 John 3 : 8–12). Hence the Christian is always as much bound by religious principle to speak the truth, as if he had taken an oath to that effect. Every form of deceit, falsehood and insincerity is evil and worthy of abhorrence alone (Rom. 12 : 9). The subject is renewed by the Lord below (23 : 16–22).

38 Ye have heard that it was said, An eye for an eye, and a tooth for a tooth;

A. The Lord illustrates in the following verses (ch.

5 : 38 ; 6 : 4) the Gospel law of love ; He refers to different situations in which a believer may be placed, in each of which peculiar temptations to violate that law are encountered.—B. **It hath been said**—in Exod. 21 : 24 ; Lev. 24 : 19, 26 ; Deut. 19 : 21. The primary object of the penalties inflicted on offenders by the public law is the protection of society. These passages contain the law which the "judges" are to administer ; private revenge is strictly forbidden (Lev. 19 : 18 ; Prov. 20 : 22 ; 24 : 29). The ancient law of retaliation, as observed in a rude state of society, allowed the injured party to exact a punishment far greater in amount than the injury sustained by him ; he avenged the loss of an eye, for instance, by taking the life of the offender. This severity was not tolerated by Moses. Modern laws, while they have changed the forms of punishment, still recognize the principle involved in the laws of Moses, namely, that the punishment should be proportioned to the enormity of the offence.—C. **An eye . . . tooth**—thou shalt give an eye for, etc. (see Exod. 21 : 23–25). The principle of this law is : Thou shalt suffer harm in the same form and measure in which thou hast wantonly inflicted it on another. This law of retaliation was administered by the legal tribunals established by Moses.

[39] But I say unto you, Resist not him that is evil : but whosoever smiteth thee on thy right cheek, turn to him the other also.

A. **But I say unto you.** The difficulties sometimes found in interpreting this verse and the following may possibly be removed by observing that in reference to insults or injuries, the Lord condemns two extremes, and prescribes a middle course. On the one hand, He forbids anger, hatred and a revengeful spirit ; on the other, He desires His followers to guard against that state of feeling, which is variously termed *weakness, timidity* and *passive* *submission.* The middle course, which is here prescribed, consists, first, in the suppression of angry and revengeful feelings, and, secondly, in the active exercise of a forgiving, disinterested love; such love prompts to acts of kindness and generosity even towards a persecuting and rapacious enemy. This magnanimous spirit is perfectly consistent with a fearless self-defence, as described in Matt. 10:19 (that is, a firm remonstrance against false accusations), and as illustrated in John 18:23; Acts 16:37. The Lord does not require non-resistance in such a form as would lead to a useless sacrifice of our lives, or to violations of conscience.—B. **Resist not evil** —" recompense to no man evil for evil" (Rom. 12:17-19; 1 Thess. 5:15; 1 Pet. 3:9). *To resist* here signifies *to withstand* (as the same word is rendered in Acts 13:8; 2 Tim. 3:8; 4:15), or to oppose in a direct manner, in the same hostile spirit in which the attack is made. The whole duty is illustrated in John 18:33-37; 19:9-11. The *evil* is malice, ill-treatment, provocations, proceeding from evil men (comp. 2 Thess. 3:2, 3).—C. **Smite . . . cheek, etc.** The act of smiting on the face was always regarded as the most grievous insult which could be offered to a person (2 Cor. 11:20); it is here an image of insulting and abusive treatment of any kind. The Lord requires that ill-treatment should be met by such calmness and submission as would be indicated by the act of offering the other cheek. The meaning is best explained by the conduct of the Lord Himself (John 18:22, 23; comp. with Isai. 50:6). When the officer struck Jesus, He neither exhibited anger, nor submitted the other cheek literally, but performed an act of love by appealing to the offender's judgment and conscience. When He was betrayed and seized, He manifested neither anger nor weakness, but returned good for evil by healing the high priest's servant (John 18:10; Luke 22:50, 51). When Paul received permission from the magistrates of Philippi to depart from his prison, he refused to go forth until the alarmed magistrates had publicly acknowledged his innocence (Acts 16: 36–39).

⁴⁰ And if any man would go to law with thee, and take away thy coat, let him have thy cloak also.

A. The Lord here describes the Christian's course of conduct in another case, that is, when the hostile person seeks a sanction for his injurious conduct by instituting legal proceedings.—**B. Coat . . . cloak.** The coat or tunic (Greek, *chiton*, always translated *coat* in the N. T., except in Mark 14 : 63 ; Jude 23), was an under garment, adapted to the form of the body, sometimes furnished with sleeves, and extending from the neck to the knees (John 19 : 23). Over it was loosely thrown the cloak or mantle (*himation*, variously translated, particularly in the plural, e. g. 17 : 2, as a general name for all articles of clothing, cloak, garment, raiment, clothes, apparel and vesture, 21 : 7; 24 : 18, and see 26 : 65, A.). The latter was a piece of cloth nearly square, of far greater value than the under garment; hence the loss of it was more severely felt than the loss of the former. These images the Lord employs to express the following principle: If another attempts to deprive thee by legal means of an object of value, rather than that thou shouldst encourage a contentious spirit in others by thy example (if devout men cannot arrange the matter, 1 Cor. 6 : 1–7), do thou bear the loss, and disarm thy enemy (Rom. 12 : 20), by meeting him with a disinterested and kind spirit, and granting him peaceably an object of even greater value than he seeks; thou wilt eventually not suffer harm or loss by imitating Me. This precept of the Lord, like the former, respecting the right and left cheek, is intended, by means of a particular case, to illustrate the general principle of Christian peaceableness, forbearance and magnanimity.

⁴¹ And whosoever shall compel thee to go one mile, go with him twain.

A. **Compel thee to go.** The original word refers to an ancient Persian law, by which public couriers were authorized to press into their service men, horses, ships or any object that might serve to facilitate their progress, and also to employ the personal service of the owners. Hence the word designated any demand that was oppressive, but, nevertheless, authorized by the government. —B. **Go ... twain.** *Twain* is a nearly obsolete English word, for which *two* is now used. The Lord here adds to the foregoing principles the following: If thou art required to perform an act which thou canst not decline, but dost nevertheless regard as oppressive, exercise thyself in self-denial; withhold complaints, and, in order to testify a willing and cheerful spirit, generously increase the task imposed on thee, by a voluntary addition to it. The sense is: Do not selfishly think only of thy personal rights, but be kind-hearted and generous, even when such a spirit is not manifested towards thee (comp. Eph. 4: 31, 32).

⁴² Give to him that asketh thee, and from him that would borrow of thee, turn not thou away.

A. The Lord finally answers the question: How shall the Christian act in cases in which no legal compulsion occurs?—B. **Give, etc.** All that thou hast (money, clothing, etc.) belongs really to God (Ps. 24: 1; 50: 10-12; 89: 11). Share the gifts of God with thy destitute brother (James 2: 14-16; 1 John 3: 17). The Lord teaches that the act of giving should be guided by Christian wisdom and love in their combination; He does not, for instance, mean that a knife should be given to a madman, nor money to an impostor, nor unsuitable objects to importunate children, nor that a man should give to the actual injury of his own family (1 Tim. 5 : 8), or encourage idleness (2 Thess. 3 : 10).—C. **Borrow**—without paying interest, according to Exod. 22 : 25; Lev. 25 : 37; Deut. 23 : 20, where the word *usury* is equivalent to the modern word *interest* (see below 25 : 27). The sense is: Let not the certainty that thou wilt derive no temporal advantage from the act, prevent thy compliance with the petition. —D. **Turn . . . away**—do not turn thy back without listening and complying; so the word is used in 2 Tim. 1 : 15; Tit. 1 : 14.

⁴⁵ Ye have heard that it was said, Thou shalt love thy neighbor, and hate thine enemy.

A. The Lord concludes this part of the sermon by answering an objection to His doctrine which the Jews might derive from a perversion of God's words in the O. T.—B. **It hath been said**—by the Jewish teachers, when they explain the Law.—C. **Thou . . . neighbor** (Levit. 19 : 18). As the Jewish people alone received through Moses a knowledge of the true God, and all the surrounding nations were idolatrous, the word *neighbor* was so interpreted as to be equivalent to the word *Jew*. But in order to guard against an exclusive spirit which would so greatly restrict the exercise of love, Moses commands in ver. 34 of the same chapter, compared with Lev. 24 : 22, that the Jew should love as himself "the stranger" also, who dwelt with him. The *neighbor*, as the Lord interprets the word (Luke 10 : 27–37; Matt. 22 : 39, 40), is every fellow-man (comp. 7 : 12, and see 19 : 18, 19, B., and 22 : 39, C.).—D. **And hate thine enemy.** The false teachers of the Jews regarded every one who did not belong to their community—any Gentile or heathen—as an enemy. No command like the one here mentioned is found in the O. T. The Jewish teachers wickedly combined with the former precept of God, respecting love, their own precept of hatred, and pretended to derive it from passages like Exod. 34:11-14; Deut. 7:1-5; 23:6; 25:17-19. In these, however, God directed His people to avoid all contact with the idolatrous nations around them, and to destroy every trace of idolatry; but His law did not refer to the individual, nor permit the Jews to *hate* a single human being.

⁴⁴ But I say unto you, Love your enemies, and pray for them that persecute you.

A. Love your enemies—not only do not entertain angry or revengeful feelings against those who are hostile to you and who injure you, but rather cultivate a spirit of forgiveness and kindness, and manifest a willingness to render them the same kind services to which you believe your friends to be entitled (comp. Eph. 4:31, 32). The feelings of the heart are here viewed as the springs of our actions.—**D. Pray for, etc.** The sense is: Let the unjust treatment which you receive only urge you to beseech God to forgive the offenders, to change their hearts and to give them a new and holy spirit (see Rom. 12:20, 21; 1 Cor. 4:12, 13; 1 Pet. 3:9. Illustrations in the O. T. are found in Gen. 50:15-21; 1 Sam. 26:23, 24—in the N. T. Luke 23:34; Acts 7:60). The Lord requires not only words and acts of kindness towards enemies, but also sincere good-will in the heart. Our whole deportment towards enemies is viewed in its influence on our own religious life before God. We are accordingly commanded to love our enemies, etc., for God's sake, *and for our own sake.*

⁴⁵ That ye may be sons of your Father which is in heaven: for he maketh his sun to rise on the evil and the good and sendeth rain on the just and the unjust.

A. That ye ... in heaven. There is here undoubtedly a reference to ver. 9; there the peacemakers are declared to be blessed, because they are the sons of God. Here the Lord further explains those words by declaring that none can be children of God, who do not resemble Him iu their disinterested, tender love towards all men (comp. ann. to 25 : 35, 36.)—**B. He maketh ... rain.** These gifts of God, the sun and rain, to which we are indebted for all the enjoyments of life, are impressive witnesses of the divine existence, power, bounty and universal love (Acts 14 : 17 ; Exod. 34 : 6); the goodness of God is intended to move men and lead them to repentance (Rom. 2 : 4; comp. 2 Pet. 3 : 9).—**C. Evil—good—just—unjust.** The last word, translated *unrighteous* in 1 Cor. 6 ; 9, designates those who show their contempt of God by an obstinate perseverance in unrighteouness (Rom. 1 : 18 ; 2 : 8 ; 2 Thess. 2 : 10 ; 2 Pet. 2 : 15). With this interpretation as a guide, the gradation in the terms here used may be thus determined. The people of God and the people of the world are viewed in two aspects: the *good* are those whose conduct before the world exhibits no gross violations of the divine law—but they are *just* only when they are controlled by strict religious principle, by a living faith (see. 1 : 19, B.); the *evil* (and unthankful, Luke 6 : 35) are those who have obviously never respected the laws of the Author of every blessing; they are really *unjust*, that is, unrighteous in the eyes of God, as they obstinately disobey the call to repentance and faith, and remain in a state of sin.

⁴⁶ For if ye love them that love you, what reward have ye ? do not even the publicans the same ?

A. In this verse and the following, the Lord sets forth the doctrine explicitly, that Christian love, in its genuine form, is not only disinterested in its operations, but that it also proceeds itself from a holy source—from that love to God, which is the fruit of faith (Gal. 5 : 6 ; 1 Thess. 1 : 3). The Lord contrasts Christian love with that love which policy, or which the usages of society require men to express in words, but which is altogether different in its origin and operations from the former.—B. **What reward have ye ?**—what reward will ye receive for it from God? Disinterested acts of love, as they proceed only from holy sentiments, reward the doer by the pleasure and increased blessedness which they impart ; the believer is made by grace a partaker of the divine nature (2 Pet. 1 : 14), which is eminently *love*, disinterested love (1 John 4 : 8, 19); for the blessed God takes pleasure in performing deeds of love in behalf of the unworthy (ver. 45 ; Rom. 5 : 8). The selfish, calculating love (friendly or polite acts) which is bestowed on them alone who can pay for it in kind, resides in a heart which is incapable of receiving and enjoying the " reward " of a consciousness of resembling the divine nature (comp. the witness of the Spirit, Rom. 8 : 16).—C. **The publicans.** The Lord strikingly illustrates the thought which He here expresses, by the remark that such a calculating love, which is so base in its character, is confessedly manifested by the vilest class of men ; the term *publican* was proverbially used to describe the character of unprincipled and ungodly men (Matt. 18 : 17). The word *sinners* in Luke 6 : 32 is an equivalent term.

⁴⁷ And if ye salute your brethren only, what do ye more *than others ?* do not even the Gentiles the same ?

A. **Salute**—express a friendly feeling, when you meet (comp. 10 : 12).—B. **Your brethren**—your kinsmen, or those whom you regard as associates and equals, and whom you distinguish from mere strangers or heathens **and** from enemies, by acts of courtesy and kindness in private life.—C. **What do ye, etc. ?** The sense is: There are only two kingdoms, that of light or of God, and that of darkness or of Satan; every individual belongs to the one or the other (Matt. 12 : 30 ; Eph. 2 : 11–13 ; 5 : 8–14 ; 1 Cor. 10 : 21 ; 2 Cor. 6 : 14–16). Now, if ye do not entertain a disinterested love towards others, derived from God, the source of all pure love, ye belong in reality to the class of the Gentiles, whom ye regard as enemies of God.

[48] Ye therefore shall be perfect, as your heavenly Father is perfect.

Ye therefore . . . perfect, etc. The explanation is readily found in 1 John, ch. 4, in which love is repeatedly set forth as the nature of God, who is perfect. Hence, love in its purest form, implanted in the soul by the Divine Spirit, constitutes the highest perfection to which the sanctified believer can attain in this life; absolute perfection or sinlessness is not here attainable, but the believer constantly follows after it (Phil 3 : 12–14).

CHAPTER VI.

¹ Take heed that ye do not your righteousness before men, to be seen of them: else ye have no reward with your Father which is in heaven.

A. The Lord had warned His hearers (5 : 20) against the dangerous doctrines of the Pharisees, who held that righteousness consisted in outward works. He then showed that such a superficial and false mode of interpreting the O. T. was a prolific source of error. He now considers a class of errors, consisting not so much in perversions of particular scriptural passages, as in false views of three moral duties; these, in their outward combination, were vainly supposed to constitute righteousness in its most advanced degree; they were :—alms-giving (ver. 2), prayer (ver. 5), and fasting (ver. 16). These three acts (representing respectively the three familiar classes of duties to our neighbor, to God, and to ourselves) are acceptable only when they are performed in an humble and devout spirit, as in the case of Cornelius (Acts 10 : 2, 4, 30, 31.)—**B. Take . . . righteousness.** Let not your righteousness (—the *doing* or performance of religious duties) be like that of the Pharisees, a mere hypocritical display before men; let it rather be the result of a living faith in your Heavenly Father.—**C. Before men . . . of them**—while your light should shine before men (5 : 16), let it not be your first object, in any works of righteousness, to gain the applause of men. Such a low and selfish feeling, which prompts to no benevolent acts unless there are spectators present, is inconsistent with sincere love to

God, to whom alone all praise and glory belong (Ps. 115 : 1).—D. **Else, etc., etc.**—if your good works proceed from vanity or any other corrupt feeling, your Heavenly Father will withhold every blessing from you (comp., Isai. 1 : 10–20).

² When therefore thou doest alms, sound not a trumpet before thee, as the hypocrites do in the synagogues and in the streets, that they may have glory of men. Verily I say unto you, They have received their reward.

A. **Therefore**—since, then, no outward works are acceptable in the eyes of God, that proceed from corrupt motives.—B. **Alms**—here representatives of all manner of benevolent acts.—C. **Do not sound . . . thee.** This is a proverbial expression like many others, e. g. *casting pearls before swine* (Matt. 7 : 6) ; it is derived from the form of public proclamations, as in 1 Sam. 13 : 3 ; Isai. 18 : 3, and is here applied to the ostentatious charity of the Pharisees, who eagerly sought to attract public attention to their good works.—D. **Hypocrites**—who feign to be that which they are not, like the spies mentioned in Luke 20 : 20 (comp. 22 : 18, C.). This Greek word was applied by the Greeks to a theatrical performer, whose appearance and language on the stage were only assumed. It was afterwards applied to dissemblers, and especially to those who profess religious principles and feelings which they do not possess. Hypocrites are frequently rebuked by the Lord (15 : 7; 16 : 3); a woe is pronounced repeatedly in ch. 23, and their eternal punishment is taught in 24 : 51.—E. **In the streets.** In the *synagogues*, alms were publicly collected before the usual prayers were offered— in the *streets*, they were afterwards distributed. In both cases the Pharisees gave with great pomp, with a view to have glory of men.—F. **Verily, etc.** A similar phrase occurs in Luke 6 : 24; the sense is: They desire only the praise of men (see John 12 : 43; Rom. 2 : 29), and this fleeting and valueless reward is all that they will ever obtain.

³ But when thou doest alms, let not thy left hand know what thy right hand doeth.

Let not . . . doeth. The Psalmist, by a beautiful figure of speech in Ps. 19 : 2, represents each day as transferring, at its close, to the next day, and each night to the next, the duty of praising the great Creator; that is: The praise of God shall never cease. Here, by a somewhat similar figure, employed for an opposite purpose, an interruption of the communication between the two hands is required. The sense is: Make no display of thy good works, and indulge as little in spiritual pride, as if thou didst not thyself know that thou hadst done them. The most zealous Christian is still an unprofitable servant (Luke 17 : 10). Such unconsciousness of personal merit is illustrated in 25 : 37.

⁴ That thine alms may be in secret: and thy Father which seeth in secret shall recompense thee.

A. **That . . . secret**=so that thy benevolent acts, being performed with a lowly mind, and not with a view to attract public attention, may be acceptable to God.—
B. **Thy Father . . . secret**=who knows every secret thing (see 2 Chron. 16 : 9; Ps. 139 : 1-16; Hebr. 4 : 13).—
C. **Recompense.** While the blessing of God attends the faithful Christian in this life, the highest reward will be bestowed in the world to come (Matt. 25 : 34-40; Luke 14 : 14).

⁵ And when ye pray, ye shall not be as the hypocrites: for they love to stand and pray in the synagogues and in the corners of the streets, that they may be seen of men. Verily I say unto you, They have received their reward.

A. When prayer had lost its life, and ceased to call all the emotions of the heart into exercise, the want of devout feeling was supplied, after the manner of the heathen (ver. 7), by outward forms and words, which availed nothing (James 5 : 16).—**B. They love . . . synagogues.** The hours of private prayer were three (Ps. 55 : 17 ; Dan. 6 : 10)—nine o'clock (the third hour, Acts 2 : 1, 15), noon (the sixth hour, Acts 10 : 9), and three o'clock (the ninth hour, Acts 3 : 1). The posture varied; the Jews prayed standing, which the Lord mentions in Mark 11 : 25 as usual and acceptable—sitting (2 Sam. 7 : 18 ; 1 Chron. 17 : 16)—kneeling (Luke 22 : 41 ; Acts 9 : 40; 20 : 36)—bowing the head (2 Chron. 29 : 30), or with the whole body prostrate.—**C. In the corners . . . men.** If the hour of prayer arrived before the Jew had reached the synagogue, he was expected to pause wherever he was, and to perform his devotions. The Pharisees could easily regulate their movements so as to be found in the street at the hour of prayer; by taking a position at a corner, they were seen by the largest number of spectators (23 : 5), and could thus gratify their spiritual pride.

⁶ But thou, when thou prayest, enter into thine inner chamber, and having shut thy door, pray to thy Father which is in secret; and thy Father which seeth in secret shall recompense thee.

A. But thou. The manner and spirit of Christian prayer is now described. The Lord indicates by the use of the word *thou* that He refers to private prayer, as distinguished from public worship.—**B. Enter . . . inner chamber.** A retired apartment which is not in daily use. To such a spot the Lord directs those who desire to commune with God in prayer (see below ver. 18, A.). Indeed, secret prayer may be acceptably offered in any place—on the deck of a vessel, in a public conveyance, in a crowded room—provided that the heart seeks after God and not after the praise of men. But the Lord implies that private devotions are best performed when no spectator is present to disturb the mind. His own practice is incidentally mentioned in Matt. 14:23; 26:36; Mark 1:35; 6:46, and elsewhere.—C. **Thy Father ... secret** —who is a spirit (John 4:24) and therefore invisible (Col. 1:15), but omniscient and omnipresent (Ps. 139:1-12).

⁷ And in praying, use not vain repetitions, as the Gentiles do: for they think that they shall be heard for their much speaking.

A. Vain repetitions. The original word refers either to the numerous but unmeaning sounds emitted at times by those who stammer, or to an idle and unmeaning use of words. Compare the unmeaning repetition of the same words for hours by the prophets of Baal, with the brief but believing prayer of Elijah (1 Kings 18:26, 37). For an acceptable repetition of "the same words," see 26 : 42-44.—B. **Much speaking**=multitude of words (Prov. 10:19). The abuse which is here condemned is the practice of making prayers as a mere mechanical act, the value and efficacy of which were supposed to depend on their number or length. But earnest, believing prayer, even when continued for hours, as in the case of the Lord (Luke 6:12; Hebr. 5:7), or the repetition of "the same words," when, as in the case of the Lord (Matt. 26:44), they proceed from the heart, is not forbidden; unceasing visits to the throne of grace (Luke 18:1-7; Acts 12:5; 1 Thess. 5:17) are acceptable to God and essential to the believer's security and peace.

⁸ Be not therefore like unto them: for your Father knoweth what things ye have need of, before ye ask him.

These words do not imply that believers pray to God for the purpose of informing (John 16:20) Him of their wants, which He understands even better than they do (Rom. 8:26); they pray for the purpose of acknowledging His wisdom, power and goodness, of confessing their own uuworthiness and helplessness, and of cultivating in the heart and manifesting before God a spirit of faith, humility and love, by which they become prepared to receive the gifts of His grace.

⁹ After this manner therefore pray ye: Our Father which art in heaven, Hallowed be thy name.

A. **After ... pray ye.** The Lord now exhibits a prayer which, in form, in matter, and in spirit, would be acceptable to God. According to Robinson's Harmony, it was pronounced by the Saviour between the second and third passover which occurred during His public ministry. It was, according to that Harmony, *after* the third passover, and not in Galilee but near Jerusalem, that the disciples solicited the Lord to "teach them how to pray, etc." (Luke 11 : 1-5). On that occasion He *repeated* the form of prayer which He had previously given in this Sermon on the Mount (see Prel. Obs. to ch. 5). This repetition of the prayer plainly shows that while it is, in general, designed, as a model, to exhibit the manner and spirit of prayer, it is also given as a form of prayer which the believer should not fail to repeat. The "Lord's Prayer" was recited regularly at the worship of believers at an early period. It is still repeated by the Church at public worship, as a perfect and complete prayer, comprehensively introducing every subject appropriate to that solemn act. The whole prayer consists of an introduction, seven petitions, and a doxology as the conclusion. The first three petitions, each of which refers more directly to the honor due to God, seem to point specially to the three Persons of the Holy Trinity: the *name* of the *Father*, who first chose us in Christ (Eph. 1 : 3-5); the *kingdom* of the *Son*, the Redeemer; the gracious operations of the *Spirit* who renews and sanctifies the inner man (Eph. 3 : 16; 1 Cor. 6 : 11) and thus subjects man's will to God's *will*. The remaining four petitions comprehend the whole history of man: his birth and nature as a creature of flesh and blood, needing *bread;* his fall and *sins;* the *temptations* which his life is to be spent in resisting; and his final departure from this *evil* world (Gal. 1 : 4).—B. **Our Father.** The O. T. occasionally applies the name of *Father* to God, chiefly in the sense of *Creator,* protector and benefactor (Deut. 32:6; Isai. 63 : 16; 64:8; Jer. 3:4, 19; Mal. 1:6; 2:10.) The name occurs in a higher sense in the N. T. There we learn that all men are, by nature, destitute of spiritual life (Eph. 2:1); the new life imparted to believers is like a new creation or a second birth (John 3:5; 2 Cor. 5: 17). This new creation is a work of divine grace through faith (John 1:12, 13). The believer is now accepted for Christ's sake, restored to communion with God (1 John 1 : 3, 6), and made a child of God, and is loved and treated by the Lord as a son (Eph. 1:5). Hence it is Christ who restores fallen men to that blessed state in which he can say: My Father! (1 John 3:1; Rom. 8:15). The Lord prefixes the word "Our," as the prayer is intended to be pronounced by the people of God in behalf of themselves and of all their brethren; it is, therefore, specially suited for public and for family worship.—C. **Which ... heaven.** The words raise the heart to the contemplation of the infinitely exalted and adorable God. He is at all times invisibly present in all places (1 Kings 8 : 27; Ps. 139 : 7–12; Acts 17 : 27, 28), but all His glory is not revealed (Exod. 33 : 18–23; 1 Tim. 6 : 16). In heaven, the abode of the blessed angels (Matt. 18 : 10; John 1 : 51), that divine glory is more fully revealed (Isai. 66 : 1; Acts 7 : 55, 56), and hence heaven is called God's holy habitation (Deut. 26 : 15; 1 Kings 8 : 39).—D. **Hallowed.** To *hallow* or *sanctify* (the former being an Anglo-Saxon word, the latter, Latin) is, first, to render anything holy which was unholy, that is, to set apart for God's especial service (Matt. 23 : 17) ; secondly, as in this verse, to regard and treat that which is holy as a holy object (Isai. 8 : 13), to honor and revere, to glorify (Numb. 20 : 12; Deut. 32 : 51).—E. **Name.** The *name of God* is an expression which, in cases like the present, and in many others (Exod. 23 : 21 ; Numb. 6 : 27 ; John 17 : 6 ; Acts 3 : 16 ; Rom. 9 : 17), reverentially designates God Himself (Isai. 29 : 23), the great and only object of all true adoration (Ps. 5 : 11 ; see 18 : 20, B.). Hence the whole petition is equivalent to the words : Be thou sanctified, revered and glorified *in* and *by* us—in our hearts (1 Pet. 3 : 15), language (Ps. 51 : 15), and outward life (1 Cor. 10 : 31).

[10] Thy kingdom come. Thy will be done, as in heaven, so on earth.

A. Thy . . . come. The prophet Daniel said in reference to the Messiah : " The God of heaven shall set up a kingdom, which shall never be destroyed " (Dan. 2 : 44). That kingdom " is not of this world " (John 18 : 36) ; it has not the character of an earthly kingdom, but is spiritual, according to Rom. 14 : 17. It comes wherever the Gospel is preached and received in faith, and a union with God is restored. It cannot be overthrown by all the powers of darkness (Matt. 16 : 18). We pray : " Thy kingdom come," whenever we pray that the Church of Christ may prosper and extend, or, that we ourselves may become the true children of God.—**B. Thy will . . . earth**—may Thy will be fulfilled, etc. Every creature of God, whether an angel or man is bound to be guided by the will of God alone (Matt. 12 : 50). The Lord Jesus submitted to the divine will (Hebr. 5 : 7, 8 ; Matt. 26 : 39, 42). Now God " worketh all things after the counsel of his own will " (Eph. 1 : 11), but " we pray in this petition that it may be done by us also " (LUTHER), namely, with an intelligent mind, and with a willing and believing heart (Hebr. 13: 20, 21), even as the angels in heaven, who rejoice in every victory of divine grace (Luke 15 : 7, 10), do all the commandments of God (Ps. 103 : 20, 21) gladly, promptly and continually.

¹¹ Give us this day our daily bread.

A. Give, etc. The first three petitions referred primarily to God and His glorification; the last three refer specially to the spiritual wants of man; between these two series the present petition is inserted. Thus our Lord permits us to introduce in our prayers our earthly wants and difficulties also (Phil. 4 : 6); this petition is, however, the only one which refers to them. It is immediately succeeded by others which refer to more urgent wants than those of the body (Matt. 6: 25 ; 16: 26). The words **this day** imply that the believer daily offers prayer to God.—**B. Our daily bread.** Bread, as the most prominent and important article of food, is often employed in the Scriptures for *food* in general, or the means of subsistence (Exod. 23:25 ; 1 Sam. 2 : 5 ; 2 Sam. 3 : 29; Nehem. 5 : 18). The possession, or the eating of bread, indicates, in the same manner, not only a festival or meal (Gen. 31 : 54; Jer. 41 : 5 ; Matt. 15 : 2), but also freedom from want, and, generally, from any earthly sorrow or distress (Lev. 26: 5 ; 1 Kings 21 : 4, 7; 2 Kings 25 : 29; Amos 7: 12). A similar usage appears in the New Test. The expression "*daily* bread" in this petition has been variously explained. It probably corresponds in sense to the phrase in James 2 : 16: "Things which are needful to the body," and to the words in Prov. 30: 8, which may be thus understood: Feed me with the bread of my allowance (margin)—feed me with the bread appointed for me (my *portion*, as the same Hebrew word is rendered in Gen. 47 : 22), so that I may neither suffer from want nor be corrupted by abundance. Hence the words *daily bread* imply all things that pertain to the wants of this present life (1 Tim. 6 : 17), such as food, raiment, etc. " God gives indeed without our prayer even to the wicked also their daily bread (5 : 45); but we pray in this petition that He would make us sensible of His benefits, and enable us to receive our daily bread with thanksgiving " (Eph. 5 : 20, Luther's Catechism).

¹² And forgive us our debts, as we also have forgiven our debtors.

A. And . . . debts. The act of injuring another is expressed in different languages by different images. Thus it is called in English a *trespass*, which word literally signifies *to pass across*, namely, over the boundary, into the property of another—to injure him. The Orientals call the same act a *debt;* they regard the offender as one who has, by his act, failed to render to another that which was due to him; he is therefore a debtor. Hence the word *debts* occurs in the present verse. The Greek language, again, represents the same act as an interruption of a regular or natural course of things, and applies a word signifying a *stumbling* or *falling at* or *by the side of*, that is *against* the party injured, translated *trespass*, ver. 14, 15 below, and in Matt. 18 : 35. Such offensive acts or violations of duty occur, whenever any divine law has been violated; all these are *sins* according to 1 John 3 : 4. As this is the *Christian's* prayer, it implies that the Christian too has many sins to confess.— B. As we . . . . debtors—even as we freely, without measuring the extent of the injury (18 : 21, 22), forgive those who have not rendered us that which was our due. This prayer, as taught by the Lord, is not offered by Him for Himself, for He was without sin (see 1 : 16, C.); it is given to believers and designed to be continually repeated by them, inasmuch as they continue to offend in many things (James 3 : 2 ; 1 John 1 : 8), and never become perfect in this world (Phil. 3 : 12). The petition does not imply that the forgiveness which we extend to others is a good work, whereby we purchase God's forgiveness of our sins, neither does it mean : forgive us *in as far as* we forgive others ; it rather expresses the unclouded faith of the believer in the divine pardon, and may be thus rendered : Inasmuch as Thy grace has been bestowed upon us in such a manner that we can and do now heartily forgive others, so we pray to Thee for our own forgiveness with a cheerful faith, being assured that we shall receive it for Christ's sake. God first shows mercy to the sinner—that sinner, being now endowed with spiritual life and strength (Col. 2 : 13), is enabled to forgive others (see Matt. 18 : 15 ; Eph. 4 : 32). The Christian's sins, which he involuntarily commits (for he cannot, as a Christian, sin deliberately and consciously (1 John 3 : 6; 5 : 18), require him daily to seek pardon anew.

¹³ And bring us not into temptation, but deliver us from the evil *one.*

A. And . . . temptation. (For the expression *to tempt,* see above, 4 : 1, D.) The temptation here mentioned, in as far as it is an impulse to do evil, does not proceed from God, but from man's own bad heart (James 1 : 13, 14); to such temptations, which Satan continually renews (Luke 22 : 31 ; 1 Cor. 7 : 5 ; 1 Pet. 5 : 8), men are continually exposed. Hence watchfulness and self-examination, combined with a diligent use of the means of grace, are continually necessary ; the words : " Watch and pray that, etc." (Matt. 26 : 41), refer to the Christian's experience during his whole earthly existence. From the words which the Lord addresses to Simon : " Satan hath desired, etc." (Luke 22 : 31, 32), we learn that He did not pray for Simon's entire exemption from such trials (which always beset us, Eph. 6 : 11, 12), but for the steadfastness of his faith during the contest. The sense of the petition may be thus stated: Preserve us, O Lord, from entering into temptation, for the flesh is weak (Matt. 26 : 41), and we cannot overcome by our own strength; but if thou permittest the temptation to come (1 Cor. 10 : 13), for the purpose of exercising our faith, then abandon us not; let Thy presence go with us (Exod. 33 : 14, 15), and grant us sufficient grace to bear the trial. This longing of the soul to be delivered from sin and its consequences is then briefly expressed in the words of this petition—suffer us not to fall (comp. 26 : 41).—**B. But ... the evil one** — Satan, or his power. The word *deliver* is applied in 1 Thess. 1 : 10 to the redeeming work of Christ. This seventh petition, accordingly, asks for more by far than the preceding; it expresses the longing of the soul for redemption (Rom. 8 : 23; 1 Cor. 15 : 54, 55). Comp. Luther's explanation in the Catechism.

[14,15] For if ye forgive men their trespasses, your heavenly Father will also forgive you: But if ye forgive not men their trespasses, neither will your Father forgive your trespasses.

A. When our Lord (Luke 11 : 2-13) repeated this prayer (see above, ver. 9, A.), He subjoins certain instructions relating to the duty and the benefit of earnestness and perseverance in prayer. On the present occasion He appends a general declaration referring to the condition on which the divine acceptance of prayer depends. In the spirit of His former words in 5 : 48, He shows that God will not hear the prayers of those who do not seek to resemble Him in His attribute of love—forgiving love. The lesson is frequently taught by Him that those alone who show mercy will find mercy (comp. the illustrative parable, 18 : 21-35). On one occasion (Mark 11 : 24-26) when the Lord describes faith as essential to success in prayer, He employs again language like that which is before us here, and teaches that none can pray acceptably, who are not governed by that spirit of brotherly love, which is the result of faith (Gal. 5 : 6).—**B.** The sense of these two verses, therefore, is: If ye forgive men from your hearts (18 : 35), that holy love which prompts you to do so, proceeds from a faith which leads to your justification (Rom. 5 : 9); your prayer will then be heard, as well when you pray for pardon, as for other mercies. The want of love, on the other hand, betrays a want of faith, which will render all your prayers unavailing.

[16] Moreover when ye fast, be not, as the hypocrites, of a sad countenance: for they disfigure their faces, that they may be seen of men to fast. Verily I say unto you, They have received their reward.

A. The Lord now adduces a third instance of the outward, mechanical religion of the Pharisees (see ver. 1, A.). The laws of Moses, which contain no directions respecting the fasts of individuals, viewed as special duties, prescribe only one public fast-day (26 : 31, D.), which was to be strictly observed every year; it was the solemn day of atonement (Exod. 30 : 10; Lev. 16 : 29-34; 23 : 27; Numb. 29 : 7). The phrase in these passages: "afflict your souls," is equivalent to: "fast strictly," as it may be shown from Ps. 35 : 13; Isai. 58 : 5 (margin of the English Bible). Other fast-days, both public and private, not divinely appointed, but voluntarily observed, were subsequently added, particularly after the return of the people from the Babylonian Captivity. In the course of time, when human devices and mere formal religious acts were substituted for the worship of God in the heart, fasting began to be regarded as one of the chief duties of religion, and was even pre-eminently supposed to constitute it (see below, 17 : 21, B.). The practice of fasting, combined with devout prayers, was observed by

the most sincere worshippers (Luke 2 : 37). But the Pharisees made a parade of their piety by voluntarily observing the second and fifth days of every week as fast-days (Luke 18 : 12 ; Matt. 9 : 14). As their fasting was only intended to gain the praise of men, and not to promote their own progress in the love and fear of God, they are here called *hypocrites*. Deep grief often causes men to forget or even loathe food; when fasting, as a religious exercise, is not connected with godly sorrow (2 Cor. 7 : 10), a sorrow created by a sense of sin, but is only an outward rite, it easily degenerates into a mere Pharisaic and self-righteous exercise. The Saviour's disciples were not trained to observe the ordinary Jewish fasts (Matt. 9 : 14).
—**B. Of a sad countenance.** The single Greek word, so translated, occurs also in Luke 24 : 17; the corresponding Hebrew term is translated *sad* in Gen. 40 : 6; but in Dan. 1 : 10 it is translated, in the comparative degree, faces *worse liking*=sadder=looking worse. The term designates the gravity and even wanness and gloom which grief of heart spreads over the countenance. Here it was mere affectation or pretence, "that they may appear unto men to fast" (comp. Isai. 58 : 5). Such fasting strikingly resembles the trade or *business* of the hired mourner at an oriental funeral (9 : 23, B.); it scarcely deceives men; it cannot deceive God.—**C. Disfigure their faces.** The original word *disfigure*, is translated, according to the connection, *consume* (Matt. 6 : 19), *perish* (Acts 13 : 41), *vanish away* (James 4 : 14). It here signifies that the Pharisees, who practised various mourning rites (11 : 21, D.) when they fasted, scattered earth or ashes on their heads (2 Sam. 1 : 2; Isai. 61 : 3; Lament. 2 : 10; Jonah 3 : 6; Matt. 11 ; 21), or at least refrained from removing the filth from their faces and beards, thus presenting an unsightly and squalid appear.

ance; possibly, like mourners (2 Sam. 15 : 30; 19 : 4; Esth. 6 : 12), they covered their heads; thus they either gave an unnatural appearance to their faces or concealed them entirely.—D. **They . . . reward** (see ver. 2, G.).

¹⁷ But thou, when thou fastest, anoint thy head, and wash thy face;

Anoint, etc. The Lord supplies entirely different motives from those of the Pharisees, for fasting, and restricts its purposes to the intercourse of the soul with God. The anointing and washing here mentioned indicate, in conformity to Jewish customs, the special preparations of one who is cheerful, who proposes to attend a joyful festival (Amos 6 : 6; Luke 7 : 46), or who has passed through and completed a period of mourning (2 Sam. 12 : 20; 14 : 2; Dan. 10 : 3; see 26 : 7, C.). The sense is: Seem to be, what thou really art, but never make a display of those holy emotions which thy communion with God awakened in thy soul. When thou dost worship God with a believing heart, let thy inward peace and comfort relieve themselves naturally in thy countenance, thy words and thy acts. The worship of God is not a gloomy, but a cheerful and blessed service.

¹⁸ That thou be not seen of men to fast, but of thy Father which is in secret: and thy Father which seeth in secret shall recompense thee.

A. That thou . . . fast—let thy Father know the feelings of thy heart, and do not display them before men. The communion of the soul with God is the most holy exercise in which it can engage. It is not intended to attract public attention, nor to flatter human pride, but to strengthen the soul in faith and deepen the intensity of its love to God. This unrestrained communion of the soul with God is too sacred to be revealed to the inquisitive eyes of spectators. The Lord clearly refers to the private or closet devotions of the believer, as distinguished from the public worship, in which it is also his duty to engage.—**And thy Father ... thee.** The sense is: Let thy faith and holy love be revealed by the light which they shed around thee (1 Cor. 6 : 20), in thy holy walk and conversation, which thy Heavenly Father, as a reward of thy faith, grants thee grace to maintain consistently and *openly* before men. The reward is not bestowed in view of the fasting, which, as a "bodily exercise, profiteth little" (1 Tim. 4 : 8), but in view of the holy sentiments of the heart.

[19] Lay not up for yourselves treasures upon the earth, where moth and rust doth consume, and where thieves break through and steal:

A. The Lord now proceeds to furnish general instructions to His hearers on the duty and manner of cultivating those devout sentiments, without which all outward worship is unacceptable to God and unprofitable to man.—**B. Treasures.** This word properly designates in the Scriptures a large quantity or collection (see 31 : 52, D.), not so much of the precious metals, as rather of other objects, e.g. wheat, oil, honey (Jer. 41 : 8), snow, hail, wind (Job. 38 : 22; Jer. 10 : 13), also, clothing (Job 27 : 16; James 5 : 2); it is hence equivalent to the terms: stores, stock or supply. Thus, too, figuratively, the predominating sentiments and feelings of the heart constitute a good or an evil treasure, acccording to their character (Matt. 12 : 35). With a similar reference to *abundance* or fulness, we read that in Christ "are hid all the treasures of wisdom and knowledge" (Col. 2 : 3). In view of the *value* of such treasures or stores, any object which is valued or loved is a treasure (Exod. 19 : 5 ; 2 Cor. 4 : 7). Now all earthly treasures, such as costly apparel, deposits of grain, and gold and silver, are liable to be destroyed.

[20] But lay up for yourselves treasures in heaven, where neither moth nor rust doth consume, and where thieves do not break through nor steal:

A. Treasures in heaven—collect those treasures of which heaven is the appropriate place of deposit. The Lord points out the "true riches" (Luke 16: 11) as the only abiding source of comfort and happiness—*in heaven*—with God, as in Luke 20 : 4. Various passages, e. g. James 2 : 5 ; 1 Peter 1 : 4 ; 2 Cor. 8 : 9, in which similar images occur, conclusively show that the incorruptible heavenly treasure, in its most comprehensive sense, is the love of God towards us in Christ Jesus, in whom He has made us accepted (Eph. 1 : 6) ; from that love all true happiness in this world and in the world to come, proceeds, such as, our adoption, spiritual joy and peace, and final salvation. *That* divine love is unchanging and eternal ; " no creature shall be able to separate " us from it (Rom. 8 : 39).—**B.** Such is the treasure which the believer is here commanded to lay up ; it is secured to him ("laid up") when he receives Christ in faith, and follows Him even unto death.—**C.** As the Lord, on one occasion, when the disciples misunderstood His remark respecting the possession of riches, explained that He referred, not to the mere possession, but to the *trusting* in riches (Mark 10 : 23, 24), so here (as it appears plainly from 1 Tim. 6 : 17), the Lord does not forbid the reasonable accumulation of property for lawful purposes (such as are mentioned in Prov. 3 : 9; 2 Cor. 12 : 14); but He forbids us to make the laying up of earthly treasures the chief purpose of our lives. The reasons are given in 1 John 2 : 15, 17, and here in ver. 21 ; the true path of duty is described in ver. 33 below ; see also ver. 24, D.

²¹ For where thy treasure is, there will thy heart be also.

A. Heart—a collective name for all that is in man, his views, feelings, tendencies, inclinations, etc. (see Prov. 4 : 23, and above, 5 : 8, A.). **B.** The sense of the verse, which is repeated, Luke 12 : 34 (see Prel. Obs. to ch. 5), is: If earthly advantages are the chief objects of your desire, and constitute the treasure which you seek, you cannot seek God with all the heart (ver. 24; 1 John 2: 15). Your thoughts and feelings (your heart) will be so absorbed by these objects, that you will fail to "work out your own salvation with fear and trembling" (Phil. 2:12).

^{22, 23} The lamp of the body is the eye: if therefore thine eye be single, thy whole body shall be full of light.—But if thine eye be evil, thy whole body shall be full of darkness. If therefore the light that is in thee be darkness, how great is the darkness!

A. When the eye itself is guided by a light (—lamp), it is enabled to control the movements of the body; in a spiritual sense, the mind of man, when guided by the light of divine truth, directs him in the way of life and peace—the body is full of light. The neglect of that light leads to death. Hence these two verses contain the following solemn admonition, founded on the words in ver. 21: Inasmuch as earthly treasures perish, and only heavenly treasures abide forever (see 1 John 2:17), if your soul (judgment, feelings, conscience, will) be guided by the light of revealed truth, then your whole condition in time and in eternity will be happy and blessed. But if your soul be misguided or led astray, then the light of truth shines in vain for you; for, like one who obstinately closes his eyes and will not be guided by the light of the sun, you close every avenue by which divine truth could reach you.—B. **Eye . . single . . evil.** The eye is often introduced as an image of an internal light ("the light that is in thee"). It is either *single* or *evil*. Its singleness or simplicity consists in its natural and healthy action, when it truthfully conveys correct impressions; it is *evil*—deceitful, a bad, diseased eye (as the unbelieving heart is evil, Hebr. 3:12), when it furnishes clouded, distorted and false views and impressions; for a special case, see 20 : 15, B. Now, even as the eye of the soul receives divine light, or else refuses to be guided by it, so will the whole condition ("thy whole body") of the individual be prosperous or wretched. In the latter case, no possibility of salvation exists, when the Gospel, the only appointed means of salvation, is denied and rejected, and mere earthly objects, the applause of men, riches, etc., alone are valued. How great, how dangerous is the darkness, how great will be the misery of the impenitent and unbelieving! (Rom. 2 : 5–9; comp. Luke 13 : 34, 35).

²⁴ No man can serve two masters: for either he will hate the one, and love the other; or else he will hold to one, and despise the other. Ye cannot serve God and mammon.

A. The Lord now unveils a dangerous opinion which often lies hidden in the human soul; the heart cannot be divided between the world and God, who alone is entitled to our devotion and love (1 John 2 : 15; James 4 : 4; 2 Cor. 6 : 14–16; Gal. 1 : 10).—B. **No man . . . masters** —no man can serve two masters whose whole nature and course of action are opposed to each other; he cannot at the same time be guided by worldly-mindedness and by the love of God.—C. **For either . . . the other.** The man will, when the two masters are in direct opposition, *prefer* in his heart the one to the other (as the words *love* and *hate* are sometimes used, John 12 : 25; Rom. 9 : 13; Malachi 1 : 2, 3); when the choice must be actually made, he will not fail to betray in his conduct his real sentiments by *holding to*—sustaining, vigorously assisting or *supporting* the one (as the same word is rendered in 1 Thess. 5 : 14), and *despising*—slighting, disregarding the other (as the word *despise* means in Rom. 2 : 4; Hebr. 12 : 2; 2 Pet. 2 : 10).—D. **Mammon**—*riches*. The same word occurs in Luke 16 : 9, 11, and is rendered *riches* in the margin. Even if this Chaldaic, or rather Syriac, word is

not, as some have, without sufficient historic evidence, supposed, the name of a Syrian god or idol, still "covetousness is idolatry" (Col. 3 : 5). The Lord uses this word in place of the terms: *money, riches*, etc., because He does not intend to condemn the possession and proper use of the latter, but rather the sin of making it our idol or God. The sense is: Ye cannot give your hearts to the service of the true God, and, at the same time, regard earthly advantages as the sovereign good. A clear distinction between the mere possession of riches, and a predominating thirst for them, is thus made (see above, ver. 20, C.). The divine rule is given in Ps. 62: 10. "If riches increase, set not your heart upon them." "It is not a sin to possess property and a family; but thou art forbidden to convert thy possessions into thy masters; thou must remain *their* master, and cause them to serve thee."
—LUTHER.

[25] Therefore I say unto you, Be not anxious for your life, what ye shall eat, or what ye shall drink : nor yet for your body, what ye shall put on. Is not the life more than the food, and the body than the raiment?

A. Therefore—lit. *on this account;* because the service of the world, and confidence in earthly objects can only betray and conduct to ruin.—**B. Be not anxious.** The parallel passage, Luke 12 : 29, contains another term descriptive of *a mind excited*, uneasy, tossed about by various fears. The same word, equivalent to "cares of this life" (Luke 21 : 34), and the same lesson occurs in Phil. 4 : 6. The apostle explains the Saviour's words as distinguishing, on the one hand, between anxiety and care without faith in God, as if He cared not for us (1 Pet. 5 : 7), and, on the other hand, calm submission in faith of all our affairs to God.—**C. Is not . . . raiment?**—anxiety respecting your subsistence, arising from want of confidence in God, is as unwise as it is offensive to Him. If

God has hitherto been able to sustain your very life (which is *more*—of more importance than the food of a day), and to preserve your body itself from decay, is His power not sufficient to furnish the inferior gifts of food for the support of the former, and of clothing for the latter?

⁲⁶ Behold the birds of the heaven, that they sow not, neither do they reap, nor gather into barns; and your heavenly Father feedeth them. Are not ye of much more value than they?

A. Four reasons are furnished by the Lord for repressing in ourselves all needless anxiety respecting our temporal interests. The first is expressed in the words immediately preceding this verse. Here the second reason is given, derived from the beautiful provision which God makes for inferior creatures; they cannot, like man, by sowing and reaping, provide even to that extent, for their wants. Are ye not much better than they? How much more tenderly will God care for you! (Matt. 10 : 29, 31.)—**B. Feedeth.** The divine care of inferior creatures, extending from the largest quadruped to the smallest insect, teaches man to value them, and avoid all wantonness or cruelty in dealing with them (Deut. 22 : 1–7 ; 25 : 4 ; Prov. 12 : 10).—**C. More value than they**—ye, who have immortal souls; ye, to save whom the Son of God is come.

²⁷ And which of you by being anxious can add one cubit unto his stature?

A. The third reason is derived from the fact that such anxiety is, nevertheless, utterly unavailing, and as fruitless as the attempt would be to *add one cubit*, etc. —**B. Cubit . . . stature.** The cubit (John 21 : 8) was a linear measure equal to the length of the arm from the elbow to the extremity of the middle finger. It varied somewhat (from 17½ to 22 inches) among different nations, but it is usually defined to be equal to 18 inches. But the word translated *stature* also means *length of life* ("of age" in John 9 : 21, 23), and, indeed, measures of length are figuratively applied to the life-time (Ps. 39 : 5, "my days as a handbreadth"). Hence the sense here may be—no anxious efforts of our own can add hours or even moments to our life, or prolong it beyond the divinely appointed limit. This interpretation is confirmed by the well-known more frequent desire of men to add to their *lifetime*, than to their *stature*.

[28,29] And why are ye anxious concerning raiment? Consider the lilies of the field, how they grow; they toil not, neither do they spin :—Yet I say unto you, That even Solomon in all his glory was not arrayed like one of these.

A. The third reason (ver. 27, A.) is here further illustrated, thus: All the skill of man is exerted in vain to equal the splendor, beauty and delicacy revealed in common objects belonging to inanimate nature.—B. **Lilies.** They grow spontaneously in the field in great abundance in Palestine, and are occasionally mentioned in the O. T. (1 Kings 7 : 25; Song of Sol. 2 : 1, 2, 16; Hos. 14 : 5). These flowers have not the ability to toil or spin for the purpose of adorning themselves: nevertheless, they have their daily nourishment furnished to them, and are, besides, distinguished for their beautiful colors, delicate forms, and rich fragrance.—C. **Solomon . . these.** The proverbial glory of king Solomon, whose magnificence exceeded that of all other monarchs, was manifested in the rich apparel, gold, silver, and ivory appearing on his person and throne. Still, these did not really constitute a part of himself, as the delicate colors of the lilies and their delicate forms essentially belonged to them.

[30] But if God doth so clothe the grass of the field, which to-day is, and to-

morrow is cast into the oven, *shall he* not much more *clothe* you, O ye of little faith?

A. Grass of the field—herbage and wild flowers.—**so clothe**—so richly. All the works of God are invested with beauty to the eye of faith; that beauty impressively proclaims the tenderness of divine love.—**B. Oven.** When an east or south wind prevails only two days in the east, vegetation suffers extremely; the grass withers under its influence. The scarcity of wood compelled the people to employ withered grass, stalks and shrubs as fuel for heating the ovens which they used in baking bread.—**C. Shall he not, etc.**=if God takes pleasure in bestowing beauty on a mere flower, He will not fail to supply those with the necessaries of life, who occupy a far higher grade in creation, inasmuch as they have rational and immortal souls, which are capable of exercising faith. The expression, *O ye of little faith* (found also in 8:26; 14:31; 16:8=*distrustful*), reminds them of the capacity given to them, and not to birds and flowers, to exercise faith, and gently rebukes them for not anxiously seeking a higher degree of spiritual life.

[31] Be not therefore anxious, saying, What shall we eat? or, What shall we drink? or, Wherewithal shall we be clothed?

[32] For after all these things do the Gentiles seek: for your heavenly Father knoweth that ye have need of all these things.

A. For ... seek. This clause should be connected with the foregoing verse, as it at once points out the true character of such questions.—**Gentiles**=the other *nations* of the world, as the word is translated in Luke 12:30. All these were heathen nations, and such is the meaning of the word *Gentiles* as here used (see 4:15, 16, A.). The sense is: Do not ye imitate blind heathens, who do not know the true God, who have no joyful trust or faith, and who therefore anxiously seek for these things, as if they were themselves the sole guardians of their temporal interests.—B. **For your ... things.** The fourth reason (see ver. 26, A.) for dismissing anxious cares is here derived from the fact that the omniscient God already knows the wants of His children, and that His mercy and power will not fail to supply these.—C. Such admonitions are not intended to teach that we should lead a life of carelessness and idleness, and expect a miraculous supply of our wants. Errors of this kind are already exposed in Prov. 6 : 9–11 ; 24 : 30–34, and condemned in 1 Thess. 4 : 11 ; 2 Thess. 3 : 10. The Lord designs to warn against the tendency to accumulate property as the great object of life.

[33] But seek ye first his kingdom, and his righteousness; and all these things shall be added unto you.

A. **Seek ye**—let your desires and efforts be directed towards higher objects. The Christian's duty in this respect is described in Phil. 3 : 13–15.—B. **First**—as the soul is more precious than the body (Matt. 16 : 26), let the great object of all your anxious cares and seeking be your own salvation (Phil. 2 : 12); let it be your *first* great care. " There are many ways devised by men for *seeking* the kingdom of God, but there is only one way of *finding* it, namely, to believe in Christ and study the Gospel diligently with watching and prayer, so that its divine truth may take deep root in the heart, and bear fruit in the life."—LUTHER.—C. **The kingdom of God**—the kingdom mentioned in 5 : 3, 10, 19, 20, and frequently. It is here a general term for the Messiah's kingdom and its blessings which reward the true worship and service of God (John 4 : 23, 24). At the same time, the fundamental idea of the term is also referred to, that is, a cheerful recognition of God as the Lord and Father of all, and an

intimate communion of spirit with Him (Rom. 14: 17).
—D. His (=God's) righteousness—that righteousness
which is of faith (see Rom. 9: 30–32), which alone avails
before God (comp. Rom. 1: 17; 3: 21, 22), and to which
the Lord had already referred in 5: 20, as distinguished
from the righteousness which the Jews had vainly devised.
—E. And all . . . you—you shall not suffer real harm
even in your temporal affairs, by seeking after God with
all the heart (Mark 10: 28–30; 1 Tim. 4: 8). He is the
shield and exceeding great reward of all His believing
people (Gen. 15: 1), and He will supply their daily wants
(Ps. 145: 15). The sense is best explained in Rom. 8: 32;
if God's love bestows the most precious gift, namely, His
only-begotten Son, *that* love will also bestow things of
inferior value.

³⁴ Be not therefore anxious for the morrow: for the morrow will be anxious for itself. Sufficient unto the day is the evil thereof.

A. Be not . . . morrow. These words contain a prohibition of anxiety occasioned by a want of confidence in God; they do not render it unlawful to gather the products of the field for future use and consumption, or to provide for other ordinary and constantly recurring events. Indeed, the company of the disciples possessed a purse or treasury for the wants of the next day (John 12: 6).— Morrow—next day, as the same word is translated in Acts 4: 3, here equivalent to the *future* time in this world. —B. The morrow . . . itself. As a day, by a beautiful figure of speech, is personified in Ps. 19: 2 (see ver. 3 above), and represented as speaking to the next day, illustrative of the uninterrupted glorification of the Creator, so here Christ describes the next day as occupied with cares respecting itself, doubtless meaning that the same Lord who provides for the present day will be able to provide again when the next day shall arrive.—C.

Sufficient etc.—thy present evils (evil things, Luke 16: 25), sickness, want, care, sins, in short, all the sorrows and evils originating in Adam's fall (Rom. 5:12), and which oppress thee *now* (to-day), are sufficient to occupy thy attention; thy searching after deliverance and grace, so that thou mayest inherit eternal life, if properly conducted, will leave no time for dwelling on possible evils of a future time, which may never be experienced.—Comp. Hebr. 3:7, 13, and Eccl. 9:10. "Seek ye the Lord while, etc. (Isai. 55:6).

CHAPTER VII.

1, ² Judge not, that ye be not judged.—For with what judgment ye judge, ye shall be judged: and with what measure ye mete, it shall be measured unto you.

A. "The Lord had, in the preceding chapter, described the good works which are acceptable to God, revealed the spirit of genuine prayer, and warned against covetousness, etc. He now proceeds to utter a solemn warning against another vice of man—the tendency to rely on his own wisdom, and to judge and censure others."—LUTHER. The text does not allude to official trials, judgments or sentences either in the Church (Matt. 18 : 15–17 ; 1 Cor. 5 : 12, 13 ; 6 : 5) or in the State (Rom. 13 : 3, 4); nor to cases in which the well-known facts themselves pronounced a sentence on others before the tribunal of our own understanding and conscience, as in ver. 16, 20 (see also John 7 : 24 ; 1 Cor. 2 : 15). But it forbids hasty judgments (1 Cor. 13 : 7), uncharitable and self-righteous or arrogant and censorious reflections on others, concerning whose moral and religious character, or whose motives we have neither the authority nor the ability to pass sentence, even in the silence of our own hearts (see Rom. 14 : 4 ; James 4 : 12). That the act of thus judging others in our own minds, even independently of any expression of our opinion in words, is forbidden, appears from 5 : 22.—**B. For with . . . judged** —by the Supreme Judge of all men (5 : 7 ; 6 : 15).—**C. And with . . . again**—the patient love, or the severity of your judgment of others, being an evidence of your true spiritual state, will thus decide hereafter on your admission into heaven or exclusion from it (see Luke 6 : 36–38).

³ *And why beholdest thou the mote that is in thy brother's eye, but considerest not the beam that is in thine own eye?*

A. Mote—any particle of straw, wood, etc., a splinter here representing a defect or fault.—**B. Beam**—a rafter, a heavy piece of timber supporting the roof. "It is an image of a sin that is immeasurably greater than one represented by a mote."—LUTHER.—**C. Thine own eye.** The eye represents the moral and religious character and conduct. The sense is : Thou hast faults of thine own ; thou hast a better opportunity to read thine own heart and judge of its iniquity than thou hast to ascertain the state of thy neighbor's heart. Thy own faults should therefore appear to thee far more heinous than those of thy neighbor. His motives, which thou canst not know, may be in reality less censurable than thine own. (Comp. 23 : 24, B., " thy brother "—thy equal in knowledge, etc.)

⁴ *Or how wilt thou say to thy brother, Let me cast out the mote out of thine eye ; and lo, the beam is in thine own eye?*

How wilt—how canst thou presume to say, etc. (Luke 6 : 42). The sense is : Thou dost contract guilt already by thy neglect of strict self-examination, and by an unwarranted condemnation of another; thy iniquity is still greater when thou dost hypocritically assume the character of a well-meaning friend and adviser, while thy heart is filled with self-righteousness and pride ; these vices exclude all knowledge of thyself, and all sincere regard for the welfare of thy brother (see Rom. 2 : 21–23, " Can the blind lead the blind ? " Luke 6 : 39).

⁵ *Thou hypocrite, first cast out the beam out of thine own eye; and then shalt thou see clearly to cast out the mote out of thy brother's eye.*

Thou hypocrite—who pretendest to be wiser and better than another, study the divine law, and ascertain first thy own sinful state. Then only, when the light of truth guides thee, and when thou hast, as an humble believer, found joy and peace (Rom. 15 : 13), mayest thou, with the wisdom which faith imparts, "see clearly" how to teach transgressors (Ps. 51 : 12, 13) and to strengthen thy brethren (Luke 22 : 32 ; see Rom. 2 : 17–24).

⁶ *Give not that which is holy unto the dogs, neither cast your pearls before the swine, lest haply they trample them under their feet, and turn and rend you.*

A. Proverbs have always been much employed by the oriental nations. Many are found in the O. T.; they are often introduced in the N. T. also (e. g. Matt. 9 : 12; 10 : 16 ; 12 : 34 ; 13 : 57 ; 23 : 24 ; John 4 : 37 ; Acts 9 : 5 ; 1 Cor. 5 : 6 ; 15 : 33). Our Lord frequently quoted proverbs, and then illustrated their true application, without intending the terms to be strictly understood and applied in their whole extent. Thus, in Matt. 24 : 43, 44, His second coming is compared to the sudden approach of a *thief;* the *thief's visit* was a proverbial phrase, simply descriptive of that which is unexpected (see 1 Thess. 5 : 2 ; 2 Pet. 3 : 10, and below, 18 : 3, C.). So a carcass may furnish a proverb (Matt. 24 : 28). In the same way, dogs and swine provided the Jews with various proverbs; an instance occurs in 2 Peter 2 : 22; another occurs in the present text. The common usage led our Lord to employ these familiar images here; it was His object to be readily understood by His hearers. They at once gathered from His words the sense : Do not waste or destroy that which is valuable by an unnatural or unworthy application of it, for such a course would resemble that which your proverb forbids : "Give not, etc."—**B. Dogs.** The dog was not only regarded by the

Jews as an unclean animal (Isai. 66 : 3), but also served as an image of all that was contemptible (1 Sam. 17 : 43 ; Isai. 56 : 11), and base or malicious (Ps. 22 : 16 ; Phil. 3 : 2 ; Rev. 22 : 15).—**C. Swine.** The laws of Moses declared the swine (Lev. 11 : 7; Deut. 14 : 8) to be unclean. The proverbially filthy habits of the animal (2 Pet. 2 : 22) led the Jews to regard it as an image of all that is unclean, vile and disgusting.—**D. Holy**—connected with God and His service, or proceeding from the holy God. The proverb doubtless originated in a saying like this : Do not profane that which is holy—do not throw to dogs the holy flesh of animals (Hag. 2 : 12) which had been offered as a sacrifice to God (see Lev. 22 : 14, and comp. Exod. 22 : 31).—**E. Pearls**—substances, usually white and round, and of a peculiar lustre, found in certain bivalves ; the most valuable are obtained from the pearl-oyster of Ceylon. Large pearls, intended as ornaments (for which in antiquity almost incredible sums were readily paid), have always been held in very high estimation on account of their beauty, and hence their commercial value has been proportionately great (Matt. 13 : 45, 46). The pearls are here images of the precious truths taught by divine wisdom.—**F.** The sense of the whole verse appears to correspond to that in Prov. 9 : 7–9, and 23 : 9, and is illustrated in Matt. 10 : 13, C. The dogs and swine doubtless designate the same class of persons, that is, sinners, despisers of divine truth, as described below (10 : 13–6). The Lord cannot here mean that believers should ever hesitate to proclaim the Gospel, since He Himself preached its truths to all men indiscriminately, and commanded His apostles to adopt the same practice (Mark 16 : 15 ; Matt. 10 : 27; 2 Tim. 4 : 2). To the believing and penitent soul, the truths of the Gospel are even more precious than pearls ; but to him who despises and scornfully rejects them, they are as little adapted as pearls are to satisfy the hunger of dogs or swine. "We preach and we exhort every man who will receive the truth; but he who tramples upon us, who despises and rends us, may follow his own will (Rev. 22 : 11, 15). We withdraw from him, shaking off the dust of our feet (Matt. 10 : 14). From such scoffers we take back our pearls, although very unwillingly; we would gladly unite with them, but they were not of us (1 John 2 : 19). We give our pearls to others, who can understand their value."—LUTHER.

⁷ Ask, and it shall be given you; seek, and ye shall find; knock, and it shall be opened unto you:

A. The Lord resumes the subject of prayer (6: 5–13); He designs to offer additional encouragement to the believer to engage and persevere in that holy exercise. —**B. Ask—seek—knock.** "We have here both a command and a promise respecting prayer."—LUTHER. The gradation in these terms, which are all descriptive of the act of prayer, as well as in the promises respectively corresponding to them (*given*, *find*, *opened*), is remarkable. The believer *asks* of God in prayer; the answer may seem to be withheld, as in 15 : 23. Then the believer, like the woman of Canaan, conscious that God will not close His ears to prayer, *seeks*, that is, with still deeper feeling (Deut. 4 : 29), like one who has not yet found, but perseveres in seeking; he continues the exercise (comp. Ps. 27 : 4). If the answer is still delayed, he redoubles his earnest efforts (he cries the more, 20 : 31), and the earnestness of his prayer, demonstrating his faith or his firm conviction that God will hear, at length prevails (James 5 : 16)—like continual *knocking* on the door by a visitor who will not be denied (Acts 12 : 16) by the inmates of the house (Luke 11 : 5–9). Hence, when men merely " say their prayers," without *feeling* them, such lip-devotion is not genuine prayer (15 : 8). The same lesson of perseverance in prayer is given in Luke 18 : 1–7, and illustrated in the case of the woman of Canaan, referred to above, whom no apparent refusal could repel, because her faith was great. "The Lord does not here multiply words in vain; He knows that we are often timid in prayer, fearful of approaching the great God, conscious of our many wants, but still restrained by a sense of our utter unworthiness. And therefore He says: *Ask, seek, knock*, in order that He may the more powerfully encourage us to persevere in prayer. Oh! how blessed is the man who has faith in these words, who daily and hourly calls on God in prayer, and constantly receives new gifts from the grace of God. Alas! how cold and torpid is our faith in the divine promise that prayer shall always be heard. O Lord! increase our faith."—LUTHER.—C. The words before us are, according to 1 John 3 : 22, addressed to true believers, and are to be understood with certain limitations, like similar promises in Ps. 50 : 15; Zech. 13 : 9; Matt. 21 : 22. Such success in prayer, as the whole tenor of the words in 18 : 19, 20; John 14 : 13, also shows, is found only when the prayer is offered in a child-like spirit (ver. 11 ; Rom. 8 : 15), and in faith (Matt. 21 : 22; Mark 11 : 24; James 1 : 6), and when it considers in all things the glory of God (James 4 : 3).

* For every one that asketh receiveth ; and he that seeketh findeth ; and to him that knocketh it shall be opened.

For, etc. The Lord very graciously extends in this verse the foregoing promise to *every one* ("whosoever will," Rev. 22 : 17), for the purpose of removing all doubt and fear from the praying soul. The word *for* reminds the believer of the sure foundation of his faith—the presence and power, the truth and mercy of God, as revealed in the whole history of His dealings with His believing people.

⁹,¹⁰ Or what man is there of you, who, if his son shall ask him for a loaf, will give him a stone?—Or if he shall ask for a fish, will give him a serpent?

What man, etc. Consider the power of love even in a mere human being. Parental love will not refuse a needful gift, much less, in cruel mockery, place a stone before a hungry child, or alarm and endanger him by offering a serpent (see 3:7, B.). Can you think, when your souls seek after peace in God, that He who is so abundant in goodness (Exod. 34:6) will refuse you His comfort, and send you only new and still more painful doubts and fears? The Lord selects familiar objects, bread and fish, the ordinary articles of food of the old and the young in Galilee (John 6:9; 21:13).

¹¹ If ye then, being evil, know how to give good gifts unto your children, how much more shall your Father which is in heaven give good things to them that ask him.

If then an earthly parent, whose heart is by nature corrupt and evil, is nevertheless prompted to bestow " good (—appropriate, useful) gifts " on his child, how much more readily will your heavenly Father, who is infinitely holy, kind, wise and mighty (Ps. 103), bestow on His believing children, when they pray, the richest gifts of His love (" good things "—pre-eminently and absolutely *good*), even His Holy Spirit! (Luke 11:13. Comp. Luke 18:6, 7.)

¹² All things therefore whatsoever ye would that men should do unto you, even so do ye also unto them: for this is the law and the prophets.

A. Therefore. The Lord here concludes one portion of His sermon with a general admonition. The sense is: Accordingly, as you may infer from an earthly parent's love the greatness of your heavenly Father's love, so too, with respect to your duties to your fellow-men, you may infer from your own personal feelings (Luke 12 : 57), when yourh appiness depends on others, the extent of their claims on your forbearance, sympathy and active aid.—B. **All things whatsoever, etc.** This precept, in its Christian sense, differs widely in its whole spirit from ancient Jewish and heathen maxims that somewhat resemble it, inasmuch as it directs our attention to the spiritual wants of our nature, which did not occur to Jewish and heathen teachers. It teaches us to consult the highest interests of others by aiding them in seeking the salvation of their souls, for we surely desire eternal happiness for ourselves.—C. **For this ... prophets—** this precept embodies the whole spirit of the laws found in Moses and the prophets respecting the duties which men owe to their fellow-men. The Pharisaic mode of interpreting the O. T. allowed that sect to practise oppression, to pursue selfish ends, etc. (23 : 13, 14, 23 ; Luke 20 : 47). The sense, as determined by passages like Matt. 22 : 40 ; Rom. 13 : 8–10 ; Gal. 5 : 14, is : Love to your neighbor, a genuine love, will prompt you to fulfil towards him all the duties which God has prescribed in the writings of Moses and the prophets.

^{13,14} Enter ye in by the narrow gate : for wide is the gate, and broad is the way, that leadeth to destruction, and marry be they that enter in thereby. For narrow is the gate, and straitened the way, that leadeth unto life, and few there be that find it.

Enter—gate, etc. Life is frequently compared to a journey or pilgrimage (Gen. 47 : 9 ; Ps. 39 : 12 ; Hebr. 11 : 13 ; 1 Pet. 2 : 11); the road (=the course of conduct) which man, the traveller, follows, leads him either to *destruction* (ver. 13) or to life (ver. 14). The life into which men enter is the kingdom of heaven, as Matt. 18, ver. 3, comp. with ver. 8 and 9, demonstrates ; the destruction (perdition, Phil. 1 : 28 ; Hebr. 10 : 39 ; 2 Pet. 3 : 7) is the eternal loss of the soul in hell (Matt. 5 : 29; 10 : 28 ; 16 : 26 ; 2 Thess. 1 : 9). Both gates are *at the end* of the journey, road or way of life on earth, as it appears from Luke 13 : 24, 25, and the sense is : Enter on the straitened way that conducts to the narrow gate. —With these solemn words the Lord applies the truths taught in the foregoing discourse, and thus addresses us: Be on your guard and seek divine guidance, lest you be betrayed by your corrupt nature, and choose a course of life which will conduct to your ruin. The way of worldly ease, impenitence and sin is broad and open ; the gate at its end is wide enough to admit into the place of punishment all the multitudes which approach it. Beware of following a multitude to do evil (Exod. 23 : 2), or of being influenced by your spiritual sloth to yield to sin and temptation. Many (continues the Lord) thoughtlessly wander onward, *because* (ver. 14) the straitness (= narrowness) of the opposite gate, and the contracted space afforded by the opposite way (that is, the self-denial and deadness to sin, or crucifying of the flesh, Gal. 5 : 24, required by religion), are not agreeable to man's corrupt nature. Few find the narrow way—succeed in overcoming the impediments presented by their corrupt nature. They live after the flesh, and therefore perish (Rom. 6 : 21 ; 8 : 6, 13 ; Col. 3 : 5, 6). Seek ye, therefore, the kingdom of God by faith in Me and My atoning work (John 10 : 9 ; 14 : 6); mortify the deeds of the body (Rom. 8 : 13); seek a renewal in the spirit of your mind, and put on the new man (Eph. 4 : 23, 24), and ye shall find life eternal.

[15] **Beware of false prophets, which come to you in sheep's clothing, but inwardly are ravening wolves.**

A. The Lord had, in the foregoing verses, exhibited

the danger which threatens the soul *from within* (Mark 7:21, 22), when men carelessly yield to the promptings of their corrupt nature. Here He warns against another danger which is *from without*, proceeding from the seductive influences exerted by false guides (comp. Luke 20:46).—B. **False prophets.** This term is here used for teachers of false doctrines (see 24:11). Such enemies sowed tares among the wheat (13:25); repeated complaints and warnings respecting them occur in the N. T. (Acts 13:6, 10; 20:28–30; Gal. 5:12; Col. 2:8; Tit. 1:10). Some attempted to put a yoke upon the disciples by teaching that their salvation depended on the observance of the ceremonies of the Law (Acts 15:1, 2, 10); others taught that the resurrection is past already (2 Tim. 2:18), substituted specious fables for divine truth (2 Tim. 4:3, 4), and even denied the Lord that bought them, whose doctrines are called "damnable heresies" (2 Peter 2:1), "doctrines of devils" (1 Tim. 4:1). These teachers are called "false prophets" (1 John 4:1; Matt. 24:11).—C. **Sheep's clothing.** The lamb or *sheep* has always been regarded as an image of innocence or harmlessness, and the *wolf* as one of violence, ferocity, injustice and evil in every form (see Matt. 10:16; John 10:12). The sheep's *clothing* describes the plausibility, apparent honesty and piety of deceitful teachers. Hence we find the following description of their language: "perverse things" (Acts 20:30); "vain words" (Eph. 5:6); "enticing words" (Col. 2:4); "feigned words" (2 Peter 2:3); "good words and fair speeches" (Rom. 16:18); "a show of wisdom" (Col. 2:23). Such deceivers (Tit. 1:10; 2 John 7) are, however, inwardly (in their real character) *ravening* (=ravenous) *wolves*, grievous (ruinous) wolves (Acts 20:29). Their presence and influence bring destruction on those who follow them

(2 Thess. 2 : 10–12 ; 2 Peter 2 : 1). Hence believers, who are now forewarned by the Saviour (24 : 25), are commanded to "try the spirits whether they are of God" (1 John 4 : 1). "Do you ask: How shall I try them, and detect the wolf? I answer: Let every man acquire a clear and sure knowledge of Gospel doctrine, namely, that God has given unto us His Son, and will forgive and save us through Him alone (1 Tim. 1 : 15); and then let him be fully persuaded in his own mind (Rom. 14 : 5 ; Eph. 4 : 14), having his heart established with grace (Hebr. 13 : 9), insomuch that he will abide by the doctrine and 'hold fast the form of sound words' (2 Tim. 1 : 13 ; Tit. 1 : 9), although all that dwell on earth should teach a different doctrine (Gal. 1 : 8). At the same time, false doctrines can be detected and exposed only by him who is spiritual, for the truth must be spiritually discerned. (1 Cor 2 : 14, 15)."—LUTHER.

¹⁶ By their fruits ye shall know them. Do *men* gather grapes of thorns, or figs of thistles?

A. Fruits. These constitute the signs by which false teachers may be detected. They are of two kinds: first, according to the Lord's own declaration in 16 : 12, the *doctrines* which they teach; when these contradict the Gospel doctrine, the teacher is a false prophet (1 John 4 : 1–3 ; Luke 6 : 45); secondly, their *practice*, their walk and conduct; when they are controlled by carnal affections (works of the flesh, Gal. 5 : 19–21), they are false prophets (Tit. 1 : 16 ; 2 Tim. 3 : 5 ; Jude 4).—**B. Grapes . . . thistles.** The *vine*, which furnishes grapes, and the *fig-tree* are both highly esteemed for their rich and wholesome fruit (Numb. 20 : 5 ; Deut. 8 : 8), and are often introduced in Scripture as images of excellence, high value, etc. (Ps. 90 : 8–11 ; Jude, 9 : 10). *Thorns* and *thistles* are, on the contrary, images of that which is worthless, evil or desolate (2 Sam. 23:6, 7; Isai. 32:13; Ezek. 2:6; Micah 7:4), since God originally cursed the ground, saying: "Thorns and thistles shall it bring forth to thee" (Gal. 3:18).—The sense is: Pure doctrines and salutary lessons will not be set forth by a corrupt man consistently and earnestly.

[17] Even so every good tree bringeth forth good fruit; but a corrupt tree bringeth forth evil fruit.

Good tree ... evil fruit. The two trees represent respectively the faithful and the false teacher. When a teacher's doctrines, on the one hand, agree with the revealed Word, and obviously tend to the glory of God and the welfare of man, and when his consistent conduct, on the other, exhibits the power of divine truth, he is a trustworthy teacher. The opposite case is that of the false teacher (1 John 4:1-3). The original word, here translated *corrupt*, designates that which is decayed, foul, worthless, etc., as in Matt. 13:48 "bad"—worthless (Eph. 4:29), "corrupt"—filthy, foolish (comp. Eph. 5.4); the tree is not one that is rotten, but one that always was of a *bad* kind.

[18] A good tree cannot bring forth evil fruit, neither can a corrupt tree bring forth good fruit.

This verse contains the divine declaration, very distinctly expressed, that holy purposes in the heart, on the one hand, and unholy purposes, on the other, viewed as sources, cannot possibly produce respectively results of a character opposite to themselves (comp. 12:33, 34; 1 John 5:18). Christ and Belial can never have the same aims (2 Cor. 6:15).

[19] Every tree that bringeth not forth good fruit is hewn down, and cast into the fire.

A. The end of the false teacher is here revealed in figurative language; it is described in other terms in 2

Thess. 2 : 8 ; Hebr. 10 : 27 ; 2 Peter 2 : 1, 3, 9.—**B. Hewn . . . fire** (see 3 : 10, B.).

⁸⁰ Therefore by their fruits ye shall know them.

The Lord, in conclusion, renews His warnings, and implies that none who suffer themselves to be led astray can hope for indulgence hereafter, since they have ample opportunities to detect and shun false teachers, whose doctrine and walk are inconsistent with the written word (Rom. 16 : 17 ; comp. Deut. 32 : 32, 33, and John 13 : 35).

⁸¹ Not every one that saith unto me, Lord, Lord, shall enter into the kingdom of heaven ; but he that doeth the will of my Father which is in heaven.

A. The Lord now proceeds to consider the case of those who, without being teachers, are unfruitful branches (John 15 : 2)=who profess to follow Him, but continue to serve sin.—**B. Saith . . . Lord.** The evil course which is here rebuked consists in the mere adoption of the form of sound words (that *saith* Lord), by those who refuse to open their hearts to the influence of the divine truth which they outwardly profess (comp. 15 : 7, 8). The repetition of the word *Lord* refers to ostentatious professions of religion which are unaccompanied by a living faith, and a corresponding spirit of obedience (comp. Luke 6 : 46).—**C. Shall . . . heaven**—inherit the eternal kingdom of glory (25 : 34).—**D. He that doeth, etc.** The distinction between empty professions of religion and a life of obedience is frequently noticed in the Scriptures, for instance (Matt. 15 : 7, 8 ; Rom. 2 : 13 ; James 1 : 22 ; 1 John 3 : 18). Here profession and practice are contrasted ; when the former stands alone, it not only possesses no value, but is in truth the result either of hypocrisy or self-deception, so that the Christian name, without a living faith, cannot conduct to salvation (comp. Tit. 1 : 16). The phrase, *to do the will of God*, which often occurs (Matt.

12 : 50), is of deep import. The will of God, as revealed in the Scriptures, refers, on the one hand, not simply to the outward walk, but also to the sanctification of the heart; hence none do the will of God who do not cultivate holy affections in the soul (John 7 : 17).

²² Many will say to me in that day, Lord, Lord, did we not prophesy by thy name? and by thy name cast out devils? and by thy name do many mighty works?

A. In ver. 15-19 the Lord had declared the doom of false teachers; in ver. 21 He added that those also should be excluded from heaven whose confession of faith was apparently sound, but who did not demonstrate the power of faith by a life of obedience; here He teaches further, that even those who have seemingly led a moral life, and performed many good works outwardly, shall nevertheless perish, if a living faith had not been the source of their good works. "Without faith it is impossible to please him" (Hebr. 11 : 6; comp. Rom. 14 : 23). So, also, all those who had been made "partakers of the Holy Ghost," but had fallen away (Hebr. 6 : 4, 6), who had sinned wilfully after they had received the knowledge of the truth (Hebr. 10 : 26), and who, after escaping the pollutions of the world, had again been entangled therein (2 Pet. 2 : 20), will perish with those who had pleasure in unrighteousness (2 Thess. 2 : 12).—B. **Many**—large numbers. The word is used where there is no intention to state the number precisely, as in 8 : 11.—C. **In that day**—the day of judgment (Matt. 24 : 36, B.; 25 : 31-46, and comp. Luke 10 : 12 with Matt. 11 : 24), when Christ will judge all men (Acts 17 : 31; 2 Thess. 1 : 7-10), and when all secret things will be made manifest (Rom. 2 : 16; 1 Cor. 3 : 13; 4 : 5).—D. **Prophesied.** To prophesy, strictly speaking, is *to foretell future events*, as in Acts 11 : 27, 28. But the Hebrew and Greek words generally include the idea of declarations, exhortations and warnings uttered by inspired men, in reference to the past, the present or the future, while they are immediately controlled by the divine influence. The gift of prophecy was granted in different degrees and to individuals of various classes (comp. the cases of Balaam, Numb., ch. 22, and of Saul, 1 Sam. 19 : 23). The possession of the gift did not change the nature of the prophet, or exempt him from his personal religious duties. If the apostle Paul had not diligently watched over his spiritual state, he might, even after having preached to others, have been himself a castaway (1 Cor. 9 : 27).—E. **In thy name**—by thy authority and power, in which we professed that we had faith. The individual mentioned in Mark 9 : 38, 39, believed in Christ, and by his faith wrought miracles (see Matt. 17 : 20) ; the sons of Sceva, mentioned in Acts 19 : 13-16, did not sincerely believe, and therefore failed. " The devils believe " (James 2 : 19). All these truths the understanding of the impenitent sinner may fully admit ; but *saving faith* consists in an humble and grateful *acceptance* of the pardon which God has offered through Christ.—F. **Cast out devils**—from demoniacs=persons possessed with unclean spirits, as in 4 : 24.—G. **Wonderful works**—*miracles*. As the Lord does not imply that the statements of those who here speak respecting their prophesying and miracles are untrue, and as the speakers are nevertheless disowned by Him in the next verse, we may view them in the following light. There were many persons who could not resist the evidence of the divine origin of the Gospel, when it was proclaimed by Christ and His apostles, and who accordingly believed, and were admitted as members of the Church. Thus Simon the sorcerer believed and was baptized (Acts 8 : 12, 13) ; nevertheless Peter afterwards declared that his heart was not right in the sight of God=it was unchanged (ver. 21-23).

Ananias and Sapphira, mentioned in Acts, ch. 5, were not only Christians by profession, but could also have said with truth : Lord, did we not sell land, and lay certain proceeds at the apostles' feet ? (Acts 4 : 37 ; 5 : 8). Yet they dared to lie unto God. Members of the congregation in Corinth, possessing the gifts of prophecy, healings, etc. (1 Cor. 12 : 28), are severely rebuked by the apostle for their unchristian conduct (1 Cor. 11 : 17–22). Judas, the traitor, received the gift of working miracles (Matt. 10 : 4, 8). Even at a much earlier period, Balaam, " who loved the wages of unrighteousness " (2 Pet. 2 : 15), possessed the gift of prophecy in an eminent degree (Numb., ch. 24). Caiaphas, who thirsted for the blood of Christ, also prophesied as high-priest of the Jews (John 11 : 49). It thus appears that the miraculous powers granted to the early Christians were exercised by members of the Church in some cases, who were, nevertheless, not truly renewed and sanctified in heart. Precisely so, in our day, the fulfilment of external duties, like praying, teaching, giving, etc., by no means furnishes decisive evidence that the heart is renewed.—The fatal defects of such persons are here revealed—a want of love, and a want of humility. Such defects betray ultimately the want of saving faith, in which these holy sentiments originate. The language in the text indicates not only the want of genuine love, the sign of a true disciple (John 13 : 35), but also the presence of Pharisaic self-righteousness ; they speak of *their* showy works, but can give no praise to the Lord, who had endowed them with His gifts in this life, in order to secure their hearts for His service.

²³ And then will I profess unto them, I never knew you : depart from me ye that work iniquity.

A. **Will I profess**—I, who am the Judge of all men, will openly declare a sentence corresponding to their false professions.—**B. I never knew you.** When the believer is said to know the Lord (John 10 : 14 ; 17 : 3), the sense is that he fears and loves Him with an intelligent faith. When God perceives such holy sentiments in his soul, He recognizes him as the work of His own grace, and pronounces that work—that new creation (2 Cor. 5 : 17)—to be "very good" (Gen. 1 : 31). On the other hand, the impenitent, who have not put on the new man (Eph. 4 : 24), and do not bear the image of Christ in their souls (Col. 3 : 10), are, in reality, strangers to God (Eph. 2 : 12)—He does not know them as His children in Christ. When we now compare the language in 2 Tim. 2 : 19: "The Lord knoweth them that are his," with the text, the sense of the latter appears to be: I did not see in you an abiding faith that produced love and humility in your souls; hence I never numbered you among the heirs of eternal life. "Wherefore let him that thinketh he standeth take heed lest he fall" (1 Cor. 10 : 12. See below, 25 : 12).—**C. Depart.** The unalterable sentence of the Judge consigns the impenitent to the regions of endless woe and despair (see Matt. 25 : 41). These words teach that the unrighteous who have no real fellowship with Christ on earth (2 Cor. 6 : 14–16), and claim it only in pretence (1 John 1 : 6), will never be partakers with the redeemed of His glory in heaven (Rom. 8 : 17; 1 Pet. 4 : 13; 5 : 1, 4).—**D. Work iniquity.** They are not accused of special vices or crimes; man is by nature a child of wrath (Eph. 2 : 3), and is "condemned already" (John 3 : 18), because of the corruption of his nature; the wrath of God abides on him already (John 3 : 36), and he is saved from that wrath only by a living faith in the crucified Redeemer (John 3 : 16; Rom. 5 : 9). The rich man, in the parable (Luke 16 : 19–31), is declared to have found an eternal abode in hell (ver. 26), not on account of his wealth, nor on account of unusual vices or crimes; none of these are mentioned; he is lost because he never became a new creature. He was unfeeling and selfish (ver. 21), a lover of pleasure (ver. 19, 25) more than a lover of God (2 Tim. 3 : 4; now "whosoever will be a friend of the world is the enemy of God" (James 4 : 4).— The word here translated *iniquity* is always so rendered in the English N. T., except in 1 John 3 : 4, where it is rendered "lawlessness." The latter is strictly the meaning of the word; in that passage the term is applied to sin in every form. *Workers of iniquity* are therefore all who do evil in thought, word or deed.

"Every one therefore which heareth these words of mine, and doeth them, shall be likened unto a wise man, which built his house upon the rock:

A. **Therefore**—as the result of all the foregoing lessons, and specially of those taught in ver. 21 and elsewhere, respecting the importance of seeking, preserving and exemplifying in the conduct a living faith. He alone "heareth these sayings and doeth them," who possesses such a faith; for it purifies the heart (Acts 15 : 9); it justifies (Gal. 2 : 16); it worketh by love (Gal. 5 : 6); it teaches us to pray acceptably (Matt. 21 : 22); it inspires a cheerful confidence in God's protecting care (Matt. 8 : 26), and it overcomes the world (1 John 5 : 4) and the power of death (1 Cor. 15 : 55).—B. **A wise man**—a true believer (comp. 25 : 2); "the fear of the Lord" (true godliness, Ps. 34 : 18–22), "that is wisdom" (Job. 28 : 28). True wisdom consists in the choice of the best ends, and the employment of the most appropriate means to obtain them. The Saviour's words in Mark 16: 16 indicate the best end and the best way to reach it: "He that believeth, etc."—D. **Which ... rock.** God is called a *Rock*, a sure dependence of His people (Deut.

32 : 15, 18; Ps. 18 : 22; Isai. 17 : 10). Jesus Christ is called a *corner-stone* (Isai. 28 : 16; Rom. 9 : 33; 1 Peter 2 : 6), and the only foundation (1 Cor. 3 : 11); His redeeming work is the only foundation on which our comfort and hope in this life and our salvation in heaven can be properly established.

²⁵ And the rain descended, and the floods came, and the winds blew, and beat upon that house; and it fell not: for it was founded upon a rock.

A. Under the image of a tempest with all its attendant circumstances, copious discharges of water, high winds, etc., the Lord exhibits the trials to which faith is exposed. As the descending *rains* assail the roof, the *floods* attempt to undermine the foundation, and the *winds* beat against the walls, so the whole moral nature of man is exposed to the wiles of the devil. On this account the apostle says: "Put on the *whole armour* of God," which he proceeds to describe in Eph. 6 : 11–18; "above all," says he, "taking the shield of faith." When the understanding is perplexed by doubts, the heart allured by the world, the conscience in danger of being lulled asleep, and when, finally, in the struggle with the last enemy, which is death (1 Cor. 15 : 26), the believer's heart and flesh might fail, then God is the strength of his heart (Ps. 73 : 26), the rock of his refuge (Ps. 94 : 22; comp. Hebr. 6 : 18–20). B. It fell not . . . rock. The apostle Paul obtained mercy, that in him first Jesus Christ might show forth all long-suffering, for a pattern to them which should hereafter believe on Him, Jesus Christ, to life everlasting (1 Tim. 1 : 16). In his weakness, the Lord's strength was made perfect (2 Cor. 12 : 9), so that he could do all things through Christ who strengthened him (Phil. 4 : 13). Now when he speaks of the many trials which befall the Christian, he refers to his own joyful experience of the preserving grace of God, which, like an immovable rock, sustained him; and he gratefully says: "In all these things we are more than conquerors through him that loved us" (Rom. 8 : 37). The atonement of Christ is a rock on which the believer builds all his hopes of salvation—human works and merit are a foundation of sand.

²⁶ And every one that heareth these words of mine, and doeth them not, shall be likened unto a foolish man, which built his house upon the sand :

A. A foolish man. The foolish man, that is, the unenlightened, impenitent man, may apparently make provision for his future safety, like those mentioned in ver. 21, 22, or like the Pharisees and hypocrites described in ch. 5 and ch. 6, who practised external religious duties. An outwardly moral life is all the preparation which many believe to be essential to salvation. (For "foolish," see 25 : 2.)—**B. Sand**—a foundation without solidity, incapable of sustaining a pressure. Outward good works, as described in ch. 5 and ch. 6, which proceed from a desire for the praise of men, and not from a living faith, afford no solid foundation of the hope of eternal life. "Other foundation, etc." (1 Cor. 3 : 11).

²⁷ And the rain descended, and the floods came, and the winds blew, and smote upon that house; and it fell: and great was the fall of it.

When religious principle—love to God, faith in the atoning work of Christ—has not taken entire possession of the soul, and when, consequently, a spirit of watchfulness and prayer is not maintained, the heart easily yields to temptation, and a fall may at any time occur. When the hour of death arrives, the false hopes which had lulled the soul asleep must pass away with the breath of the body; the soul, unsupported by the righteousness of a Saviour who had been practically rejected, perishes forever (Matt. 24 : 42–51).

²⁸ And it came to pass, when Jesus ended these words, the multitude were astonished at his teaching :

A. The effect of the whole discourse in ch. 5–7 is described.—**B. Astonished.** The people were deeply moved by the divine words.—**C. His teaching**—the matter and the manner of His preaching (Mark 4 : 2), its unusual mode of presenting the truth, its new topics, and, above all, the power with which it reached the conscience and the heart (see 16 : 12, B.).

²⁹ For he taught them as *one* having authority, and not as their scribes.

A. Authority. The people deeply felt the weight and divine power of His words. So, too, the officers who were directed on a certain occasion to apprehend the Saviour, returned to their employers without Him, excusing their failure to obey by alleging the overwhelming power of His words: " Never man spake like this man " (John 7 : 32, 45, 46; comp. Mark 1 : 22, 27).—**B. As their scribes**—not such a lifeless mode of teaching as theirs was, not such puerile lessons, which neither instructed the mind nor influenced the heart, not as the scribes of that day, who merely repeated the sayings of their predecessors, but as a lawgiver who spoke in His own right (e. g. 5 : 18 : " *I* say unto you ").

CHAPTER VIII.

¹ And when he was come down from the mountain, great multitudes followed him.

A. Matthew had exhibited the Lord's knowledge and wisdom in the preceding chapters; he now proceeds in a series of narratives, of which miracles form the subject, to set forth the Lord's divine power and goodness. The statements are arranged rather according to the nature of the subjects than the order of time, and hence the events differ somewhat in their order from that which is adopted by Mark and Luke.—**B. The mountain** (see 5 : 1, C.).—After descending from the mountain, the Lord performed the miracle which is here recorded.—**C. Great multitudes, etc.**—eager to learn more from one who had so deeply impressed them (7 : 28). They appear to have been dismissed by Him (as on other occasions, 14 : 22, 23), before the leper approached (see ann. to ver. 4, A.).

² And behold, there came to him a leper and worshipped him, saying, Lord, if thou wilt, thou canst make me clean.

A. Worshipped (see 2 : 2, D.).—**B. Lord**—an honorary title of address, translated *Sir*, when applied to a man (Matt. 13 : 27; 21 : 30; John 12 : 21). It is frequently used in the N. T. in reference to God, in addressing Christ, etc.; it is then translated *Lord*.—**C. If thou wilt**—if thou dost decide to do it (comp. James 4 : 15). This prayer ("beseeching," Mark) has many excellences. It is short, avoiding "vain repetitions" (6 : 7); it is sincere, proceeding from the heart; it is humble, for the leper is conscious that he has no claim nor right to any divine gift; it prevails, since it is made in fath. " The leper does not say: Lord, I have prayed, I have fasted, I have given tithes (Luke 18 : 12), as if he had thereby acquired any merit, but he is conducted to Christ by his deep conviction of his uncleanness and unworthiness, and he relies on divine mercy alone."—LUTHER.—D. **Clean**—Thou canst deliver me from my legal uncleanness, by restoring me to health. Besides the bodily evils which the leprosy occasioned, this hideous disease also created a legal or ceremonial uncleanness (Lev., ch. 4), which excluded the sufferer from all intercourse with society. Now if the Saviour should make him *clean* or restore him to society, this blessing would imply that he had already been restored to health.

³ And he stretched forth his hand, and touched him, saying, I will; be thou made clean. And straightway his leprosy was cleansed.

A. **Jesus . . . touched him.** The Jew who touched anything declared by the Law to be unclean, as a dead body, a leper, etc., became ceremonially unclean himself, until the prescribed means of purification had been applied (Lev. 5 : 3; ch. 13–15; ch. 22: Numb., ch. 19). But the "Holy One and the Just" (Acts 3 : 14), who here touched a leper, could not Himself be defiled (Hebr. 7 : 26). Besides, at the moment when He touched the man, the latter was healed and virtually cleansed. So the act of touching the dead, whom the prophets were empowered to restore to life, did not defile the latter (1 Kings 17 : 21; 2 Kings 4 : 34).—B. **I will**—I am willing, I have so determined. The Lord Jesus, being moved with compassion (Mark), and seeing the lowly spirit and the faith of the leper, immediately granted his petition.— C. **Be thou clean.** The word of the Saviour is almighty. Men employ human means when they desire to produce an effect, and, nevertheless, are not always successful. But Christ "spake, and it was done" (Ps. 33 : 9).—**D. Straightway.** It is one of the peculiar features of a miracle, that the object in view is at once attained, while in the ordinary operations of nature certain extended periods of time are usually employed.

⁴ And Jesus saith unto him, See thou tell no man ; but go thy way, shew thyself to the priest, and offer the gift that Moses commanded, for a testimony unto them.

A. See thou . . . man. These words indicate that the multitudes mentioned in ver. 1 are no longer present.— " See "—see thou to it that, etc. The command : *tell no man*, was given on other occasions (Matt. 9 : 30 ; 12 : 16 ; Mark 3 : 12 ; 5 : 43). In some of these cases, it may have been the Saviour's desire to avoid a certain notoriety, which, as in this instance (Mark 1 : 45), afterwards attracted those who merely from an idle curiosity desired to see signs and wonders (12 : 38, 39 ; 16 : 4 ; John 5 : 14), and who interrupted Him in His great work of preaching the Gospel (Luke 4 : 43 ; Mark 1 : 38). At other times, He desired to prevent an undue excitement of a political character, which was inconsistent with the nature of His kingdom (Matt. 16 : 20, B. ; John 6 : 14, 15 ; 18 : 36). But He had, no doubt, often a direct reference to the spiritual welfare of the persons for whom He wrought a miracle ; retirement from society and silence would enable them to discern His divine character clearly, while the distraction of mind connected with the recital of all the details to inquisitive listeners might tend to efface the good impressions which they had received. Such was probably His motive in Luke 8 : 56, and, possibly, in the present case also ; the leper is directed not to pause on his journey from Galilee to Jerusalem, where his gift should be offered. When such considerations did not require silence, the

Lord even directed that the miracle should be proclaimed (Mark 5 : 19).—**B. Shew . . . priest.** He could not be restored to society until all the ceremonies prescribed in Lev., ch. 14, had been duly performed. "The authority to pronounce a sentence in the case of a leper belonged to the priest; the Saviour directed the leper to respect the office of the priest, in order to show by his example that even when we perform works of charity, we must always respect the rights and interests of all others."—LUTHER. **C. Offer the gift.** This gift or offering consisted of two lambs, or, in the case of a poor person, of one lamb only, and two turtle doves (Lev. 14 : 10, 21, 22). Moses received the law from God; the Saviour desired, accordingly, that it should be observed in all its parts until He who was "the end of the law" (Rom. 10 : 4) should have fulfilled it (Matt. 5 : 17, 18). Afterwards the laws of Moses respecting the ceremonies of religion, etc., were abolished (Acts, ch. 15 : Gal., ch. 4 ; ch. 5 ; Col., ch. 2).— **D. For a testimony unto them**—the priest and those who were associated with him, or the people generally. A similar phrase occurs in 10 : 18 ; 24 : 14. The sense probably is the following : The priest who should inspect the case of this man could not fail to ascertain the manner in which the latter had been healed, and could thus obtain a twofold testimony from him, first, respecting the Saviour's power, which exceeded that of man (see John 5 : 36), and, secondly, respecting His conformity to the divine law. The latter circumstance refuted the charge often made against Christ, that He did not keep the law (for instance, John 9 : 16), while the former was an evidence that He *was* "of God" (John 3 : 2 ; 9: 32, 33). Thus the whole occurrence was a "testimony," or source of information and faith to the priest and to all others.

⁵ And when Jesus was entered into Capernaum, there came unto him a centurion, beseeching him.

A. **Capernaum** (see 4 : 13, B.).—B. **A centurion.** The military officer in a Roman army, who commanded a company of infantry, forming one of the smaller divisions of an entire legion (see 26 : 53, C.), and orginally consisting of 100 men, was styled a *Centurion* (from *centum*, the Latin word for one hundred). Of the several Roman centurions mentioned in the N. T. (Acts 21 : 32 ; 22 : 26 ; 27 : 1, etc.), two others, besides the one here introduced, deserve special notice (Matt. 27 : 54 ; Acts 10 : 1). The centurion here mentioned was originally a heathen (ver. 10), but appears from Luke 7 : 3-5 to have become acquainted with the revealed religion of the O. T., like Cornelius (Acts 10 : 2), and to have worshipped the true God. "God had sent him to Capernaum, where he obtained from the Jews a knowledge of the Ten Commandments, and, generally, of the truth taught by Moses and the Prophets."—LUTHER.—C. **There came, etc.** The particulars are stated more fully in Luke, from whose narrative it appears that the centurion, in his deep humility, did not personally apply to the Lord, but requested his Jewish friends to intercede for him (Luke 7 : 6, 7). As their well-known dislike to associate with heathens (Acts 10 : 28) does not appear in this case, and his love of their nation (Luke) is, on the contrary, mentioned to his praise, it is possible that this centurion had already been received as a member of their community; in this case his liberal act of building a synagogue for them (Luke) may be the more readily explained. He built it for the honor of that God whom he had found and desired to adore publicly. Matthew, who intends to describe the miracle simply, without detailing all the circumstances, omits those which are connected with these Jewish friends. The miracle described in John 4 : 46–54, in the case of a nobleman's son, was wrought on another occasion.

⁶ And saying, Lord, my servant lieth in the house sick of the palsy, grievously tormented.

My servant, etc. The Romans are said to have been usually severe masters, and to have felt but little sympathy for their servants or slaves in the personal afflictions of the latter. This centurion shows a very different spirit; he is warmly attached to his servant ("who was dear unto him," Luke 7 : 2), as if the latter were a relative; and he beautifully illustrates the principle that sincere love disregards the external distinctions of rank which the world has established, independently of the personal character of individuals. The same principle of the Christian faith was afterwards forcibly presented by Paul in Gal. 3 : 28; Col. 3 : 11. "A devout master will teach his servants also to fear the Lord."—LUTHER. (Comp. Acts 10 : 2.—For **palsy**, see 4 : 24, E.).

⁷ And he saith unto him, I will come and heal him.

A. Jesus saith—through messengers, as afterwards John, when in prison, *said* to Him : Art thou, etc., through the medium of others (11 : 2, 3; comp. also Luke 14 : 18).—**B. I will come, etc.** Why does the Saviour so readily grant the prayer of this man, when He seems to refuse His aid to the woman of Canaan (15 : 24), and even forbids the twelve disciples, on one occasion (10 : 5), to preach to the Gentiles? In these two latter cases He referred to the fact that "salvation is of the Jews" (John 4 : 22), namely, that the Messiah was to come forth from the Jewish nation—in other words, that the first covenant had been made with the Jews, and that, according to the counsel of God, the second or new covenant in

Christ was also to be offered to them ("to the Jews first," Rom. 1:16; 2:9, 10; Acts 13:46) as the "heirs of promise" (Hebr. 6:17; Rom. 11:26-29); from them it was to extend to the Gentile world. At the same time the Lord designed to test the earnestness of the woman of Canaan, and, in His address to the disciples, refers only to the early period of their labors, or the first preaching of the Gospel, and not to their later operations, when they *did* preach to the Gentiles also. Now, in the case of the centurion, in which the circumstances were different, the Lord, probably intending to give a practical illustration of His words in ver. 10:11, promptly afforded relief. "Here, again, we see that the centurion did not rely on any works or righteousness of his own, but solely on the mercy of Christ."—LUTHER.

⁸ And the centurion answered and said, Lord, I am not worthy that thou shouldest come under my roof: but only say the word, and my servant shall be healed.

A. Answered=through the friends whom he had sent (Luke 7:6).—**B. I am . . . roof.** The centurion confesses that the Lord is greatly his superior in rank, as the words, "I am not worthy, etc.," indicate. As intimate relations existed between him and the Jewish elders (Luke 7:3), he can scarcely have alluded to his heathen origin, nor can he have referred to any earthly rank or distinction, inasmuch as the Lord held neither any military nor any civil office; it must be the divine character and power of the Lord to which he refers It is possible that he regarded Christ as invested with a divine commission like Elijah or one of the distinguished prophets with whose history he had become acquainted. "He humbly expresses his unworthiness of the Lord's favor, while, among the Jews, the Lord is despised and rejected (Isai. 53:3). This is genuine faith and genuine humility, when we feel our entire unworthiness, and, nevertheless, 'hope in God's mercy,' according to Ps. 147 : 11."—LUTHER.—**C. Only say the word**—the mere utterance of Thy will is sufficient, without Thy personal attendance, which I am too unworthy to expect; disease and death yield obedience to Thy commands.

⁹ For I also am a man under authority, having under myself soldiers: and I say to this one, Go, and he goeth; and to another, Come, and he cometh; and to my servant, Do this, and he doeth it.

The centurion was familiar with the conception of power and authority, on the one hand, and of immediate obedience, on the other, under a powerful government like that of the Romans. He himself obeyed without delay his own superior officer, under whose authority he was placed ("set," Luke 7 : 8—placed under him as a subaltern); he exacted and received the same obedience to the commands which he issued to the men under his command. In his household, his servants at once obeyed him, knowing that he had sufficient power to enforce his commands. Without having at this time very clear views of the exalted nature of the Lord, he knew that He could always accomplish His will by merely expressing it, without employing visible means. " In this man—says the centurion in his heart—God Himself dwells, for His works show that He has power over sickness, death and the devil. Therefore, I am not worthy that He should come under my roof."—LUTHER.

¹⁰ And when Jesus heard it, he marvelled, and said to them that followed, Verily I say unto you, I have not found so great faith, no, not in Israel.

A. Marvelled. The sense is, not that Christ was Himself unprepared for such a demonstration of faith, since He, the giver of all grace, " knew all," and " what was in man " (John 2 : 24, 25). As He was grieved when He encountered hardness of heart (Mark 3 : 5), so He was pleased when He saw a degree of faith which the circumstances of the individual could not have led an ordinary spectator to expect, as in this case and in 15 : 28. The same Greek word frequently refers to events which were not naturally expected to occur (Mark 12 : 17; Luke 4 : 22, " wondered ;" 11 : 38), and here chiefly describes the great pleasure which the faith of this heathen gave the Lord, in whom the unbelief of the Jews around Him (who had Moses and the prophets) could scarcely have led Him to expect such sentiments.—B. **So great faith** —a faith so intelligent, unhesitating and sure of success. The Lord does not specify other beautiful traits of this man's character, his tender love, his generosity, his humility or his liberality, but at once refers to the source of all—his *faith* (comp. 15 : 28; Luke 7 : 50).— C. **No, not in Israel.** The name *Israel*, signifying *Prince* (warrior) *of God*, was given to Jacob by the angel (Gen. 32 : 28; Hosea 12 : 4), and was afterwards extended as a collective term to his descendants, the Jewish people (Exod. 4 : 22; Deut. 33 : 28, 29; Matt. 10 : 6); in this sense it is used here. The " house of Israel" in 10 : 6, as in 2 : 6, F., is the people of Israel. The language of the Lord indicates great sorrow, arising from the unbelief of the mass of the Jews, who denied His divine character and mission ; it seems to indicate that He very unwillingly uttered the sad truth. " I have found so great faith, so sincere, so firm——;" here He pauses, as if the question had arisen : Can it be that, after so many mercies have been granted to the chosen people, none of them show such faith? Then He completes the sentence: " No ; such faith as this heathen possesses I have not found in the chosen people of God."

[11] And I say unto you, That many shall come from the east and the

west, and shall sit down with Abraham, and Isaac, and Jacob, in the kingdom of heaven.

A. I say. The same solemn words, occurring in this and the next verse, were repeated by the Lord on a later occasion (Luke 13 : 28, 29).—**B. Many**—pagans or Gentiles, converted to God, of whom this man is a representative (see 21 : 41, C.).—**C. East and west.** These terms are intended to convey the lesson that no geographical limits shall be assigned to the Church of Christ on earth, nor any national or other earthly distinctions exist in it (Acts 10 : 35 ; Rom. 10 : 12). "The field is the world" (13 : 38; see also Gen. 28 : 14 ; Isai. 11 : 9 ; Habak. 2 41:). —**D. Sit down**—literally recline. At that period, guests ordinarily reclined on cushions placed around the table, and supported the upper part of the body on the left arm or elbow (John 13 : 23, 25 ; comp. 26 : 7, A.).—**E. With Abraham, etc.**=the Gentiles shall be received into the new covenant (26 : 28, B.), which succeeds the one made with Abraham, and is an expansion and fulfilment of it (see below 21 : 41, C., and comp. Hebr. 12 : 22–24). The calling of the Gentiles (the "many") was contemplated (John 10 : 16) in the divine promise that "all families of the earth shall be blessed" in Abraham (Gen. 12 : 3). In this verse the Lord designates the privileges and blessedness of true believers (who are of all nations, Rev. 7 : 9; 15 : 4) under the figure of a banquet—a figure familiarly known to the ancients (see 22 : 2, C.), who used similar language to express the conception of the highest possible degree of enjoyment (Isai. 25 : 6; Matt. 26 : 29; Luke 14 : 15 ; Rev. 19 : 9). "Our salvation does not depend on our heathen or Jewish birth, but on our living faith in Christ, when we humbly seek His grace (Gal. 5 : 6)."—LUTHER. (Comp. 21 : 31, C.)—**F. Abraham . . . Jacob.** These three patriarchs, the founders of the

Jewish nation, to each of whom the same divine promise was given (Gen. 22:18; 26:3,4; 28:14), are the representatives of the true people of God (Gal. 3 : 7), who collectively constitute a kingdom of which God is the acknowledged King.

¹² But the sons of the kingdom shall be cast forth into the outer darkness: there shall be the weeping and gnashing of teeth.

A. Sons of the kingdom. The Hebrews were accustomed, in view of the near connection between a father and a son, to designate the near or intimate connection of any two objects, circumstances or events, by calling the one the *son* of the other (see below, 23 : 15, D., and for *daughter*, 21 : 5, B.). Thus the " sons of the resurrection " (Luke 20 : 36) are those who shall certainly share in the resurrection; the " sons of the bride-chamber " (9 : 15) are the most intimate companions (Judg. 14 : 11) of the bridegroom, and specially wait on him. The " rebels " in Numb. 17 : 10 are called in the original " sons of rebelliousness." Now, the " kingdom of God " consists of those who know and worship Him as the only true God and King. The Jews alone, of all the nations of the earth, were acquainted with the true worship of the Creator, and, as the chosen people (Exod. 19 : 5, 6) and children of those who received the promises (Acts 3 : 25; Rom. 9 : 4, 5), they were thus connected in the most intimate manner with the "kingdom" of truth. They claimed such an honorable name in view of prophetic passages like Gen. 28 : 14, and natural and spiritual pride concealed from them the truth that " they only who are of faith " are the children of the kingdom (Gal. 3 : 7). The true "children of the kingdom " (13 : 38) are believers only (Rom. 4 : 14–16; Gal. 3 : 29). The kingdom of God was taken from the Jews (Matt. 21 : 43) because of unbelief (Hebr. 3 : 19; 4 : 6; Rom. 11 : 20).

—B. **Shall be cast out**—cast out, in accordance with the image, from the banquet-chamber, by which a final exclusion from the happiness of heaven is signified.—C. **Into the outer darkness.** The banquet is at night, as in Matt. 22 : 13; the outer darkness, particularly if the image is derived from the gloom of a remote prison, as in Isai. 42 : 7, is the opposite of the light and enjoyment found in the banquet-chamber.—D. **There shall ... teeth.** These terms (Ps. 112 : 10), expressive of the agony, wrath and despair of those who are cast out, describe the eternal punishment of those who reject Christ, and die in impenitence and unbelief (Luke 16 : 23, 26). The phrase often occurs (13 : 42; 22 : 13; 24 : 51; 25 : 30).

¹³ And Jesus said unto the centurion, Go thy way; as thou hast believed, *so* be it done unto thee. And the servant was healed in that hour.

A. **Go thy way.** The original word so translated here, like the similar word translated *go to* in James 4 : 13; 5 : 1, is a term of exhortation, incitement, etc. Here it is equivalent to: *Be of good cheer.*—B. **As thou ... unto thee** (see 15 : 28, C.). "The Lord seems to say here to him: Not only in this case, but in any other case also, if thou shouldst ask even more, or if thou wert thyself in great distress, and shouldst only believe, thou shouldst have all for which thou dost ask. For, even as thou conceivest of Me and believest, so shalt thou find Me to be. If thou believest that I will have mercy on the poor sinner who comes to Me in penitence and faith, thou wilt find Me to be such a Saviour."—LUTHER.—C. **That hour**—*at the same time.* The healing of the servant, who had been at the point of death (Luke 7 : 2), was immediate and complete.

¹⁴ And when Jesus was come into Peter's house, he saw his wife's mother lying sick of a fever.

A. **Peter's house,** in Capernaum (ver. 5). Bethsaida was his birthplace (John 1 : 44; see 4 : 18, B.; 16 : 18, B.).
—B. **Wife's mother.** History, as distinct from tradition, has not preserved any facts respecting the members of Peter's family, except the circumstance mentioned in 1 Cor. 9 : 5, that, at a later period, his wife accompanied him at times, during his missionary travels; in that passage Peter bears the name of *Cephas*, for which see 16 ; 18, B.
—C. **Sick of a fever,** a " great fever " (Luke 4 : 38). " There is here no mention made of the faith of this sick woman, but Luke adds (4 : 38) that *others* besought the Lord for her. She may have been lying in a state of unconsciousness at the time. Here we perceive how acceptable in the eyes of God that office of love is, which we perform when we pray to Him in faith, in behalf of others."—LUTHER.

¹⁵ And he touched her hand, and the fever left her: and she arose, and ministered unto them.

A. **He touched . . . left her**—at the moment when He took her hand to raise her up, the fever left her. Luke adds (4 : 39) that He "rebuked" the fever, as in ver. 26 below He rebuked the winds and the sea.—B. **She arose, etc.** She **ministered**—either, as in Luke 10 : 40, *served* them at the table, or, in general, waited on the guests in the house. This circumstance is mentioned for the purpose of showing that her restoration was immediate (Mark 1 : 31 ; Luke 4 : 39) and complete.

¹⁶ And when even was come, they brought unto him many possessed with devils: and he cast out the spirits with a word, and healed all that were sick.

A. **Even**—evening, "when the sun was setting" (Luke 4 : 40).—B. **They**—the inhabitants of Capernaum.
—C. **Brought unto, etc.** The tidings of the miracle wrought by Christ when He first entered the house were

soon conveyed to others. As many of the "sick with divers diseases" (Luke) were necessarily *carried* by their friends, as in Mark 2 : 3, and as it was the Sabbath-day (Mark 1 : 21, 29) when He had entered the house the people waited until sunset, or the close of the Sabbath (Lev. 23 : 32); even such works of mercy were regarded by the self-righteous Jews as unlawful, when performed on that day (Luke 13 : 14).—D. **Possessed with devils** (see EXCURSUS II.).—**Spirits**=*unclean* spirits, as they are termed in 10 : 1.—**E. With his word**—without even touching them, as in 12 : 13. He employed no visible means; His divine power, when He expressed His will, was sufficient to deliver men from any evil.

¹⁷ That it might be fulfilled which was spoken by Isaiah the prophet, saying, Himself took our infirmities, and bare our diseases.

The passage quoted occurs in Isai. 53 : 4. The prophet there teaches that the atonement of Christ was vicarious, that is, He suffered and died *in our place*, in order that He might deliver us from sin and all its mournful effects (see 1 Peter 2 : 24, and comp. 20 : 28, E.). Now sickness and death were originally introduced into the world by sin (Rom. 5 : 12). The evangelist here very beautifully refers to the words of the prophet, and shows the *completeness* of the work of Christ; His atoning work and grace will effectually deliver the believer from all sin; the illustration or proof is found in the circumstance that the Lord here exhibited His power to deliver men already in this world from the consequences of sin, which affect the body as well as the soul, such as sickness, etc. (Gen. 3 : 16–19). He *took* and *bore* our whole burden (Isai. 53 : 4–6, 12). " Although the prophet primarily refers to the sufferings which Christ endured, in order to deliver us from our sins, Matthew here very happily refers to the *whole work* which Christ performed, by which

He delivers us from all evils, whether they are those of the body or those of the soul."—LUTHER.

[18] Now when Jesus saw great multitudes about him, he gave commandment to depart unto the other side.

A. Jesus . . . multitudes. The events now related occurred some time after the foregoing, "on a certain day" (Luke 8 : 22, and comp. Mark 4 : 35). The three evangelists adopt a different order in relating them. It is not important to us to know the precise days on which the events may have occurred, while it is important to us to be made acquainted with the words and acts of the Lord.—**B. To depart . . . side**—opposite to Capernaum, namely to the eastern side of the Sea of Tiberias. These multitudes were at times burdensome, and interrupted Him in the work of teaching (Mark 3 : 9), their continued presence also tended to inflame the hatred of His enemies, and led them to plot against His life (Matt. 12 : 14-16). Such a motive probably influenced Him in the present case, as the circumstance that He desired to depart when He saw the multitudes seems to imply.

[19] And there came a scribe, and said unto him, Master, I will follow thee whithersover thou goest.

A. Master. There are several Greek words which are translated *Master* in the N. T., and are equivalent to *Teacher ;* the present term occurs in 12 : 38; 19 : 16; 22 : 16, 24, 36. They are all respectful titles given to religious teachers of the Jews (see 23 : 8, A., and for *Rabbi*, 23 : 7, B.).—**B. I will follow thee.** This man was already a *disciple* of the Lord, as the word *another* in ver. 21 implies. That word, which originally means a *learner*, and then an attendant or *follower* (5 : 1, D.; 11 : 29, B.), was afterwards specially used to designate the Twelve Apostles (10 : 1, 2). It is sometimes applied in a general sense to those who frequently came to *learn* of Jesus, or seemed disposed to attach themselves to Him, as in John 4 : 1. Many of these on one occasion abandoned Him permanently (John 6 : 66).—C. **Whithersoever, etc.** This offer or promise, like those of Ittai (2 Sam. 15:21) and Ruth (Ruth 1 : 16), seems to express sentiments of attachment and confidence ; nevertheless, promises are often made with apparent sincerity, but without due knowledge and reflection. This scribe perhaps expected, as the Lord's answer implies, that his personal attendance on Christ wonld not require self-denial, nor subject him to losses and persecution, but rather secure for him temporal advantages and conveniences.

²⁰ And Jesus saith unto him, The foxes have holes, and the birds of the air *have* nests ; but the Son of man hath not where to lay his head.

A. Foxes, etc. The Saviour replies : Animals and birds have their fixed abodes, and men provide for themselves homes. But I came to labor for others, not to seek My own gratification (Matt. 20 : 28). Thou canst not follow Me in a proper spirit, unless thou dost renounce the world and give thyself wholly to God. "The Christian is a stranger on earth (Ps. 119 : 19; Hebr. 11 : 13), and does not fix his affections on the things of this world ; he must be willing to renounce all for the sake of Christ. This scribe, perhaps, had not pure motives, when he said : I will follow, etc., and the Lord therefore replies to him : Thou shouldst look to heaven alone for place and joy ; expect no earthly honors by entering My service; thy only kingdom here will be the cross, and thy palace, the contempt of the world."— LUTHER.—**B. Son of man.** The Saviour applies this term, which is of deep import, to Himself exclusively. After referring to the prophet Daniel in Matt. 24 : 15, He speaks in ver. 27 of the "coming of the Son of man," and when He again employs the term in Matt. 26 : 64, He there, too, refers to the prophet Daniel, who in ch. 7 : 13, 14, gives this name to the promised Messiah, ascribing to Him everlasting dominion. Hence the Lord implies, by assuming this title, that he is the Messiah ; the same truth He distinctly revealed to the woman of Samaria (John 4 : 25, 26). In Matt. 26 : 63, 64, He applies both this appellation and that of " Son of God" to Himself. The actual fulfilment of the divine promise in Gen. 3 : 15 respecting the woman's seed, that is, the descendant who should crush the serpent, also seems to be indicated by the term. The name, as its application in Matt. 9 : 6 ; John 3 : 13 ; 5 : 26, 27, shows, refers to the mystery (1 Tim. 3 : 16) of the incarnation of the Word, the Son of God (John 1 : 1, 14). The Son of man, " very man and very God," who is now on the right hand of God (Acts 7 : 55), will hereafter appear in all His divine glory as the Judge of men (25 : 31).—C. **Hath not** (=a place) **where to lay his head.** In 4 : 13 it is said that the Lord "dwelt in Capernaum," which is called " his own city " (9 : 1). It may have been temporarily His place of abode. The words " hath not, etc.," are not so much intended to convey to the scribe the idea that the Lord was absolutely poor and destitute, as, rather, to state the fact that He led a life of disinterested labor, enjoying none of the comforts of a fixed home. The whole life of Christ was a period of humiliation and sorrow (comp. Phil. 2 : 7, 8 ; 2 Cor. 8 : 9). The scribe is thus taught to "count the cost " (Luke 14 : 26–33.

[21] And another of his disciples said unto him, Lord, suffer me first to go and bury my father.

A. Another of, etc.=one of those who temporarily accompanied the Lord, not one of the Twelve (see 5 : 1, D., and 8 : 19, C.).—B. **Suffer me, etc.** In this man the Lord perceived a better spirit, and, accordingly, desired him to become permanently a follower, as Luke relates (9 : 59), saying, Follow Me. The man readily consents, but refers to an obstacle which seems to render immediate obedience inexpedient—the death of his father. It was customary among the Jews at that time to inter their dead very soon after life was extinct, without waiting till the next day (Matt. 9 : 23; Acts 5 : 6, 7). The sons (Gen. 25 : 9; 35 : 29; 1 Kings 13 : 31), or the nearest friends (Matt. 14 : 12), usually performed the last offices connected with the burial. As the act of touching a deady body created a legal uncleanness, the priests were not allowed to assist at any funerals except those of their nearest relatives (Lev. 21 : 1–3). The high-priest, "upon whose head the anointing oil was poured" (ver. 10), was not permitted to bury even his father (ver. 11); the same prohibition applied to the Nazarite (Numb. 6 : 7). It was, therefore, well known to the Jews that cases could occur in which a higher religious duty prevented a son from performing that office. If this man at that moment received the tidings that his father had just expired, the command of the Saviour implied that such a higher duty now called him away under very urgent circumstances, which are not here specially related. It was perhaps necessary to teach him that neither our natural affections nor our domestic duties are ever permitted to interfere with our duties to God, even as Abraham learned when he was commanded, as a trial of his faith, to offer up his son Isaac (Gen. 22 : 1–19). James and John immediately left their father, when the Lord assigned to them the duty to follow Him (4 : 21, 22). The present case is, therefore, peculiar; without such a direct divine call, the duties of children to their parents, as the Lord teaches in 15 : 3–6, can never be neglected without sin.

²² But Jesus saith unto him, Follow me; and leave the dead to bury their own dead.

The terms **death, dead,** etc., are frequently employed in the Scriptures in a figurative sense. Those who have in faith renounced the service of sin are "dead to sin," or simply "dead," having no connection with it (Rom. 6 : 7–11). Again, those who are destitute of saving faith are destitute of spiritual life, and are emphatically said to be "dead" (Eph. 2 : 1 ; Col. 2 : 13 ; 1 Tim. 5 : 6 ; Rev. 3 : 1). The Saviour intends to say : Let thy friends who are spiritually dead render the last offices due to the dying or the dead—to thy father; thou hast at present a higher and more solemn duty to perform. "The Lord does not mean that this man, or any other one, should ever neglect the duty prescribed in the commandment: 'Honor thy father, etc.' (Exod. 20 : 12), but intends to say, as He likewise does in Luke 14 : 26, that no apparent duty, obligation or necessity in this world can ever excuse us from fulfilling the duties which we owe to God." —LUTHER.

²³ And when he was entered into a boat, his disciples followed him.

Entered, etc.=after the foregoing conversation with two of His usual attendants.

²⁴ And, behold, there arose a great tempest in the sea, insomuch that the boat was covered with the waves: but he was asleep.

A. **The sea**—of Galilee; it was subject to very sudden and dangerous tempests.—B. **He was asleep.** When the Lord assumed our human nature, He clothed Himself with all the attributes which belonged to it, as far as these are without sin (Phil. 2 : 7, and see 1 : 16, C.). We read, accordingly, that He hungered (4 : 2 ; 21 : 18), thirsted (John 19 : 28), was wearied (John 4 : 6), wept (Luke 19 : 41 ; John 11 : 35). His hunger and His tears are mentioned in connection with acts of divine power (Matt. 21 : 18, 19; John 11 : 35, 43). Mark informs us (4 : 35) that the evening had already arrived, when the Lord proceeded to the vessel; on the way the events occurred which are described in Matt. 8 : 19–22, and which occupied some time. After the vessel had left the shore, and when, doubtless, night, the natural period of repose, had already come, Luke says (8 : 23) that the Lord "fell asleep." " In seasons of sorrow, when we cannot find relief or comfort, the Lord seems at times to have forgotten us, or, as here, *to be asleep*. In such cases He desires to teach us that we can do nothing without Him (John 15 : 5). When we cease to trust in ourselves (2 Cor. 1 : 9), and look to Him for aid, His grace affords relief (2 Cor. 3 : 5 ; 12 : 9)."—LUTHER.

[25] And his disciples came to *him*, and awoke him, saying, Save, Lord; we perish.

Save, Lord. The disciples are terrified. They forget for the moment that, after the labors which He had performed, a deep sleep had fallen upon Him, and almost seem to reproach Him, when they say in their trepidation: " Master, carest thou not that we perish ? " (Mark.) Their prayer, which refers to deliverance from bodily death, is most appropriately repeated by us when, without the doubt which it concealed, but with deep humility and confidence, we beseech Him to save our souls from eternal death.

[26] And he saith unto them, Why are ye fearful, O ye of little faith ? Then he arose, and rebuked the winds and the sea; and there was a great calm.

A. Why . . . fearful. The Lord calms the tumult in their souls by asking : Has My power ever failed ? Is not My presence itself a sure protection ? Do ye not yet understand that I came from God, and that, as I have chosen you, the great work which you are to accomplish cannot be hindered or defeated by any present danger? —**B. O ye ... faith.** The disciples are thus again rebuked in 16 : 8, where the miracle to which the Lord refers should have taught them that His resources never failed; the same lesson is taught in 6 : 30. In 14 : 31 these words are addressed to Peter. The disciples were not absolutely *faithless*—without faith (John 20 : 27); they *believed*, it is true, but their prayer shows that they permitted doubts and fears to disturb their faith. A genuine Christian faith is always characterized by cheerfulness, and entire, unhesitating confidence in the power and grace of God.—**C. Rebuked ... sea.** In the direct address which Mark (4 : 39) has preserved: " Peace, be still," it would "be absurd (says TRENCH, *Miracles*, p. 12) to suppose a mere oratorical personification. There is (continues he) in these words a distinct recognition of Satan and the powers of evil as the authors of the disharmony in the outward world—a carrying of all these disorders back to Him as their ultimate ground. The Lord elsewhere uses the same form of address to a fever, for it is said that He *rebuked* it (Luke 4 : 39), where the same remarks will hold good." That this interpretation is correct, is proved by the Saviour's own words, when He publicly ascribed the bodily affliction of a certain Jewess to Satan (Luke 13 : 16; see also below, 16 : 23, B.).—**D. There was ... calm.** " Jesus sleeps, for He is a man ; He controls the winds and storms with a word as God (Ps. 65 : 7; 89 : 8, 9; Nahum 1 : 4), for He is God. God and Man are one Person in Christ. Our blessed Lord also teaches us here that His believing people should never fear nor despair, for He is always near (Rom. 8 : 31). If the faith of the disciples had been stronger, they might have boldly said:

Blow, ye winds, and dash against us, ye waves; ye can do us no harm, for Christ is with us."—LUTHER.

27 And the men marvelled, saying, What manner of man is this, that even the winds and the sea obey him?

Marvelled=*wondered* (8 : 10, A.). In Mark and Luke the terms *feared, wondered,* seem to refer to the disciples. But the expression in Mark, "the men," indicates the other persons who were present, partly in this ship, and partly in the other ships which were in company (Mark 4 : 36). If the disciples are included, they marvelled because they saw in this new miracle a manifestation of authority which controlled the action of the most powerful natural agents, the winds and the waves. They obtained new views of the power and glory of their Master. "Perhaps some of those present who accompanied the disciples had previously looked on Christ with unbelief. The danger through which they had just passed opened their eyes and touched their hearts. Trials and afflictions lead many souls to Christ, and strengthen believers in their holy faith (2 Cor. 12 : 9, 10)."—LUTHER.

28 And when he was come to the other side into the country of the Gergesenes, there met him two possessed with devils, coming out of the tombs, exceeding fierce, so that no man might pass by that way.

A. **Country of the Gergesenes**—in Mark and Luke, *of the Gadarenes.* The city of Gadara was the metropolis of Peræa, according to Josephus (War, 4. 7. 3). This city was situated east of the Jordan, on the south of the lake, and not far from it; it was one of the ten cities which bore the collective name of Decapolis (see 4 : 25, B.; Mark 5 : 20; 7 : 31). This region was inhabited chiefly by pagans. The ancient boundary lines of this "country" are not now known, and the want in modern times of precise geographical knowledge respecting the ancient divisions of the country has occasioned a diversity of opinions respecting the reason for which the same country is called that of the *Gergesenes*. Some have supposed that this region was originally occupied by the ancient *Girgashites* (Gen. 15 : 21 ; Deut. 7 : 1 ; Josh. 24 : 11 ; Nehem. 9 : 8), and that their name, with a slight alteration in the orthography, was perpetuated, after their extinction, in that of the country, that is, *Gergesa*, while the later name was *Gadara*.—**B. Two ... devils.** (For DEMONIACS see EXCURSUS II.) Mark and Luke mention only one. So, too, Matthew speaks of two blind men (20 : 29, A.), one of whom, named Bartimeus, was better known than the other. It is, no doubt, on this account that Mark (10 : 46) and Luke (18 : 35) refer to him alone (comp. Matt. 28 : 5 and Mark 16 : 5 with Luke 24 : 4) ; the former evangelists mention only the angel who speaks. So Mark and Luke here select the one whose case was more striking than that of the other.—**C. Tombs**. The limestone rocks of the mountains (Mark 5 : 5) in the vicinity of Gadara abounded in natural and artificial cavities (27 : 60, A.) or grottos, which were much used as places for depositing the dead. To such gloomy abodes the demoniacs were driven by the unclean spirits dwelling in them.—**D. Exceeding fierce.** " No man could bind him, no, not with chains " (Mark). " He was driven of the devil into the wilderness " (Luke). " He was always, night and day, in the mountains " (Mark 5 : 5). Even in ordinary cases of madness, uncommon muscular power is developed ; maniacs often refuse to associate with men. " God sometimes permits Satan to manifest in such awful forms the great power which He desires to exercise over man, in order that we, who are made acquainted with these facts, may the more deeply feel our need of divine grace in overcoming our unbelief and the power of Satan, the god of this world (2 Cor. 4 : 4), and also that we may learn that God alone can deliver us from sin, from Satan, and from eternal death."—LUTHER.

²⁹ And, behold, they cried out, saying, What have we to do with thee, thou Son of God? art thou come hither to torment us before the time?

A. Cried out, saying. This is not language which the demoniacs used consciously, or uttered as expressive of their own sentiments, but is really the language which the unclean spirit addressed to the Lord, who had previously said: Come out of the man, thou unclean spirit (Mark 5 : 7).—**B. What ... with thee.** This phrase, occurring also in 2 Sam. 16 : 10 ; 19: 22 ; 2 Chron. 35 : 21, often expresses an unwillingness to hold any intercourse or connection with the person addressed, whose presence, opinions and acts are indicated as offensive ; it also implies entire alienation (2 Kings 9 : 18 ; Ezra 4 : 3) ; it occurs again in Matt. 27 : 19. The spirits know (Mark 1 : 24) that one "stronger than Beelzebub" (Luke 9: 21, 22) is before them. "The devils seem to accuse Christ of injustice in expelling them ; the world often complains that religion exacts more of man than is reasonable and just."—LUTHER.—**C. Thou Son of God.** This name was already applied by the angel to the Lord when His birth was foretold (Luke 1 : 35), for He had no earthly father. John the Baptist, His forerunner, " bare record that He was the Son of God " (John 1 : 34, and see Matt. 3 : 17). This name is not applied to the Saviour by the Scriptures in the sense in which believers are called the "children of God," as in Matt. 5 : 9 ; John 11 : 52 ; Rom. 8 : 14 ; 9 : 26. They owe their adoption to God's only-begotten Son, while Christ was from all eternity (John 17: 5) *one* with the Father (John 10: 30), and begotten of Him (Hebr. 1 : 5-8), and is therefore called the "Only-begotten Son" of God (John 1 : 14, 18 ; 3 : 16, 18 ; 1 John 4 : 9). As the Son of God, He possesses all the attributes of the divine nature, and is to be honored as the Father (John 5 : 23). The devils confess the truth here, and tremble (James 2 : 19). The first occasion on which believing men give Him that divine name is described below (14 : 33 ; see 26 : 63, F).— **D. To torment us.** The demoniacs could not, from their own knowledge, have styled Jesus "the Son of God," hence we may believe that the whole of the language in this verse, referring to the misery which their apostasy had brought on them, really proceeded from the unclean spirits dwelling in them.—**E. Before the time**—art thou come before the time of judgment? From Matt. 25 : 41 ; 2 Peter 2 : 4 ; Jude, ver. 6 ; Rev. 20 : 10, we learn that while the present condition of the fallen angels is unutterably miserable, they are, nevertheless, reserved for a final sentence of eternal condemnation, which will be pronounced on the judgment-day. It is, probably, to that "time" that the words which they here utter refer.

³⁰ Now there was afar off from them a herd of many swine feeding.

These swine were unclean animals, which the Jews were not allowed to eat or even touch, and which they abhorred (see 7 : 6, C.). Very ancient Jewish authorities had declared it to be illegal even to own them, and their presence was deemed to be a pollution. The owners of this herd of 2,000 swine (Mark) may have been the pagan inhabitants of that region, who denied the Lord God Jehovah to be the true God ; if they were Jews, which is, however, not probable, they treated the laws of Moses with contempt, by keeping such animals for purposes of traffic. In either case, a pecuniary loss occasioned by the destruction of the herd would naturally assume the character of a solemn warning. No reproach could fall on the Lord Jesus, on account of the loss, on the ground that He destroyed private property, even if He had caused the destruction of the swine (which was really occasioned by the unclean spirits); He is, in the first place, the Lord of all, and, in the second place, any such reproach uttered against Him would really be a condemnation of God, who sometimes "suffers," as here, that is, *permits* animals to die in large numbers of contagious diseases, or perish by inundations, earthquakes, etc.

³¹ And the devils besought him, saying, If thou cast us out, send us away into the herd of swine.

According to Luke (8 : 31), the devils besought the Lord that He would not command them to go into the *deep*, that is, literally, the *abyss*, which word in Rom. 10 : 7 designates the place that is the opposite of *heaven*, and in Rev. 9 : 1, etc., describes the pit which is "bottomless." Here it appears to stand for *hell* (2 Peter 2 : 4), the place of punishment. The devils desired to remain on earth temporarily. Many circumstances connected with the present state, operations, etc. of lost spirits are yet unknown to us.

³² And he said unto them, Go. And they came out and went into the swine: and, behold, the whole herd rushed down the steep into the sea, and perished in the waters.

A. Go=*depart, get you hence*, as the same word is sometimes rendered, without referring to any place of destination (Matt. 4 : 10 ; James 2 : 16). The word therefore does not imply that Jesus Himself directed them to go into the swine, but simply (as Mark and Luke also say) that He *gave them leave* or *suffered* them to depart. He refrains from directing their movements, after they leave the two men.—B. Went . . . swine=

by divine permission, for the purpose of giving unquestionable evidence in this aggravated case that the evil spirits had really been banished from the two men. Still, there is much here that is mysterious. We do not completely understand the nature of the human soul, nor the precise mode in which it influences the body. Much less can we expect to understand fully events so remarkable as those which are here mentioned, and in which invisible evil spirits are bound to act on the bodies of animals. But, as Christians, we believe all the facts which the Lord has been pleased to make known to us in this portion of His word.

[33] And, behold, all the city came out to meet Jesus: and when they saw him, they besought *him* that he would depart from ther borders.

A. **All the city.** All the inhabitants were astonished when they received the tidings, and, following a natural impulse, went out to see Jesus.—B. **They besought**, etc. They could not comprehend the greatness of the mercy of Christ, and, looking only at the destruction of their temporal property, were filled with fear lest His presence would produce additional losses.—" These people are more afflicted by the loss of their swine than impressed by the deliverance of the two wretched men from the power of Satan. Our carnal feelings often cause us to consider only the calamities which are inflicted, and which are richly deserved, and to overlook entirely the riches of divine grace given to believers."—LUTHER.

CHAPTER IX.

¹ And he entered into a boat, and crossed over, and came into his own city.

A. Crossed over—returned to the west side (see 8: 18). The Gergesenes, like the Jews of Antioch (Acts 13 : 46), "put from themselves" the word of God; so, too, all who scorn the Gospel pronounce themselves to be unworthy of everlasting life. "In this whole narrative, faith and forgiveness are again presented as inseparably connected."—LUTHER.—**B. His own city**=Capernaum (4 : 13, B.; Mark 2: 1); here He temporarily dwelt (comp. 1 Sam. 8 : 22 ; see below, 11 : 23, C., and 13 : 54, A.).

² And, behold, they brought to him a man sick of the palsy, lying on a bed: and Jesus seeing their faith said unto the sick of the palsy: Son, be of good cheer; thy sins are forgiven.

A. They brought—the four men (Mark 2 : 3) brought, not a costly gift, but a wretched, dying sinner. And yet, the most acceptable offering which the poor sinner can bring is his own evil heart.—**D. Jesus seeing their faith** =the faith not so much of the sick man who needed his aid, as of the four bearers, as seen in the measures which they adopted to reach Christ. "We do not read that these persons uttered one word aloud ; nevertheless, their *silent* prayers were heard and accepted, as an encouragement for us. When our silent prayers are made in faith, they sound so loudly that, like the cries of Moses (Exod. 14 : 15), they are at once heard in heaven."—LUTHER.—
E. Son—a soothing term of address, expressive of kind

feeling, like " Daughter " in ver. 22 below, and " Children " in Mark 10 : 24.—**F. Be . . . cheer**—maintain thy confidence and hope, for thy help is near. The force of the original word may be ascertained by comparing the following passages in which it occurs : Matt. 14 : 27 ; Mark 10 : 49; Acts 23 : 11.—**G. Thy sins etc.**—I grant thee at this moment forgiveness.—The greatest evil in the world, and, indeed, the source of all other evils is, not sickness, but sin (Gen. 3 : 16–19). Of this man's personal history nothing is known. As a son of Adam, he was, however, a sinner, according to Rom. 5 : 12. The Saviour does not simply announce the divine forgiveness to this man, as Nathan addressed David (2 Sam. 12 : 13); the Pharisees rightly understood Him as meaning that He, by His own authority, granted forgiveness.

³ And, behold, certain of the scribes said within themselves, This man blasphemeth.

A. Certain of the scribes. Luke adds (5 : 17, 21) "and Pharisees." We may account for their presence on this occasion by referring to the circumstance that the report of His extraordinary mode of preaching had been extensively circulated by the multitudes who heard the Sermon on the Mount, and that the suspicions and jealousy of the Pharisees induced them to watch Him closely.—**B. Said within themselves**—did not utter their thoughts ; but these could not be concealed from the all-seeing eye which rested on them (ver. 4).—**C. Blasphemeth.** The original term here translated *blaspheme* indicated among the Greeks the act of *slandering*. In the N. T., however, it is applied to irreverent, contemptuous or malicious language in reference to God and divine things, as in Matt. 12 : 31 ; Rom. 2 : 24; Tit. 2 : 5; it designates, also, any language or expression which claims for man the power and honor belonging to God alone.

In this latter sense it is used here, and in Matt. 26 : 65 ; John 10 : 33, 36. In 27 : 39 it is translated *railed*, and also in Luke 23 : 39. These scribes reasoned in their hearts: "Who can forgive sins but God only?" (Mark 2 : 6, 7)—does He not usurp an office which belongs to God alone?

⁴ And Jesus knowing their thoughts said, Wherefore think ye evil in your hearts?

A. Knowing (literally, *seeing*) **their thoughts** (ver. 3, B., above). Mark says: "Jesus perceived in his spirit, etc.," referring to His divine nature and attributes.—**B. Wherefore, etc.** They correctly believed that God alone can forgive sin (Ps. 32 : 5; Acts 5 : 31). Wherein consisted the *evil* of their thoughts? As they could not discover a single blemish in His life and conduct (John 8 : 46), they attempted at least to "entangle him in his talk" (22 : 15 ; comp. Mark 12 : 13; Luke 20 : 20), and accuse Him of falsehood, blasphemy or any other offence which would place Him in their power. They now maliciously rejoice that the opportunity is found, and this unhallowed feeling, in addition to their unbelief, is the *evil* which He exposes (comp. Zechar. 8 : 17).

⁵ For whether is easier, to say, *Thy* sins are forgiven ; or to say, Arise, and walk.

A. For—I will therefore convince you by an act of divine power, that your thoughts concerning Me are evil. —**B. Whether** (=which of the two) **is easier, etc.** The sense is: It is alike beyond the power of a mere man, on the one hand, to free a sinner actually from guilt, and, on the other, to restore a sick man to health by a word; such power belongs, as you rightly think, to God alone. Now He who can exercise sufficient power to accomplish the one work, seeing that such power must be divine, can also accomplish the other divine work (comp. Ps. 103 : 3).

⁶ But that ye may know that the Son of man hath power on earth to forgive sins (then saith he to the sick of the palsy), Arise, take up thy bed, and go unto thy house.

A. But (—now) **that ye may know, etc.** Of the two works, that of *forgiving* belongs to the spiritual world, and cannot be seen with the bodily eye; but the other, the *healing*, is one concerning the reality of which men can have the testimony of their own senses.—**B. That the Son . . . earth**—in order to give you this evidence that I possess divine authority, and that " all things that the Father hath are mine " (John 16:15).—Here, the sentence, if completed, would be in substance: I will now, by performing visibly an act of divine power (healing), prove to you that I can perform another act of divine power (forgiving), which cannot be seen. Here God was " manifest in the flesh " (1 Tim. 3:16; John 1:1, 14; comp. Matt. 16:19; 28:18. For " Son of man," see 8:20, B.).—**C. Then saith . . . palsy.** Here the Lord evidently pauses, without completing the sentence; He had addressed the scribes sitting near Him (Mark 2:6), but He now turns towards the sick man with a gesture which seemed to say: Look, and then judge for yourselves.—**D. Arise, etc.** The man is perfectly restored. He is commanded to carry away his bed himself, in order to silence enemies by such undeniable evidence of his entire restoration to health.

⁷, ⁸ And he arose, and departed to his house. But when the multitudes saw *it*, they were afraid, and glorified God, which had given such power unto men.

A. And he . . . house—the wondering and amazed multitude (Mark, Luke), respectfully opening a passage for one whose misery had previously not moved them, but whose miraculous restoration filled them with awe.— **B. Glorified God**=ascribed honor and praise to God (comp. 15:31, A).—**C. Which**(=who)**. . . men.** Of the several Greek words translated *power* in the N. T., the one which Christ had used in ver. 6, to designate His authority and ability to forgive sin (translated sometimes *authority*, as in 7 : 29 ; 21 : 23), is here also employed by the multitude, showing that they were now convinced by the power revealed in this miracle that He had also power to forgive sin.

⁹ And as Jesus passed by from thence, he saw a man, called Matthew, sitting at the place of toll and he saith unto him, Follow me. And he arose, and followed him.

A. A man ... **Matthew** (signifying *gi, t of Jehovah*). He was so named after he became an apostle ; his earlier name was Levi (Mark 2 : 14 ; Luke 5 : 27). So the apostle Simon was afterwards usually called *Peter* (Matt. 16 : 18), and Saul of Tarsus is generally mentioned by the name of Paul (Acts 13 : 9). Mark or Marcus, the nephew of Barnabas (Col. 4 : 10), and the writer of the second Gospel, had originally been known as John (Acts 12 : 12, 25 ; 15 : 37).—B. **Place of toll**—where the taxes were paid.—C. **Follow me** (see 4 : 19, A.). As Matthew appears to have resided in or near Capernaum, where the Lord frequently taught, he had doubtless at a previous period been converted, and had become a believer ; he now receives a direct call to become a constant attendant of Christ. Although he is the author of the present Gospel, his humility does not allow him to commemorate the temporal sacrifices which he cheerfully made. Luke says (5 : 28) " he left all," in order to follow Christ.

¹⁰ And it came to pass, as he sat at meat in the house, behold, many publicans and sinners came and sat down with Jesus and his disciples.

A. **In the house**—of Matthew, who had invited " a great company of publicans and of others " (Luke 5 : 29). —B. **Publicans and sinners.** These terms, used in a reproachful sense, are often combined (11 : 19). The latter term comprehended various classes of persons, namely, those who did not respect the rules of the Pharisees (John 9: 16, 24), those who had been cast out of the synagogue, whose reputation was sullied in the public eye, as in Luke 7: 37, 39, and all heathens (Gal. 2; 15), or Jews who associated with them. The word in its deeper import, describing the evil in the heart, the source of sins against God, occurs in Luke 18: 13; Rom. 5: 8; 1 Tim. 1: 15.—C. **Sat down** (8 : 11 D.) . . . **disciples.** The blessed Saviour, who came into the world in order to cleanse men from the leprosy of sin, freely associated with the vile and unholy, in order to touch their souls, and thus fulfil the merciful design of His mission (ver. 13).

¹¹ And when the Pharisees saw *it*, they said unto his disciples, Why eateth your master with the publicans and sinners?

A. **The Pharisees saw it.** They and the scribes (Mark, Luke) were, unquestionably, not guests themselves, but residents of the place ("their scribes," Luke 5 : 30), and may have addressed these words to the disciples as the latter were leaving the house.—**Saw**—made aware of, *knew*, as the same word is translated in ver. 4 and 6.—B. **Said . . . disciples**—either for the malicious purpose of impairing the confidence of the latter in the Lord, or from a secret dread of the Lord's rebuke, if they addressed Him personally.—C. **Why eateth, etc.**—if he fears God and reveres Moses, why does He pollute Himself by associating with such vile people? The Pharisees here, as in Luke 19: 7, unintentionally bear testimony to the holy character of Jesus.

¹² But when he heard it, he said, They that are whole have no need of a physician, but they that are sick.

A. **But . . . said**—interposed, and gave an answer in which all His mildness, wisdom, holiness and love are revealed.—B. **They that are whole need, etc.** (Compare an analogous proverb in Luke 4 : 23.) The Lord employed proverbs, when they could be spiritually applied (see 7 : 6, A.). In the present instance, the grace of God which heals the soul is to be understood. The Saviour says: If men were "whole," and not lost sinners (18 : 11 ; 1 John 3 : 5), the work which I came to finish (John 17 : 4), would not have been necessary (8 : 17). But now, can I be more appropriately occupied than when I guide lost wanderers back to heaven and to peace?

¹³ But go ye and learn what *this* meaneth, I desire mercy, and not sacrifice: for I came not to call the righteous, but sinners.

A. **Go ye ... meaneth**=ye have no true conception of divine mercy, neither do ye comprehend the purposes of God in His dealings with men. Search out the meaning of these words of the prophet, before you constitute yourselves judges of others.—B. **I desire mercy and not** (=rather than) **sacrifice** (Hosea 6 : 6). The same passage is quoted again in 12 : 7. The prophet had complained (ch. 4 : 1), that the divine gifts of truth (right views of the divine will), mercy (the forgiveness of penitent sinners), and religious knowledge (knowledge of God), had been ungratefully and wickedly spurned by the children of Israel. God Himself deplores the infatuation of the Israelites, who despised the gifts of divine grace, and, in place of kindly *receiving* from God (that is, of accepting His offered mercy), thought, in their self-righteousness, only of *giving* to Him (that is, of acquiring merit and a right to temporal prosperity by their outward worship). Therefore the prophet was commanded to announce the coming wrath (6 : 5, "I hewed, etc."), in order to lead men to repentance, and incline them to seek divine mercy. Then follow the words quoted by the Saviour. Hence the sense appears to be:—For I, thy God, desired mercy—I desired to find a contrite spirit in you, and *to exhibit* mercy (2 : 19, 20), more than I desired to *receive* your sacrifices (5 : 6). Ye Pharisees (as the Saviour now applies the text) still expect to earn the gifts of God by your religious ceremonies, and, like your fathers, ye undervalue that mercy which God desires to grant to the poor and humble sinner.—**C. For.** The connection is the following: To reclaim lost sinners, in accordance with the gracious will of God, precisely corresponds to the great purpose of My mission, *for* I came, etc.—**D. To call**—to repentance, and, ultimately, to eternal life (comp. 1 Cor. 1 : 9; 1 Thess. 2 : 12; 1 Peter 2 : 9; 5 : 10). The Lord called men personally during His ministry on earth; He now calls them by the word and Spirit.—**E. The righteous.** If men were righteous, it would not have been necessary that I should come into the world and call them to repentance; but as they are sinners, I appropriately seek them out. As Christ came to call all men to repentance, "for that all have sinned" (Rom. 5 : 12), and, consequently, including the scribes and Pharisees, whom He now addresses, it cannot be supposed that He here excludes them as objects of His call, or that in this solemn moment, when His words overflow with tender love and pity, He would ironically term them *righteous*. We read in Luke 15 : 7 of "righteous *ones*" (the word *persons* is not in the original) which need no repentance. If the Lord does not here refer to man as he existed before the fall, He may mean "the spirits of just men made perfect" (Hebr. 12 : 23) whose redemption is secured, or the angels who are holy (Mark 8 : 38; Acts 10 : 22), who kept their first estate (Jude 6), and who consequently need no repentance (see below, 18 : 12).

¹⁴ Then come to him the disciples of John, saying, Why do we and the Pharisees fast oft, but thy disciples fast not ?

A. **The disciples of John.** They are mentioned on several occasions (Matt. 11 : 2; 14 : 12; John 3 : 25); the apostle Andrew and probably the apostle John were originally his disciples (John 1 : 37, 40).—B. **Why . . . oft.** As John still belonged to the old covenant (11 : 11, and see ann. to 3 : 1, B.), and was, moreover, the preacher of godly sorrow and repentance, his disciples observed a rigid mode of fasting (6 : 16, A.).—**Oft**—on many private fast-days appointed by themselves. While John's abstinence and rigor even exceeded that of the Pharisees (Matt. 3 : 4), the Saviour conformed to the ordinary usages of society (11 : 19), for the purpose of teaching mankind the mode in which these may be hallowed by a heavenly mind. Paul teaches in reference to these points (Rom. 14 : 2-5) that an enlightened conscience conducts to purity and peace.—C. **But they . . . not.** The disciples of John had, on the one hand, learned from the testimony of their teacher that Christ's mission was divine; but, on the other, they believed, like the Pharisees, that frequent fasting ("often," Luke 5 : 33) constituted an essential part of religion. They accordingly solicit the Lord to explain the reasons in consequence of which He refrained from enjoining the some duty on His disciples (comp. 15 : 2, B.).

¹⁵ And Jesus said unto them, Can the sons of the bride-chamber mourn, as long as the bridegroom is with them? but the days will come, when the bridegroom shall be taken away from them, and then will they fast.

A. **Sons of the bride-chamber**—friends of the bridegroom—an image of the disciple (John 3 : 29), or companions (Judg. 14 : 11), who took part in the usual marriage ceremonies (see ann. to 25 : 1, D.). The Saviour reminds John's disciples that their master had already compared Him (John 3 : 29) to the bridegroom, indicating by the figure that His presence on earth denoted peace and joy. Indeed, the same image had been employed by Hosea (2 : 19, 20), to whose writings the Lord had just referred (see 8 : 11, E.).—B. **Mourn.** Fasting indicated grief of heart, unsatisfied desire, longing after a happier state (Acts 10 : 30). The prophet Zechariah had been directed to announce (8 : 19) that in the days of the Messiah, the Jewish *fasts* should be changed into " cheerful *feasts*." Would it not—asks He—be inconsistent with the joy which My presence is intended to diffuse, if I should prescribe regular fast-days, that is, periods of mourning, as if the blessings of the Gospel were still insufficient to supply all the spiritual wants of men and fill them with joy? (comp. Luke 1 : 67-80).—C. **But the days, etc.**= nevertheless, I shall, on a future day, withdraw My visible presence from the disciples under circumstances that will indeed cause them to mourn; they will then experience for a season (" your sorrow," John 16 : 20) all that grief which causes men to fast (comp. 2 Sam. 12 : 16, 21). The Lord alludes to the finishing of His work on the cross, John 19 : 30. The fulfilment of this prediction is illustrated in Matt. 26 : 56; Luke 24 : 17; John 16 : 6; 20 : 11, 19. The words, " they will fast," do not contain a command, but simply announce a future event. Hence the Church of Rome totally perverts this passage by adducing it as authority for meritorious fasts. When the true Christian observes a fast, he is influenced by some sorrow of the heart, not by a mere mechanical rule.

[16] And no man putteth a piece of undressed cloth upon an old garment; for that which should fill it up taketh from the garment, and a worse rent is made.

A. The occasion seemed to the Lord so well adapted for explaining both to the disciples of John and to those of the Pharisees the true nature and spirit of the Gospel, as contradistinguished from Judaism, that He continued the discourse.—**B. A piece of new cloth**—new, not yet fulled or dressed. Before cloth is ready for use, it is fulled or milled, that is, cleansed, scoured and pressed, in order to render it firmer, stronger and closer. As a patch of such cloth, when sewed on an old garment, would shrink on becoming wet, and tear from the seam, it would be totally unsuited to the purpose of repairing or improving the old garment.—**C. That ... it up**=the patch of *new* cloth (marg. *raw* or *unwrought* cloth).—**D. Taketh ... garment**=tears away still more of the old garment.—**E. Worse rent**=the whole purpose is defeated, and additional loss is sustained by an unwise combination of things unsuited to each other. The disciples of John, although they were taught by their master, according to 3 : 7–9, that the religion of the Jews of their day consisted of "dead works" (Hebr. 6 : 1 ; 9 : 14), could not yet comprehend the exalted purposes of the Gospel; they possibly supposed that a mere reformation of various Pharisaic abuses was sufficient. The Lord teaches them that it would be as inappropriate and destructive to combine the Christian religion with Jewish forms, as it would be to attempt to repair an old garment in the manner described.

¹⁷ Neither do men put new wine into old wine-skins: else the skins burst, and the wine is spilled, and the skins perish: but they put new wine into fresh wine-skins, and both are preserved.

A. Neither do men, etc. (see ver. 16, A.).—**B. New wine**=the expressed juice of the grape, called *must* before fermentation, during which process a gas is set free, to which vent must be given.—**C. Wine-skins.** The oriental nations, as in ancient times, still carry fluids, water, milk, wine, etc., in prepared skins of animals, generally goat or sheep-skins. The fermentation of the new wine could easily burst the old skins; hence new and strong skins were selected for new wine.—D. **They put ... wine-skins.** There must be an adaptation of means to the end, where success is expected. If—said the Saviour, addressing the disciples of the Pharisees—I should incorporate the ceremonies and usages of the Law, or your religious usages, with the Gospel, these would conflict with each other; their union is impossible. The Law has only a "shadow of good things to come" (Hebr. 10:1), and was intended only to conduct you to the Gospel (Gal. 3:23–25; Col. 2:16–23). It prefigured the blessings of the Messiah's kingdom, but could not impart them (Hebr. 9:7–10). The Gospel, on the other hand, teaches men to worship in spirit and in truth (John 4:23, 24).

¹⁸ While he spake these things unto them, behold, there came a ruler, and worshipped him, saying, My daughter is even now dead: but come and lay thy hand upon her, and she shall live.

A. **A ruler**—one of the rulers of the synagogue, who guided the public services (comp. Luke 13:14; Acts 13:15). His name was Jairus (Mark 5:22). The Hebrew form of the same name is Jair (Numb. 32:41; Esth. 2:5). Matthew had described the Lord as a deliverer from sickness and from sin; he now presents Him as a deliverer from death.—B. **Worshipped**—fell at His feet (Mark 5:22; see 2:2, D.), demonstrating his sincerity and faith.—C. **My daughter.** She was his "only daughter, about twelve years of age" (Luke 8:42). The prayers which parents offer for their children proceed from a very holy feeling which the Creator implanted in the soul, and are very acceptable to Him.—D. **Is even now dead.** The distracted father had watched at her bedside till she was at the last gasp (Luke); in his agony and despair he announces the inevitable issue—she expired while he was on the way (ver. 23, A.). He utters all his sorrows: She lies—he exclaims—at the point of death (Mark); she is even now dead.—E. **Lay . . . her**=exert Thy mighty power in her behalf (comp. 2 Kings 5 : 11, and see below, 19 : 13, B.).—F. **She shall** (=will) **live** =although now dead, she will then be restored to life.

¹⁹ And Jesus arose, and followed him, and *so did* his disciples.

Jesus arose=moved by the man's faith. " Much people followed " (Mark), eager to witness the result.

²⁰ And, behold, a woman, who had an issue of blood twelve years, came behind him, and touched the border of his garment.

A. A woman, etc. Her situation had long been most distressing; she had, according to Mark (5 : 26), been injured rather than benefited by painful remedies, the cost of which had reduced her to poverty (Luke 8 : 43). She was, moreover, excluded by the ceremonial law (Lev. 15 : 19–27) from intercourse with society.—B. **Came behind**=hoping to obtain relief without attracting public attention.—C. **Border . . . garment.** Four purple or blue ribbons were placed, as the Law directed (Numb. 15 : 37–40; Deut. 22 : 12) on the border of the square mantle worn by the Jews, forming tassels or tufts at the four corners; these were designed to remind them continually of their duty to God (see 23 : 5, C.).

²¹ For she said within herself, If I do but touch his garment, I shall be made whole.

A. If I do but (=only) **touch**=without publicly addressing Him.—B. **I shall be made whole**—literally, I shall be *saved*. This word of deep import, here equivalent to *saved from sickness* (comp. 8 : 25), as Peter also used it once (Acts 4 : 9), almost invariably refers, in the N. T., since the angel first used it (Matt. 1 : 21, B.), to a spiritual salvation or deliverance—the salvation of the soul.

22 But Jesus turning and seeing her said, Daughter, be of good cheer, thy faith hath made thee whole. And the woman was made whole from that hour.

Thy faith, etc. Faith is the hand which takes the offered grace, but that grace itself is always unmerited and free. From the details given by Mark and Luke, we learn that this woman's faith was sincere, but not enlightened. The Lord, who designed to heal her soul as well as her body, induced her to overcome her false shame, in order to convert her into a fearless and public confessor of her faith. He then teaches her that it was not His garment which relieved her, but His own conscious power, in consequence of her confidence in Him. He looked to the sincerity of her heart, more than to the original want of light in her understanding.

23 And when Jesus came into the ruler's house, and saw the flute-players and the crowd making a tumult,

A. And when ... house—after the miracle performed on the way, as stated by Mark (5 : 35) and Luke (8 : 49); the fears of the father had been well-founded, his daughter had expired while he was seeking Jesus.—**B. Flute-players**, who accompanied the singing of mournful dirges. At Jewish funerals, which, in ordinary cases, speedily followed the death of the individual (8 : 21, B.), the presence of hired mourners (Mark 5 : 38; Amos 5 : 16), chiefly females ("mourning women," Jer. 9 : 17; 2 Chron. 35 : 25), was required by the customs of the times.—**C. Making a tumult**=of lamentation: all wept and bewailed her " (Luke).

24 He said unto them, Give place: for the damsel is not dead, but sleepeth, and they laughed him to scorn.

A. Give place=withdraw, *depart ye*, as the original word is usually translated. The Lord, as Mark and Luke indicate, directed the mourners to retire, as the interment which they expected to attend would not take place. Those whom an idle curiosity alone had conducted to the spot are also removed, and none witnessed the miracle except the parents and three apostles (Mark 5 : 37-40).— **B. For . . . sleepeth.** The sense is not: She is merely in a swoon, trance, etc., for the term *sleep* is not applied to such a condition or to asphyxia. But the Saviour does apply it to the condition of one who was really dead (John 11 : 11-14). When we consider the expression in Luke 8 : 55, " her spirit came again," which implies that it had previously left the body, the sense must be as in the case of Lazarus.—C. **Laughed him to scorn** =they *derided* Him ; the hired mourners and others who had no accurate knowledge of Christ and no faith, "knowing that she was dead" (Luke), impiously ridiculed the Lord's language : " She sleepeth."

[25, 26] But when the crowd was put forth, he entered in, and took her by the hand, and the damsel arose.—And the fame hereof went forth into all that land.

A. When . . . put forth—dismissed, *sent away* (as the same word is translated, Mark 1 : 43), being too heartless and profane to be admitted as spectators of this exhibition of divine power and grace.—**B. Took . . . arose.** The touch of the Prince of life (Acts 3 : 15) restored life to her (Mark 5 : 41). The parents seem unable to credit the testimony of their own senses, until the Lord recalls their thoughts, by directing them to supply the child with food (Luke).—C. **The fame** (=report) **hereof, etc.** Do the scornful, in the presence of the living child, still laugh Him to scorn ? " Blessed is the man —that sitteth not in the seat of the scornful " (Ps. 1 : 1).

[27] And as Jesus passed by from thence, two blind men followed him, crying out and saying, Have mercy on us, thou son of David.

A. Two blind men—whom their common misfortune,

like that of the ten lepers (Luke 17 : 12), had associated together, and whose attention had been arrested by the tumult before the house of Jairus.—B. **Followed him, crying**—calling aloud, not knowing whether He were sufficiently near to observe them, and unable to control their feelings.—C. **Thou ... David**—the promised Messiah, as in 12 : 23 (see 1 : 1, C.). At this period large numbers of the people, besides these blind men, already regarded Christ as the Messiah, Even the woman of Canaan (15 : 22) had learned to know Him in this exalted character.—D. **Have mercy on us** (comp. Ps. 123 : 3). They knew that it lay in His power to afford relief. Possibly the prophet's beautiful description of the Messiah's kingdom (ver. 5 of Isai., ch. 35), which they had heard read in the synagogue, often formed the subject of their reflections. All men, whatever their sorrows may be, are permitted to appeal to the same divine pity and compassion, and all who believe will receive a gracious hearing.

[28] And when he was come into the house, the blind men came to him: and Jesus saith unto them, Believe ye that I am able to do this? They say unto him, Yea, Lord.

A. **The house**—in Capernaum where He lodged.—A. **The blind ... him.** Their perseverance is an evidence of their earnestness and faith. They *followed*, as He would not pause on the way (see ver. 30, B.).—C. **Believe ye, etc.** Since Jesus knew their thoughts, as well as those of the scribes mentioned above (ver. 3, 4), He cannot have asked this question for the sake of information ; so, too, as our Father knoweth our wants (6: 32), we do not pray for the purpose of giving Him information. An open and fearless confession of the truth, and a distinct recognition of the claims of God, essentially belong to a living faith. Such a declaration is therefore required in Rom. 10 : 9, 10, as well as in Matt. 10 : 32;

Acts 8 : 37. The confession of faith, in this instance, also included a recognition of Christ as the promised Messiah.

⁹⁹ *Then touched he their eyes, saying, According to your faith be it done unto you.*

A. **Touched . . . eyes**=to furnish evidence that He personally healed them by His divine power, independently of any visible means.—A. **According to, etc.** The sense is: Since ye have such faith, ye shall obtain divine mercy; a weak faith would have impaired the power of your prayers; the want of faith would have excluded you from all participation in the gifts of God.

³⁰ *And their eyes were opened; and Jesus strictly charged them, saying, See that no man know it.*

A. **Their eyes were opened**=their sight was perfectly restored; this figurative expression, in the sense of *to see, to perceive*, frequently occurs.—A. **Strictly charged, etc.** =with deep feeling impressed the prohibition. The original word indicates a very powerful emotion, translated *groaned* in John 11 : 33; here it seems to imply that the Lord was painfully moved by the circumstances which required such a prohibition. Inasmuch as He had just performed a very striking miracle (ver. 25), which already attracted public attention, the prohibition apparently refers not so much to the publication of the fact that their sight had been restored, as specially to the premature communication that He was the Son of David, a title of the Messiah, which, more than any other, was adapted to arouse the carnal hopes of the Jews, and produce political tumults (comp. 16 : 20).

³¹ *But they went forth, and spread abroad his fame in all that country.*

Spread abroad=both indirectly, by appearing to many who knew their previous condition, and directly, by communicating the fact that He possessed power to heal. Matthew does not, however, state that they violated the Lord's command to withhold for a season the fact from the public that He was the true Messiah. The word here translated *but* (Greek, *de*) is rendered by *and* in ver. 28. Here it is merely a term continuing the narrative, and introducing the statement of the circumstance that they were the means of spreading, etc. There is another Greek word which strictly signifies *but*, as in 4 : 4 ; 5 : 15, and which indicates things that are opposite, but it does not occur here (see 5 : 1, A.).

³² And as they went forth, behold there was brought to him a dumb man possessed with a devil.

A. As they—the Lord and His attendants, the disciples, were leaving the house, after the departure of the blind men.—**B. They brought**—certain persons, doubtless friends of the man, encouraged by the recent evidences of the Lord's power and kindness.—**C. A dumb . . . devil.** This demoniac had not been originally mute. Matthew introduces the case as an illustration of the power of the unclean spirit, which either fettered the organs of speech, or produced that total prostration of the mind, which, even in cases of ordinary madness, results in an apparently sullen and obstinate silence.

³³ And when the devil was cast out, the dumb man spake; and the multitudes marvelled, saying, It was never so seen in Israel.

A. Spake—as an evidence of the entire liberation of his mind and body from the influence of the unclean spirit. May we not imagine that his first words were those of grateful praise ? (comp. Ps. 35 : 28).—**B. It was, etc.** What was never so seen in Israel (—among the Jews, 8 : 10, C.). The analogous case in 12 : 22-24 indicates that there is here a reference to the character of Christ as the Son of David, the Messiah, so that the sense is : No one ever before among the Jews furnished such evidences tnat he was the Messiah. Such a tendency of the people to regard the Lord as the Messiah (ver. 27, C.) induced the Pharisees in their madness to employ the blasphemous language found in the next verse, in order to account for a miracle, the reality of which they could not deny.

³⁴ But the Pharisees said, By the prince of the devils casteth he out devils.

Casteth he out, etc. This is the first recorded instance of the malignity of the Pharisees in ascribing a glorious work of divine power to the agency of Satan. They were unable (precisely as in John 9:16 and Acts 4:16) to deny the actual performance of the miracle, but they gratified their hatred by impiously pretending, in opposition to their own convictions, that an agreement existed between the Lord and Satan. (This charge, to which there is a reference in 10:25, was repeated in 12:24, in a case in which a man was also dumb as well as blind.)

³⁵ And Jesus went about all the cities and the villages, teaching in their synagogues, and preaching the gospel of the kingdom, and healing all manner of disease and all manner of sickness.

A. **Jesus went about** (see 4:23, where a similar sketch of the labors of Christ in Galilee is given). On this occasion He takes a southerly direction towards Jerusalem.—B. **Cities and villages.** The extraordinary fertility of the soil of Galilee enabled a vast multitude to dwell within its comparatively narrow limits. Josephus says that there were 240 cities and villages in Galilee, of which the smallest contained above 15,000 inhabitants (Life, ch. 45; J., War., III. 3, 2. For **Gospel** see 4:23, C.).

³⁶ But when he saw the multitudes, he was moved with compassion for them. because they were distressed and scattered as sheep not having a shepherd.

A. **The multitudes**=resorting to Him (Mark 2:13).—

A. **He was . . . compassion.** The words which now follow doubtless furnish the sense of the language in which the Lord expressed His pity (comp. 14: 14 and Mark 6 : 34; see Matt. 18 : 27, A. for the original term). —C. **They were distressed**—*were harassed*, exhausted by the burdens which the evil times laid on them, and the exactions of their religious teachers (Matt. 23 : 4; comp. Ezek. 34 : 2–6).—D. **Scattered**—left unguarded, were *cast down*, as the same word is rendered in 15 : 30; 27 : 5, that is, contemptuously *cast* aside by the scribes and Pharisees; hence they are called "lost sheep" (10 : 6). They received from their callous teachers none of the consolations of religion.—E. **As sheep, etc.** There is here apparently an affecting allusion to the words of Moses, who entreats the Lord to provide a successor after his death, that the people may not be "as sheep which have no shepherd" (Numb. 27 : 17 ; comp. also 1 Kings 22 : 17; Isai. 53 : 6; Jer. 50 : 6; Ezek. 34 : 5.); the same image is expanded by the Lord Himself in John 10 : 12, and see below, 10 : 6.

[37] Then saith he unto his disciples, The harvest truly is plenteous, but the labourers are few.

A. The gathering of men into the kingdom of God was elsewhere compared to the labors of the harvest field (John 4 : 35). The view of the spiritual state of the Jews induced Him to send forth the seventy disciples (Luke 10 : 1, 2), to whom he addressed the same language.—B. **Plenteous**—large abundant, while the *harvest* here refers more immediately to the Jewish people, the *field* is the world (13 : 38). As a saving knowledge of the truth is designed for all men without exception (1 Tim. 2 ; 4), the parting words of the Lord to His messengers, are: "Go ye into all the world, and preach the Gospel to every creature" (Mark 16 : 15).—C. **The labourers, etc.**

—the heralds of the Gospel are few, compared with the vast numbers composing the entire human race, "all nations" (28: 19). The words, too, possibly allude to the comparatively small number of those who had hitherto become the Lord's disciples.

³⁸ Pray ye therefore the Lord of the harvest, that he send forth labourers into his harvest.

A. **Pray**—*beseech*, as the word is often rendered (Luke 8: 38), or, *entreat*, without the divine blessing, all human labors are vain (1 Cor. 3: 6, 7; Ps. 127: 1).—B. **The Lord of the harvest.** This title corresponds to the one in Mark 12: 9, the *Lord* (master, owner) of the vineyard. The householder in Matt. 13: 27, who sowed good seed, is declared by Christ to be an image of Himself (13 : 37). According to this interpretation, the Lord of the harvest is Christ, the head of the Church (Eph. 1 : 22). Hence, the admonition: Pray, beseech Me to send, etc., must involve the following sense: If you sincerely desire the coming of the kingdom, you will not only be willing to go forth yourselves, but you will also express your sympathy for the lost sheep around us, by entreating Me to associate many others with you.—The Lord desires to awaken a missionary spirit in the hearts of His people, and encourage a spirit of prayer (comp. 1 Tim. 2 : 1–3); He also desires them to manifest the sincerity of their prayers by furnishing the means to send forth laborers to heathen nations.—C. **Send forth.** The original employs the same word which is translated *driveth* in Mark 1 : 12, descriptive of a divine impulse. While a call to the ministry in the Church at the present day is not of a miraculous nature, still, the sacred office cannot be rightly assumed, unless the individual is altogether governed by holy impulses, and gives his whole heart to the " good work " (1 Tim. 3 : 1).—D. **His harvest**—the glory resulting from the conversion of the world—the inheritance of the Lord Jesus (Ps. 2 : 8)—belongs to Him; the joy and happiness which thence result are imparted to the redeemed.

CHAPTER X.

¹ And he called unto him his twelve disciples, and gave them authority over unclean spirits, to cast them out, and to heal all manner of disease and all manner of sickness.

A. And . . . disciples. The Lord had, according to Mark (3 : 13 ff.) and Luke (6 : 13), selected the Twelve from the whole number of His disciples. Matthew, who had hitherto mentioned the calling of only five of the whole number (4 : 18, 21 ; 9 : 9), here implies, by mentioning " the twelve," that the twelve *Apostles* (as the Lord Himself called them, Luke 6 : 13) already constituted a regularly organized company. He had reserved the full list of their names until he reached this point of time, when he designed to record the instructions which he and his eleven associates received on the eve of their first mission.—The motive of the Lord in selecting *twelve* disciples, and not enlarging the number antecedently to His ascension, is not revealed. They are an entirely distinct company from the Seventy whom He afterwards sent forth (Luke 10 : 1), and who seem to correspond to the seventy elders of Israel (Exod. 24 : 1 ; Numb. 11 : 16). The founders of the twelve tribes constituting the Jewish nation were the twelve sons of Jacob (Gen. 35 : 23–26 ; ch. 46) ; the whole nation was subsequently represented by the twelve princes or heads of the tribes (Numb. 1 : 44).—**B. He gave, etc.**—by the exercise of that almighty word which gave soundness to a withered hand (12 : 13) life to the dead (John 11 : 43, 44), and forgiveness to the sinner (Matt. 9 : 2). This divine authority of Christ now invests the Twelve with power to work the miracles here mentioned. " He does not send them forth with carnal weapons, but gives them others which are far more mighty (2 Cor. 10 : 4), whereby they can overcome sin, the devil and death."—LUTHER.

^{2, 4} Now the names of the twelve apostles are these: The first, Simon, who is called Peter, and Andrew, his brother; James, *the son* of Zebedee, and John his brother; Philip, and Bartholomew; Thomas, and Matthew the publican; James *the son* of Alpheus, and Thaddeus;—Simon the Canaanæan, and Judas Iscariot, who also betrayed him.

⁵ These twelve Jesus sent forth, and charged them, saying, Go not into *any* way of the Gentiles, and enter not into any city of the Samaritans.

A. Several portions of this extended address of the Lord, referring to the first mission of the Twelve, were afterwards repeated in their presence, and also combined with the instructions which He gave when He sent forth the Seventy (see Luke, ch. 9, ch. 19 and ch. 12). They contain the essential principles by which the heralds of the cross were to be governed in all their future labors. **B. Go not in any way of**—into the vicinity or territory. —**C. Gentiles**=heathens (see 4 : 15, 16, A.).—**D. Samaritans**—the people of Samaria.—**E. Enter ye not.** This prohibition to visit Gentiles and Samaritans was merely temporary (8 : 7, B.); indeed, the Lord proved by His example that the Samaritans (John, ch. 4) and the Gentiles (Matt. 15 : 21) were not rejected. He designed to establish His Church first of all among the Jews, to whom the promises had been given (Rom. 9 : 4; 15 : 8–12), and then receive all the nations of the earth into it (see Matt. 28 : 19, C.). In this sense His words are to be understood in 15 : 24. At the present period, the Gentiles and Samaritans (Luke 9 : 52, 53) were not prepared to receive the Gospel. Besides, this mission of the Twelve was not of a general nature, but rather constituted a part of the training or education of the disciples, while they were "with Him" (Mark 3 : 14). "At this period they resemble students of theology, whose preparatory course is not yet completed."—BENGEL. When the proper time had arrived (24 : 14 ; 28 : 19), the Lord, before His ascension, removed all restrictions and enlarged the commission of the apostles to the fullest extent (as in Acts 26 : 17) by saying : "Ye shall be witnesses unto me both in Jerusalem, and in all Judæa, and in Samaria, and unto the uttermost part of the earth" (Acts 1 : 8. Comp. Acts 2 : 39 ; 3 : 26 ; 13 : 46 ; Rom. 2 : 9, 10 and ch. 11, as well as Isai. 49 : 6, on the order of the time in the calling of the Jews and the Gentiles).

⁶ But go rather to the lost sheep of the house of Israel.

The Lord alludes to His own words, which Matthew appears to quote in 9 : 36, and which are suggested by affecting images of the religious wants of the Jews, in the prophets (see 9 : 36, E., and comp. Luke 15 : 4 ; 1 Pet. 2 : 25). They are **lost**—not merely led astray by false doctrines, but, as far as human aid avails, inextricably lost, helpless, perishing (comp. 18 : 12, 14) ; the good Shepherd alone can save them. For *Israel*, see 8 : 10, C.

⁷ And as ye go, preach, saying, The kingdom of heaven is at hand.

Preach (3 : 1, C.) **saying, etc.** (comp. 3 : 2 and 4 : 17). A gradation in the use of this general theme—"the kingdom of God"—may be assumed. When John discoursed on it, he announced that the Lord would speedily appear ; when the Lord Himself began to proclaim it (4 : 17), He announced that He had really appeared, bringing the gift of eternal life with Him (John 1 : 17 ; 2 Tim. 1 : 10). The disciples are now sent forth to furnish to all the proof (comp. 11 : 5) that the work itself of man's salvation was actually begun (comp. the commission given after the

Resurrection, Mark 16 : 15, 16). "Here, too, we learn that ministers of the Gospel are to preach, not on worldly matters, but on the 'things pertaining to the kingdom of God' (Acts 1 : 3), that is, to eternal life, including the scripture doctrines respecting righteousness, remission of sins, etc."—LUTHER.

⁸ Heal the sick, raise the dead, cleanse the lepers, cast out devils : freely ye received, freely give.

A. **Heal ... devils** (comp. for illustrations Mark 6 : 13 ; Luke 10 : 17 ; Acts 9 : 36 ff.; 20 : 10–12). The chief purpose for which the apostles received the power of working miracles was, to prove that God had really sent them ; thus the word was confirmed "with signs following" (Mark 16 : 20; comp. Acts 4 : 29, 30).—B. **Freely ... give.** The original word for *freely* (translated *for nought* in 2 Thess. 3 : 8) is here equivalent to *gratuitously* (comp. its use in Rev. 21 : 6 ; 22 : 17, and the prophet's analogous expression in Isai. 55 : 1). The Lord's own words (alluding to Deut. 24 : 15), in ver. 10 below : " The workman is worthy of his food," as well as those which He addressed to the Seventy (Luke 10 : 7), and the lessons taught by the inspired apostle (1 Cor. 9 : 7–14 ; Gal. 6 : 6 ; 1 Tim. 5 : 18), show that He does not forbid His disciples to receive an adequate support. He reminds them that they had not earned nor merited the gift of the Spirit, and forbids them to perform miracles and preach the Gospel only for the sake of pecuniary gain. The grace of God which had been imparted to them, and which was to be communicated by them to others, is incapable of being bought or sold (comp. Acts 8 : 18–23).

⁹ Get you no gold, nor silver, nor brass in your purses.

A. **Get you no gold, etc.**—procure as a supply on the road. In the present case, divine providence would

always furnish a supply for the wants of the disciples.—
B. Nor . . . brass—not only not gold and silver coins, but not even the smallest copper or brass coin in circulation, called a *lepton* (translated *mite*, Mark 12 : 42; see 5 : 25, 26, B.).—**C. Purses**—girdles or belts, which secured the money carried on the person (3 : 4, B.).

[10] Nor wallet for your journey, neither two coats, nor shoes, nor staff: for the laborer is worthy of his food.

A. Wallet—a sack or pouch, often made of leather, in which travellers carried provisions, as bread (Mark 6 : 8). David carried the stone in his wallet, with which he slew the Philistine (1 Sam. 17 : 40, 49).—**B. Two coats**—an additional *chiton* or under-garment (5 : 40, B.), besides the one already carried on the person.—**C. Shoes.** The word here translated *shoes* may possibly describe an article which covered the traveller's entire foot; in Mark 6 : 9 *sandals* or soles of wood or leather are allowed; but see 3 : 11, C.—**D. Nor staff.** The Lord desires to educate His disciples for their future more important apostolic labors, and train them for future trials by the present experience of God's protecting power. Such was the great lesson which He desired to inculcate practically. The sense of His words then is: Go forth, in dependence on the presence and direct aid of God. Take no money with you, for God will provide (comp. Deut. 31 : 6); encumber yourselves with no articles of clothing which you do not now wear on your persons. If you have no staff, do not seek for one. Depend solely on the presence and power of God. In our day, when such promises are not specially given, no *miraculous* supply of the ordinary wants of an individual can be expected by him.—**E. For . . . food**—*maintenance* (see 3 : 4, C.). In 1 Tim. 5 : 18, the word is hire—stipend, remuneration. The sense of the whole is: As laborers in the service of God, you will not be forgotten by Him; all your wants shall be supplied either through the instrumentality of those among whom you minister, or otherwise (see above, ver. 8, B.). " Hence, those who call themselves Christians, and who nevertheless withhold their contributions, and do not support the ministers of the Word, commit a grievous sin, and shall hereafter give an account of their stewardship to Him who here says: ' The workman, etc.' "—LUTHER.

¹¹ And into whatsoever city or village ye shall enter, search out who in it is worthy; and there abide till ye go forth.

B. Search out—by presenting the Gospel, and observing, for your own information the spirit in which it is received.—**C. Worthy.** The Greek word usually translated *worthy*, often (e. g. 22 : 8, B.) conveys the sense of *corresponding* or *adapted to* anything, as in Eph. 4 : 1. The **worthy** here are, not any who *deserve* the grace of God, which is always unmerited and free, but the poor in spirit (5 : 3), who hunger and thirst after righteousness (5 : 6), who feel that they labor and are heavy laden (11 : 28), and in deep penitence seek the forgiveness of their sins (Luke 18 : 13).—**C. There abide**—in that house, while you remain in the city or town ; do not change your place of lodging, for the sake of finding elsewhere greater personal comforts (Luke 10 : 7, " eating, etc."), and, on the other hand, do not go from house to house, as if you were simply mendicants or vagrants.

¹² And as ye enter into the house, salute it.

Salute it—the inmates or family (John 4 : 53; 1 Cor. 16 : 15) by saying: " Peace be to this house " (Luke 10 : 5 ; comp. Ruth 2 : 4). This ancient mode of greeting (Judg. 19 : 20; John 20 : 19) is still observed in the eastern countries. When this salutation proceeds from the Lord Jesus, as in Luke 24 : 36, it is not a mere formality (Matt. 5 : 47), but really conveys a divine blessing, as the Lord Himself declares (John 14 : 27). A genuine, unaffected politeness is the natural result of the holy principle of Christian love, and is inspired by the benign spirit of the Christian faith (see Isai. 52 : 7). When the apostles wrote letters (Acts 15 : 23; James 1 : 1) to brethren of Greek origin, they courteously used the corresponding Greek salutation—"Greeting" (for which see 26 : 49, B.). In Luke 10 : 4 mere ceremonious greetings *by* (—on) *the way* are prohibited.

¹³ And if the house be worthy, let your peace come upon it; but if it be not worthy, let your peace return to you.

A. If . . . worthy—if the members of the family meet you in a spirit indicating a thirst after divine truth and grace, or, at least, a willingness to hear.—**B. Let your . . . it**—then communicate to them the tidings of the kingdom, and bestow upon them the blessings which I empower you (ver. 1 and ver. 7) to impart. Indeed, a Christian salutation addressed to another, and proceeding from a holy frame of mind (1 Thess. 5 : 17), is not a mere formality, but a prayer which has power with God.—**C. Let your peace. etc.** (comp. Isai. 55 : 11). The sense is: Withdraw from those whose rejection of the offered mercy demonstrates that they are not ready and prepared to receive divine grace (see 7 : 6, F.).

¹⁴ And whosoever shall not receive you, nor hear your words, as ye go forth out of that house or that city, shake off the dust of your feet.

A. Whosoever . . . words—when the people of a city or town altogether and obstinately refuse to receive the message and the blessing which I send through you, thus in reality despising God (1 Thess. 4 : 8, and below, ver. 40).—**B. When . . . city**—and when ye withdraw in sorrow.—**C. Shake . . . feet.** Symbolical actions, designed to express some thought or feeling with great emphasis, are frequently described in the O. T. (see, for instance, Nehem. 5 : 13, and also Acts 18 : 6). Even Pilate understood the force with which such an act appealed to the judgment and feelings of a spectator (27 : 24). The act of shaking off the dust from the feet, when performed by one who was departing, implied that between him and those whom he abandoned not the slightest bond or connection, represented by particles of dust, any longer existed. (Comp. Acts 13 : 50, 51, where Paul and Barnabas do not by any means, like ordinary Jews, express a feeling of contempt or spiritual pride by that act, but imply that the unbelieving people had thus cast off God and His word.)

¹⁵ Verily I say unto you, It shall be more tolerable for the land of Sodom and Gomorrah in the day of judgment than for that city.

A. **Verily** (see 5 : 18, A.).—A **More tolerable**—a less heavy punishment shall be inflicted, one more easily endured (comp. 11 : 22).—C. **The land**—the inhabitants, as in Isai. 37 : 11.—D. **Sodom and Gomorrah.** These two cities were situated in the vale of Siddim; after their destruction in the days of Abraham (Gen. ch. 19), the whole territory was occupied by the Salt Sea (Gen. 14: 3; Deut. 3 : 17), now called the Dead Sea (Lake Asphaltites). The awful judgment which overwhelmed the wicked inhabitants made them " an ensample (=example), etc." (2 Pet. 2 : 6; Jude 7, and comp. Deut. 29 : 23; Isai. 1 : 9; Lam. Jer. 4 : 6; Amos 4 : 11.—E. **Day of judgment**—at the end of the world, when the living and the dead shall appear before the Judge and receive their final sentence (John 5 : 22–29; Matt. 25 : 31 ff.; Rom. 2 : 5; 2 Thess. 1 : 7–10).—F. **Than for that city.** The cause that the judgment and punishment of those who reject the Gospel are more severe than those of the people who " vexed the righteous soul " of Lot (2 Peter 2 : 6–8), lies in the greater guilt of the former. These had received a greater amount of light and knowledge (Moses and the prophets, Luke 16 : 29; John the Baptist, and Christ Himself and His apostles), and hence their impenitence was still less excusable than that of Gentiles (comp. 11 : 21–24, and Luke 12 : 47, 48; Rom. 1 : 20; 2 : 17 ff.).

¹⁶ Behold, I send you forth as sheep in the midst of wolves; be ye therefore wise as serpents, and harmless as doves.

A. I send. The original here (by inserting the pronoun *I*, which is ordinarily omitted) indicates an emphasis—I, who am guided by unerring wisdom, *I* send you on this dangerous mission.—**B. Sheep . . . wolves.** In such proverbial expressions only one point of comparison is introduced, and the terms are not to be interpreted beyond that one point. (See the case in which the Lord compares His unexpected coming to that of a thief, Matt. 24 : 43, 44, and comp. 7 : 6, A.) The *sheep* is an image of gentleness and unresisting endurance (Isai. 53 : 7), the *wolf*, of violence and oppression (comp. 7 : 15, C.; John 10 : 12). "What a wonderful struggle we see here! Twelve sheep are sent out to meet an innumerable multitude of wolves! Now, the Lord sends, not lions but sheep among the wolves, in order to manifest, unto His own glory, that the cause of the mighty result lies, not in the wisdom of man, but in the power of God (1 Cor. 2 : 5),"—LUTHER.—**C. Serpents . . . doves.** Two proverbial phrases are here combined, so that one may limit the other. The *serpent* (3 ; 7, B.) was regarded already in the earliest ages as a symbol of wisdom or prudence, and even of artfulness or cunning (Gen. 3 : 1; see 13 : 33, B.). Its habit of gliding away noiselessly when danger is near, is selected here as the sole point of comparison. The disciples are commanded to retire quietly, when their preaching finds no response. On account of its gentle traits, the Lord presents the dove as an image of the candor, sincerity and purity of motives by which He desires the disciples to be characterized (comp. Phil. 2 : 15 ; 2 Cor. 1 : 12). He teaches them that they should not needlessly provoke opposition to the Gospel by any imprudence, by passion or by selfish feelings on their part.

¹⁷ But beware of men: for they will deliver you up to councils, and in their synagogues they will scourge you ;

A. Beware of men—" see that ye walk circumspectly " (Eph. 5 : 15) among hostile men ; do not commit yourselves unto them (John 2 : 24), so that if any *deliver you up*, you may not suffer as those who are really evil-doers (1 Peter 4 : 15). Such severe persecutions are not to discourage, for, in the case of the believer, they " turn to his salvation " (Phil. 1 : 19).—**B. Councils**=not only the Sanhedrin or supreme council, but also the inferior tribunals in the cities of Palestine.—**C. Scourge, etc.** (comp. 23 : 34; 24 : 9; Acts 5 : 40; 22 : 19 ; 26 : 11 ; 2 Cor. 11 : 24). The number of stripes could not legally (Deut. 25 : 3) exceed *forty*, and might be less. Thirteen blows with a scourge having three lashes were regarded by the Jews as equivalent to thirty-nine stripes (2 Cor. 11 : 25). The Romans did not observe this humane specification (Matt. 27 : 26, B.)

¹⁸ Yea, and before governors and kings shall ye be brought for my sake, for a testimony to them and to the Gentiles.

A. Governors. The original gives the Greek term for the procurators, proconsuls and proprætors, who were appointed by the Roman government as rulers over provinces; such were Pilate (27 : 2), Felix (Acts 23 : 24) and Festus (Acts 25 : 1). See 1 Peter 2 : 14.—**B. Kings** (see Acts 12 : 2, 3; 25 : 2).—**C. For my sake** (see 9 : 11, D. and Acts 5 : 41).**D**—. **For a testimony**=to the Jews in the councils and synagogues respecting Me and My Gospel (see 8 : 4, D., and comp. John 15 : 27 ; Acts 1 : 8 ; 22 : 15).—E. **Gentiles**—the governors and kings with their attendants. For **Gentiles**, see 4 : 15, A. In this portion of the Lord's instruction, as in Luke 21 : 12, where the same prophetic words are repeated, He appears to refer not so much to the particular journey which the disciples were now on the point of taking, as to their later experience generally in the work of preaching the Gospel.

¹⁹ But when they deliver you up, be not anxious how or what ye shall speak: for it shall be given you in that same hour what ye shall speak.

A. **Be not . . . speak**—entertain no anxiety respecting, etc. (see 6 : 25, B.) On a later occasion, when these words were repeated, the explanatory words are added: "neither do ye premeditate" (Mark 13 : 11), "meditate before" (Luke 21 : 14); they correspond to those addressed to Moses in a similar case (Exod. 4 : 10–12). They mean, not that the disciples should refrain from thinking on their approaching trials, but that they should not suppose that their deliverance would depend on their own ingenuity and well-studied addresses to the judge ; "*how*"—the manner and style; "*what*"—the matter to be introduced into the address.—B. **It shall . . . speak**—ye shall receive such wisdom, as to utter in these circumstances precisely the words best suited to the case, and such as none can gainsay nor resist (Luke 21 : 15 ; comp. Isai. 50 : 4). The promise was invaribly fulfilled, for instance, in Acts 2 : 14 ; ff. ; 3 : 12 ff. ; 5 : 19, 20 ff. ; ver. 29 ff. ; 7 : 2 ff.

²⁰ For it is not ye that speak, but the Spirit of your Father that speaketh in you.

A. **For . . . Father**—not your own mind or spirit (2 Sam. 23 : 2), but the Holy Ghost, one of the Persons of the blessed Trinity, by whom the prophets and apostles were inspired (see John 16:13, 14; 1 Cor. 2 : 10-13; 1 Peter 1:10-12; 2 Peter 1: 21). In the whole work of grace, whereby the sinner is called, enlightened, awakened, enabled to believe and to pray, justified, sanctified and ultimately saved, the author of all is God, through Christ, by His Spirit.—B. **Which speaketh, etc.** By this gift of inspiration the apostles were qualified to become infallible teachers of divine truth. That gift disappeared after the age of the apostles. At present, men are neither inspired, when they preach the Gospel, nor enabled to work miracles like the apostles; but the converting and sanctifying influences of the divine Spirit, as connected with the means of grace, are now as fully granted to those who will receive the Gospel, as they were in the earliest periods of the Church.

[21] And brother shall deliver up brother to death, and the father his child: and children shall rise up against parents, and cause them to be put to death.

The Saviour here glances at the future trials of His followers, and alludes prophetically to the bitterness of feeling which the persecutors of His people will manifest (see below, 24: 10). Their hatred of religion (sanctioned by their erring judgment, John 16:2; Acts 26:9), will be so intense as to extinguish all natural affection ("without natural affection," Rom. 1: 31). During the early persecutions of the Christians, cases repeatedly occurred in which pagans delivered their nearest relations to torture and death.—**Deliver up**—inform against, surrender.—**Rise up**—as witnesses against (comp. 12 : 41). Both terms here imply an active, persecuting spirit, as in ver. 17.

[22] And ye shall be hated of all men for my name's sake: but he that endureth to the end the same shall be saved.

A. **Ye ... hated of** (—*by*) **all**—the unbelieving Jews and Gentiles whom you encounter, and whose evil deeds your religion condemns (John 3 : 19, 20; 15 : 18; · 1 John 3 : 13, and see below, 24 : 9, B.). The various religious systems of the heathens tolerated or recognized one another; the Christian religion could recognize none of them, but rejected all, and hence it alone encountered universal opposition, and was hated by "all nations."— B. **For my name's sake**—because ye are My followers; thus the hatred of the world (James 4 : 4) of which I am the object (John 7 : 7), will be transferred to you.—C. **Endureth to the end**—of his earthly pilgrimage, the hour of death (John 13 : 1), keeping his faith until he finish his course (2 Tim. 4 : 7; Rev. 2 : 10, 26).—D. **Shall be saved**—from his sins (1 : 21), and consequently from their punishment, which is eternal death. According to the analogous passage (2 Tim. 4 : 18), the present words involve the sense : He shall (although even killed, as James was (Acts 12 : 2), nevertheless enter the heavenly kingdom—"though he were dead, yet shall he live" (John 11 : 25).

[23] But when they persecute you in this city, flee into the next: for verily I say unto you, Ye shall not have gone through the cities of Israel, till the Son of man be come.

A. **But ... the next.** This the apostles are described as having afterwards frequently done (Acts 13 : 51; 17 : 10, 33; 20 : 1).—B. **Ye ... be come.** The original may also be rendered : *Ye shall not have completed.* The original Greek word is rendered : *made an end* (11 : 1); *finished* (13 : 53); *accomplished* (Luke 2 : 39); *accomplished* (Luke 18 : 31); *fulfilled* (Acts 13 : 29, and elsewhere). It unquestionably involves the idea of *completion.* It is not probable that the Lord refers in the words: *till . . . come* to His own journey mentioned in 11 : 1, in the sense that He would soon come to them —*overtake* them, since it is on the contrary stated (Luke 9 : 10) that they came back to Him. The following is probably the sense of the words: Do not expend your time in any city where your labor is fruitless, for you can always find a field elsewhere. If you should even survive till the Son of man be come, you would not have fully completed the great work assigned to you. Now the *first* coming of the Lord occurred when He assumed our nature (John 1 : 14; 6 : 38; Matt. 2 : 6; 5 : 17; 18 : 11). His *second* coming will occur at the end of the world, and will be visible. But, while Christ appears personally and *visibly* on both occasions, the first, and the second, there may be various *intermediate comings*, in which *His presence will not be visible*. His visible and invisible presence are carefully distinguished in John 14 : 25 (comp. with Matt. 28 : 20, "I am, etc."). There is a coming in the spirit (Matt. 18 : 20); there is a coming (John 14 : 3; 21 : 22; 24 : 44, C.), whenever a believer dies. It might therefore be expected that several Greek words of the same general signification would be employed in connection with the Lord's coming. The first (apokalupsis) in 2 Thess. 1 : 7; 1 Peter 1 : 7, 13; the second (eisodos) in Acts 13 : 24; the third (eleusis) in Acts 7 : 52; the fourth and most usual (parousia) in Matt. 24 : 3, 27, 37, 39; 1 Cor. 15 : 22; 1 Thess. 2 : 19; 3 : 13; 1 John 2 : 28, and frequently in the epistles. A fifth term (epiphaneia), in 1 Tim. 6 : 14; 2 Tim. 4 : 1, 8, is usually translated "appearing."—*That* coming which is strictly the *second visible* coming is distinguished from every intermediate or invisible coming by significant terms indicating *manifestation* (2 Thess. 2 : 8), or *visibility* (the fifth term just mentioned), or *revelation* (the first), or an actual, visible

16

presence (the fourth).—One of the *intermediate* comings of Christ, marked by His power but not by His visible presence, is revealed in Matt. 16 : 28 ; according to these words, this coming will occur during the lifetime of "some standing" there when the words were pronounced. It appears from the parallel passages (Matt. 16 : 28; Mark 9 : 1 ; Luke 9 : 27), that those persons would, before they "tasted of death," that is, within a period shorter than an ordinary lifetime, "see the kingdom of God come with power." The expression therefore means that the Son of man would come in "power," but not visibly. Now, when the Lord said to His disciples : " I will not leave you comfortless: I will come to you " (John 14 : 18), *that* coming was spiritual and invisible, according to ver. 23 of the same chapter, "we will come, etc. ;" and, as ver. 16, 26, show, the promise was fulfilled in the outpouring of the Holy Ghost. This event or coming of Christ with power occurred on the day of Pentecost. On that day the Church of Christ was founded (Acts 2 : 47). But it is this Church of Christ, in its different aspects, which often receives precisely the name of *kingdom* in the parables (see 13 : 24, B.; ver. 31, A.; ver. 44, A.; ch. 16 : 18, D.). That kingdom truly came "with power" according to Peter's words (Acts 2 : 16, ff.), and it was, according to ver. 33 of Acts, ch. 2, the fulfilment of "the promise of the Holy Ghost." Hence, the coming of the Lord in the present text refers, not to His transfiguration, described in ch. 17, nor to His resurrection, nor to the destruction of Jerusalem, but to His coming in power when He poured out the Spirit, who was to "abide with them forever" (John 16 : 16). The sense of the whole passage then is : The work of preaching the Gospel is so vast, that you will not have proclaimed it even to all the inhabitants of Palestine before the day of

Pentecost, when "ye shall be endued with power from on high " (Luke 24 : 49 ; Acts 1 : 8).

²⁴ *A disciple is not above his master, nor a servant above his lord.*

This saying was often repeated by the Lord (Luke 6 : 40; John 13 : 16; 15 : 20). The word in the two latter passages translated *greater* (equivalent to *superior, better*) explains it when translated *above* in this text. The sense is: Complain not that you suffer persecution while you disinterestedly labor for the welfare of your fellow-men, for I, your Master and Lord (John 13 : 13), have voluntarily exposed Myself to even greater trials.

²⁵ *It is enough for the disciple that he be as his master, and the servant as his lord. If they have called the master of the house Beelzebub, how much more shall they call them of his household ?*

A. **It is enough**—*it may suffice*, as the word is rendered in 1 Peter 4 : 3—it should satisfy you.—A. **For the . . . lord**=that the disciple or servant should experience joys and sorrows like those of his lord. Those who by self-denial, fidelity and a living faith participate in the sorrows, shall also participate hereafter in the joy of their Lord (John 17 : 22 ; Rom. 8 : 29 ; 2 Cor. 3 : 18 ; Phil. 3 : 21 ; 2 Tim. 2 : 12 ; 1 John 3 : 2).—C. **Beelzebub.** Baal, often mentioned in the O. T. (Judg. 2 : 13), was an idol worshipped by the ancient Phenicians and others, and coincides with the Babylonian Bel (Isai. 46 : 1) ; the Philistines of Ekron (2 Kings 1 : 2, 3, 16) called this god Baal-Zebub=Lord of the flies, alluding, according to some interpreters, to a supposed deliverance of the land by him from swarms of the poisonous fly (gad-fly) mentioned in Isai. 7 : 18. Others suppose that he was worshipped in the form of a summer-fly, in allusion to Baal, the god of the sun. The fly was thus an image of the sun-god. By simply changing the final letter, the name assumes the form of Beelzebub, as the translators print it in the margin. This latter name, signifying *Lord of filth* (dung), was now given by the Jews in derision to the idol, according to the most probable of several explanations, and was then applied to the prince of devils.—D. **How much more, etc.**=if they have not hesitated to apply such a contumelious term to Me, how much more readily will they calumniate you. The original (see 20 : 11, B.), here translated *master of the house*, is translated *householder* in 13 : 27. The latter is declared in ver. 37 to be Christ Himself, who accordingly in this text means Himself by the term, and, in harmony with the image, speaks of the company of His disciples as His *household*.

²⁶ Fear them not therefore: for there is nothing covered, that shall not be revealed; and hid, that shall not be known.

A. Fear ... therefore—since your lot on earth will thus resemble My own; as you bear My reproach willingly (Hebr. 11 : 26; 13 : 13), you shall also share in My triumph (13 : 43; Col. 3 : 4); *therefore*, " be of good cheer; I have overcome the world " (John 16 : 33; comp. Acts 4 : 29).—B **For there, etc.** The sense of this oft-repeated saying (Luke 8 : 17; 12 : 2) in the present connection is: Although we are now dishonored, although My doctrine is scorned by many, and My person and nature seem to be covered with a veil (comp. Hebr. 10 : 20; Phil. 2 : 7), nevertheless the truth shall yet be acknowledged and My honor and glory be made known (John 12 : 28); divine truth is too mighty to be suppressed by man (2 Tim. 3 : 8, 9).

²⁷ What I tell you in the darkness, speak ye in the light: and what ye hear in the ear, proclaim upon the housetops.

A. The *darkness* refers to the humble and private labors of the Lord, who holds no public and honorable station; the *light* indicates the subsequent wide diffusion of divine truth throughout the world.—B. **What . . . ear**—what is whispered to you; Gospel truth is received by so few, that it seems to be whispered in your ears alone.—C. **Proclaim, etc.** That which is proclaimed on the housetops becomes known to all; it is a proverbial expression, referring to the practice of walking on the flat roofs of the houses (Deut. 22 : 8, and Matt. 9 ; 2, D.); it indicates the utmost publicity. So, too—says the Saviour—let your preaching be bold, free, public, accessible to all.

²⁸ And be not afraid of them which kill the body, but are not able to kill the soul: but rather fear him which is able to destroy both soul and body in hell.

A. **And be not afraid . . . soul.** Even if you suffer death in consequence of your adherence to My cause, meet death without fear, rather than incur the displeasure of God by " shunning to declare all His counsel " (Acts 20 : 27). When Polycarp was brought before the proconsul, the latter said : " Renounce Christ, or I will cause you to be consumed by fire." Polycarp answered : " You threaten me with fire that burns for a moment, and is then extinguished, for you know nothing of the judgment to come, and of the fire of *eternal* punishment reserved for the wicked."—B. **But rather, etc.** Some interpreters suppose that the Lord here indicates Satan as the object of fear, and as the possessor of the vast power of destroying both soul and body in hell. But such an interpretation would assign to the fallen angel the same omnipotent power which belongs to God. Now Satan is always under the control of the Almighty, who will destroy his power (Hebr. 2 : 14). There would indeed be an incongruity in this verse, if in the former part the Lord should command His disciples not to fear Satan's instruments, and then command them to fear Satan himself. St. James says: "Resist the devil, etc." (James 4 : 7). The language in the parallel passage (Luke 12 : 5) cannot possibly describe any power, except that of God. Moreover, the language of James (4 : 12), "Who is able to save and to destroy," refers undeniably to the Lord and not to Satan. Consequently, Christ presents, in this solemn warning, the divine attributes of almighty power and justice—fear the displeasure of God, and the loss of your souls more than bodily death. In the next words, which are intended to console, he reveals those of omnipresence and tender love (for "hell," here *Geenna*, in the original, see 5 : 22, G.). The bodies of the unrighteous as well as those of the righteous, according to John 5 : 28, 29, will be re-united with the souls that once dwelt in them, and then be assigned respectively to the regions of eternal bliss, or of eternal despair (25 : 46). The words *destroy* and *perish* do not indicate the extinction or annihilation of the soul or body, but *that* misery or ruin which the wicked will suffer when their peace and happiness are forever destroyed.

²⁹ Are not two sparrows sold for a farthing? and not one of them shall fall on the ground without your Father.

A. **Sparrows** (comp. the *swallow*, Ps. 84 : 3)—small harmless birds, of such little value that two were sold for one farthing, and five for two farthings (Luke 12 : 6). The farthing here mentioned (assarion) is different from the coin (equal to four mills) also named *farthing* in the English translation in 5 : 26, B. (which see). The *assarion* was equal perhaps to one cent and six mills, or four times as much as one *kodrantes*. Ten were equal to the silver coin called a *penny* (plural, *pence*) in 8 : 28; 20 : 2; see 17 : 24, B.—B. **And not one, etc.**—not one of them is struck by an arrow or stone, and falls or dies from cold or want of food without the knowledge and permission of your heavenly Protector. How much more (ver. 31), will he watch over you? (comp. 6: 26, 30).

³⁰ But the very hairs of your head are all numbered.

But the, etc.—an ancient proverbial expression. In the form in which it occurs in Luke 21 : 18 ; Acts 27 ; 34, it is found in 1 Sam. 14: 45 ; 2 Sam. 14: 11 ; 1 Kings, 1 : 52.

³¹ Fear not therefore, ye are of more value than many sparrows.

A. This application of the foregoing words very clearly involves the doctrine of a special Providence, by which is understood the constant active superintendence of God over all the affairs, acts, etc., of men, from which not even the most unimportant circumstance is excluded. The doctrine is here presented as an unfailing source of comfort and faith.—**B. Of more value**—referring to the value of the immortal soul (16 : 26), and the price paid for its redemption (1 Peter 1 : 18, 19).

³² Every one therefore who shall confess me before men, him will I also confess before my Father which is in heaven.

A. The Lord, after giving these admonitions, which exhibit the divine presence as a sure support, directs the attention of the Twelve to the respective consequences of fidelity and of a weak faith.—**B. Confess . . . men.** The confession consists not simply in words, as when an individual is publicly recognized as a member of the Church ; nor in the act of commemorating the Lord's death in the Lord's Supper, but also in the whole course of conduct; the faith or convictions of the mind and heart must overcome even the terrors of death. (Comp. Rom. 10 : 9, 10, on the duty and importance of " confessing the Lord Jesus with the mouth," in connection with the faith dwelling in the heart.)—**C. Him will—heaven.** The language in Luke 12 : 8, which introduces the holy angels as witnesses whose ministry, will be employed at the end of the world (Matt. 13:39, 49), and, especially, the terms employed in Mark 8:38, prove that the time when Christ will confess or acknowledge believers, will be the day of judgment (2 Thess. 1:7). His confession will consist in the invitation contained in Matt. 25:34, as illustrated in ver. 10 and 21 of the same chapter.

³³ But whosoever shall deny me before men, him will I also deny before my Father which is in heaven.

A. But ... men. The denial of Christ before men consists not simply in avowed infidelity, but in continued impenitence also, in the neglect or refusal to own Him as the Head of the Church, and, generally, in a conformity to the world (Tit. 1:16), which is enmity with God (James 4:4; comp. 1 Tim. 5:8). The term is applied to the conduct of Peter (26:70) when he disowned his Master. —**B. Him will etc.**—by saying "in that day: I never knew you" (7:22, 23; 25:12), and by pronouncing the sentence: "Depart from me, etc." (25:41; 2 Tim. 2:12). Such solemn language powerfully enforces the lesson taught in ver. 28 above.

³⁴ Think not that I came to send peace on the earth: I came not to send peace, but a sword.

A. The Lord here meets the following objection which the disciples might make:—Why dost thou permit such opposition to Thy cause to prevail? He explains that life is a period of probation, that the means of salvation shall be offered to all, and that even as God had designed men to be free agents, so also that liberty of choice between life and death shall continue. The words of Simeon in Luke 2:34, possibly alluding to Isai. 8:13–15 (comp. Rom. 9:32, 33), seem to refer to the same liberty of choice which is recognized by Moses (Deut. 30:16, 17), Joshua (ch. 24:14, 15), Elijah (1 Kings 18:21), Ezekiel (ch. 18:30–32), the Lord Jesus Himself (John 5:40; Matt.

23 : 37), the apostle Paul (Rom. 8 : 13), and the Scriptures generally.—B. **Think not**—you cannot therefore expect, when men are free agents, that My Gospel should be welcomed or even peacefully tolerated by all; there are many who suffer themselves to be deluded by the prince of the world (John 14 : 30; 19 : 8-11; 2 Cor. 4 : 4), and are full of enmity towards God (Rom. 5 : 10; James 4 : 4).—C. **To send**=to cast. The original word is translated *cast* in 4 : 18, and frequently. In Luke (12 : 51), the word *give* is employed in a similar connection.—D. **Peace on earth.** Harmony cannot prevail between parties which are as much opposed to each other as darkness is to light (comp. 2 Cor. 6 : 14-16). The sense is: There can be no agreement between Me and the world which now lieth in wickedness (1 John 5 : 19), until all submit willingly to Me, are renewed in spirit, and become *one* as the Father and I are one (John 17 : 11, 21-23). —The contest between the flesh (the corrupt nature of man) and the Holy Spirit (Gal. 5 : 17), or between Christ and the world (John 17 : 14-16), is often described in the Scriptures; it is one which, according to the Saviour's words (Matt. 12 : 30), suffers none to be neutral. When the Prince of Peace (Isai. 9 : 6) shall have united men in one spirit of faith and love (Eph. 2 : 14-18), reconciled the world to God (2 Cor. 5 : 19), established peace on earth (Luke 2 : 14; Isai. 11 : 6-9), and destroyed the last enemy (1 Cor. 15 : 26), eternal peace will prevail.—E. **A sword**—division (Luke 12 : 51), strife, contests between divine truth and human corruption. The *sword* which is used in warfare is frequently introduced as an image of war and strife (comp. Lev. 26 : 6; Jer. 14 : 13). The Lord here, obviously (see Luke 12 : 49), does not intend to say that He came for the purpose of producing strife in the world, for the true Christian's weapons are all spiritual

(Eph. 6 : 12), and he never persecutes (13 : 29, 30 ; 26: 52, B.). Neither can the Lord refer to the Roman soldiers who destroyed Jerusalem, as His own explanation in ver. 35 excludes the idea here of a public or national war. He means rather that the appearance of His holy religion in a sinful world will arouse all the opposition of the powers of darkness, and that this opposition will be manifested on the part of the servants of sin (comp. John 8 : 44 and Acts 7 : 54; see also 11 : 12, B.).

³⁵, ³⁶ *For I came to set a man at variance against his father, and the daughter against her mother, and the daughter in law against her mother in law.—And a man's foes shall be they of his own household.*

The prophet Micah (ch. 7 : 5, 6), after deploring the general corruption of the Jews, illustrates it by exhibiting the domestic discord which, among other evils, proceeded from the want of religious principle. In these two verses the Lord alludes to that passage in the prophet, but applies it in a new sense. When the members of a family combine in pursuing an evil course—He says—and any of them are subsequently converted, the impenitent relatives will trample on all the ties of consanguinity and affinity, and persecute those whose new principles and life condemn their own. The believer (ver. 36) will not find peace in the bosom of his own family, while his relatives remain dead in sin.

³⁷ *He that loveth father or mother more than me is not worthy of me: and he that loveth son or daughter more than me is not worthy of me.*

The Lord answers the difficult question suggested to His hearers by the foregoing words : Since the service of God and the service of sin are incompatible, how—ask they—shall we proceed, when we cannot follow Thee without rupturing the most holy ties of nature? If— answers the Lord—such a trial of your faith occurs in seasons of unusual difficulty, whom are you solemnly bound to *love more* (—to obey)—the Holy God, or His impenitent and rebellious creatures? (Acts 5 : 29). Although you should appear to hate your nearest kindred (Luke 14 : 26) by forsaking them (Matt. 19 : 29), like Abraham (Gen. 12 : 1), nevertheless, you cannot be worthy of Me (—you cannot be true disciples, Luke 14 : 26), if, in compliance with the wishes of any human being, you refuse to confess Me publicly (ver. 32) and to remain faithful to My service. (Comp. 19 : 29.)

³⁸ And he that doth not take his cross, and follow after me, is not worthy of me.

Cross (see 16 : 24, 25). Those who were condemned to suffer death on the cross as criminals were compelled, to their own infamy, to carry that instrument of torture themselves to the place of execution (27 : 22, B.). Hence the phrase, *to take* or *carry a cross*, may have been used proverbially to describe any painful duty which might expose to great suffering and contempt (1 Cor. 1 : 23). The Saviour bore His own cross (John 19 : 17) till His scourged and lacerated body tottered under the burden, and Simon of Cyrene came to His aid (Matt. 27 : 32). Still the phrase did not originate with the Jews, among whom crucifixion was not practised anciently as a mode of inflicting ignominy and death. The sense of the words is: The impenitence and persecution of your kindred may cause you to experience all the pangs of one who already suffers the first agony of a crucifixion. You may even suffer death. Nevertheless, you cannot be worthy of Me (ver. 37), but are unfitted alike to belong to My kingdom on earth, and to share in My glory, if you permit such considerations to withdraw you from My service.

³⁹ He that findeth his life shall lose it: and he that loseth his life for my sake shall find it.

A. The Lord on more than one occasion purposely used the same word in a literal and a spiritual or a higher sense (comp. "dead" in 8 : 22, and "hath—hath not," in 13 : 12). The Greek word here translated *life* is *psyche*. This word, in conformity to the usage of the corresponding Hebrew word, occurs with various shades of meaning, which the connection usually defines. It is used in the N. T. to designate (1) the vital principle of man, his spirit, principle of life (Acts 20 : 10-24), or his *life*, bodily or natural life (Matt. 2 : 20; 6 : 25; John 10 : 11); (2) the *soul*, the animating principle, viewed as distinct from the body itself (Acts 2 : 27; Rev. 6 : 9); (3) specially, the soul, viewed as spiritual in its nature (Matt. 10 : 28; 26 : 38); (4) and, pre-eminently, the rational, immortal soul (Matt. 11 : 29; 16 : 26; 22 : 37; James 1 : 21; 1 Peter 1 : 9). These, and other meanings of the word, such as in Acts 2 : 41-43, may all be arranged under two leading thoughts: First, the life of the body, as dependent on the presence of the soul; secondly, the immortal spirit of man itself.—B. To these two modes of using the word, the Lord refers in this text. In the analogous passage (John 12 : 25), two different Greek words (*psyche*, twice after the word *his*, and *zoe* before the word *eternal*), are both translated *life*, because the English language is deficient in more appropriate terms. The sense of the present text (as also of 16 : 25) appears to be: He who hopes to escape a violent death (=to save his bodily life) by denying Me, will lose his true or higher life (=will lose his soul, fail to obtain life eternal); he, on the contrary, who is willing to deny himself (Mark 8 : 34, 35), to renounce his friends and even suffer bodily death, as well as die spiritually to the world and sin (Rom. 6 : 1-11), rather than renounce Me, shall obtain the true life, eternal life in heaven.

⁴⁰ *He that receiveth you receiveth me; and he that receiveth me receiveth him that sent me.*

A. Possibly the disciples here, as in 19 : 24, 25, betrayed by their words or looks the anxiety which this revelation of their future trials had produced. The Lord now cheers them by exhibiting another view of their office, by virtue of which they become the representatives of His person (2 Cor. 5 : 20), and are authorized, as His instruments (Rom. 15 : 15-18), to distribute His heavenly gifts.—He that receives your word as the word of God (1 Thess. 2 : 13), in faith—the Lord proceeds, describing conduct opposite to that mentioned in ver. 14—receives thereby all the blessings which I Myself confer through it on the souls of men (John 17 : 22, 23); yea, such a hearer receives the gifts of the Father who sent Me, as richly as if the Father, who is one with Me (John 10 : 30; 14 : 9, 10), bestowed them directly without your agency (comp. John 17 : 18: 20 : 21; Mark 9 : 37; Luke 10 : 16).—**B.** The efficacy of Gospel truth (Rom. 1 : 16), and the blessings which it imparts, when it is proclaimed by men in its fulness and purity, are equal to those which were manifested when the Saviour Himself personally preached (see 18 : 5). This doctrine, here implied, involves another scriptural truth, namely, that the influences of the Divine Spirit are inseparably connected with the Word of God, as one of the means of grace (see John 5 : 39; Acts 16 : 14; Rom. 1 : 16; 1 Cor. 1 : 18; 3 : 6; 15 : 1, 2; 2 Tim. 3 : 16; 1 Peter 1 : 22).

⁴¹ *He that receiveth a prophet in the name of a prophet shall receive a prophet's reward; and he that receiveth a righteous man in the name of a righteous man shall receive a righteous man's reward.*

A. The Lord, after referring to the disciples themselves and all succeeding heralds of the cross, now describes the nature and extent of the divine blessing which shall be bestowed on those who receive the preached word in faith.—B. The sense is: Those who received God's ancient messengers, the prophets, because God had sent them (= " in the name of a prophet "), obtained the highest blessings which a prophet could bestow (= " a prophet's reward," as one which he is the means of conferring—instruction in the truth, miraculous gifts, etc.; see for instance, 1 Kings 17 : 16; 2 Kings 4 : 37); so, too—continues the Lord—those shall obtain the blessings of the Gospel who receive you as the prophets or teachers of the new covenant (Matt. 23 : 34; Luke 10 : 19). When " prophets and righteous men " are mentioned together, as here, and in 13 : 17; 23 : 29, if a distinction between them is intended (that is, if the terms do not, as " wise men and scribes " in 23 : 34, denote the same class generally), then the latter are probably only religious teachers, who, without possessing the gift of inspiration and the power of working miracles, are nevertheless faithful in guiding others in the way of life.

⁴² And whosoever shall give to drink unto one of these little ones a cup of cold water only, in the name of a disciple, verily I say unto you, he shall in no wise lose his reward.

A. **These little ones**—the disciples standing in the presence of the Saviour ("these"). They are called *little ones*, as in Matt. 18 : 2–6; Mark 9 : 37, either in reference to the childlike and pure sentiments of humility, confidence, etc., which must dwell in them—and then all believers appropriately receive that name; or, in reference to their meekness, which exposed them to the contempt of the Jews (see Ps. 119 : 141; and below, 11 : 25, H., and 25 : 40). In Mark 9 : 41, 42, "you" stands for the word "these" in the present text, and the "little ones" are, generally, humble and unassuming but sincere believers.—B. **A cup . . . water**—however slight the outward expression of the love and faith of the heart may be, where more cannot be done (Mark 14 : 8). A cup of cold water was of greater value to a traveller in the East than it would be in regions more abundantly supplied with water.—C. **In the . . . disciple**=shall give to one of these little ones, in consideration of his office as a religious teacher—the giver himself being prompted by a grateful sense of God's mercy in sending the Gospel and its blessings through His servants.—D. **He shall, etc.**—his faith and gratitude towards God, manifested toward His messengers, in supplying their immediate wants, shall not be unnoticed because the individual is unable to render greater services, but shall be rewarded in this life already, by increased spiritual strength and joy. The poor widow's faith and devotion (Mark 12 : 41-44) converted her two mites into a gift of greater value in the Lord's eyes than the "much money" given by others possessed. "God estimates the act according to the intention, not the intention according to the act." —GROTIUS (see ann. to 25 : 22, 23, 40).

CHAPTER XI.

¹ And it came to pass, when Jesus had made an end of commanding his twelve disciples, he departed thence to teach and preach in their cities.

A. Commanding—imparting instructions in 10 : 5–42.—**B. Departed**—continued the journey mentioned in 9 : 35.—**C. To teach—preach**—in accordance with the great purpose of His appearance in the world (Mark 1 : 38).—**D. Their cities**—the Galileans (comp. "their synagogues," 4 : 23; 9 : 35; 12 : 9).

² Now when John heard in the prison the works of the Christ, he sent by his disciples.

A. John=the Baptist. Matthew reserves his account of the circumstances which occasioned this imprisonment, until he describes the death of John (ch. 14 : 3–12).—**Q. Heard**—from his disciples (Luke 3 : 20; 7 : 18), who were allowed to visit him.—**C. The works**—course of conduct (as in John 8 : 39), or, specially, the miracles, etc., of the Lord (as in John 10 : 25, 38).

³ And said unto him, Art thou he that cometh, or look we for another?

A. Said—through His disciples (see 8 : 5, C.).—**B. Thou he . . . cometh**—of whom Moses in the Law and the Prophets did write (John 1 : 45). The prophecy of Moses in Deut. 18 : 15, which referred to Christ (Acts 3 : 21–23), had led the people generally to expect the appearance of a prophet clothed with unusual authority (John 1 : 21; 6 : 14); but they appear to have made a distinction between him (John 7 : 40, 41) and the promised Messiah Himself, to whom they correctly applied passages like Gen. 49 : 10; Numb. 24 : 17; Ps. 118 : 26. These disciples of John, however, who had heard their master's direct witness respecting Christ (John 1 : 15-34), doubtless refer to Him as the *Lord*, whose coming both Isaiah in ch. 40 : 3, and Malachi in ch. 3 : 1, had predicted. John's father had already applied the latter passage (Luke 1 : 76) to him and Christ (see also Mark 1 : 2 ff.); John himself had referred to the prophets when he announced the immediate coming of the Lord (see ann. to 3 : 11). The question, then, is equivalent to: Art thou the Messiah whose coming the prophets and John have announced?—**B. Or . . . another**—or should we *expect*, *wait for* (as the same word is rendered in Luke 1 : 21; Acts 3 : 5; 10 : 24) another, as the promised Messiah, different from thyself?—**D.** John had, at an earlier period, expressed the strongest and most joyful faith in Christ, as the true Messiah (Matt. 3 : 11, 14; John 1 : 29-34). How is then the doubt or uncertainty respecting Christ's character, which his message seems to express, to be explained? Several eminent interpreters are inclined to believe that the gloom of John's prison had temporarily clouded his faith, or that the Saviour's mode of life, to which John's disciples had already objected (see 9 : 14: John 3 : 25), and his own protracted confinement, from which Christ did not deliver him, produced doubts and impatience in his soul. These interpreters refer, by way of illustration, to those unhappy scenes of spiritual declension or sloth which sometimes occur in the experience even of sincere believers, in which their faith seems to fail. Thus, they adduce the instances of Moses (Numb. 20 : 11, 12), David (1 Sam. 27 : 1) and Elijah (1 Kings 19 : 4, 10). But John had always freely exposed himself to hardships (Luke

1 : 80; Matt. 3 : 4); he well knew that his mission terminated with the appearance of the Lord (John 3 : 30), and the wrath of the mightiest of the land, though it might lead to his imprisonment and death, had no terrors for him (Matt. 3 : 7; 14 : 4). If, after having witnessed the scene at the Saviour's baptism (John 1 : 33), he had, even temporarily, wavered in his faith, and, after reflection, still cherished doubts in his soul (unlike Peter, who denied the Lord without reflection, Matt. 26 : 69–75), he would not have been represented by the Saviour at the very time (ver. 7–11, below) as a model of firmness and tenacity of purpose. Hence it is probable that the following view of John's spiritual state, entertained by other interpreters, affords the true explanation. While he retained his own clear convictions, he could not remove the doubts of all of his disciples. Some of them, retaining the jealous feeling betrayed in John 3 : 26, never attached themselves to Christ's cause (see 9 : 14, C.).—Like Elisha in a similar case (2 Kings 2 : 16, 17), John may have ultimately said to them : If ye will not believe me, then—go, see, and judge for yourselves. "It is certain that John asked the question not for his own sake, but for the sake of his disciples who still doubted, and whom he was anxious to enroll among the Lord's believing disciples, since his own death was near."—LUTHER.

⁴ And Jesus answered and said unto them, Go your way and tell John the things which ye do hear and see.

A. "In the same hour he cured many of their infirmities, etc." (Luke 7 : 21).—**B. Go and tell, etc.**—ask John to explain to you the lessons taught both by the miracles which I perform, and also by the new subject— *the Gospel of the kingdom*—to which My discourses refer (see 4 : 23).

⁵ The blind receive their sight, and the lame walk, the lepers are

cleansed, and the deaf hear, and the dead are raised up, and the poor have the good tidings preached to them.

The predictions in the O. T. relative to the Messiah furnished the marks by which He shall be recognized when He appeared. Among these, the Lord here refers to two: His miracles and His proclamation of the *glad tidings* that God had now visited His people in mercy (Isai. 29 : 18, 19; 35 : 5, 6; 43, 8, 9; 61 : 1). The Messiah is described in these passages as the possessor of *all* power—He can control bodily and spiritual blindness, death, etc.—When John (proceeds the Lord) explains to you that these and other predictions are fulfilled in Me, then abandon your doubts, and believe.

⁶ And blessed is *he*, whosoever shall find none occasion of stumbling in me.

A. While the Lord here pronounces a blessing, He also solemnly warns John's disciples and tells them to beware of resisting the force of the evidence which they shall receive from John's explanation of the prophecies.—**B. Find none occasion, etc.**—blessed is he who shall, on such evidence, receive Me as the promised Messiah.

⁷ And as these went their way, Jesus began to say unto the multitudes concerning John, What went ye out into the wilderness to behold? A reed shaken with the wind?

A. It is possible that the multitudes present on this occasion were not able to understand the true motive of John in sending the message (ver. 3, D.), and may have manifested surprise that he almost seemed to recall the testimony respecting Jesus which he had himself pronounced. The Lord removes this impression by reminding them of the firmness, consistency and fearlessness which John had always displayed.—**B. Reed**—a water-plant, growing on the banks of the Jordan, which flowed through the wilderness where John had preached (3 : 1, 6). It had a long, hollow stem which yielded to the most gentle wind; it possessed little strength (1 Kings 14 : 15, and see Matt. 12 : 20, A.). Ye well know (the Lord says) that John's character, precisely because it was not like a reed, made a powerful impression on you.

⁸ But what went ye out for to see? A man clothed in soft raiment? behold, they that wear soft raiment are in kings' houses.

Soft raiment—ye well know that John's exalted and firm spirit, which discarded such luxuries, is so little capable of betraying irresolution and fear or doubt, that it was in reality his unconquerable boldness in rebuking the sins of the king's house which led to his present imprisonment. His language (3 : 7), which was not marked by courtly and hypocritical phrases, was very different from that of the false prophets of old (Jer. 6 : 13, 14).

⁹ But wherefore went ye out? to see a prophet? Yea, I say unto you, and much more than a prophet.

A. A prophet?—did ye not all truly regard him as a messenger whom God had sent to you? (see 14 : 5; 21 : 25, 26).—**B. More than, etc.**—higher in rank (for the reason given in the next verse) than the prophets of the O. T.; it was, namely, his high office, agreeably to the predictions respecting him, to be the immediate forerunner and witness of the Messiah (Luke 1 : 76), whom he saw personally—a privilege which none of the ancient prophets were permitted to enjoy (1 Peter 1 : 10–12)

¹⁰ This is *he*, of whom it is written, Behold, I send my messenger before thy face, who shall prepare thy way before thee.

It is written=in Matt. 3 : 1. Christ here intimated to those who have ears to hear (ver. 15), that if John is the messenger mentioned by the prophet, then He Himself is the *Lord* whose coming is thus announced. The fidelity of John, in fulfilling the duties of his peculiar office, is described in ch. 3 above, and John, ch. 1. In Malachi the Lord of Hosts speaks of Himself: " before *me*; " Christ here reveals (comp. ver. 27 below), that He who speaks is God the Father addressing God the Son: " before *thee*," indicating that the Persons of the Trinity, distinct but not separate, are *one* God.

" Verily I say unto you, Among them that are born of women there hath not arisen a greater than John the Baptist : yet he that is but little in the kingdom of heaven is greater than he.

A. Born of women—human beings, mortals (see Job 14 : 1 ; 15 : 14), as contradistinguished from the Son of God.—**B. Not a greater** (one)—with respect to privileges and knowledge. John, who did no miracle (John 10 : 41) like the ancient prophets, nevertheless occupied a higher rank than their own (ver. 9, B. above).—**C. Kingdom of Heaven**—the condition of God's people in this life, not in the eternal world (see EXCURSUS I.).—**D. He that is least, etc.** As He places this " least " one above John, He cannot mean a mere nominal Christian, nor one whose mind alone has received the light of the Gospel. Much less can He refer to Himself, as some interpreters have supposed, forgetting that the *Founder* of the Church can in no sense be the *least* member of it. He, rather, speaks of one who, like John, possesses a living faith. The sense of the passage is : He who cordially embraces My doctrine, and is a member of My body (Eph. 5 : 30, 32), even though he be slower than his brethren in learning (comp. 5 : 19, B.), will still have a more exalted view of God, the Atonement and eternal things, than that which has been granted to John. The Christian's privileges in the Church are far greater than those which John enjoyed, and in this sense, too, he is greater—more highly favored (Hebr. 11 : 39, 40).

¹² And from the days of John the Baptist until now the kingdom of heaven suffereth violence, and men of violence take it by force.

A. **From . . . now**—from his first appearance as a messenger and public teacher (Luke 1 : 80, "the day of shewing") until the present moment.—B. **The kingdom, etc.** Compare a similar saying of the Lord on a later occasion, in Luke 16 : 16. If the word (*biazetai*) in Matthew and Luke is taken in an active sense in both places, which the laws of the language confessedly allow, and if the connection is also noted, the meaning of the whole may be thus conceived:—John had encountered great opposition from the influential classes of the Jews (Matt. 21 : 25, 32; Luke 7 : 30); such was also the experience of the Lord. The cause lay in the uncompromising spirit of divine truth, which tolerates the existence of no sinful feeling or practice, and demands self-denial and the surrender of the whole heart to God. Such a holy religion, which opposed the sins that men naturally love (John 3 : 19), accordingly *offered violence* to their habitual modes of thought, feeling and action. The Lord Himself had said: "I came not to send peace, but a sword" (Matt. 10 : 34). Here, too, he employs a word signifying "to offer violence," in the same manner. As in Matt. 10 : 22 he had said: "Ye shall be hated of *all* men" (=who do not believe) so, in Luke 16 : 16, He declares, that, in consequence of this holy standard which religion erects, "every man *offers violence* to it"—his evil heart rebels against its demands; nevertheless (adds the Lord, ver. 17), that opposition shall not prevail. Here in Matthew when we compare the uninterrupted series of persecutions which the teachers of religion had always experienced among the Jews, as described in Matt. 23 : 34-37, the sense appears to be:—Earlier prophets brought messengers which were unwelcome to the Jews, and came in conflict with their vices and sins; they were thus exposed to a violent death (Luke 11 : 47-51). So, too, John was impiously charged with "having a devil," ver. 18 below. The kingdom which he preached offered (not *suffered*) violence, namely, to the unholy passions of men, and men of violence (Herod and his lawless instruments) now forcibly assail it in its representative, and coerce John, or snatch him (as the same Greek word is rendered in Matt. 13 : 19, John 10 : 12)—alluding to John's undeserved imprisonment.

¹³ For all the prophets and the law prophesied until John.

This verse certainly is intended to set forth more than the obvious fact that the *prophets prophesied, etc.* The intermediate thought, occurring in Matt. 5 : 12; 23 : 34-37; Acts 7 : 52, may be:—Such has always been the lot of the messengers of God; opposition to divine truth is characteristic of the corrupt heart of man (Jer. 17 : 9, and see 17 : 12, B.). John's experience does not differ from that of Moses, who gave the law, and that of the succeeding prophets.

¹⁴ And if ye are willing to receive *it*, this is Elijah, which is to come.

A. Receive—into the mind and heart, understand it correctly, and believe it (comp. "receiveth" in Cor. 2 : 14).
—**B. This is, etc.**=that Elijah whose coming was foretold by the prophet Malachi (4 : 5), is really John the Baptist. The name of Elijah is applied to John as if he were identically the same, but really in the sense that he came "in the spirit and power of Elias" (Luke 1 : 17)—with the same earnestness of purpose and fearless devotion to the interests of religion (see 1 Kings, ch. 17—ch. 21 ; 2 Kings, ch. 1, and 2). When John denied that he was Elijah (John 1 : 21), he merely denied the truth of a popular Jewish interpretation of the words of Malachi,

according to which the deceased Elijah himself was to rise up from his grave and go before the Messiah (see 14 : 2, B.; 16 : 14, A.; 17 : 10, 11).

¹⁵ He that hath ears to hear, let him hear.

This oft-repeated proverb (13 : 9, 43), representing man as accountable for the use which he makes of his privileges and opportunities, here specially refers to the word *receive* in ver. 14; the sense is : Let the hearer give all the attention of which he is capable, and meditate carefully on the meaning and true application of My words (comp. Luke 9 : 44).

^{16, 17} But whereunto shall I liken this generation? It is like unto children sitting in the market-places, which call unto their fellows,—And say, we piped unto you, and ye did not dance, we wailed, and ye did not mourn.

A. Whereunto shall, etc.—What is there (as Jeremiah had asked, Lam. 2 : 13) that can illustrate the inconsistent conduct of the Jews?—**This generation**=the people then living, who heard the preaching both of John and of Christ (see 24 : 34).—**B. Like unto children, etc.** The *markets* were open places where miscellaneous articles were exposed for sale, public meetings held (Acts 16 : 19), laborers engaged (Matt. 20 : 3), and where children played. The children here introduced are capricious, easily dissatisfied, and of different humors. Some propose to imitate a marriage ceremony, with its usual cheerful songs and instrumental music ("piped"=played on pipes or flutes (1 Cor. 14 : 7; 1 Kings 1 : 40; Isai. 30 : 29; Jer. 33 : 10, 11). Others reject the plan, and propose the imitation of a funeral procession with its mournful cries. They are described as wayward children (see Luke 7 : 32); the conflicting propositions of the whole number set forth the contradictory expressions of the Jewish people.

¹⁸ For John came neither eating nor drinking, and they say, He hath a devil.

John neither ate nor drank according to your usages (namely, bread and wine, Luke 7 : 33), as his earnest purpose to live solely for his great mission led him to disregard ordinary comforts and enjoyments (see ann. to 3 : 1, B.). Hence you allege that his self-denying course resulted from melancholy or madness (John 10 : 20). You said: "He hath a devil," wickedly ascribing the divine influence which guided him to the presence of an unclean spirit, like those that control demoniacs, forbidding them to use the organs of speech (9 : 32), or driving them from society to the tombs (8 : 28).

¹⁹ The Son of Man came eating and drinking, and they say, Behold, a gluttonous man and a winebibber, a friend of publicans and sinners! And wisdom is justified by her works.

A. The Son . . . sinners—I have (for the purpose of confirming the faith of my disciples, of obtaining access to sinners, etc.) conformed to the usages of the people, eating and drinking " such things as are set before Me " (Luke 10 : 8). At the beginning of My miracles, I furnished the guests in Cana with wine (John 2 : 11), and recently I was found eating in the house of Matthew (9 : 10, 11) with publicans and sinners, whom I sought to lead into the kingdom of heaven. As you exaggerated in the case of John, so you have calumniated Me by ascribing My conformity to the ordinary forms of social life, and My earnest seeking after penitent sinners, to gluttony and a love of wine.—The latter terms were regarded as infamous (Deut. 21 : 20; Prov. 23 : 20, 21).—**B. But wisdom is justified, etc.** Wisdom, in its highest sense, belongs to God alone (Rom. 16 : 17; 1 Tim. 1 : 17). Wisdom in man is the gift of God (James 1 : 5). That heavenly gift—the Lord here says—will preserve men from pernicious errors, and teach them to discern in John, on the one hand, the evidence of his heavenly mission, in Christ, on the other, the evidence of His divine nature and power. And my followers, by their decision to obey me, which will result in their holy life, or works, will furnish evidence to themselves, and to others, that man's highest wisdom consists in faith in Me.—For "justify," see 12 : 37, A.

[20] Then began he to upbraid the cities wherein most of his mighty works were done, because they repented not.

A. **Then**=at the time when the people had already found sufficiently favorable opportunities to understand His doctrines, and to repent and believe.—B. **Upbraid**=chide, *reproach* (comp. "anger" and "grieved" in Mark 3 : 5, and see Mark 16 : 14).—C. **Cities**=inhabitants dwelling in them.—D. **Mighty works**—miracles (see 7 : 22, G.).—E. **Repented not** (see 3 : 2, A.). He rebuked them for not being convinced by His miracles that He was a messenger of God, and for not obeying His call to repentance (4 : 17).

[21] Woe unto thee, Chorazin! woe unto thee, Bethsaida! for if the mighty works had been done in Tyre and Sidon which were done in you, they would have repented long ago in sackcloth and ashes.

A. **Woe**=an exclamation of sorrow (24 : 19), sometimes mingled with indignation (23 : 13).—B **Chorazin . . . Bethsaida.** Both places were on the shore of Lake Gennesaret. The former was not far from Capernaum; the latter, the western Bethsaida, lay on the northwestern shore of the lake. There was another Bethsaida, mentioned in Mark 8 : 22; Luke 9 : 10, according to several eminent authors (von Raumer: Palästina, p. 122), which lay on the east of the Jordan, where the latter flows into the lake, and was also called *Julias* (Josephus, Antiq. 18, 2, 1; War. 2, 9, 1). At the latter place the miracle recorded in Matt. 14 : 15 ff. occurred.—C. **Tyre . . . Sidon.** Tyre was a large commercial city, founded long before the age of Solomon (1 Kings 5 : 1), being mentioned already in Josh. 19 : 29. All the arts known to the ancients flourished there (2 Chron. 2 : 7). It was situated on the eastern coast of the Mediterranean Sea (Luke 6 : 17), and was distant about thirty-five miles, north-west, from the Sea of Galilee.—Sidon, somewhat more than twenty miles north of Tyre, was a still older city, having been founded by a son of Canaan (Gen. 10 : 15, 10); it was known as early as the days of Joshua as "great Sidon" (Josh. 11 : 8; 19 ; 28 ; see 15, 22, A.). In the O. T. the wealth, vices and ruin of the Phœnician cities were repeatedly mentioned by the prophets (Isai. 23 : 14; Jer. 25 : 22 ; 47 : 4 ; Ezek. ch. 26–28).—D. **Sackcloth**—coarse cloth, worn as a mourning-garment (comp. Isai. 50 : 3; Rev. 6 : 12). Mourners also threw **ashes** and dust (Ezek. 27 : 30) on their heads (see 6 : 16, C.).— E. As in 10 : 15, the Lord here declares that even heathen did not exhibit such hardness of heart.

²² Howbeit I say unto you, It shall be more tolerable for Tyre and Sidon at the day of judgment, than for you.

The same expressions, with a similar application, occur in 10 : 15 above.

²³ And thou, Capernaum, shalt thou be exalted unto heaven ? thou shalt go down into hades : for if the mighty works had been done in Sodom which were done in thee it would have remained until this day.

A. **Capernaum** (see 4 : 13, B.). The Lord often addressed the inhabitants of a city collectively, by a well-known figure of speech, as if He addressed one person (comp. 23 : 37; Ps. 137 : 5, 6: Isai. 40 : 9). In such cases deep and powerful emotions are expressed.—B. **Hades.** This Greek word occurs in ten other places in the N. T. (Matt. 16 : 18; Luke 16 : 23; Acts 2 : 27, 31, etc.). In 1 Cor. 15 : 55 it corresponds to the Hebrew word (Sheol) in the passage quoted from Hosea 13 : 14. Christ was the "mediator of a *better* covenant" (Heb. 8 : 6); He "brought life and immortality to light through the Gospel" (2 Tim. 1 : 10; see 27 : 52, 53, A., and comp. John 1 : 17; 4 : 23). Passages like these explain the indistinctness of the allusions in the O. T. to the state of the dead; even the ancient prophets did not receive the full revelations concerning the eternal world, which are now found in the N. T. The ancient Jews gave the name of *Sheol* (somewhat in the sense of the modern phrase: *beyond the grave*) to the region or receptacle in which the souls of all (1 Sam. 28 : 19) of the dead were gathered together. Jacob refers to his death, when he says that he is to be *gathered unto his people* (Gen. 49 : 29); but on a former occasion he called it *a going down into the Sheol* (Gen. 37 : 35; comp. Ezek. 31 : 15, 17). The word, in its general sense, referred less to the grave literally, than to that unseen world to which the grave was the gate, and designated both a condition or state and a region or locality. In that Sheol, with its vast divisions, all the dead found an abode (see Isai. 5 : 14). Clearer views could not prevail until the Gospel revealed the great truths that in the eternal world there are two distinct regions: first, *heaven*, the abode of the divine glory (also called Paradise, Luke 23 : 43 ; 2 Cor. 12 : 4; Rev. 2 : 7, or the eternal home of the blessed, where are "many mansions," John 14 : 2); and, secondly, the eternal abode of Satan and all the wicked, the place of punishment (Matt. 25 : 41, 46; 2 Pet. 2 : 4). The Greek *Hades*, corresponding to the Hebrew *Sheol*, thus came to signify, after the Gospel was given, not the grave in which the body is placed, nor, any longer, the world of the dead in a general sense, but, specially, that region of the eternal world occupied by the wicked. Thus, in Matt. 16 : 18, *Hades* already means the powers of darkness that are opposed to God. This is demonstrated by the words in Luke 16 : 23, where the "torments" of *Hades* are mentioned. Thus Hades and Geenna (5 : 22, G.) now coincide in meaning. There is a third word, occurring in the N. T. in 2 Peter 2 : 4, having the same sense, which in English is expressed by the word hell.—**C. Exalted . . . to hell.** Capernaum, even in a more eminent degree than Chorazin and Bethsaida, had been honored and favored by the residence and teachings of the Lord (4 : 13; 9 : 1), and by the numerous miracles (ch. 8 : 19; Luke 4 : 23) which He had wrought in it. By these privileges and advantages that city had been "exalted unto heaven "—received the most decisive evidences of divine pity and love. The impenitence of the people " brought them down to hades "—robbed them of divine favor and of the saving grace of Christ, caused them to retain their whole burden of guilt, and plunged them into everlasting ruin. The modern traveller, who in vain seeks for positive traces of the site of that city, sees in its utter destruction and actual disappearance from the face of the earth a solemn image of the divine judgment on continued hardness of heart and impenitence.

²⁴ Howbeit I say unto you, That it shall be more tolerable for the land of Sodom in the day of judgment, than for thee.

As in ver. 22, the Lord announces the awful doom of those who undervalue and despise their exalted religious privileges.

²⁵ At that season Jesus answered and said, I thank thee, O Father, Lord of heaven and earth, that thou didst hide these things from the wise and understanding, and didst reveal them unto babes.

A. When the Lord on a later occasion uttered a similar prayer (Luke 10 : 21, 22) it was the language of holy joy. We may ascribe the same general character to the present prayer.—A. **At that season.** This phrase, which occurs in precisely the same form below (12 : 1), may designate a period of time including several days or even weeks. Matthew probably means that the prayer, even if uttered after the events mentioned in ver. 2, ff., 20, ff., nevertheless referred to the general subjects presented in the present chapter.—C. **Answered.** The phrase "answered and said," as in 22 : 1, occurs very frequently in the sense of the corresponding Hebrew term, which does not necessarily imply a foregoing question, but is equivalent to the general expression: *began*, or, *proceeded*, or, *continued to speak* (here, in a direct prayer ; comp. 12 : 38 ; 15 : 15 ; 17 : 4 ; and see 28 : 5, A.) Thus, in Job 3 : 2, according to the original, Job *answered* (margin) *and said;* in Deut. 21 : 7, the Hebrew signifies : They shall (begin to) speak, and shall say, etc.—D. **I thank thee**—I confess to Thee (to Thy honor, Rom. 14 : 11 ; 15 : 9, or) I praise Thee (Gen. 29 : 35).—E. **Lord . . . earth**—Creator and Sovereign, Ruler of all that exists (Gen. 1 : 1 ; 14 : 19 ; Deut. 10 : 14, 17 ; Rev. 14 : 7.—F. **that . . . understanding.** The sense may be gathered both from Isai. 5 : 21 ; 29 : 14, to which passages the Lord appears to allude, and also from the subsequent explanations of Paul (1 Cor. 1 : 17–29). Impenitent and ignorant men, in place of submitting to the wise and holy precepts of God, prefer to obey the dictates of their own erring judgment. This sin punishes itself by closing their minds and hearts to the influences of divine grace (see below 13 : 14). The Lord employs no compulsion, but, after revealing His will and furnishing men with sufficient facilities to seek and find Him, He suffers the obstinate to choose death rather than life (Rom. 1 : 28 ; comp.

13 : 14-16, below). The blindness which succeeds (2 Cor. 3 : 14), is wrought by Satan (2 Cor. 4 : 4), by whom they that disown God, suffer themselves to be taken captive (2 Tim. 2 : 26). The **wise and understanding** here are, therefore, the worldly wise, who are " wise in their own conceits" (Rom. 11 : 25 ; 12 : 16), and whose "wisdom is foolishness with God " (1 Cor. 3 : 19, 20). Their wisdom is carefully distinguished from true or divine wisdom in 1 Cor. 2 : 4-16. " The words mean, not that God intentionally concealed a knowledge of Gospel truth, which, on the contrary, He commands His people to proclaim to all the world, but that He was pleased to make known a system of divine truth, without being governed by the wisdom of the world, which is really foolishness, or being induced to withhold it, because it did not suit the tastes of foolish men."—LUTHER.—G. **These things**—the new Gospel truth respecting the Son and His mediatorial work (ver. 27), or, the way of salvation through faith in a crucified Redeemer, as we learn from Luke 10 : 21-24.— H. **And hast revealed, etc.** A *babe* or little child may serve, on the one hand, as a representative of persons of very limited knowledge and skill, as in 1 Cor. 3 : 1 ; Hebr. 5 : 13, and, on the other, of persons who exhibit docility, who are not yet accustomed to the practice of deceitful arts and to the strifes of ambition, as in Matt. 18 : 2-6. In the latter sense the word is used here (comp. 10 : 42) —the humble, unassuming and docile, who are willing to learn of Jesus, and to be made wise unto salvation.

²⁶ Yea, Father, for so it was well-pleasing in thy sight.

A. **Yea.** It is often, as here, an emphatic affirmation. The sense, after supplying from ver. 25 the words which are here understood, is : Truly, I thank Thee, Father, for *so* (—after this manner) it seemed, etc.—B· **It seemed good**—it was Thy good pleasure (namely, to hide, etc., to reveal, etc.), as the same word is translated in Eph. 1 : 5, 9; Phil. 2 : 13; 2 Thess. 1 : 11. (Comp. 1 Sam. 12 : 22.)—C. **In thy sight**—before Thee, as the unerring Judge. The sense is: All that Thou doest is holy, just and good, and claims all praise. Since Thou hast hid—revealed, etc., I rejoice in these acts of Thine, because they are Thy acts—they are right and acceptable to me, because Thou doest them.

²⁷ All things have been delivered unto me of my Father: and no man knoweth the Son, save the Father: neither doth any know the Father, save the Son, and he to whomsoever the Son willeth to reveal *him*.

A. The Lord here addresses the people who surround Him, and implies that the revelations mentioned in ver. 25, are made by the Father through Him (comp. Hebr. 1 : 2). He sets forth the solemn truth that He alone is competent to reveal all that the Gospel contains, since He alone, as one person of the blessed Trinity, and not a mere prophet, possesses "all the treasures of wisdom and knowledge" (Col. 2 : 3).—**B. All things . . . Father.** "No mere human being, nor any angel, could employ such language (Isai. 42 : 8). But He, who is the 'true God and eternal life' (1 John 5 : 20), is here the speaker. Again, when He says: 'delivered unto me,' since God does not deliver to God, Christ refers to His human nature, which is inseparably united with the divine. Hence the words apply to the whole Person of Christ."—LUTHER.—The term: *all things*, necessarily includes all things in heaven and earth, of which, according to ver. 25, the Father is the Lord, and corresponds to the language used by Christ at His ascension (Matt. 28 : 18; comp. also John 3 : 35; 13 : 3; 17 : 2; Phil. 2 : 10; Hebr. 1 : 6). Hence Christ (called the *Word*, John 1 : 1), who is God, the Creator (John 1 : 3; 1 Cor. 8 : 6), the Ruler of the world (Hebr. 1 : 3), in whom the Father is seen

(John 14 : 9), will also be the Judge of all men (John 5 : 22 ; 2 Cor. 5 : 10), and is thus "over all, God-blessed forever" (Rom. 9 : 5). Men often think of the Son, who is God-Man, rather according to His human than according to His divine nature. And, indeed, Christ exhibited during His earthly ministry all the attributes of human nature which are without sin ; He was, therefore, a man. But, after His divine nature, He is a spirit (John 4 : 24), of which it is difficult for us to form a clear conception. —**C. And no man . . . save the Son.** The Lord here alludes to the mystery of the Holy Trinity (3 : 17, B. ; comp. John 1 : 18 ; 6 : 46 ; 10 : 30, 38 ; 17 : 21 ; 1 Cor. 2 : 10, 11). The same perfect knowledge of the Son which God the Father possesses, the Son also possesses in reference to the Father ; thus He is able to make a full and unerring revelation.—**D. And he . . . reveal him.** There is a twofold knowledge of God among those who read or hear the Gospel. The understanding of men may be made acquainted with revealed doctrines, e. g. the Trinity, Atonement, etc., as the Pharisees understood better than heathen the nature and will of God, as revealed by Moses (Matt. 23 : 2, 3) ; such intellectual knowledge, without love, is of no avail (1 Cor., ch. 8). There is another form of religious knowledge ; it exists in the soul, when faith and love abide there, and when the individual's religious experience constantly enlarges it. To this experimental knowledge of divine truth the present words refer. The revelation to the true believer will be adapted in fulness to his increasing capacity for receiving it (comp. 13 : 12).

²⁸ Come unto me, all ye that labour and are heavy laden, and I will give you rest.

A. Come unto me (comp. John 14 : 6). The word translated *come,* is not the verb usually rendered *come,* as in ver. 3, 14, 18, 19 of this chapter, and in the analogous passage (John 7 : 37), but is a Greek adverb equivalent to : *hither, here, come ye*; its use may be seen in ch. 21 : 38; 25 : 34; 28 : 6. The emphasis lies on the word *me*—for, without *me*, your Saviour, ye can do nothing (John 15 : 5). There is doubtless an allusion here to the Jewish teachers, whose formal and superficial instructions afforded neither light to the mind, nor comfort to the heart, while He, the Saviour, was able and willing to impart life and salvation to the hungering and thirsting soul (John 4 : 14; 6 : 27). Hence He exclaims : Ye lost sheep, hither, to *Me!* (Comp. Prov. 8 : 1–4; Isai. 45 : 22.) —B. **All ye that labor** (=toil, 6 : 28) . . . **laden.** A previous description of the spiritual state of the people, given in 9 : 36, illustrates the spirit of this gracious invitation. Many, doubtless, whom the preaching of John, or the reading of the O. T. in the synagogue had awakened, were painfully seeking after peace ; they *labored* or *grew weary* (as the words also implies) in observing not only the ceremonial law, but also the mechanical rules of their teachers, from which the burdened conscience obtained no relief. They assumed the *heavy burdens* mentioned in 23 : 4 and Luke 11 : 46, that is, the additional exactions of their teachers, which, by their number and minuteness, had become well-nigh intolerable, but still they found no peace (Hebr. 9 : 9). The word *all* authorizes every one who knows "the plague of his own heart" (1 Kings 8 : 38) to come with confidence to Him whose love is as tender as His power is great, according to Hebr. 4 : 16. " Wait not, do not hesitate because you are unworthy to come, but come because you are unworthy (Isai. 55 : 1), and need such grace."—LUTHER.—C. **And I . . . rest**=will *refresh* you (as the word is translated in 1 Cor. 16 : 18 ; 2 Cor.

7 : 13), that is, I will give you repose and comfort by supplying all the wants of your souls (comp. Isai. 57 : 15).

⁹⁹ *Take my yoke upon you, and learn of me; for I am meek and lowly in heart; and ye shall find rest unto your souls.*

A. **Take my yoke**—enter My service, obey My commandments (comp. 1 John 5 : 3, where "grievous" is—*heavy, oppressive*). In allusion to the instruments by which animals were attached to the plough or cart (1 Sam. 6 : 7), the word *yoke* was used proverbially to describe not only a state or condition which was felt to be oppressive (Acts 15 : 10; Gal. 5 : 1), but also, generally, the condition of those who were controlled by the will of a superior (1 Tim. 6 : 1)—B. **And learn** (=how to be saved) **of me.** The Greek word for *learn* furnishes the original term for *disciple* (5 : 1, D.)—*learner;* hence, *learn of me*—be my disciples.—C. **For I am meek**—mild, gentle (see 5 : 5, A.; 21 : 5, D.). The blessed Saviour's spirit was very different from that of the selfish and unfeeling scribes and Pharisees who are mentioned in 23 : 2-4. We can learn of him with confidence and ease, for he condescended to assume our nature in order to give us not only unerring precepts but also a perfect example (1 Pet. 2 : 21).—D. **Lowly**—*humble,* as the same word is rendered in James 4 : 6, 1 Pet. 5 : 5. The humility of the Saviour was *in heart*—genuine and sincere. He, whom all the angels worshipped (Hebr. 1 : 6), made Himself of no reputation, but humbled Himself voluntarily so far as to suffer the ignominious death of the cross (Phil. 2 : 5-8).—E. **And ye shall find rest** (=repose, peace) **unto your souls**—by being delivered from your sins and therefore from condemnation through faith in me (Rom. 8 : 1); the atonement which I shall make, will give peace and joy to your souls (Rom. 5 : 1, 11).

³⁰ *For my yoke is easy, and my burden is light.*

The original word for *easy* is translated *kind* (Luke 6 : 35 ; Eph. 4 : 32), and *gracious* in 1 Pet. 2 : 3, implying that the service of Christ is soothing, beneficent, by its very nature. That service, which, in its honorable character and blessedness, resembles the relation usually termed *friendship* (John 15 : 15), is nevertheless called here a *yoke* and a *burden ;* but these terms, without a material distinction between them, are designed to correspond to the preceding *labor* and *heavy laden.* The cause that Christ's service is in any case a yoke and burden, lies, not in the nature of religion itself, which is love and joy (Rom. 14 : 17 ; Phil. 4 : 4 ; 1 Thess. 5 : 16), but in the continued influence of original sin, as described by Paul in Rom. 7 : 22–24 ; 2 Cor. 4 : 16. The corrupt flesh of man, not completely subdued in this life (Phil. 3 : 12), still struggles to lead away the soul from God, and hence the believer is required to watch and pray continually (1 Cor. 10 : 12 ; 1 Pet. 5 : 8). Nevertheless we have the gracious promise that if we faithfully use the means of grace (Eph. 6 : 13–18), the Word and Sacraments, and, by the faith which they enkindle and maintain, resist the devil, he will flee from us (James 4 : 7), and we shall continually grow in knowledge and in grace (2 Pet. 3 : 18).

CHAPTER XII.

¹ At that season Jesus went on the sabbath day through the cornfields; and his disciples were an hungered, and began to pluck ears of corn, and to eat.

A. At that season—when the Lord uttered the foregoing memorable words (comp. 11 : 25, B.).—**went through**; pathways, without hedges or fences, often led through fields of grain, as in 13 : 4, A.—**B. Cornfields** —fields sown with grain, wheat, rye, barley and other cereals. The *corn of wheat* mentioned in John 12 : 24, means a single grain of wheat.—**C. An hungered** (see 4 : 2, C.).—**D. To pluck**—as any one was allowed to do freely (Deut. 23 : 25), provided that he merely rubbed the ears in his hands (Luke 6 : 1) and appeased his hunger without conveying the grain away. The Jewish teachers alleged, without divine authority, that this permission was suspended on the Sabbath.

² But the Pharisees when they saw it, said unto him, Behold, thy disciples do that which it is not lawful to do upon the sabbath.

A. But the Pharisees . . . it. This chapter is intended to furnish illustrations of the malevolence with which the Pharisees began to regard the Saviour.—**B. Thy disciples, etc.** When the Jewish teachers had resolved all religion into mere outward works, they enumerated many harmless acts, which, under the denomination of *work* or *labor*, were, as they alleged, violations of the law respecting the Sabbath (Exod. 20 : 8–11). As the act of plucking and then rubbing the ears in the hands while passing through a field, seemed to resemble harvest work, it had been specially prohibited by the Jewish teachers; to this human ordinance the Pharisees here refer; their reproach is not directed against the mere act of eating the grain (Exod. 12 : 16).

³ But he said unto them, Have ye not read what David did, when he was an hungered, and they that were with him ?

A. The Lord explains that the true worship of God is in spirit (John 4 : 24), and not in the letter (comp. Rom. 2 : 27-29; 7 : 6); that is, God regards rather the spirit of faith and love, or the motive of the act, than a mere formal and heartless observance of the letter of the law (Isai. 1 : 11-18).—**Have ye not read**—in 1 Sam. 21 : 3, 6, when David, that devout man (1 Sam. 13 : 14), fled from Saul, and suffered hunger, as My disciples now suffer? Did the high-priest, whose decision was final (Deut. 17 : 9, 12), judge as you now do? Are you wiser and more devout than that priest and that anointed king?

⁴ How he entered into the house of God, and did eat the shewbread, which it was not lawful for him to eat, neither for them that were with him, but only for the priests.

A. **The house of God** (comp. Exod. 23 : 19; 1 Kings 8 : 13); this term includes the priest's habitation in the precincts of the tabernacle (1 Sam. 3 : 15); the latter still retained the ark until David's successor had built the temple (1 Kings 8 : 3–6). So, too, one of the Greek words translated *temple* (see 4 : 5, E.; 21 : 12, A.) comprehended also the external courts surrounding the sacred edifice.—B. **Shewbread**—twelve loaves of bread, placed every Sabbath-day upon the table in the sanctuary before the Lord, hence called in Hebrew *bread of the face* or *presence* of God.—C. **Which** (it) **was not lawful, etc.**—Aaron and his descendants alone were permitted in ordinary cases to eat the shewbread, after it gave place to the new bread (Exod. 29 : 32, 33 ; Lev. 8 : 31 ; 22 : 10; 24 : 9). Now the devout David, who was already anointed and endowed with the Spirit of the Lord (1 Sam. 16 : 13), demonstrated, as the Saviour here declares, to all succeeding generations, that true religion consists rather in holiness of mind and purpose than in a mere outward conformity to the letter of the ceremonial law, when, in a case of necessity, He departed without sin from the mere letter.

⁵ Or have ye not read in the law, how that on the sabbath day the priests in the temple profane the sabbath, and are guiltless ?

A. The former case illustrated the general principle that religion did not consist exclusively in mere forms; the present shows, further, that a literal cessation of manual labor without any exception whatever, was never intended by the Lord when He gave the law respecting the Sabbath. The same principle is illustrated by another practice, in John 7 : 22, 23—**B. Or have . . . law** (of Moses)=in Lev. 24 : 8, and Numb. 28 : 9, 10, that besides the exchange of shewbread, certain burnt-offerings are required every Sabbath, in addition to the daily sacrifice, although the preparation of the wood for fire, the slaying of the lambs and the incidental duties connected with the sacrifice, certainly constituted *work* or labor.— **C. Profane the sabbath**=perform manual labor on the Sabbath day. According to your religious views—the Lord says—the priests, whom none condemn, literally "do work" on the Sabbath, and yet thereby strictly obey the commandments of God. My disciples—He continues, may have equally good authority for disregarding one of your sabbatical rules. Thus, too, Christ refers in John 5 : 17, to the ceaseless action of God as another illustration of the truth that total inaction by no means corresponds to the divine nature and will.

⁶ But I say unto you, That one greater than the temple is here.

The Lord, after this appeal to the judgment of His hearers (comp. Luke 12 : 57), now speaks authoritatively in His own divine majesty. The sense is: The honor of God is the great end of all His laws; the honor due to His name required that His service in the temple should never be interrupted. If the claims of the temple-service (sacrifices, etc.), take precedence before every other duty, much more shall every institution yield before the will of Him, from whose presence not the temple only, but the heaven of heavens itself (2 Chron. 6 : 18) derives its holy character. That Greater One am I! The glory of the second temple was greater than that of the first, which Solomon built (Hagg. 2 : 7, 9), because it was honored with the presence of the Saviour, " in whom dwelleth all the fulness of the Godhead bodily " (Col. 2 : 9), and whose body is, as He Himself declares, therefore the true temple (John 2 : 19, 21 ; Rev. 21 : 22).

⁷ But if ye had known what this meaneth, I desire mercy, and not sacrifice, ye would not have condemned the guiltless.

See above 9 : 13, B. The sense is: That saying of God teaches that He is better pleased when He bestows a blessing on man, than when a heartless, hypocritical and unprofitable worship is offered to Him ; if ye had rightly understood it, ye would not have so maliciously censured My disciples for being guided by My divine authority and benevolent purposes, and for doing as they have done.

⁸ For the Son of man is Lord even of the sabbath day.

In Mark 2 : 27 an additional saying of the Lord is recorded (" The sabbath was made, etc.") which, when combined with the present verse, gives the following sense of the whole: The sabbath law and all other laws of Moses were intended to promote the welfare of man, and train him for the service of God. Now I, the Son of man, and the Lord from heaven (1 Cor. 15 : 47), who have authority to appoint, alter or abolish laws relating to the service of God (John 5 : 23), have allowed the act of My disciples. The sabbath day was originally designed for holy rest, and spiritual improvement. Have these disciples violated the spirit of the divine institution by acknowledging My authority, and, in a case of necessity, gratefully partaking of food? The Saviour here, by declaring that the divine law receives its authority from Him, unequivocally reveals His divine nature.

⁹ And he departed thence, and went into their synagogue.

Their synagogue—in the same town ("their" the people of the place) in which the foregoing conversation was held, but on a subsequent sabbath day (Luke 6 : 6).

¹⁰ And, behold, a man having a withered hand. And they asked him, saying, Is it lawful to heal on the sabbath day? that they might accuse him.

A. Withered hand=the right hand (Luke 6 : 6) was paralyzed, shrivelled and useless.—**B. They asked him, etc.** When the scribes and Pharisees observed that Jesus had called the man forward (Luke), they objected to the act of healing him, as a profanation of the sabbath, even though that act should involve no outward work. The principle which the Lord explains in this case, according to Mark 3 : 4, is the following: The divine law respecting the sabbath does not forbid actions simply because they are *actions*, as opposed to total inaction, but only *evil actions*=evil in themselves, or evil by being inconsistent with the true design of the sabbath ; on the other hand, it requires *good* actions (" do good—evil ? "). Hence devout and benevolent acts, or those which are good in the eyes of God, are always appropriate on that day.—C. **Accuse him**=denounce him as a profane person and sabbath-breaker.

^{11, 12} And he said unto them, What man shall there be of you, that shall have one sheep, and if this fall into a pit on the sabbath day, will he not lay hold on it, and lift it out? How much then is a man of more value than a sheep? Wherefore it is lawful to do good on the sabbath day.

A. The sense is the following: Even you yourselves admit that God does not intend to teach in any of His commandments a lesson of needless cruelty. Now, shall the humane relief which an animal may claim, be denied to a human being? (Matt. 6 : 26; Luke 13 : 15, 16; 14 : 5; Mark 3 : 4).—**B. Wherefore, etc.**—any act which proceeds from a holy motive, and which honors God, or confers a substantial benefit on a human being, is acceptable in the sight of God, and therefore "lawful"—*right, permitted*, by the divine author of the Law.

¹³ Then saith he to the man, Stretch forth thy hand. And he stretched it forth; and it was restored whole, as the other.

A. Stretch forth, etc. At the Lord's word, this man, like Peter (Luke 5 : 5), attempted to do an apparently useless or impossible act. It is not our part to determine the possibility or probability, but simply to believe and obey, when God has commanded and promised.—**B. Restored whole**=to entire health or soundness; the corresponding Greek verb is translated in Luke 15 : 27, "safe and sound," and "be in health" in 2 John 2.

¹⁴ But the Pharisees went out, and took counsel against him, how they might destroy him.

A. But . . . went out—filled, according to Luke 6 : 11, with *madness* (the original word for *madness* indicates both folly and wickedness, as in 2 Tim. 3 : 9). It was their own hatred of the Lord (to which they yielded, and which proceeded from Satan (John 13 : 2; 2 Cor. 4 : 4; Eph. 4 : 27) that produced such awful hardness of heart, and closed their eyes to the divine glory of Christ.—B. **Took counsel.** They consulted with the Herodians (Mark 3 : 6), the political adherents of Herod Antipas, the ruler of Galilee, who resided in Tiberias (2 : 22, C. ; 22 : 16, B.). The Pharisees appear to have represented Christ to the Herodians as dangerous to the government in a political respect (see below, 21 : 38 ; 27 : 11, B.). "What power Satan possessed over their hearts! They hear the wisdom of God; they are convinced by the miracles wrought before them ; they listen to unanswerable arguments of the Lord ; every appeal is made to them ; yet, in place of repenting, they seek to destroy Christ."—LUTHER.

¹⁵, ¹⁶ And Jesus perceiving *it*, withdrew from thence: and many followed him; and he healed them all;—And charged them that they should not make him known.

A. **Withdrew**—from the neighborhood of these hostile men (to the sea, Mark 3 : 7), as the hour of the completion of His work (26 : 45) had not yet arrived.—C. **Healed them all**—all the sick persons among them. The miracles which are related in detail in the four Gospels, do not exceed those here mentioned in such general terms, either in glory or in power, but are intended to serve only as specimens or as illustrations of that whole class of the Saviour's works (John 20 : 30, 31).—D. **Charged . . . not make him known**—spread abroad (as in Mark 6 : 14), publish everywhere ; His object was to avoid an unwelcome notoriety (comp. Mark 3 : 11, 12), and he refrained from irritating his enemies needlessly (see 8 : 4, A.):

¹⁷ That it might be fulfilled which was spoken by Isaiah the prophet, saying,

A. **That . . . fulfilled** (see 1 : 22, A.).

¹⁸ Behold my servant, whom I have chosen; my beloved, in whom my

soul is well pleased: I will put my Spirit upon him, and he shall declare judgment to the Gentiles.

A. My servant. The lofty description of the "servant" here introduced (Isai. 42 : 1–4), cannot possibly refer to Cyrus (mentioned in ch. 44 : 28 ; 45 : 1, the Persian king, Ezra 1 : 1 ff.) nor to any prophet, nor to the people of Israel viewed collectively, but only to the Son of God, even as the corresponding passage (Isai. 52 : 13 ; 53 : 12), refers to Him alone, according to Matt. 8 : 17 ; Luke 22 : 37 ; John 12 : 38, and, especially, Acts 8 : 30–35.—**B. Whom I have chosen**—whom I uphold, *sustain*, and thus acknowledge as My chosen one (see an illustration in John 9 : 30–33).—**C. My beloved . . . pleased** (see above, 3 : 17, B.).—**D. I will . . . him** (comp. Isai. 11 : 2 and 61 : 1 with Luke 4 : 18, 21, and see also Matt. 3 : 16 ; John 3 : 34).—**E. And he shall . . . Gentiles.** The Greek word here translated *judgment*, like the Hebrew word in the passage in Isaiah, is used with various shades of meaning. It sometimes refers to the final judgment (Matt. 10 : 15 ; 12 : 41) ; it also indicates a decision of the mind (John 7 : 24), a sentence, or the punishment which is decreed (Rev. 16 : 7), or the tribunal itself (Matt. 5 : 21), and also justice, equity, righteousness (23 : 23, D.), or the righteous will of God, in accordance with the original Hebrew word in passages like Lev. 18 : 4 ; Ps. 119 : 108. In the last sense it appears to occur here, and may be explained from Rom. 3 : 26, thus :—He (Christ) shall declare to the Gentiles God's righteousness and justice, in devising a plan of salvation.

¹⁹ He shall not strive, nor cry aloud; neither shall any one hear his voice in the streets.

Oriental imagery is here introduced by the prophet, when he intends to declare that the Messiah will not exhibit a spirit of strife (—contention or wrangling), which reveals itself in loud, warlike shouts (Exod. 32 : 17), nor will He designedly create confusion, but will diffuse a spirit of love and peace. The latter part of the verse alludes to the well-known habits of the people of the East, of whose loud reproaches, violent vociferations and angry shouts all travellers complain.

²⁰ A bruised reed shall he not break, and smoking flax shall he not quench, till he send forth judgment unto victory.

A. **A bruised . . . quench.** A reed, originally feeble (11 : 7, B.), and moreover bruised or crushed by a blow, can no longer sustain itself, and is totally unsuited to serve as a supporting staff (comp. 2 Kings 18 : 21).— **Smoking flax.** The name of the material sometimes stands for that of the article itself; so *silk* in Ezek. 16 : 10 means *garments made of silk*. Thus, the wick, made of flax, and placed in a lamp, is here meant. It was lighted, but, at length, it merely smokes ("dimly burning," as the translators render the original Hebrew in the margin), in consequence of the want of oil (see 25 : 1, E.), and the flame is on the point of expiring. Both of these images describe the state of fallen man, robbed of light, strength and peace by sin, and ready to perish. They correspond to those already presented in Matt. 9 : 36; 11 : 28. The former, the bruised reed, describes man as a fallen creature; the smoking flax or expiring light represents his want of spiritual life and holiness. The sense is :— The meek and merciful Messiah, who brings with Him, not despair and death, but joy and life, will not repulse the humble and helpless sinner (John 6 : 37), who implores Him to pity, forgive and save him, but will infuse new spiritual life into his soul. The reed is bruised—man is helpless; the flax merely smokes and has no clear light —man's faith is weak; still, even the most feeble effort to seek divine grace shall not only not be discouraged ("not break—not quench") but be graciously recognized and sustained by the compassionate Redeemer.—B. **Till ... victory.** Matthew explains the prophet's word—"truth"—thus:—The Messiah will demonstrate the truth, justice and righteousness of God in all His ways, as well in the plan of salvation, as in the final judgment of men. That divine *truth,* however violent its conflict with error and sin may be, will, sooner or later, be acknowledged by all, and thus gain the "victory" over all errors and delusions.

²¹ And in his name shall the Gentiles hope.

A. **In his name**—in the power and mercy (atoning work) of Him who alone can save (Acts 4:12; comp. Phil. 2:10).—B. **Gentiles** (see 4:15, A.). The prophet's word, for which Matthew gives the equivalent word *Gentiles*—heathen nations, is *isles;* this term often occurs in Isaiah and the prophetic writings generally (Ps. 72:10; Jer. 31:10; Ezek. 39:6; Dan. 11:18; Zeph. 2:11).—C. **Hope**—*confide in,* equivalent to the prophet's term: *wait for.*

²² There was brought unto him one possessed with a devil, blind, and dumb: and he healed him, insomuch that the dumb man spake and saw.

The bodily afflictions of this man were occasioned by the unclean spirit dwelling in him. The demoniac described in 9:32, 33, was only dumb; here, the blindness of the man gives additional interest to the case. For **possessed,** see EXCURSUS II.

²³ And all the multitudes were amazed, and said, Is this the Son of David?

Is this, etc. (as in 9:27)—Is not He who can work such a miracle, the promised Messiah? (see 1:1, C.).

²⁴ But when the Pharisees heard it, they said, This man doth not cast out devils, but by Beelzebub the prince of the devils.

A. But when, etc. The same reproach had been uttered before (see 9 : 34). The connecting remarks may have been these:—He is not the Messiah—said the Pharisees. But how then—others asked—shall we explain His miracles? These He performs with the aid of Beelzebub—exclaimed the Pharisees.—**B. Beelzebub** (see 10 : 25, C.). He is revealed in the Scriptures as the head, ruler or prince of all the unclean spirits (see 4 : 1, E.).

^{25, 26} And knowing their thoughts he said unto them, Every kingdom divided against itself is brought to desolation; and every city or house divided against itself shall not stand:—And if Satan casteth out Satan, he is divided against himself; how then shall his kingdom stand?

A. Knowing, etc. (see 9 : 3, B., and 4, A.).—**B. Said unto them, etc.** The Lord refers in these words to the kingdom of darkness, the head of which is **Satan** (see 4 : 1, E.), who rules over the fallen angels (Matt. 25 : 41; 2 Pet. 2 : 4); their acts are consequently his own acts. In answer to the blasphemous charge of the Pharisees, that our Lord was acting by Satan's power and authority, He says: "If the ruler of a country, or the governor of a city, or the head of a family ("house"), should invariably act against his own interest, and defeat his own plans, he would necessarily accomplish his own ruin. Apply this principle to Satan—proceeds the Lord (ver. 26) in His appeal to the understanding of His enemies—and say whether you can really believe that this watchful and cunning enemy of man (2 Cor. 2 : 11; Eph. 6 : 11, 12; 1 Pet. 5 : 8) would intentionally convey to Me the power to rescue from his grasp invariably all his victims whom I meet. Would he, by these miracles, give currency to My doctrines, which undeniably operate against his influence? Does not your charge that Satan casts out Satan (=himself), carry its own refutation with it?

²⁷ And if I by Beelzebub cast out devils, by whom do your sons cast them out? therefore shall they be your judges.

A. After showing that the charge is inconsistent with itself, the Lord next exhibits its inconsistency with the avowed opinions of the Pharisees themselves.—**B. Your sons** (Luke 11 : 19). This title was given to the pupils of religious teachers; comp. the phrase: "Sons of the prophets" (1 Kings 20 : 35; 2 Kings 2 : 3). Here it designates any Jews who recognized the scribes and Pharisees generally as their religious teachers, and who, with the approbation of the latter, endeavored to relieve demoniacs. Of the real nature of their proceedings no satisfactory accounts have been preserved. According to the statements of early Christian writers (quoted by Grotius on this passage), these exorcists expelled demons by invoking the name of the God of Abraham, of Isaac, and of Jacob. Josephus relates that some Jews in his day, styled exorcists, claimed that they could expel demons by means of certain charms, roots, etc. (Antiq. 8 : 2, 5 ; War, 7, 6, 3). Compare the case described in Acts 19 : 13–19.—These men—says the Lord—may be regarded as judges in this case; according to their decision, from which you cannot appeal, since you have always approved of their acts, demons may be expelled without the aid of Satan.

²⁸ But if I by the Spirit of God cast out devils, then is the kingdom of God come upon you.

A. By the Spirit of God—the creative Spirit of God (Gen. 1 : 2; Job. 33 : 4; Ps. 104 : 30); Luke says (11 : 20): "with the finger of God." The latter is a figurative term of the same general meaning, that is, indicates the divine power (comp. Exod. 8 : 19; 31 : 18, and Ps. 8 : 3). **C.—Then the kingdom, etc.** The Lord declares that His miracles are wrought neither by the aid of Satan, nor by the arts practised by the Jewish exorcists, but directly by divine power. Learn, therefore, from My miracles—

He adds—that God, by whose power alone they are wrought, is here present (the kingdom, not of Satan but of God, is come unto you—the Messiah's kingdom (Dan. 7 : 14).

²⁹ Or how can one enter into the house of the strong man, and spoil his goods, except he first bind the strong *man?* and then he will spoil his house.

A. House of the strong man—this world, in which Satan exercises his influence (John 12 : 31 ; Acts 26 : 17, 18.—**B. Spoil.** Several Greek words are translated in the English Test. *to spoil*, which English word there never means *to mar, to render useless*, but *to despoil*, that is, to take away by forcible or other means (Col. 2 : 8,— to carry off as booty ; here, the English word signifies to wrest from another by superior power.—**C.** Satan is like a strong man, who takes captive the unwary and impenitent (2 Tim. 2 : 26), but Christ is stronger, and hence *binds*—curbs him, despoils him of his prey when He expels unclean spirits from their victims, and will ultimately, when the wisely chosen time arrives, destroy him (Hebr. 2 : 14 ; John 16 : 11 ; 1 John 3 : 8 ; comp. Isai. 49 : 25, 26).

³⁰ He that is not with me is against me ; and he that gathereth not with me scattereth.

A. Two proverbs are here combined, both referring to the inevitable and continued conflicts in the world between sin and holiness (2 Cor. 6 : 14–16). The former (repeated in Mark 9 : 40) indicates that neutrality in feeling, and the latter, that neutrality in action, cannot be tolerated by the Lord, in matters of religion.—**With me** —*on my side*, as in 26 : 69, C. ; 1 Kings 1 : 8 ; 2 Kings 6 : 16 ; 9 : 32.—**Against**—*hostile*, as in Matt. 10 : 35.— **Gathereth**—by living and laboring for the glory of God.

—**Scattereth**=actually wastes the grain (Matt. 3 : 12) or, disperses the flock (John 10 : 12 ; 11 : 52 ; 16 : 32), which I and my servants have gathered.—**B.** At all times, while the contest between light and darkness is maintained in the world (2 Cor. 6 : 14-16; Gal. 5 : 17), every individual practically espouses the cause either of God or Satan (Rom. 6 : 16 ; 8 : 7; Matt. 6 : 24). Hence he who does not give his heart to the Saviour, as an humble, contrite sinner, or a true believer, is still a servant of sin (see 13 : 43, A.).

³¹ Therefore I say unto you, Every sin and blasphemy shall be forgiven unto men: but the blasphemy against the Spirit shall not be forgiven.

A. Therefore, lit. *On this account*=as every man serves either God or Satan, and will receive hereafter a corresponding reward, I urge you to consider well your true position, if indeed you may yet find "repentance to the acknowledging of the truth" (2 Tim. 2 : 25, 26).— **C. Blasphemy**=irreverent, malicious, slanderous language employed in reference to God and divine things (see 9 : 3, C.).—**Shall** (=will) **be forgiven unto men**=if they sincerely repent (Acts 8 : 22 ; 2 Cor. 7 : 10) and exercise faith (Acts 16 : 31; 20 : 21 ; Hebr. 11 : 6).—**D. The blasphemy . . . Spirit.** It is specially the office of the Holy Spirit (1 : 18, D.; Acts 15 : 8), to call, enlighten (Eph. 1 : 17, 18), convert, renew (Eph. 5 : 9 ; Tit. 3 : 5) and sanctify man (2 Thess. 2 : 13 ; Eph. 4 : 30; 1 Cor. 6 : 11 ; 1 Pet. 1 : 22). Hence Paul says: " No man can say [with deep, inward conviction of the soul] that Jesus is the Lord, but by the Holy Ghost " (1 Cor. 12 : 3). When, therefore, the sinner, to whom, under the Gospel dispensation, the most efficacious means of grace have been given, resists all the influences of the divine Spirit, and does this consciously and purposely, he closes every avenue to his future conversion and sanctification; for this sin is not so much a particular act as a certain state or condition of the soul. Further, he who has already been influenced in any degree by that Holy Spirit, the only author of man's conversion, but afterwards deliberately quenches (1 Thess. 5 : 19; Eph. 4 : 30) the light, and resists (Acts 7 : 51) the life-giving power of the Spirit, thereby renders a renewed conversion impossible ; for he wilfully and consciously scorns and disowns the only means given for man's conversion, namely, the influences of the divine Spirit. Nothing more could be done to such a vineyard that God had not previously done (Isai. 5 : 4). It is impossible for such persons to be renewed, according to Hebr. 6 : 4–6, inasmuch as they deliberately and consciously suppress those holy influences which are the exclusive means of conversion. So, too, no other sacrifice can atone for those who " sin wilfully," and scorn the Saviour's atoning death (Hebr. 10 : 26). This is a " sin unto death " (1 John 5 : 16); any prayer of another for the pardon of that sin, independently of the sinner's sincere repentence, would be altogether fruitless, involving the unscriptural thought that God would pardon the impenitent and scornful (see ver. 32, C.).—**E. Shall not be forgiven**—because, by the very nature of this sin, which consists in a deliberate and conscious resistance to the converting influences of the Divine Spirit, it excludes that genuine " believing " (faith and joyful trust in God's grace through Christ), in reference to which the Lord says : " He that believeth not shall be damned " (Mark 16 : 16). When the apostle John accordingly declares : " The blood of Jesus Christ His Son cleanseth us from all sin " (1 John 1 : 7), he restricts, by the introduction of the word " us," that blessed influence of Christ's atoning work *to them that believe.*

[32] And whosoever shall speak a word against the Son of man, it shall be

forgiven him; but whosoever shall speak against the Holy Spirit, it shall not be forgiven him, neither in this world, nor in that which is to come.

A. **And . . . forgiven him**—provided that he yields to the converting grace of God, repents and believes. So Paul, once the persecuting Saul (Acts 8 : 1–4), was forgiven, for while he spake and acted against the Son of man (Acts 9 : 5), denying that he was the Messiah and the Son of God, he was led astray, not by a deliberate design to dishonor God, but by erroneous views of religious duty, according to Acts 26 : 9 ; 1 Tim. 1 : 13. Hence he describes his own case as a glorious illustration of the grace of Christ (1 Tim. 1 : 16). Even in the case of the murderers of the Lord, an avenue was open for the penitent (Luke 23 : 34 ; Acts 2 : 23, 37, 38).—B. **But whosoever . . . not be forgiven him**—for the reason stated above (ver. 31, D.). The forgiveness of the *impenitent* sinner is incompatible with the holiness of God, and cannot therefore occur, until the sinner humbles himself before God in sincere repentance. Now, since no man can come to Christ except the Father draw him (John 6 : 44) by giving the Holy Spirit (Rom. 5 : 5), and since the sinner wilfully and contemptuously scorns such divine grace, no other avenue to pardon exists for him.—C. **Neither . . . world to come.** The Greek word (*aion*) here and elsewhere (see ann. to 24 : 3, E. and comp. Luke 16 : 8 ; Hebr. 11 : 3) translated *world* is peculiar, and different from the ordinary word (*kosmos*) which occurs very frequently (e. g. Matt. 4 : 8 ; 13 : 38 ; 26 : 13). According to a usage of the N. T., conforming to very early views (illustrated in 13 : 39 ; 24 : 3), the end of the world which we inhabit constitutes a broad line of demarcation between two great divisions of all time, or, rather, duration, regarded as the past and the future. (The phrase: *the end of the world*, occurring in 13 : 39, 40 ; 24 : 3 ; 28 : 20, designates the time to which there is a reference in 2 Pet. 3 : 10 when "the earth—shall be burned up"). The some word (aion), in the sense of *continuance* or *duration*, is applied to both. In the former case, the phrases are: *this present world* (Gal. 1 : 4; 2 Tim. 4 : 10; Tit. 2 : 12), *this world* (Luke 20 : 34; 1 Cor. 1 : 20; 2 : 6; Eph. 1 : 21); in the latter, *the world to come* (Mark 10 : 30; Eph. 1 : 21), *that world* (Luke 20 : 35), *ages to come* (Eph. 2 : 7). Hence, " this world " in Matt. 13 : 22 designates the period which extends to the day of judgment; again, when the word occurs in the phrase: *the end of the world* (Matt. 13 : 39, 40; 24 : 3; 28 : 20), the sense is precisely that which the English words convey—the end of all things, when this earth shall pass away. But when these two divisions are *not* contrasted (as they are in Luke 20 : 34, 35), the term indicates eternity itself—*forever*, as in Matt. 6 : 13; John 6 : 51; Rom. 9 : 5; 1 Tim. 1 : 17, and very frequently. When, therefore, the Lord combines both expressions (comp. also Luke 18 : 30) in the present verse, he comprehends man's entire existence, or both the whole period preceding the end of this world, and the whole endless or eternal existence of man after that event. His language therefore by no means indicates that there may be cases in which forgiveness might be obtained after death (which would be a contradiction of the whole system of Bible doctrine as set forth even before the Gospel age, Eccl. 9 : 10), but is intended, like " and ever" in the phrase: *for ever and ever*, to be an emphatic expression for the word: *Never*, the word used in Mark 3 : 29. (So, too, the phrase: *day and night*, in an emphatic sense, often signifies *continually*, as in Acts 20 : 31; 26 : 7; 2 Tim. 1 : 3). The explanatory statement added in the parallel passage, Mark 3 : 30, seems to sanction the inference, that, as the Pharisees were conscious of the truth that God's power wrought miracles through Christ, but, nevertheless, in their excessive impiety and with deliberate blasphemy ascribed these works of God to Satan, therefore (according to John 9 : 41), they practically renounced God forever, and their sin would remain unforgiven. The whole tenor of the Lord's words authorizes us to assume that the unpardonable sin consists in a bold and contemptuous spirit in reference to God. Hence, he who is distressed by the fear that he may have committed that sin, proves, by the distress which controls him, and by the entire absence of all desire to dishonor God, that he is certainly *not* the sinner of whom the Lord is speaking in this passage.

³³ Either make the tree good, and its fruit good; or make the tree corrupt, and its fruit corrupt: for the tree is known by its fruit.

A. Good . . . corrupt (see 7 : 17, 18.—**B. Make**—assume, constitute and declare, represent as a truth or fact ; in this sense the same Greek word (*making, makest, made*) occurs in John 5 : 18 ; 8 : 53 ; 10 : 33 ; 19 : 7. The Saviour says: Recognize the simple fact that the tree and its fruit are alike, both being either good or bad. The sense is: If My fruit (=the expulsion of unclean spirits) is good, then I, the tree (the author of the work), cannot be evil. But if I am evil, then it is also an evil thing to expel unclean spirits.

³⁴ Ye offspring of vipers, how can ye, being evil, speak good things? for out of the abundance of the heart the mouth speaketh.

A. Ye offspring, etc. (see 3 : 7. B.—**B. How can . . . things?** This language is intended to establish the Lord's declaration just made respecting the spiritual state of those whom He addresses. The sense is: You are in spirit the children of the serpent (23 : 33 ; John 8 : 44 ; 1 John 3 : 8 ; Rev. 12 : 9), and your conduct is in accordance with your spiritual character ("being evil");

you resemble the thorn and thistle (7 : 16), from which none would expect to gather grapes or figs (comp. James 3 : 11, 12).—C. **For out, etc.** The sense of the proverb as here applied is: Your blasphemous language, which demonstrates that you are not Abraham's children in spirit (John 8 : 39; Gal. 3 : 7), is the result of the entire ascendancy which the Serpent (—Satan, Gen. 3 : 1 ; Rev. 12 : 9) possesses over your hearts (comp. 15 : 19 and John 8 : 44).

[35] The good man out of his good treasure bringeth forth good things: and the evil man out of his evil treasure bringeth forth evil things.

A. Good . . . evil man. The difference between a devout and a wicked heart is indicated by the terms *good* and *evil* (see 19 : 17, A.); the whole verse is explanatory of the one which precedes it.—**B. Treasure**—the ruling sentiments of the heart (see 6 : 19, B.). The state of the heart, or its decided inclination to obey God or Satan, determines the good or evil character of the individual.

[36] And I say unto you, That every idle word that men shall speak, they shall give account thereof in the day of judgment.

A. And—further.—**B. Idle.** The Greek word originally signifies *inactive*, as in 20 : 3, 6, and then, *slothful*, as in 1 Tim. 5 : 13, and 2 Pet. 1 : 8. As sloth, in its spiritual aspects (neglect of watchfulness, etc.) readily exposes the heart to the influence of sin, the word is applied in the text in an unfavorable sense (as equivalent to *evil*) to language proceeding from an evil heart, and uttered when there is no fear of God before the eyes (Ps. 36 : 1) of the speaker. Comp. the phrase: *vain* (—empty) *words* (Eph. 5 : 6).—**C. Give account**—be tried, judged respecting its character (comp. 25 : 19; Luke 16 : 2; Rom. 14 : 12; Hebr. 13 : 17; 1 Pet. 4 : 5).

[37] For by thy words thou shalt be justified, and by thy words thou shalt be condemned.

A. Justified. *To justify*, when the act is performed by God, signifies usually in Paul's epistles, particularly in those to the Romans and Galatians, *to forgive* and admit the penitent believer to the full enjoyment of divine favor through the imputation of the merits of Christ. Here, however (and comp. 11 : 19, B.), the word occurs (as in 1 Cor. 4 : 4; Luke 10 : 29) in its original sense—to declare or set forth that an individual is free from all blame, and has conformed to his duty.—**B.** The Saviour reveals here the important principle, that, in the eyes of God, words are regarded as if they were *actions* (comp. James 3 : 5–8, and two of the Ten Commandments (Exod. 20 : 7, 16). He desires to remove from the minds of men the dangerous opinion that, because the words of the lips seem to be mere breath or air, they are of less account than the deeds of the hands. He means to say: Watch well over your words, for God will judge them as evidences of the spirit in you which dictates them, and which rules you.

[38] Then certain of the scribes and Pharisees answered him saying, Master, we would see a sign from thee.

A. Certain=not the same mentioned in ver. 24, but "others" according to Luke 11 : 16.—**B. Master** (see 8 : 19, B.).—**C. A sign.** The original word is frequently translated *miracle* (Luke 23 : 8; John 2 : 11); sometimes it is associated with kindred words, as in John 4 : 48; Acts 2 : 22; 2 Cor. 12 : 12). It specially designates a miracle intended as a *mark, token, indication*, and wrought for the purpose of demonstrating the truth of some declaration, claim, etc.—**D.** A later occurrence of the same kind (see below, 16 : 1) conveys the idea that the unbelieving and malicious Pharisees alleged that the miracles already wrought on earth (healing the sick, etc.) were not sufficient to demonstrate the Lord's divine mission ; they scornfully ask Him to exhibit a still more striking miracle. On the second occasion they ask for some phenomenon in the skies, such, for instance, as those described in Joel 2 : 30, 31, or the fall of manna or bread from heaven (comp. John 6 : 30-32).

³⁹ But he answered and said unto them, An evil and adulterous generation seeketh after a sign ; and there shall no sign be given to it, but the sign of Jonah the prophet.

A. An evil . . . generation (Deut. 1 : 35). The same answer is given again on a later occasion (16 : 4). Christ alludes, in the word "adulterous" to language frequently occurring in the prophets, according to which the relation between the Lord and His people, in a spiritual sense, resembled that established by a marriage contract; this language referred to the fidelity which the Lord justly claimed from the people of His covenant, viewed as His spouse (Isai. 54 : 5 ; Jer. 3 : 14 ; 31 : 32 ; Hosea 2 : 19, 20. See 22 : 2, C. ; comp. also Eph. 5 : 25 ; Rev. 19 : 7-9 ; 21 : 9).—**B. There shall no, etc.** As the request proceeded, not from a spirit of faith, but from unbelief and malice (comp. 27 : 42), the Lord refuses to gratify such unholy feelings. Unreasonable demands of men, which come in conflict with the ways and means appointed by divine wisdom, are never granted (comp. Luke 16 : 27-31). —**C. The sign . . . Jonah**—such as occurred in the case of Jonah ; the Lord refers to His own resurrection, as the next verse shows. (The "sign of the Son of man in heaven," mentioned in 24 : 30, B. refers to a different subject.)

⁴⁰ For as Jonah was three days and three nights in the belly of the whale : so shall the Son of man be three days and three nights in the heart of the earth.

A. Jonah, etc. He lived about eight centuries before the Christian era. The original Greek word here translated *whale*, properly signifies, in accordance with the original phrase in Jonah, a *sea-monster* or *great fish*. The occurrence took place in the Mediterranean Sea, on the eastern coast of which the city of Joppa (Acts 9 : 43, Jaffa) was situated, from which Jonah sailed. The Hebrew word translated *prepared* (=arranged, appointed, procured) in Jonah 1 : 17, occurs also in 4 : 6, 7, 8, and indicates that, like the gourd, the worm, and the scorching wind, it was miraculously adapted by divine power to the occasion.—The **three days and three nights** here mentioned, and quoted from Jonah 1 : 17, do not necessarily mean thrice twenty-four hours. Among the Jews, as among several other ancient nations, the civil day of twenty-four hours commenced at sunset, and extended to the next sunset (see Lev. 23 : 32). According to the Jewish mode of reckoning, any *portion* of the whole division of time constituted by one day and one night, was called "a night and a day;" the later Greek combined both words in one (=night-day) which Paul uses in 2 Cor. 11 : 25 (comp. Gen. 1 : 5, 8). Hence, a few hours of a certain *night-day* of twenty-four hours, were counted as the whole. The Rev. Mr. Osborn relates in his work "PALESTINE, etc.," p. 65, that his confinement for five days in quarantine actually extended only from Friday evening to Tuesday morning, or little more than three days, but "orientally, five consecutive parts of days are accounted so many days." According to different estimates, our Lord's body lay in the grave from thirty-three to forty hours, that is, during certain hours of the first and of the third day-nights (=periods of twenty-four hours) respectively, and the whole of the intermediate day-night—in modern language, from Friday afternoon till Sunday morning, before the sun rose. Such a period would constitute, according to the Hebrew mode of describing it, three night-days. The **heart of the earth** here is a phrase corresponding to the Hebrew in Jonah 2 : 3, where we read "the heart (=the interior or midst) of the seas" (see the margin of the English Bible ; in ver. 2, the Hebrew word for *hell* is *Sheol*, for which see above, 11 : 23, B.).—B. The Lord here refers prophetically to His resurrection from the grave on the third day (16 : 21); He announces the occurrence by divine appointment (and not as an answer to their presumptuous demand) of a greater miracle than the one for which they do ask ; He refers to His own restoration to life on the third day,—an event which had been foreshadowed by Jonah's return to the land of the living. But even this sign of the Saviour's divine mission, to which the apostles afterwards appealed with great power (Acts 2 : 24; 3 : 26; 5 : 30), made no salutary impression, after it had been given, on the obdurate hearts of His enemies (28 : 11–15).

[41] The men of Nineveh shall stand in the judgment with this generation, and shall condemn it; for they repented at the preaching of Jonah; and, behold, a greater than Jonah is here.

A. The Lord now speaks prophetically ; He refers with deep solemnity to the consequences of the blindness and unbelief of that generation, which will not yield even to the powerful testimony furnished by His resurrection (Rom. 1 : 14).—B. **The men of N.**=the Ninevites (Luke 11 : 30; see Jonah 3 : 5 ff.). Nineveh, the chief city of Assyria, on the river Tigris (2 Kings 19 : 36), was one of the oldest cities mentioned in the Bible (Gen. 10 : 11).— C. **Shall rise . . . condemn it**=their prompt and sincere repentance, after they heard the preaching of Jonah (whose restoration to the world they had not even seen, and who was, moreover, a stranger and foreigner, and yet was not asked to work miracles), is itself a condemnation of the unbelief and impiety of the Jews. So the conduct of the good Samaritan (Luke 10 : 30 ff.), condemned that of the priests and Levites (comp. 10 : 15 ; 11 : 21-24).— **Stand up**=as a witness (comp. Job 16 : 8 ; Matt. 10 : 21). —D. **A greater**=in nature, power, and fulness of His revelations.

⁴² The queen of the south shall rise up in the judgment with this generation, and shall condemn it; for she came from the ends of the earth to hear the wisdom of Solomon; and, behold, a greater than Solomon is here.

A. **The queen of the south**—of Sheba, lying south of Judea (1 Kings 10 : 1 ; 2 Chron. 9 : 1). Her country is now known as Yemen or Arabia Felix, in the southern part of Arabia, bordering on the Red Sea. The oriental phrase: **the uttermost parts** or *ends* (comp. Rom. 10 : 13 and Ps. 19 : 4), was employed in early ages, when a very limited knowledge of geography existed, and travelling was tedious and difficult, to indicate *a great distance.* —B. This queen, a heathen, travelled a vast distance to see a wise *man ;* the Jews rejected Him who was as much greater, wiser and better than Solomon, as God is greater than man; therefore their guilt was even greater than that of the heathen.

⁴³⁻⁴⁵ But the unclean spirit, when he is gone out of the man, passeth through waterless places, seeking rest, and findeth it not. Then he said, I will return into my house whence I came out; and when he is come, he findeth it empty, swept, and garnished. Then goeth he, and taketh with himself seven other spirits more evil than himself, and they enter in and dwell there: and the last *state* of that man becometh worse than the first. Even so shall it be also unto this evil generation.

A. The conclusion of these three verses: " Even so, etc.," show that the Lord has here introduced a parable, like one in 11 : 16 ff. where, as well as here, the Jewish people in general (" this generation "), and not an individual, constitutes the subject of the comparison. Such comparisons, which are brief, and which contain no details as a narrative, occur elsewhere, as in Matt. 24 : 32 ; Luke

12 : 41, and are then termed *parables*. The leading image here presented was familiar to the Jews. It was an ancient opinion among them that unclean spirits occupied desolate regions. To this circumstance Isaiah refers in 13 : 21, 22; 34 : 14, as well as Jeremiah in 50 : 39. The explanation of the several names which occur in these passages in the original Hebrew, is attended with great difficulties; hence, while the translators of the English Bible render them "wild beasts," "doleful creatures," "satyrs," they substituted in the margin the Hebrew names *Züm, Ijim, Ochim,* or the English "night monster." In Rev. 18 : 2, Babylon, the desolate and abandoned city, is represented as "having become the habitation of devils, and the hold (—haunt, prison) of every foul spirit, etc." The **unclean spirit** is such a one, subject to the prince of the devils, ver. 24, and had been expelled from his victim by a divine agency. The **waterless places** are the desolate regions to which he then proceeds. Here he wanders without finding **rest.** Dissatisfied and wretched, he determines to return, not humbled, but with Satanic arrogance presuming to claim man as his own, saying: **my house.** His absence had allowed an apparent moral improvement to take place in the subject who had been previously possessed by him. The unclean spirit associates others of the powers of darkness with himself, in order to regain his abode, by applying new and powerful temptations. Now that man in whom he had formerly dwelt merely exhibits an outward moral reform, without having acquired available means of defence (a living faith) against Satan. Hence, as every avenue to his soul is still left open and exposed, the evil spirit, returning with augmented power, meets with no serious resistance, and the moral and religious state of that man becomes more deplorable than at any previous period.—

The **house** is **empty**—not occupied by faith and love.—**Garnished**—*adorned,* as in Luke 21 : 5, *embellished* or *furnished*—an image of an increase of religious knowledge, of outward good works, as alms, etc. The number **seven** (see 18:21, A., ver. 22, B.), is probably here equivalent to *many,* or a comparatively large number (comp. 1 Kings 18 : 43 ; Job 5 : 19; Ps. 12 : 6; 119:64; Prov. 24: 16 ; 26: 16, 25 ; Matt. 18 : 21), and designates iniquity in its most repulsive forms.—**More evil**—prompting to even more grievous sins than the first spirit.—**B.** The concluding words ("this generation") as well as the preceding historical allusions to heathen in ver. 41, 42, indicate that the Lord here compares the generation of the Jewish people then living with the Jews of earlier periods, to whom God had spoken by the prophets only, and not by that Greater One, His Son (Hebr. 1 : 1, 2). The application of the parable may be viewed in the following manner. The Jewish people had betrayed a tendency from the earliest periods to maintain the worship of idols. The wickedness of the nation in forsaking the true God finally involved them in the awful punishment known in history as the Babylonian Captivity. The horrors of the Captivity made so deep an impression on the people that, after their return, every trace of idolatry disappeared. The original fall of man had exposed him to the snares of Satan, whose enmity against God urged him to promote idolatry and vice in the world, according to passages like Acts 26 : 18; 2 Cor. 4 : 4; Eph. 2 : 1, 2; 2 Thess. 2: 9; 1 John 3 : 7-12. But on the return of the people, the unclean spirit of idolatry was expelled, and, at a later period, the absence of idolatry and the diligent observance of the ceremonial law, caused it to resemble a house "empty, swept and garnished." The extinction of idolatry, however, unhappily, was not succeeded by a devout and submissive spirit of faith in God and of love for His spiritual service. The house remained "empty" in place of receiving God as its occupant, and a mechanical religion, in which the heart had no share, was gradually introduced. The enemy of man now resolved to resume his empire over the Jewish nation, and promoted a new and still more dangerous form of iniquity—the Pharisaic spirit, or a spirit of self-righteousness and pride, which prompted men to make idols of their passions, and to despise the true worship of God. Such views alienated them more fully than ever from God. The ancient idolatrous Jew, like those persons mentioned in 21 : 31, could not deny that he disobeyed the Mosaic law; hence he was still open to conviction; the more recent Pharisee, blinded entirely and hardened in heart, believed that he had fully obeyed the divine law. Hence the spiritual state in which the Lord now found the Jewish nation was more deplorable than at any earlier state. Formerly, the prophets produced a certain impression on the minds of the people—now, even the Son of God was scorned and blasphemed.

[46], [47] While he was yet speaking to the multitudes, behold his mother and his brethren stood without, seeking to speak to him.—And one said unto him, Behold, thy mother and thy brethren stand without, seeking to speak to thee.

For the Lord's **brethren**, see 13, 55, C. Their special purpose in calling Him away (Mark 3 : 31) is not stated; possibly they apprehended that His enemies, who closely pressed around Him (Luke 8 : 19), would offer personal violence to Him, if He were not speedily extricated—**without**—on the outside.

[48] But he answered and said unto him that told him, Who is my mother? and who are my brethren?

After the Lord had commenced His public ministry

and His special work as the Saviour of the world, it was fitting that He should be publicly known as the Son of God, and not as a mere member of a private family. His question, which expresses this truth, implies: When My true nature as the Son of God, through whom believers receive the adoption of sons (Gal. 4 : 5), is fully revealed, who shall be recognized as My true relatives— **my brethren?** (John 20 : 17; Rom. 8 : 15, 29; Hebr. 2 : 11). Who are they that constitute the "household of God" (Eph. 2 : 19)?

⁴⁹ And he stretched forth his hands towards his disciples, and said, Behold my mother and my brethren!

A. **Disciples**="them which sat about Him" (Mark 3 : 34), whose faith He perceived, and not the persons mentioned in ver. 38; the word *disciples* is here used in the sense of *customary attendants* (see 5 : 1, D.; 8 : 19, C.; 11 : 29, B.—B. **Behold, etc.**=I call those My brethren, who come to the Father by Me (John 14 : 6), and who by that faith which worketh by love (Gal. 5 : 6), become His children (Matt. 5 : 45 and 48).

⁵⁰ For whosoever shall do the will of my Father which is in heaven, he is my brother, and sister, and mother.

A. **Whosoever** (whether now present, or even not yet born) . . . **Father**=with the same joy and pleasure with which I do it (John 4 : 34). The emphasis, according to Luke 8 : 21, lies on the word **do**, as contra-distinguished from *hear*.—B. **The same, etc.** The sense is: Such believers enter into the closest connection with Me, and gain all My love; they receive the adoption of sons through me (Gal. 4 : 4, 5). As they thus become the children of God, have the same mind that is in Me (Phil. 2 : 5), and are united with Me (John 17 : 21), they are heirs of God and joint-heirs with Me (Rom. 8 : 17); hence, I call them my *brethren* (Hebr. 2 : 11; comp.

28 : 10, B.).—After the solemn warnings and awful revelations uttered in the foregoing verses, the blessed Saviour cannot dismiss His hearers without pronouncing merciful and encouraging words for the humble and believing hearer. This visit of Mary is related for the sake of these exalted words of comfort and holy hope.

20

CHAPTER XIII.

Preliminary Observation.—Matthew has recorded in this chapter a number of parables, in conformity to the plan which he appears to have adopted (see *Prel. Obs.* to ch. 5) of arranging his materials rather according to the class of subjects than according to the chronological order. Luke presents a similar illustrative collection of parables in the passage 14 : 28 ; 16 : 31, although a comparison of several of the connecting words (14 : 25 ; 15 : 3, 11 ; 16 : 1) indicates that the parables themselves were pronounced at different times. The words in Matt. 13 : 53 do not necessarily imply that the seven parables in the present chapter were set forth by the Lord in immediate succession ; hence, while according to ver. 2 he is in a boat, nevertheless in ver. 10 and 36 the disciples are represented as coming to him privately. Indeed, his hearers could not have remembered and understood words of such deep import, if all had been uttered without interruption ; the words rather refer to an earlier period of time during the Lord's abode in the region. The private conversation of Christ and His disciples, inserted in ver. 10-23, and which, according to Mark 4 : 10, compared with ver. 1 (" into a boat "—" when he was alone "), occurred at another time and place, as well as the conversation inserted in ver. 36-43, together with the difference in the order found in Mark, ch. 4, and Luke, ch. 8, lead to the following conclusions :—Matthew has made a selection of parables pronounced on different occasions, and it is his purpose to illustrate the Lord's mode of revealing the nature, etc., of the kingdom of heaven by means of *Parables* (comp. *Prel. Obs.* F. to ch. 24). Possibly the four parables which precede ver. 36 were delivered in succession before the people; the words in ver. 51 and 53 indicate that the remaining portion of the parables, three in number, must be assigned to private conversations with the disciples (see ver. 36).

¹ On that day went Jesus out of the house, and sat by the seaside.

Seaside—sea of Tiberias.

² And there were gathered unto him great multitudes, so that he entered into a boat and sat; and all the multitudes stood on the beach.

So that he entered into a boat—in order to address the people without being interrupted. Other vessels, employed by fishermen, were near at hand; before the Lord a richly cultivated region extended to a great distance, and the great highway was seen from the shore. The scenery appears to have suggested some of the images in the following parables.

³ And he spake to them many things in parables, saying, Behold, the sower went forth to sow.

A. **Spake, etc.**—on the present occasion. His purpose is explained below (ver. 10 ff.; 34 : 35).—B. **To sow**—grain. This parable is designed to illustrate the mode in which the Messiah's kingdom (ver. 19), in its external aspects, was to be established, and to exhibit the losses and gains of the Church of Christ on earth. (See Excursus I.) Another lesson which the parable is designed to teach, may be gathered from the thought which pervades the whole narrative, namely, that the bearing of fruit is not the inevitable result of the sowing of good seed, but also depends on the proper preparation of the soil; the lesson is :—Divine truth will not save men, unless the mind and heart be properly disposed to receive it. Hence searching views into the recesses of the human heart are also here presented. The parable assumes a prophetic character. It represents the preaching of the Gospel, which is "the power of God unto salvation" (Rom. 1 : 16), as the great means of introducing men into the kingdom of heaven. Gospel truth, however, even though it always possesses vital power, is, in various cases, proclaimed without success. The causes of this mournful result are not to be traced either to the sower, whose course is assumed to be natural and appropriate, nor to the seed—the word, which retains all its life-giving power, but exclusively to the peculiar character of the hearer (—the spot where the seed falls), that is, to evils in his heart, and to the influence of Satan. Those who really belong to the kingdom, are expected to "bring forth fruit" abundantly.—The **sower,** in this parable, is not explained by the Saviour as constituting exclusively an image of Himself; it doubtless represents any messenger to whom the office is assigned of proclaiming divine truth, or any agency by which pure religious knowledge is communicated (see ver. 37 below).

⁴ And as he sowed, some *seeds* fell by the wayside, and the birds came and devoured them.

A. **Wayside** (lit. *road, highway*)—where the ground "trodden down" by passengers (Luke 8 : 5), and, therefore, hard, was *not prepared* to receive seed. The **way** (as in 12 : 1, A.) is represented as conducting through a cultivated field.—B. **Birds, etc.** These birds found the seed *lying exposed*, that is, not received into appropriate furrows and thus sheltered.

⁵ And others fell upon the rocky places, where they had not much earth: and straightway they sprang up, because they had no deepness of earth.

A. **Rocky places**—a rock, as in Luke 8 : 6; in this spot

there was a thin covering of earth, under which a large rock extended.—**B. Straightway ... of earth.** The rock near the surface prevented the formation and development of suitable roots; the radiation of heat from its surface maintained the heat of the shallow earth above it, and thus forced a more rapid and an unnatural growth of the stalk upwards, by turning all the strength and moisture in that direction.—**Deepness of earth**—*deep earth*, according to the Hebrew idiom (comp. Ps. 18:11), where "dark waters," are, in the Hebrew, *darkness of waters*.

⁶ And when the sun was risen, they were scorched; and because they had no root, they withered away.

When the sun, etc. This is an allusion to the burning heat of the sun in the eastern countries (Ps. 121:6; Isai. 49:10), and its influence on vegetation, particularly when adequate supplies of moisture are not furnished.

⁷ And others fell upon the thorns; and the thorns grew up, and choked them.

A. Thorns. These indicate a soil which might be rich and free from rocks, but which had not been properly cleansed, and was hence unfavorable to the growth of valuable plants.—**B. Choked,** an expressive word occurring also in Luke 8:33. In this case the seed germinated, but the roots of the thorns had not been previously removed by a careful husbandman. Their growth was more rapid than that of the grain; they absorbed the moisture of the ground and excluded the light and air, thus effectually hindering the growth of the grain.

⁸ But others fell upon the good ground, and yielded fruit, some a hundredfold, some sixty, some thirty.

A. Good ground—well prepared for the reception of the seed, sufficiently moist and rich, and free from other roots and seeds.—For the word **good** see below, ver. 23.

—B. **Some a hundredfold, etc.** The soil of Palestine was originally so productive that sixty, and even a hundredfold rewarded the labor of the cultivator, when the divine blessing "prepared rain for the earth" (Ps. 147:8). For an illustration see Gen. 26:12, and comp. Exod. 3:8; Deut. 8:7–9; Ezek. 20:6.—**Hundredfold**—a specified amount multiplied by one hundred, so that one measure of grain which the sower scattered produced one hundred measures.

⁹ He who hath ears, let him hear.

Who hath, etc. (see 11:15). These concluding words indicate the divine will that the hearer or reader of the parable should meditate on its spiritual import and its particular application to himself.

¹⁰ And the disciples came, and said unto him, Why speaketh thou unto them in parables?

The disciples asked: "What might this parable be?" (Luke 8:9). The question indicated a reflecting and inquiring spirit, which the Lord would gladly have seen and rewarded in the case of all his hearers. As even the disciples did not "know (=understand) this parable" (Mark 4:13), they express their surprise that the Lord should veil His doctrines in parables which the people were even less prepared to understand.

¹¹ And he answered and said unto them, Unto you it is given to know the mysteries of the kingdom of heaven, but to them it is not given.

A. Unto you, etc. The Lord explains His reason in verses 11–15, which cannot be separated from one another without obscuring the whole passage. **B. It is given**—by divine grace (see the explanation of 11:25 f.). All pure religious knowledge is a divine gift (John 3:27); those who, like the disciples and certain other persons

(Mark 4 : 10), receive it with an humble and inquiring mind and in a spirit of faith and obedience, obtain an increased measure of knowledge, according to Mark 4 : 24. The docility and faith hitherto manifested by the disciples (but not by those who were "without," Mark 4 : 11—remained separate from Christ, 1 Cor. 5 : 12, 13) prepared them for still further revelations of divine truth.—C. **The mysteries.** The word *mystery* in the N. T. is applied to any divine decree or purpose, or to any Gospel truth (Rom. 11 : 25 ; 1 Cor. 15 : 51 ; Eph. 5 : 32 ; 1 Tim. 3 : 16) which human reason could not possibly discover, and which therefore could not be known without a special revelation (1 Cor. 13 : 2); *after* such a revelation these may be intelligible. Even when such truths are made known, they retain the name of "mysteries," because we are indebted to revelation exclusively for the knowledge of them (see Rev. 16 : 25, 26 ; 1 Cor. 2 : 7, 10; Eph. 3 : 3 ; 6 : 19). In the present verse the word refers to circumstances or truths hitherto not distinctly revealed.—E. **To them it is not given**— except through the veil of parables (see ann. B. above).— While the parable furnished new light to those who had already learned to value divine truth, it was unintelligible to those who had previously undervalued and neglected such religious instruction as had already been offered to them.

¹² For whosoever hath, to him shall be given, and he shall have abundance: but whosoever hath not, from him shall be taken away even that which he hath.

A. A similar declaration occurs in 25 : 29, which passage (Parable of the Talents), like the present, appears to contain the following sense:—He who conscientiously and faithfully avails himself of the means and the time for growing in knowledge and grace, which God affords, will be more and more enriched spiritually; on the other hand, he who exhibits a spirit of levity, of contempt towards God, of impenitence and unbelief (—who *hath not* any interest, docility and faith), will not only derive no benefit from such opportunities, but that indulgence of God and that security which he did enjoy temporarily, will be converted into wrath and punishment (—*from him shall be taken*, etc.) It is to be observed that in Matt. 25 : 29, the man who " had not," had received at least *one* talent (precisely as all men, even heathens Rom. 1 : 20, have certain favorable opportunities afforded to them), but he did not endeavor to profit by it.—B. The disciples, in consequence of their past fidelity and zeal, receive from the Lord an explanation of the spiritual import of the parable; the people, who disregarded Christ and His doctrine, lost, in consequence of such sloth and hardness of heart, even those advantages which they might have derived from the possession of the writings of Moses and the prophets. The nominal Christian, who fails to seek the sanctifying grace of God, will ultimately lose " even that which he hath "—will lose all the benefits which he might have enjoyed, and, finally, lose his soul, although he bore the Christian name, and was acquainted with the letter of the divine word.

¹³ Therefore speak I to them in parables: because seeing they see not; and hearing they hear not, neither do they understand.

A. Therefore—for the reason that they have not properly applied the religious knowledge which they already possess or can acquire (Matt. 23 : 2, 3). As they, therefore, undervalue truth, I veil the deeper truths respecting My kingdom in the form of parables. This explanation is sustained by the words in the parallel passage: " With many such parables spake He the word unto them, *as they were able to hear it*" (Mark 4 : 33).—

B. They seeing see not, etc.—they have had sufficient opportunity to perceive the importance and truth of my doctrine (they could see and hear), but they voluntarily turn away from me; they resemble a man endowed with sight, but who sees nothing because he closes his eyes (comp. Jer. 5 : 21 ; Ezek. 12 : 2 ; Isai. 32 : 3, from which passages the peculiar sense of the language may be gathered).

¹⁴ And unto them is fulfilled the prophecy of Isaiah, which saith, By hearing ye shall hear, and shall in no wise understand; and seeing ye shall see, and shall in no wise perceive.

A. Unto them is fulfilled. As these words of the prophet, like those quoted in 15 : 7, 8, describe the conduct of other individuals also, besides those to whom they are here applied (of which fact Acts 28 : 25 ff. afford a proof), the sense must be :—The words of the prophet are in this case again fulfilled. They may thus be fulfilled in the case of many who bear the Christian name. —**B. The prophecy**—in Isai. 6 : 9, 10. It is quoted not only here, and in the parallel passages Mark 4 : 12; Luke 8 : 10, but also in John 12 : 40, and Acts 28 : 26, 27. When the prophets are commissioned to announce future events, particularly divine judgments, their commission is sometimes so expressed as if they were themselves commanded to perform that which will afterwards occur without their personal agency. Thus the words in Jer. 25 : 15 contain a divine command to the prophet to announce the coming of divine judgments. In Jer. 1 : 10 the sense is that he should *predict the future*, rooting out, pulling down, etc. Hence in Ezek. 43 : 3, the words: "The vision that I saw when I came to destroy the city," which allude to several foregoing chapters (ch. 1 ; ch. 10; ch. 30), are equivalent to : " I came *to prophecy that* the city should be destroyed," as, indeed, the translators have explained in the margin of the English Bible; see also Gen. 41 : 13; 49 : 7; Ezek. 9 : 1; 32 : 18; Hosea 6 : 5, where similar expressions are used (comp. 23 : 32 below). In the present passage, the words in Isai. 6 : 10, "Make, etc.," simply imply, as a prediction, according to Matthew's rendering: The heart of this people is waxed (or, will wax) gross.—C. **By hearing, etc.**—*ye will hear indeed*, according to the intention of the original Hebrew in Isai. 6 : 9; the sense is: Although this people can and do hear, nevertheless they will not understand, etc. (Comp. Mark 8 : 18.) The next clause: "and seeing, etc." expresses the same sense more emphatically—ye will overlook that which lies before your eyes. (The repetition of the same word, *hearing—hear, seeing—see*, is the Greek mode of expressing a Hebrew form of speech, according to which a finite verb with the infinitive absolute denotes an emphasis, intensity, etc. Thus in 1 Sam. 20 : 6, the original is: If thy father missing (to miss) miss me—asking, asked, etc.; here the English *at all* and *earnestly* indicate the emphatic meaning. So, too, compare Gen. 43 : 3, where the Hebrew words signifying "protesting (to protest) he protested" are given: "did solemnly protest" (see marg. of Engl. Bible).

¹⁵ For this people's heart is waxed gross, and their ears are dull of hearing, and their eyes they have closed; lest haply they should perceive with their eyes, and hear with their ears, and understand with their heart, and should turn again, and I should heal them.

A. **Waxed gross**=*fat*. (*To wax*, like the German *wachsen*, signifies to *grow, increase* in any respect.) As *fat* is not supplied with veins, arteries and nerves as abundantly as the flesh or muscular part of the body is, and is consequently far less sensitive, it is sometimes, as here and in Ps. 17 : 10; 119 : 70, employed as an image of moral or spiritual insensibility.—B. **Lest haply.** The sense then is: They closed every avenue to conviction, so that they may not be enlightened ("see, etc.")—they do not desire to know and obey God.—C. **And shall turn again, etc.**—" they have chosen their own ways, and their soul delighteth in their abominations" (Isai. 66 : 3 ; comp. John 3 : 19). For additional illustrations of man's wilful rejection of the offered grace of God (see Jer. 27 : 13 ; Ezek. 18 : 31 ; 33 : 11 ; John 5 : 40).—**Heal**= forgive, sanctify and save. (Comp. Ps. 103 : 3 ; 147 : 3 ; 1 Peter 2 : 24).—**D.** The sense of the whole prophecy is accordingly the following :—" Predict to the people—the Lord says to the prophet—that their evil course will harden them against My word, etc.—It may be that such warnings will cause them to return to Me." Such is at times the purpose of the divine words, as in Jer. 26 : 3 ; 36 : 3, 7, and compare the illustration found in Jonah 3 ; 4-10. A reference to the same prophetic passage occurs in John 12 : 39, 40. Here the apostle, who *interprets* rather than *quotes* the prophetic words, finds in the case of the hearers of Christ a mournful illustration of the effect produced on the heart by slighting the prophetic warning ; " they could not believe," because when God permitted them to choose between life and death, they preferred to close their eyes and ears ; they closed every avenue to the converting influences of the divine Spirit. When the offered mercy is despised, divine justice permits the sinner to harden himself effectually and permanently, as a judicial punishment ; hence Paul says: "Wherefore God also gave them up, etc." (Rom. 1 : 24; also 2 Thess. 2 : 11): " For this cause God shall send them strong delusion,"—He suffers them to walk in their own ways (Acts 14 : 16). After they had thus repelled the grace of God, and were now abandoned to themselves, John accordingly says : " they could not believe."

¹⁶ But blessed are your eyes, for they see: and your ears, for they hear.

Eyes—ears. The Orientals sometimes designate the person or agent by particularizing the members of the body or the senses specially employed (see Job 29 : 11, and Eccl. 1 : 8, *eye—ear;* Deut. 3 : 21, *eyes;* Acts 5 : 9, *feet*). The Lord sets forth the blessed state of His disciples, arising from the docility and faith which they had already manifested, and by which they were prepared for other still more glorious revelations and divine gifts.

¹⁷ For verily I say unto you, That many prophets and righteous men desired to see the things which ye see, and saw them not; and to hear the things which ye hear, and heard them not.

Comp. 1 Peter 1 : 10–12, "of which salvation the prophets, etc." Prophets and righteous men, long before the days of Simeon and Anna (Luke 2 : 25, 38), longed for the coming of the Messiah, and exclaimed : " Oh that the salvation of Israel were come out of Zion ! " (Ps. 14 : 7). The Saviour represents it as an exalted privilege which those enjoy who do not merely hope for redemption, but who also see in Him " the salvation of God " (Luke 3 : 6; Tit. 2 : 11 ; 3, 4).—For **prophets and righteous men,** see 10 : 41, B.

¹⁸ Hear then ye the parable of the sower.

Ye—emphatically, *Ye* who have been "faithful in that which is least " (Luke 16 : 10).—The following explanation, which specifies four classes of hearer of the word, is given by the Lord in the absence of the people (Mark 4 : 10). "The seed is the word of God " (Luke 8 : 11)— revealed truth, made accessible to men in any way (preaching, writing and printing, etc.), and connected with the influences of the Holy Spirit.

¹⁹ When any one heareth the word of the kingdom, and understandeth it not, *then* cometh the evil *one*, and snatcheth away that which hath been sown in his heart. This is he that was sown by the wayside.

A. The *first* class—the **wayside** (ver. 4). The **word of the kingdom**—the Gospel of Christ, is proclaimed to some hearers whose spiritual state resembles the hard, beaten public road. They are so addicted to the world and its sinful ways, that divine truth can find no entrance. —The **evil one,** that is, Satan (Mark 4 : 15 ; Luke 8 : 12) while "seeking whom he may devour," namely, those who are not "sober and vigilant" (1 Pet. 5 : 8), finds such worldly-minded hearers willing victims. He comes successfully *only* to such thoughtless and profane hearers (2 Cor. 4 : 4). He flees from those who resist him (James 4 : 7), but " he worketh in the children of disobedience " (Eph. 2 : 2). Their own continued impenitence and folly protect them from understanding ("understandeth not") or applying to themselves and feeling the force of the word, and thus they render the influences of divine truth ineffectual.—B. **Sown in his heart.** The *heart*, according to the usage of the Scriptures, represents generally the moral nature of man (his mind or judgment, feelings, will, etc.) as distinguished from his bodily nature (5 : 8, B.). It has sometimes a more specific sense, as here, and in Mark 2 : 6 ; Luke 2 : 19 ; Rom. 1 : 21, where the understanding is principally meant (see 15 : 19, A.). The Gospel, "the power of God " (Rom. 1 : 16), always retains its regenerating influences through the Spirit (James 1 : 18 ; 1 Pet. 1 : 23), but like good seed which retains all its vitality, it must find a soil prepared for it, before it can bear fruit. " Many of us imagine that when we listen without benefit to the preaching of the gospel, no great harm has been done *by* us or *to* us, and we forget the solemn truth here taught by the Lord, that in such cases we have been actually under the influence of Satan. Many are willing to lose a sermon for the sake of some petty, earthly gain or amusement, and forget that here too the devil has successfully tempted them to take this course."—LUTHER.

^{20, 21} And he that was sown upon the rocky places, this is he that heareth the word, and straightway with joy receiveth it;—Yet hath he not root in himself, but endureth for a while: and when tribulation or persecution ariseth because of the word, straightway he stumbleth.

The *second* class—the **rock** (ver. 5, 6). Such hearers, betraying none of the insensibility of the former class, promise by their ready and even joyful acceptance of the word, an abundant harvest of works of faith. But while they are charmed with the "beauty of virtue," they fail to abhor the loathsome disease of sin, and to repent in dust and ashes (Job. 42 : 6; Ps. 38 : 3-7). Their wilful ignorance of the evils of their own hearts and of the unutterable power and greatness of the Saviour's love towards poor sinners, operates disastrously. That faith in Christ, and that grateful love which are described in 1 Pet. 1 : 5-8, and which can be produced only when fuller instructions in Christian doctrine are obtained, find no room in their souls. They have "no deepness of earth," no "root" through which "moisture" (Luke 8 : 6) can flow, that is, no deep and abiding faith in Christ's mercy to the contrite sinner, and no Christian humility. Hence they are unprepared for such struggles with the world, the flesh and the devil, as Paul describes in 2 Cor. 4 : 7-11. When therefore they are commanded by religion ("because of the word") to practise self-denial and to follow a Saviour who is beaten with stripes, who wears a crown of thorns and bears a heavy cross, they forsake Him. Their return to the ways of sin betrays that they had acquired no perfect knowledge, no true faith, no pure love (comp. Hebr. 10 : 34 and 2 Cor. 4 : 17, 18). They stumble in the path of duty, and fall into sin. The word translated **tribulation** originally signifies a *pressure*, and thence is applied to any pressure on the heart, or any trial or sorrow—often also rendered *affliction*, as in 2 Cor. 1 : 8 and 2 Cor. 4 : 17.

²² And he that was sown among the thorns, this is he that heareth the word; and the care of the world, and the deceitfulness of riches, choke the word, and he becometh unfruitful.

The *third* class—the **thorns** (ver. 7). The first kind of hearers consists of those who evidently receive no religious impressions whatever; the second includes those who seem to be impressed, but who are governed by the impulse of the moment more than by clear and enlarged views of divine truth; the third comprehends hearers who differ widely among themselves in temperament, external condition, etc., but who resemble each other in the sincerity of their original profession of faith, and in the large amount of Christian truth which they have found. They also exhibit another common feature—the subsequent neglect of watchfulness and prayer, and of a conscientious use of the means of grace combined with a searching self-examination, after they had received the truth. Like the hard wayside and the rocky places, the thorns of this third case are an image of the corruption of the human heart. *That* inherent evil operates in various ways, affecting alike the rich and the poor, or all classes of men. Some permit earthly trials or afflictions, poverty, etc. (the " care of this world "—evils of this life, to which the Saviour (Matt. 6 : 25 ; Luke 21 : 34), and Peter (1 Pet. 5 : 7) refer,)—others permit the pleasures of the world and its profits (1 Tim. 6 : 9) and honors (like Demas, at one time a fellow-laborer of Paul (Philem. ver. 24), afterwards so unfaithful (2 Tim. 4 : 10) to interrupt their watchfulness over their souls, and to shake their faith (" the deceitfulness of richs "—money, etc., employed by Satan as a snare comp. Hebr. 3 : 13 ; 2 Thess. 2 : 10).

Original sin still clings to man and seeks to resume its empire over those who have turned to God; if they do not conscientiously use the means of grace, it "chokes the word."

²³ And he that was sown upon the good ground, this is he that heareth the word, and understandeth it; who verily beareth fruit, and bringeth forth, some a hundredfold, some sixty, some thirty.

A. The *fourth* class—the **good ground** (ver. 8). In this case the impediments which prevented the development and growth of the grain are removed from the soil. (The word here translated *good* is different from the Greek word found in Matt. 5 : 45 ; 19 : 17, also translated *good*, and more fully corresponding to the English word. The present word, translated *seemly* in 1 Pet. 2 : 12, *fair* in Acts 27 : 8, *good* in John 10 : 14, often bears the sense of *appropriate, proper, suitable*, as in Rom. 14 : 21 ; 1 Cor. 7 : 26, and is rendered *meet*—suitable, in Matt. 15 : 26. Hence, a *good* soil is one suited to good seed—properly prepared for it.) The conduct of such hearers corresponds to the divine purpose. They hear the word like others, but they also "understand"—receive it with thoughtful attention (the opposite of the *first* class) ; the " honest and good heart " (Luke 8 : 15) is a heart trained to receive divine instructions, or prepared for them ; they " receive " (Mark)—retain it and cherish its growth. They give sufficient time and attention to their spiritual concerns, and exercise an abiding faith (the opposite of the *second* class). They "keep" it (Luke)—do not allow worldly **influences** to enfeeble or destroy its power (the opposite of the *third* class). They bring forth the fruit of the Spirit (Gal. 5 : 22, 23) " with patience " (Luke), in which they differ from *all* the other classes.—B. **Some** (the one) **a hundredfold, some** (another) **sixty, etc.** They are all successful (the fruit is good and abundant), but still even they exhibit a difference in the degree of their knowledge, faith, love, etc. Even believers should "take heed how they hear" (Luke 8 : 18).

⁴⁴ Another parable set he before them, saying, The kingdom of heaven is likened unto a man that sowed good seed in his field.

A. Another parable—Of the Tares, found in Matthew alone, and obviously appended to the former as an explanation or completion of it. The interpretation is given in ver. 37–43. The former parable (1) gave prominence to individual hearers, (2) exhibited special hindrances which the Word encounters, without introducing the direct influence of "tares" as the source, (3) presented the hearers as they live and act in this world, and (4) described the immediate result. The present parable completes the former by (1) presenting these hearers as so far increased in number that they form a community—the visible Church, (2) discloses by the contrast of the two kinds of seed the original source of all opposition to the Word—the devil, (3) reveals the discriminating process which will occur on the day of judgment, and (4) sets forth the final and eternal result in the other world of the course pursued by men on earth. Hence, several of the images (sower, seed, etc.), with certain modifications, are the same in both parables.—**B. The kingdom . . . likened**—The Church in its later history and ultimate development resembles the following circumstances (comp. 18 : 23, B.), first, good seed is sown, then an enemy comes, etc.—**C. Good seed**; the original seed is the divine Word with all its regenerating (1 Pet. 1 : 23) and sanctifying (John 17: 17) influences; these holy influences furnish the Church with sanctified believers (James 1 : 18), who, in their turn, serve as *seed*, or as instruments for increasing the number of believers (see ver. 38, B.).—**D. His field** —not the public wayside, but the soil for which, as in

Isai. 5 : 4, he had done all that could have been done. The " church of God, which he hath purchased with His own blood" (Acts 20 : 28; 1 Pet. 1 : 18, 19) is designed to convert the whole world into a temple of God (John 3 : 16; see below, ver. 38).

²⁵ **But while men slept, his enemy came and sowed tares also among the wheat, and went away.**

A. **While . . . slept**—during the night (comp. Job 33 : 15). These words, which the Lord does not afterwards explain, possibly refer to times or circumstances when unusual dangers could not have been reasonably apprehended, and when unusual precautions do not seem to be required. So, the sleeping of the wise virgins (25 : 5), *who had neglected no duty*, is represented, not as a fault but as a natural occurrence. Evil does exist in the world; no ordinary precautions can entirely expel it; "it is impossible but that offences will come" (Luke 17 : 1); they must needs come (Matt. 18 : 7). No human intelligence can always detect the disguised "wolves" (Acts 20 : 29) who "privily bring in damnable heresies, etc." (2 Peter 2 : 1). The existence of *tares* (hypocrites, etc.) is no evidence that good grain cannot also grow in the field (see below, ver. 29).—B. **Enemy . . . tares** (see ver. 38, 39). The weed here called *tares*, is supposed by some to be *degenerate wheat*. It is explained by others, probably with more accuracy, to be a species of darnel (a genus of grasses), and the only deleterious species belonging to the gramineous plants. It grows among oats and wheat, somewhat resembling the latter, until the formation of the grains ("fruit," ver. 26) reveals the difference.—C. **Went his way**—unsuspected. Men are not always conscious of the evil influences which operate upon them.

²⁶ But when the blade sprang up, and brought forth fruit, then appeared the tares also.

Unholy motives, although temporarily disguised (2 Cor. 11 : 13–15), cannot avoid ultimate detection (see Acts 5 : 1 ff.).

²⁷ And the servants of the householder came and said unto him, Sir, didst thou not sow good seed in thy field? whence then hath it tares?

The incidents mentioned in this verse (the servants, etc.) are not subsequently applied in a spiritual sense by the Lord. Still, they afford a striking illustration of the truth which all history demonstrates, that men cannot explain the origin of evil in the world, independently of the aid of revelation (see Gen. ch. 3 ; Rom. 5 : 12 ff.).— **Householder**=the owner of the estate, head of the family (see 20 : 11, B.). For **Sir**, see 8 : 2, C.

²⁸ And he said unto them, An enemy hath done this. And the servants say unto him, Wilt thou then that we go and gather them up?

A. An enemy. God is not the author of *sin;* in its origin and growth, and in all its forms, it is the work of Satan (2 Cor. 4 : 4; Eph. 2 : 2). But, happily, that *enemy* is well known to God, who has revealed his devices in the Scriptures (2 Cor. 2 : 11), and destroys him through the redeeming work of Christ (Hebr. 2 : 14).—**B. Wilt thou, etc.** An illustration is here given of zeal guided by a spirit submissive to a higher authority. A zeal, on the other hand, which lacks knowledge and love, and unduly assumes authority, is discountenanced and rebuked by the Lord (comp. Luke 9 : 54, 55).

²⁹ But he saith, Nay; lest haply while ye gather up the tares, ye root up the wheat with them.

This portion of the parable, which the Lord does not afterwards specially explain, is, doubtless, designed to forbid all persecution of men on account of their faith, and to discountenance any rash judgments. At the same time, the Church is authorized and commanded to maintain strict discipline and tolerate in its own bosom no unholy doctrines or practices, according to Matt. 18 : 15; Acts 20 : 28; Rom. 16 : 17; 1 Cor. ch. 5; 1 Tim. 4 : 1–6; 2 John 10). Nevertheless, the Church may exist, and enjoy the divine presence, even when entire purity has not yet been attained. " Why did Paul recognize the church of God in Corinth (in which tares were only too plainly seen, 1 Cor. 1 : 11; 3 : 3; 4 : 14; 5 : 1 ff.; 6 : 1 ff.; 11 : 20–22; 14 : 26)? Because he beheld among them the Gospel doctrine, and Baptism and the Lord's Supper, by which symbols the Church, as such, is discerned."— CALVIN.—" The Church is authorized to exercise discipline and to excommunicate obstinate offenders, but is also directed to hope for the reformation of the latter, and to restore them when they truly repent (1 Cor. ch. 5, comp. with 2 Cor. 2 : 5–8). But while the Church employs the sword of the Spirit, which is the word, never let it employ any other sword or touch the life of the erring and profane. May not even yet the word of God reach their hearts and bring them back?"—LUTHER.

[30] Let both grow together until the harvest: and in the time of the harvest I will say to the reapers, Gather up first the tares, and bind them in bundles to burn them: but gather the wheat into my barn.

A. **Let both, etc.**—as the sun and the rain are given to all (Matt. 5 : 15), and God is pleased to tolerate all, so let men practise toleration.—B. **Harvest** (see ver. 39),— C. **I will say**—I, to whom alone " belongeth vengeance and recompense" (Deut. 32 : 35; Hebr. 10 : 30).—D. **the reapers**—agents chosen by the Lord Himself, not self-constituted judges.—E. **Burn**—an image of the divine judgment, as in 2 Sam. 23 : 7. (See above, 3 : 12, and below, ver. 41, 42.)

[31] Another parable set he before them, saying, The kingdom of heaven is

like unto a grain of mustard seed, which a man took, and sowed in his field.

A. The parables of the mustard-seed and the leaven, were either repeated by the Lord on a later occasion (Luke 13 : 18–21), or are at once transferred by Matthew to the present illustrative group. The two differ materially in intention; the former refers specially to the future growth of the visible Church of Christ, the latter to the power of divine grace manifested in the invisible Church, among true believers (comp. ver. 44–46). Both are designed to teach the consoling truth, that, while, according to the former parable, much of the seed is unproductive, the Word shall, as the prophet foretold (Isai. 55 : 11) not return void.—B. **The kingdom of heaven**—viewed in its external form, as the Church.—C. **Grain of mustard-seed.** The mustard plant assumes in the Eastern gardens, the size of a tree, the branches of which are in some cases sufficiently strong to bear the weight of a man. The seed is so diminutive ("less than all seeds"—compared with the plant itself), that the Jews proverbially referred to it as an image both of objects characterized by their small size, and also of a low degree of moral qualities (17 : 20 below ; Luke 17 : 6). There may be an allusion here not so much to the babe in the manger at Bethlehem, as rather to the company of the disciples, who were obscure and timid men and a "little flock" (Luke 12 : 32), and then, to the time when "the earth shall be full of the knowledge of the Lord, etc." (Isai. 11 : 9).

[32] Which indeed is less than all seeds: but when it is grown, it is greater than the herbs, and becometh a tree, so that the birds of the heaven come and lodge in the branches thereof.

A. **Herbs**—garden plants (see 23 : 23, A.).—B. **So that the birds, etc.**—an image of those who seek a place of refuge, often occurring, as in Ps. 104 : 12; Ezek. 17 : 23;

31 : 6; Dan. 4 : 12.—**C.** The import of the parable is the following : The Church of Christ, in its external form, proceeds apparently from an insignificant source (the despised Jesus (Isai. 53 : 3), and a band of poor and obscure men—the apostles (1 Cor. 1 : 26); but it will exhibit a vigorous growth and reveal such power and resources as to afford a home or protection and safety to all who seek its blessings.

³³ Another parable spake he unto them; the kingdom of heaven is like unto leaven, which a woman took, and hid in three measures of meal, till it was all leavened.

A. **The kingdom, etc.**—viewed in reference to the power of divine grace invisibly operating in it through the means of grace (see ver. 31, A.).—**B. Leaven**—a well-known substance employed to produce fermentation. The silent and yet powerful influence by which it produces changes in the **meal** (=flour) with which it is combined, and which it thoroughly penetrates (26 : 2 B. § 4), is here employed as an image of that divine influence which, although it is unseen by the eye ("hid"), leads to the conversion and sanctification of men. "Not by might, etc." (Zech. 4 : 6). Leaven is used in an unfavorable sense in Matt. 16 : 6, B.; 1 Cor. 5 : 7, 8.—**C. Hid**—the operations of the divine Spirit in the soul are invisible to the bodily eye (comp. John 3 : 8; Col. 3 : 3).—**D. Measures.** The original word *sæton* (Hebr. and Chald. *seah* and *sata*, 2 Kings 7 : 1, 16), indicates a certain Jewish measure for grain, flour, etc., equal to one Roman *modius* and a half (see 5 : 15, C.), or about one English peck and three quarts; hence three measures would be somewhat more than a bushel. The Lord probably specifies **three** measures, which were equal to one ephah (Ruth 2 : 17; 1 Sam. 17 : 17), in allusion to circumstances familiarly known, as Gen. 18 : 6; Judg. 6 : 19; 1 Sam.

1 : 24, without connecting any spiritual meaning with that precise number.

³⁴ All these things spake Jesus in parables unto the multitudes ; and without a parable spake he nothing unto them.

Spake he nothing—on that particular occasion, when He was describing the nature of the Messiah's kingdom ; at other times (for example, Matt. ch. 5-7) He spoke "plainly" (John 16 : 29).

³⁵ That it might be fulfilled which was spoken by the prophet, saying, I will open my mouth in parables ; I will utter things hidden from the foundation of the world.

A. **That ... spoken** (see ann. to 1 : 22, A.).—B. **By the prophet**—Asaph, the *seer*, 2 Chron. 29 : 30 (=a seer of visions, or an inspired teacher), the more ancient name for *prophet*, according to 1 Sam. 9 : 9. The words occur in Ps. 78 : 2, 3. The Spirit of Christ was in the prophets (1 Pet. 1 : 11).—C. **Parables**—*dark sayings*, as the word is explained in the second part of Ps. 78 : 2 (comp. Prov. 1 : 6). The word here designates instructions which cannot be understood without deep thought and attention. Asaph intended to disclose the divine purposes in the events to which he subsequently refers ; Christ revealed the divine purposes respecting the kingdom of God. In neither case would the *thoughtless* hearer derive instruction.—D. **I will utter ... world.** These words are substituted here for "dark sayings," etc., in Ps. 78 : 2, 3. To the "fathers" (for instance, Abraham, John 8 : 56) and the prophets (1 Pet. 1 : 12) certain revelations were granted respecting the plan of salvation which God had devised before the foundation of the world (1 Pet. 1 : 20); but the precise mode in which God designed to save men, and the precise time of the Saviour's appearance had been kept secret, until Christ appeared (John 1 : 17 ; 1 Cor. 2 : 10; Gal. 3 : 23 ; Eph.

1 : 9). He revealed the full meaning of those promises which "the fathers told" to later generations. The ancient prophetic declarations were "dark sayings," until Christ unfolded their meaning to those (ver. 11 above) whose diligence and fidelity qualified them to receive more enlarged views.—E. **The foundation of the world** —since the world began (comp. John 9 : 32).

³⁶ Then he left the multitudes, and went into the house: and his disciples came unto him, saying, Explain unto us the parable of the tares of the field.

A. **He left, etc.** The explanation which follows, and the three parables which succeed, were, accordingly, not pronounced in the presence of the multitude mentioned in ver. 2.—B. **The house**=mentioned in ver. 1.—C. **Saying, Explain, etc.** The people, as the Lord indeed implies (ver. 11-16), felt no desire to ascertain the spiritual import of his doctrine; the disciples, conscious of its unutterable importance and value, exhibit a holy desire to obtain more light and knowledge (see John 8 : 30-32). Neglect or contempt of the word punishes itself—devout attention, or deep interest in divine things, is always rewarded by an increased measure of light and grace (see ver. 12 above).

³⁷ And he answered and said, He that soweth the good seed is the Son of man.

A. The Saviour's explanation of the first portion of the parable in ver. 24-30, is brief; that of the latter portion is very full. Hence it appears chiefly designed as a revelation of the ultimate righteous judgment of God respecting true and false disciples.—B. **Is the Son of man**=Christ (see above, ver. 3, B.). As the sower in the former parable is not specially explained to be Christ exclusively, the heralds of the cross generally may be also understood, according to 1 Cor. ch. 2 (comp. Isai. 51 : 16;

John 3 : 34). The Gospel, when faithfully preached by men, is still "the power of God" (Rom. 1 : 16). At the same time, Paul says: "We have this treasure in earthen vessels, that the excellency of the power may be of God, and not of us" (2 Cor. 4 : 7).

³⁸ And the field is the world; and the good seed, these are the sons of the kingdom; but the tares are the sons of the evil *one*.

A. The field is the world. Christ is the "appointed heir of all things" (Hebr. 1 : 2; John 3 : 35; Matt. 28 : 18); the entire heathen world, which belongs to His inheritance (Ps. 2 : 8), is to hear the preaching of the Gospel (Isai. 11 : 9; 52 : 10; Jer. 16 : 19; Rom. 11 : 25). Although "we see not yet all things put under Him" (Hebr. 2 : 8), we have the promise that "this gospel of the kingdom shall be preached in all the world" (Matt. 24 : 14). The Lord in the present passage accordingly refers to the sublime purpose of the Gospel, which extends an invitation to all nations to enter the Christian Church. The latter shall extend over the whole world (Mark 16 : 15). Here we find the germ of the missionary operations of the Church.—**B. The good seed . . . kingdom**—true believers, in whom the Holy Ghost dwells (2 Tim. 1 : 14), and who, by walking after the Spirit (Rom. 8 : 1), glorify God by their works of faith (Matt. 5 : 16; John 15 : 8). The **children of the kingdom** (see 8 : 12, A.) here, are not the nominal people of God, but those who have really "received the adoption of sons" (Gal. 4 : 5) through Christ. In the former parable, the "seed is the word of God" (Luke 8 : 11); here the **seed** appears in its results, in as far as it converts men into new creatures (—righteous; see ver. 43, below). Every believer is required to become in word and deed like Noah a "preacher of righteousness" (2 Pet. 2 : 5; see ver. 24, C.).—**C. The tares . . . one**=Satan, ver. 19, A. "Ye are of your father the devil" (John 8 : 44)—ye have his nature, and do his deeds, ver. 41. All sin comes from Satan (1 John 3 : 8), even as all that is right and pure is of God. The wicked (such as Elymas, described by Paul as a "child of the devil," Acts 13 : 10), are the seed of iniquity, and destroy others by their unholy influence (comp. 1 John 3 : 10).

³⁹ And the enemy that sowed them is the devil; and the harvest is the end of the world; and the reapers are the angels.

A. **Enemy . . . devil**—the "murderer" (John 8 : 44) who introduced sin and death into the world (Rom. 5 : 12; Hebr. 2 : 14), the author of all unbelief and sin (2 Cor. 4 : 4; 2 Tim. 2 : 26), the destroyer of all who submit to him (1 Pet. 5 : 8), the great adversary of God and man (Luke 10 : 19).—B. **Harvest . . . world**—when the final judgment will be held, at the second coming of Christ (Matt. 25 : 31 ff.). For the term here translated **world**, as in ver. 22 above, see 12 : 32, C. and 24 : 3, E.—C. **Reapers . . . angels.** The angels appear as ministers (— in the service) of God (Hebr. 1 : 4-8, 13, 14), at all important eras in the Messiah's kingdom—at his birth, after His Temptation (4 : 11, B.), in Gethsemane, at His grave and ascension. So, too, they will accompany Him at His second coming (16 : 27; 24 : 31; 2 Thess. 1 : 7).

⁴⁰ As therefore the tares are gathered up and burned with fire; so shall it be in the end of this world.

A. **Tares . . . burned**, see ver. 30.—B. **In the end. etc.**—on the judgment-day (ver. 39, B.).

⁴¹ The Son of man shall send forth his angels, and they shall gather out of his kingdom all things that cause stumbling, and them that do iniquity.

A. **His angels** (see above, ver. 39, C., and below, 24 : 31; 25 : 31).—B. **Gather out**—collect and expel from. They will also, as in ver. 48, gather together God's believing people, 24 : 31.—C. **His kingdom.** Here the word is used in a wide sense, referring both to the Messiah's kingdom as manifested in the Church on earth, and to its ultimate form, when it shall embrace holy men and angels alone.—**D. Things that cause stumbling.** As these " things " are here distinguished by the word " and " from " them which do iniquity " (=sinners, 7 : 23), the latter are specially those whose impenitence and sins unfit them for heaven, while the former are not so much persons whose example is pernicious, as, rather, all temptations or causes that lead men to the commission of sin, such as false doctrines, unholy customs, evils in the Church, etc. These will not distress the redeemed in the state of glory.

⁴² And shall cast them into the furnace of fire: there shall be the weeping and gnashing of teeth.

A. Furnace of fire—an image (derived from death by fire, Dan. 3 : 6) of the horrors attending the eternal punishment of the wicked (comp. 2 Sam. 23 : 6, 7 ; Matt. 25 : 41 ; Luke 16 : 23, 24). The intense heat, which melts the hardest metals, is the basis of the image.—**B. Weeping, etc.** (see 8 : 12, D.).

⁴³ Then shall the righteous shine forth as the sun in the kingdom of their Father. He that hath ears, let him hear.

A. The righteous; these are, in passages like the present, those believers whose faith in the crucified Redeemer (Rom. 10 : 4) is imputed to them " for righteousness " (Rom. 4 : 3, 21–24; James 2 : 23). True righteousness proceeds from a living faith alone (Rom. 1 : 17; 5 : 1 ; 9 : 30) and not from human works (Gal. 2 : 16); see 1 : 19, B. In ver. 41–43, as in many analogous passages (see 12 : 30, B.), the Lord arranges *all* men in two classes, the evil and the good.—**B. Shine . . . sun**—after their bodies are " raised in glory " (1 Cor. 15 : 43) and reunited with their souls. Their exceeding glory and felicity, derived from "the sun of righteousness" (Mal. 4 : 2), are illustrated by the image of the sun—the most splendid object in nature known to man (comp. Dan. 12 : 3 ; 1 Pet. 5 : 4). —**C. Kingdom . . . Father**=the "heavenly kingdom" (2 Tim. 4 : 18), the future abode of the redeemed.—**D. Who hath**, etc. see ver. 9 above. These closing words, as well as the very full reference to the judgment, indicate that one chief object of this parable is to teach that a mere external connection with the Church alone will not save the ungodly from eternal punishment.

⁴⁴ The kingdom of heaven is like unto treasure hidden in the field; which a man found, and hid, and in his joy he goeth and selleth all that he hath, and buyeth that field.

A. In ver. 31, 32, two successive parables illustrate two different aspects of the Church, the visible and the invisible ; so here two different modes in which religious life commences in the soul are exhibited (see ver. 45, A.). —**B. Kingdom . . . field.** The kingdom is here viewed in its influence on the soul ; the result thus produced is the union of the true believer with Christ, that is, "righteousness, and peace, and joy in the Holy Ghost" (Rom. 14 : 17).—**C. And hid . . . field.** This whole image is intended to illustrate the carefulness and zeal of the truly converted (see 7 : 6, A., and 10 : 16, B.).—Their conviction of their own helplessness and misery as now made known to them, is so deep, their joy when the way of salvation is revealed to them is so great, and their gratitude to the Saviour so ardent, that they are eager to secure the precious gift, and, like Paul (Phil. 3 : 7–11), they are willing to sacrifice all the world and resign even life, rather than lose so mighty and precious a Saviour.

⁴⁵ Again, the kingdom of heaven is like unto a man that is a merchant, seeking goodly pearls.

A. In the former parable the case of those is illus-

trated who, like the Samaritans in John 4 : 41, 42, are awakened from their sleep of sin and conducted by divine grace to a saving knowledge of the truth, at a period when they were far from God. In this parable, on the other hand, those are introduced under the image of the merchant, who seek, but have not yet found, peace of conscience and joyful hope in God. These resemble the inquiring young man, "loved" by Jesus (Mark 10 : 21), but still lacking somewhat, or, the inquiring scribe who was," not far from the kingdom of God," but still not yet *in* it (Mark 12 : 34), or, like the penitent publican, who was still unable to rejoice in God's pardoning love (Luke 18 : 13). While the former parable may also serve as an illustration of the calling of the Gentiles (" I was found of them that sought me not, etc.," Rom. 10 : 20 and Isai. 65 : 1), the latter may, similarly, describe a devout Jew who "longed for the Salvation of God " (Ps. 119 : 174; Luke 2 : 29, 30) and then by faith found it in Christ.—
—B. **Seeking goodly pearls.** Those who are here represented may desire to practise the several Christian virtues and enjoy peace in God, but they do not yet understand that a living faith in Christ is the true source of all godliness and peace.

" And having found one pearl of great price, he went and sold all that he had, and bought it.

A. **One pearl . . . price.**—the one thing needful, namely, Christ (Phil. 3 : 8), the true way of life (John 14 : 6), and, consequently, "joy and peace in believing" (Rom. 15 : 13). This one pearl, the value of which exceeds that of all others, must be the image, not of any special Christian grace or virtue, nor of any particular doctrine, but rather of Him who is the "precious" Saviour (1 Pet. 2 : 7), the ultimate source of all truth, comfort and holiness—Christ, the crucified Redeemer

(1 Cor. 2 : 2); "Christ is all (Col. 3 : 11) and "filleth all in all" (Eph. 1 : 23).—B. **Sold, etc.** The Lord presents an inquirer to our view who is earnest and sincere, and who proves his deep sense of the value of the Saviour by renouncing all for His sake—all his former evil practices, and all his unholy inclinations and affections, which he daily (1 Cor. 15 : 31) crucifies, with watchfulness and prayer for divine aid (Gal. 5 : 24; comp. Eph. 4 : 21, ff.). —" His whole life is a sacrifice of self and the world (1 Cor. 9 : 27); it is devoted to uninterrupted watchfulness and self-examination; the inward man is renewed day by day (2 Cor. 4 : 16). Nothing is more dangerous to the believer than the opinion that he has already apprehended and was already perfect (Phil. 3 : 12-14); when he thinks that he stands and neglects to take further heed, he falls (1 Cor. 10 : 12; Gal. 6 : 3). Let us so think, feel and labor, as if we were *becoming* Christians, but had not yet experienced the work to be complete."— LUTHER.

⁴⁷ Again, the kingdom of heaven is like unto a net, that was cast into the sea, and gathered of every kind.

A. The parable of the Sower (ver. 3-8) illustrated the future history of the visible Church (ver. 3, B.). The parable of the Tares (ver. 24-30; 36-43, completed the former by revealing the ultimate result (ver. 24, A.). Several of the images in the latter (the separation of the evil from the good—the ministry of the angels), and, indeed, the very words of ver. 42 recur in the present— the parable of the Net, but the purposes of the parables are different. That of the Tares sets forth the sad truth that the Church of Christ will contain unsound members; but erring men have not the authority to remove these by violent means (ver. 29 above). The Lord Himself will effect the necessary separation on the day of judgment. The present parable of the Net is obviously designed to be a guide for the disciples themselves in their future labors. They are not commissioned to select the individuals to whom the tidings of the Gospel and the privilege of church-membership shall be offered (comp. Matt. 22 : 9), but are to preach the word to all, submitting the final result to the all-seeing Judge (comp. 2 Cor. 2 : 14-16.—**B. The kingdom**—the visible Church.—**C. Net**—a seine; its great length distinguishes such a draw-net, which swept the bottom, from the casting-net mentioned in 4 : 18.—**D. Gathered of every kind**—of fishes. "Those servants—gathered—both bad and good" (Matt. 22 : 10). Hence, an outward confession of faith, and even a moral life, while they may admit an individual to the Church, afford of themselves no complete evidence that he will also be admitted into heaven.

⁴⁸ Which, when it was filled, they drew up on the beach, and they sat down, and gathered the good into vessels, but the bad they cast away.

A. When it was filled—the end of the world. The lessons here taught, are more fully set forth by the Lord in 25 : 31-46.—**B. They . . . beach**—an image of the holding of judgment.—**C. Gathered** (see ver. 41).—**D. bad**—of a bad quality, the refuse, as small fish, etc. (see 7 : 17, B.). (The Law, when specifying the fishes that might be eaten, rejected certain kinds: "All that have not fins nor scales—shall be an abomination unto you" Lev. 11 : 10.)—**Good.** The same original words occurs in ver. 45, B.; here—acceptable, suitable, appropriate, etc., as in 3 : 10, "good fruit."

⁴⁹ So shall it be in the end of the world: the angels shall come forth, and sever the wicked from among the righteous.

See ver. 39. The angels are employed as God's ministers in executing the sentence of Him who "knoweth them that are His" (2 Tim. 2 : 19), while the office of those who preach the word is to invite all men to come to Jesus (2 Cor. 1 : 24). For **and of the world,** see 24 : 3, E.

⁵⁰ And shall cast them into the furnace of fire: there shall be the weeping and gnashing of teeth.

⁵¹ Have ye understood all these things? They say unto him, Yea.

According to ver. 18 ff. 37 ff., and particularly, Mark 4 : 34, when "they were alone, He (Christ) expounded (=interpreted, solved) all things to His disciples." In view of such previous explanations, He now asks the latter: Do ye at present perceive the spiritual import of these parables?—**Yea**=(yes) we do.

⁵² And he said unto them, Therefore every scribe, who hath been made a disciple to the kingdom of heaven is like unto a man that is a householder, which bringeth forth out of his treasure things new and old.

A. **Therefore**=such intelligence on your part is indeed essential to your future success as teachers.—B. **Every scribe**—every teacher of religion (comp. Ezra 7 : 6). The heralds of the cross are variously styled in the N. T. apostles, prophets, teachers, etc. (Matt. 23 : 34 ; Acts 13 : 1 ; 1 Cor. 12 : 28).—C. **Who is . . . heaven**=not every scribe who assumes that title, but one who is really fitted for his office. The religious teacher to whom the Gospel message is entrusted, and who is really fitted for his great work, must himself first become a true disciple, a living member of my Church.—D. **Treasure**—his deposit, stock or store of things which he regards as his most valuable possessions (see above, 6 : 19, B.). The faithful teacher of religion will strive not only to gather spiritual treasures, but also to make them available ("brought forth").—D. **Things new and old.** This phrase appears to be a proverb founded on the fact that some articles are more highly esteemed when they are fresh or *new*, as fruits, etc.; other articles, as wine (Luke 5 : 39), acquire additional value from **age**; thus, too, old friendships are esteemed to be of higher value than untried alliances. Here the Lord's words indicate the variety and great value of the spiritual treasures which a religious teacher must possess. A teacher of the Gospel who is properly prepared for his office, must be " apt to teach " (1 Tim. 3 : 2 ; 2 Tim. 2 : 24), that is, fitted by his own religious experience and a judicious course of educational training, to adapt his instructions to the wants of every individual. The Lord compares the faithful teacher to a provident and experienced householder, who judiciously and regularly supplies a household from his abundant stores, by adapting the supply in kind and in quantity to the actual wants of the respective individuals.

53 And it came to pass, when Jesus had finished these parables, he departed thence.

These parables—the discourses of which these parables formed the distinguishing feature (see PREL. OBS. to this chapter).

54 And coming into his own country, he taught them in their synagogue, insomuch that they were astonished, and said, Whence hath this man this wisdom, and these mighty works?

A. **His own country**—Nazareth and the region generally, in which He had been brought up (see 2 : 23 ; Mark 6 : 1).—B. **Insomuch . . . astonished**—at the power of His words, which unfolded divine truth in the most impressive and convincing manner, and at His miracles or the " mighty works " which He wrought.—C. **Wisdom . . . works.** *Wisdom*—through knowledge of the O. T., of its prophecies and their meaning, of the divine will, of the human character, etc.—**Mighty works** (see 7 : 22, G.). The people could not deny that in wisdom and power He excelled all others.

55 Is not this the carpenter's son? is not his mother called Mary? and his brethren, James and Joseph, and Simon, and Judas?

A. Carpenter. The Greek word here signifies specially an artificer in wood, a joiner, to whose occupation the construction of agricultural instruments, furniture, etc., also belonged.—**B. Is not, etc.**—are we not acquainted with his early history and family connections, and with the circumstance that he was not educated by our scribes and learned teachers? "Whence then, etc." (ver. 56). "Christ is the power of God, and the wisdom of God" (1 Cor. 1 : 24); the unbelief of these people, however, prevented them from seeing that "in Him are hid all the treasures of wisdom and knowledge" (Col. 2 : 3).—**C. His brother, etc.** The word *brother* is, according to the Hebrew usage, frequently applied to relatives in general (see above, 1 : 11, B.). In Matt. 28 : 10; John 20 : 17, the Lord gives that name to all His disciples. Hence, in the present case, that term by no means decides absolutely that the individuals now named were the children of Mary the Virgin. Indeed, the circumstance that Christ, the son of David, has no successor on His throne, seems to indicate that even after the flesh Christ, the son of Mary, was to be the last one of that royal line (for the term *first-born*, applied to Christ as Mary's son, see 1 : 25, A.). The relationship of these **brethren** has been variously explained; they were, according to some interpreters, the children of Joseph and Mary, born after the Saviour; according to others, they were the children of Joseph and a wife who died before his marriage with Mary; others again regard them as cousins of the Lord, nephews either of Joseph or of Mary. Of the different theories which have been suggested, the following, founded on various passages of the N. T., appears to be the most satisfactory. The testimony of the Scriptures alone, as far as it is furnished, and not tradition, can conduct to reliable conclusions. Among the women who witnessed the crucifixion (Luke 23 : 49), *four* are particularly mentioned in John 19 : 35, as having stood " by the cross of Jesus." The first is the Virgin Mary ; the second is the Virgin's sister, whose name, like that of Mary, is omitted ; the third is called Mary, the wife of *Clopas ;* the fourth is Mary Magdalene. Of the four, the second, described as " his mother's sister " (and *different from the third*, called Mary, is mentioned in Matt. 27 : 56 as " the mother of Zebedee's children "—James and John, according to 10 : 2 ; her name, as it appears from Mark 15 : 40 was Salome (see the ann. to 20 : 20, B.). As the Hebrews employed the word *sister* like *brother* in a very wide sense, Salome may have been the Virgin's full sister, or her half-sister (as in Gen. 20 : 12), or simply a relative (as in Gen. 24 : 59, 60; Job. 42 : 11 ; for Zebedee, see 20 : 20, B.). Three females named Mary are here introduced. The first is the Virgin Mary (1 : 16, B.), and the third is Mary Magdalene (see 27 : 56, A.). The second, called "the other Mary" in Matt. 27 : 61 ; 28 : 1, was " the mother of James the less and of Joses" (Mark 15 : 40; Matt. 27 : 56). (This James is called " the less"—the younger, in order to distinguish him from the other apostle James, the brother of John). The same Mary is described in John 19 : 25, as the "wife of Clopas." Now, " the brethren of the Lord " are, according to the present text (13 : 55), James, Joses, Simon and Judas (see also Mark 6 : 3; Gal. 1 : 19). These, with Mary and certain "sisters" appear, according to verses 55 and 56, and ch. 12 : 46, to constitute one family. The absence of Joseph, on all occasions in which the Virgin appears, beginning with John 2 : 1, and also the solemn commission of the Saviour who intrusted His mother to the beloved disciple (John 19 : 26, 27), in whose house she accordingly found a permanent home, prove conclusively that Mary was now not only a widow but also a childless woman. It may also be here mentioned that the ancient ecclesiastical historian Eusebius (III. 11) quotes from a still older author, Hegesippus, who asserts that Clopas was the brother of Joseph. There is no sufficient reason to doubt the historic truth of this statement, as in the age of Hegesippus (about the middle of the second century, or fifty years after the death of John the Evangelist) tradition, as distinct from history, had not yet assumed the form and character which later ages gave to it. On this basis, we assume the following to be the historical facts: Clopas, the brother of Joseph, having died, the latter, who was supposed by the ignorant to be the father of Jesus (Luke 3 : 23), assumed the care of the four sons and the daughters of his deceased brother. These supposed cousins of the Lord (but, more accurately, the nephews of Joseph only) were therefore regarded as the adopted or the true children of Joseph and Mary, and, accordingly, were commonly called his "brethren and sisters." These *brethren* (see above, 4 : 21 ann.), probably Joses and Simon, did not originally believe in Jesus (John 7 : 3, 5, 10), but immediately after the resurrection, all the brethren are believers, and are intimately associated with the eleven apostles (Acts 1 : 13, 14). This explanation is free from the embarrassment which attends a current theory, according to which "the other Mary" was the sister of the Virgin; for it is in that case difficult to explain the unusual circumstance that the two sisters should both bear the same name, without any plain distinction between them.

" And his sisters, are they not all with us ? Whence then hath this man all these things ?

A. **Whence then, ect.** (see ver. 55, B.).—B. **These things**—these lessons of wisdom, and these mighty works.

⁵⁷ And they were offended in him. But Jesus said unto them, A prophet is not without honour, save in his own country, and in his own house.

A. Offended—stumbled, in consequence of their wilful ignorance and their prejudices, and fell, or, were turned from the path of safety by unbelief and sin; the English word, as elsewhere (see 5 : 29, C.) is not to be understood in the sense assigned to it by modern usage.—**B. A prophet, etc.** (see John 4 : 44, and Luke 4 : 24). The sense of the proverb is: A feeling of jealousy, connected with a personal knowledge of an individual's early history and humble circumstances, or arising from early familiarity with him, often withholds men from yielding the tribute of admiration and reverence to which his subsequent high position really entitles him.

⁵⁸ And he did not many mighty works there because of their unbelief.

A. And he, etc. We learn from 9 : 28, 29 that the want of faith unfits an individual for the reception of divine gifts; hence the Lord could at this time heal only a few sick persons, according to Mark 6 : 5, in whom He discerned faith; all others were hardened and unprepared for the gifts of Christ.—**B. Unbelief**—not merely the actual denial of revealed truth, but a weak or wavering faith also, according to 17 : 20; Mark 9 : 24. The effects of unbelief are illustrated in Rom. 11 : 20; Hebr. 3 : 19.

CHAPTER XIV.

¹ At that season Herod the tetrarch heard the report concerning Jesus.

A. **Herod**=Herod Antipas (see 2 : 22, C.) was a son of that Herod who is mentioned in 2 : 1.—B. **Tetrarch.** This title originally belonged to a ruler of a territory constituting only the *fourth part* of a former extensive and undivided kingdom ; at a later period it was given, as in the present case, to rulers of limited territories, not possessing the rank and power of independent sovereigns. Antipas ruled over Galilee and Peræa, which, according to Josephus (Antiq. 17, 11, 4) might be considered a fourth part of his father's kingdom. The other portions of that kingdom, as it was constituted previously to the dismemberment, had been assigned to his brothers Archelaus and Philip.—C. **Report**=concerning the preaching and miracles of Jesus.

² And said unto his servants, This is John the Baptist; he is risen from the dead ; and therefore do these mighty powers work in him.

A. **His servants** ; these were probably his attendants or courtiers (comp. 18 : 23, D.), who had reported to him the conflicting opinions of the people (Mark 6 : 14-16 ; Luke 9 : 7-9).—B. **This is ... dead.** Herod's conscience smote him, as he had cruelly put that innocent and holy man to death. The rumor, therefore, that John was risen from the dead, at first alarmed him, and he anxiously desired to ascertain whether that statement was true (Luke 9 : 9); the discovery at a later period that his apprehensions were unfounded, so greatly relieved his mind, that he indulged in the most impious mockery of the Lord (Luke 23 : 8–11 ; comp. 27 : 18, *ann.*). These reports, which ignorant and unbelieving men propagated, and which identified Christ with John or with some one of the earlier prophets (thus virtually denying his character as the Messiah and the Son of God) long prevailed (Matt. 16 : 14). Moses had predicted the coming of Christ in Deut. 18 : 15, in terms which many misunderstood ; hence the Jews, long before the occurrences mentioned here, had inquired of John whether *he* was that Prophet of whom Moses spoke (John 1 : 21, 25). Afterwards many rightly applied the words of Moses to Christ (John 7 : 40), to whom, according to Peter (Acts 3 : 20–22) they did refer (see above, 11 : 14, B.).—C. **And therefore, etc.**—miraculous powers operate in him. Herod meets here the objection that John had not, like some of the ancient prophets, performed miracles (John 10 : 41), by assuming that because he had been sent back from the invisible world, *therefore* he was invested with new powers.

³ For Herod had laid hold on John, and bound him, and put him in prison for Herodias' sake, his brother Philip's wife.

A. **Laid hold**—caused him to be seized and *bound* (comp. Matt. 27 : 2 ; Acts 12 : 6 ; 21 : 33). The **prison** or place of confinement was Machærus, a fortress on the southern frontier of Peræa, not far from the mountains of Arabia (Joseph, Antiq. 14, 5, 2, and 18, 5, 2 ; War. 1, 8, 2 and 3, 3, 3).—**Herodias.** She was a daughter of Herod's half-brother Aristobulus, and had been married to Philip, another of his half-brothers (see above, 2 : 1, D.). This Philip, the son of Mariamne, daughter of Simon the high-priest, and distinct from the Philip mentioned in Luke 3 : 1 (whose mother was Cleopatra, had been disinherited by his father, and consigned to a private and obscure life). Her ambitious spirit now prompted her to forsake her unfortunate husband, the father of her daughter Salome (Jos. Antiq. 18, 5, 4) who is introduced below, ver. 6, and to marry Herod Antipas. The latter was induced by her to repudiate, without any just grounds, his first wife, the daughter of the Arabian king Aretas; thus a rapid succession of some of the most horrible crimes which can be committed was here exhibited. Herodias, who had attained her present rank and power by such flagitious conduct, regarded all with suspicion and hatred, who, like John, revered the divine laws which she had outraged. Hence she watched for an opportunity to gratify her revengeful spirit. Compare the threatening message sent by Jezebel to Elijah, 1 Kings 18 : 4; 19 : 1, 2.

⁴ For John said unto him, It is not lawful for thee to have her.

Such a marriage (in this case a combination of several crimes) was strictly forbidden by the divine Law (Mark 6 : 18; Lev. 20 : 21). Philip was still alive, and the father of the daughter of Herodias mentioned below.

⁵ And when he would have put him to death, he feared the multitude, because they counted him as a prophet.

A. **He would . . . death.** However dissolute Herod was, he still was compelled to respect the holy motives of John, who had touched his conscience (comp. Mark 6 : 20 with Luke 3 : 20); afterwards, fearing that John's censures would prove politically dangerous, he complied so far with the wishes of Herodias as to imprison him.— B. **He feared, etc.** The high estimation in which John was held by the people as a prophet (—a man sent from God, John 1 : 6; Matt. 21 : 6), intimidated the tyrant, and, for a season, prevailed even over the influence of

Herodias, who thirsted for the blood of John (Mark 6 : 19).

⁶ *But when Herod's birthday came, the daughter of Herodias danced in the midst, and pleased Herod.*

B. Birthday=distinguished by a banquet or festival, according to a custom of great antiquity.—**B. Daughter** (see above, ver. 3, B.). She abandoned her father Philip, and followed the rising fortune, as it seemed to be, of her depraved mother.—**C. Danced.** The ancient Jewish matrons and maidens, on certain occasions when great public blessings (for instance, Exod. 15 : 20; Ps. 30 : 11; Jer. 31 : 4) were commemorated, expressed their joy in the oriental method by artless and cheerful movements of the body, which were termed *dancing* in the sense of *moving rapidly in circles*, as the Hebrew indicates. In other cases, as in Exod. 3 : 4; 1 Chron. 15 : 29, the Hebrew word describes *leaping, bounding*, and is applied to the movement of a chariot rapidly driven (Joel 2 : 5). These dances, which were natural and unstudied movements of the happy, were usually performed by females alone. The present case is entirely different. At this period, dancing, according to Cicero (Pro Murœna, c. 6), who declares that it is a practice of drunkards or madmen alone, was the last act of a riotous banquet. On this occasion, no religious joy was to be expressed by Herod and his guests. The mere presence of females at such entertainments was deemed to be disreputable. And yet here the spectators (**before them**=in the middle of the banquet chamber, according to the Greek) were men, Herod's "lords, high captains, etc." (Mark 6 : 21). Salome, the dancer, the only female performer, violates all the rules of decorum observed at that time by cultivated and moral persons, and exhibits herself in the presence of men whom she, like a dancing-girl of no reputation, attempts to amuse. The dance was probably an Ionic dance, consisting of pantomimic or imitative movements; it was fashionable at that time among the degenerate Romans, whose customs the Herodian family basely imitated.

⁷ Whereupon he promised with an oath to give her whatsoever she should ask.

A. Promised with an oath—being carried away by the excitement produced by drinking. He is not justified in taking such rash oaths (for the word in the original, ver. 9, indicates that he swore repeatedly—lit. *the oath's sake*) by the circumstance that he could not have reasonably expected a request to perform so inauspicious an act as the issue of a death-warrant at his birth-day festival. Rash oaths are inconsistent with the true fear of God.— **B. Whatsoever she should ask**—" unto the half of my kingdom " (Mark 6 : 23), said the petty ruler, who was no independent king (ver. 1, B. above), as he learned at a later period, when the sentence of the Roman emperor consigned him to exile and a miserable end. In his pitiable folly he adopts the language characteristic of the mighty and absolute monarchs of an earlier age (Esther 5 : 3 ; 7 : 2).

⁸ And she, being put forward by her mother, saith, Give me here in a charger the head of John the Baptist.

A. She . . . mother. This shrewd young woman, observing that witnesses were present, and that she could consequently exact a literal fulfilment of the foolish words of the king, as far as that was possible, returned to her mother for advice, saying: "What shall I ask?" (Mark 6 : 24). The mother, herself a worldly-minded and ambitious woman, is, however, the slave of another unholy passion—the thirst for vengeance—which at present exceeds all others in power. She **instructs**

(=moves, urges, instigates) her daughter to claim, not jewels, rank, land, etc., but "the head of John the Baptist"—his immediate execution. The manner in which the implacable mother and the corrupt daughter take advantage of Herod's rash promise, show the little regard which they entertained for him personally, and is another illustration of the excessive depravity of the whole Herodian family.—**Give me here**=on the spot; the language is arrogant and imperious.—**B. Charger**= a large plate or dish, translated *platter* in Luke 11 : 39, a name originally given to a broad and flat wooden vessel, but afterwards applied to all vessels on which food was placed, without regard to the material of which they were made.

⁹ And the king was grieved: but for the sake of his oaths, and of them that sat at meat with him, he commanded it to be given.

A. The king was grieved.—for while John had offended and alarmed him by his rebuke, his own conscience told him that the act would be the murder of an innocent man (see below, ver. 10). He saw, too, that he himself was now simply the tool of a crafty woman, who could cherish no sincere affection for him; it would, besides, be impolitic and dangerous for him to slay a man revered by the people as a prophet of God (see ver. 5, B.). Herod is here and in Mark 6 : 14 termed a "king," not in the sense of an independent monarch, but merely in that of a *ruler*. In England, a certain officer under the government, who superintends the business of the heralds, is himself termed *king-at-arms*.—**B. Nevertheless, etc.** Two motives induce the tetrarch to comply; first, a misguided conscience, which was too ignorant to perceive that no rash oath can authorize the commission of a crime, and, secondly, a false shame, or fear of man; he forgot that the condition on which he had promised was not observed by Salome, who, as the original Greek word in ver. 7 implies, was to ask for herself—for her own pleasure or personal enjoyment, and also, that a failure to keep such an oath, could not possibly add a darker shade to his reputation, which was already infamous.

¹⁰ And he sent, and beheaded John in the prison.

He sent an executioner (Mark 6 : 27) who did the bloody deed by Herod's authority. It was not a legal execution of a convicted criminal but a murder; John had not received a public and fair trial, without which neither the Jewish nor the Roman law permitted any man to be punished (Deut. 17 : 6; 19 : 15; Acts 16 : 37 and 22 : 25. Compare the case of Daniel and Darius, Dan. ch. 6).

¹¹ And his head was brought in a charger, and given to the damsel: and she brought it to her mother.

Herodias gains her object; death has at length silenced the man whose head is on the plate before her. Is she now satisfied? Has her heart found peace? Does she forget that she has silenced a man, but cannot silence her divine and righteous Judge?—" We possess no relics of the *body* of John, as the Papists foolishly maintain, but we possess a relic of him which is of inestimable value, namely, the blessed *doctrine:* ' Behold the Lamb of God, which taketh away the sin of the world !"'(John 1 : 29). —LUTHER.

¹² And his disciples came, and took up the corpse, and buried it, and they went and told Jesus.

Some of John's faithful disciples were permitted to render the last honors to the headless body of their revered master; then they "told Jesus." They may have come to the Lord in order to ask Him for counsel in their bereavement, or to demand the punishment of Herod, or for the purpose of attaching themselves to the company of the Twelve.—" Heaven and earth rejoiced at the birth of John (Luke 1 : 13-16); he faithfully performed the duties of his high office, and began the blessed work of proclaiming the gospel tidings of the remission of sins through Christ, to whom he pointed (John 1 : 29). See, now, how the world rewards him! Nevertheless, John suffered no real and abiding harm, for God took him unto Himself in His own heavenly mansions, while Herod who triumphed, found his eternal home in the place of torment."—LUTHER.

¹³ Now when Jesus heard *it*, he withdrew from thence in a boat to a desert place apart: and when the multitudes heard *thereof*, they followed him on foot from the cities.

A. When Jesus . . . apart. The tidings brought by the disciples of John doubtless filled those of the Saviour also with horror and dread; the additional circumstance that at the same time Herod was instituting inquiries concerning the Lord (Luke 9 : 9), increased their apprehensions. For the purpose of calming their minds, the Lord temporarily withdrew to an uninhabited and uncultivated spot ("a mountain" John 6 : 3), where His attendants could also repose (see Mark 6 : 31). For **desert place**, see 3 : 1, D.—B. **When the multitude, etc.** These words imply that the retirement which the Lord sought, did not continue long. The intelligence soon circulated widely that He was sojourning in a certain " desert place apart," and *multitudes* from various cities began to assemble around Him. He had gone by water; the people went around " on foot "—by land, at the head of the lake; some appear from Mark 6 : 33 to have reached the vicinity of the designated spot before the arrival of others. The narrative of John (John 6 : 4) accounts for these large numbers by indicating that they constituted the ordinarily large companies of Jews who were on their way to Jerusalem in order to celebrate the passover. The circumstance that the people had gone considerably out of their way, and had been detained for some time, explains the fact that all were now without provisions.

¹⁴ And he came forth, and saw a great multitude, and was moved with compassion toward them, and healed their sick.

A. **He . . . forth**—when He found so many hearers assembled, He came forward, and then "began to teach them many things" respecting the kingdom of God (Mark 6 : 34; Luke 9 : 11). The locality was in the vicinity of Bethsaida (Luke 9 : 10; see Matt. 11 : 21, B.).— B. **Moved with compassion** (see 18 : 27, A.).—C. **Healed their sick**=whom they had brought for that purpose to Him, as in 4 : 24; 8 : 16.

¹⁵ And when even was come, the disciples came to him, saying, The place is desert, and the time is already past; send the multitudes away, that they may go into the villages and buy themselves food.

A. **Evening**=late in the day (Mark 6 : 35), towards sunset (Luke 9 : 12). The Jews, according to the mode adopted by the Pharisees, distinguished between the "two evenings" (see margin of English Bible at Exod. 12 : 6; Numb. 9 : 3; 28 : 4) in the following manner:— The *first* evening commenced with the declining sun, or about two o'clock in the afternoon; the *second* evening commenced at the time when the sun was setting, or about six o'clock. Between these two points of time, or about three o'clock, or later, the daily evening sacrifice was offered (see Deut. 16 : 6, and comp. Joseph. War. 6, 9, 3, and Antiq. 14, 4, 3). The evening specified here is the former; but the latter is meant in ver. 23 below, and in John 6 : 16.—B. **The time**=usual time for taking the evening meal; or, possibly—a large part of the day is already gone, as in Mark 11 : 11. The disciples express their apprehensions lest the thousands who were present (ver. 21), if not immediately dismissed, might suffer through the night from the want of food and of places of lodging.

^{16, 17} But Jesus said unto them, They have no need to go away; give ye them to eat.—And they say unto him, We have here but five loaves, and two fishes.

These two verses contain the substance of the conversation more fully related in Mark 6 : 37, 38; John 6 : 5–9. The Lord was *proving* (John 6 : 6) His disciples, that is, the strength of their confidence in His wisdom and resources, and thus educating them when He said: "Give ye, etc." Possibly He designed to indicate to them His own boundless resources by employing the very words of an ancient prophet on a similar occasion (2 Kings 4 : 42–44). The sense of ver. 17, according to John 6 : 8, 9, is: No one here is supplied with food for himself, still less for this vast multitude, with the exception of one lad who has with him five barley-loaves. (For **loaves** see 26 : 26, B.) Barley, as distinct from wheat, was usually the food only of the poorer classes of the Jews. It is frequently mentioned in the O. T. in connection with wheat, but rye and oats (for which latter barley was used, 1 Kings 4 : 28) are not mentioned in the Scriptures. " No doubt both Philip, who calculated the value of the bread which such a multitude would need, and Andrew, who pronounced the case hopeless, followed the light of human reason. We, however, who are Christians, ought not to be governed by that feeble light exclusively, but to remember that we possess a far brighter and more cheerful light in the unerring word of God. (2 Peter 1 : 19.) "—LUTHER.

¹⁸ He said, Bring them hither to me.

The Lord implies that His power will suffice to supply the deficiency. The disciples, who say: "*We* have, etc." (ver. 17), had doubtless paid the lad for the provisions (John 6 : 9) from their common purse or bag (John 12 : 6; 13 : 29).

¹⁹ And he commanded the multitudes to sit down on the grass, and he took the five loaves, and the two fishes, and looking up to heaven, he blessed, and brake, and gave the loaves to the disciples, and the disciples to the multitudes.

A. And He commanded, etc. According to Mark 6 : 39 and Luke 9 : 14, the people are arranged and recline on the grass in regular companies or messes, in order that the disciples might conveniently pass through the ranks and supply every individual. System and order in all affairs, both temporal and spiritual, constitute, as the Lord's example here shows, a part of man's religious duty (1 Cor. 14 : 33, 40).—**B. Looking . . . blessed.** John says (6 : 11): "given thanks" (comp. Matt. 15 : 36). Both terms are equivalent to the phrase : *pronounced a blessing* (see below, 26 : 26, C.)=invoked God, in gratitude and faith claimed His blessing; the former possibly designated that the words assumed the form or character of a consecrating prayer to God, asking Him to sanctify the object (1 Tim. 4 : 5); the latter, that the words were those of *grateful* praise (1 Tim. 4 : 4). According to the devout custom of the Jews, before every meal the head of the family gave thanks to God for the food before him, by pronouncing a prayer termed "the blessing." The Saviour by His example here and on other occasions (Matt. 15 : 36; 26 : 26; Luke 24 : 30), sanctions and perpetuates the practice in the Christian Church (see Acts 27 : 35; 1 Tim. 4 : 3-5).—**Brake** (see 26 : 26, B. and D.). **C. Gave the loaves** (lit. *the breads*=the pieces of bread)

to His disciples, etc. The barrel of meal and the cruse of oil mentioned in 1 Kings 17 : 16, and the pot of oil (2 Kings 4 : 2–6), like the "twenty loaves of barley, and full ears of corn" (2 Kings 4 : 42), furnished a full supply as long as a want remained unsatisfied. The same almighty power which in these cases continually renewed the bread and oil, was exercised by the Saviour, who continued to distribute from the five loaves and the two fishes, until His disciples ceased to come for more (see Ps. 145 : 16).

²⁰ And they did all eat, and were filled; and they took up that which remained over of the broken pieces, twelve baskets full.

In the midst of this abundance of food, the Saviour, according to John 6 : 12, taught a lesson of frugality, by commanding that the broken pieces of the food which God's bounty gave, and for which no demand was now made, should be reverently and thankfully preserved for future use. The quantity which remained, and which was the evidence that all were fully satisfied (Ruth 2 : 14), exceeded the original supply, and is specified as an illustration of the greatness of the miracle. The *baskets* were ordinary Jewish travelling-baskets, used as receptacles for food, etc., and were possibly transferred to the Twelve by individuals belonging to the multitudes which were on the road to Jerusalem.

²¹ And they that did eat were about five thousand men, beside women and children.

On the subsequent occasion (15 : 38) there were four thousand men. The women and children who were also present, but whose numbers cannot be estimated with any degree of confidence, are here distinguished from the men. The latter doubtless constituted the great majority on this occasion (see above, ver. 13, B.); for, although Mary, like many devout women (compare an analogous case in 1 Sam., ch. 1), accompanied Joseph, when the latter visited Jerusalem at the feast of the passover (Luke 2 : 41), it was the prescribed duty of the men only to visit Jerusalem at those times (Exod. 23 : 17).

²² And straightway he constrained the disciples to enter into the boat, and to go before him unto the other side, till he should send the multitudes away.

A. **Constrained the disciples**—as they were unwilling to leave Him alone with the people.—**Straightway**—*immediately* after having collected the remains of the food.—B. **To go before him**—by water (the sea of Galilee) to a point designated by Him, probably between the western Bethsaida (Mark 6 : 45) and Capernaum (John 6 : 17), which lay not far apart (ver. 34). For Bethsaida see 11 : 21, B.—C. **While he, etc.** The Lord had two motives in dismissing the people on that evening; the first was derived from their tumultuous efforts to proclaim Him as their temporal king (John 6 : 15), the second, from His desire to spend a season in secret prayer (see next verse).

²³ And after he had sent the multitudes away, he went up into the mountain apart to pray: and when even was come, he was there alone.

A. **Apart to pray, etc.** The example of the Saviour, to whose *private devotions* the evangelists continually refer (for instance, Luke 3 : 21; 5 : 16; 6 : 12; 9 : 28; Mark 1 : 35; Matt. 26 : 39) while illustrating His command in Matt. 6 : 6, is also a solemn admonition to all to remember that " men ought always to pray, and not to faint (Luke 18 : 1; 1 Thess. 5 : 17).—B. **The even**—the second evening (see above, ver. 15).

²⁴ But the boat was now in the midst of the sea, distressed by the waves: for the wind was contrary.

The night had now arrived, and the disciples, whose vessel had been driven far from its proper course (" contrary winds "), " toiled in rowing " (Mark 6: 48); towards morning they are exhausted by their labor. The eye of the Lord, who had passed several hours in communion with His Father, turns to them in love, and He brings divine aid.

²⁵ And in the fourth watch of the night he came unto them, walking upon the sea.

A. Fourth watch. Before the Babylonian Captivity, the Jews were accustomed to divide, for municipal and military purposes, the night, or the period between sunset and sunrise into three watches only; the first is mentioned in Lament. 2 : 19; the middle watch, in Judges 7: 19; the third or morning watch, in Exod. 14 : 24; 1 Sam. 11 : 11. The Romans, on the other hand, divided the night for military purposes (changing the guard, relieving sentinels, etc.), into four shorter divisions. Thus each quaternion or company of four soldiers mentioned in Acts 12 : 4, was on duty three hours. The name itself (=*guard*) indicates a military origin. This division was adopted by the Jews when they passed under the dominion of the Romans (or after the year 63 B. C. when Pompey, the Roman general, took Jerusalem); it is mentioned in Mark 13 : 35. The first night-watch extended from six o'clock or sunset to nine o'clock; the second to midnight; the third to three o'clock; the fourth, to six o'clock in the morning. The third is mentioned in 26 : 34, B. For the *hours* (see 20 : 3, B.).—**B. He walking, etc.** The sublime description of God's majesty and power by Job (ch. 9) contains the words: He "treadeth upon the waves (lit. *high places*=high waves) of the sea " (ver. 8). But here that divine glory is really beheld. At the Red Sea (Exod. 14 : 21) a miracle was performed; " The waters saw thee, O God ;—they were afraid (Ps. 77 : 16). So, too, the waters of the Jordan obeyed the divine word of Him who "did wonders" (Josh. 3 : 5, 16; see also 2 Kings 2 : 8, 14; 6 : 6). God's control over nature is described in the words : " He did fly upon the wings of the wind " (Ps. 18 : 10); " The Lord hath His way in the whirlwind and the storm" (Nahum 1 : 3). Here the waters furnish an occasion for exhibiting the lofty attributes of the Son of God, " by whom all things were made" (John 1 : 3) and who has "all power" (Matt. 28 : 18).

²⁶ And when the disciples saw him walking on the sea, they were troubled, saying, It is an apparition; and they cried out for fear.

A. **Saw him walking**—on the surface of the water, and nearly in the direction of the vessel (John 6 : 19 comp. with Mark 6 : 48), as no ordinary mortal could do. At that moment the approaching daylight enabled them to see objects at a distance, but not to distinguish the features.—B. **Troubled.** an expressive word, indicating deep distress or even consternation (comp. Matt. 2 : 3; Luke 1 : 12; John 14 : 1).—C. **A spirit.** Any appearance which is supposed to be supernatural, particularly in the night, will necessarily create wonder and fear (comp. Job 4 : 13–15 and Rev. 1 : 17), and, generally, the appearance of angels; for instance, Luke 1 : 12, 29; 2 : 9.

²⁷ But straightway Jesus spake unto them, saying, Be of good cheer; it is I; be not afraid.

The Lord tranquillizes the alarmed disciples by assuring them that their fears are unfounded; **it is I**—it is no other than your Master, Jesus, whom ye now see in the flesh (Hebr. 5 : 7). In every danger or trial faith in Christ gives strength and confidence to the heart, proclaiming : It is the Lord ! He is at hand !—**be . . . cheer** (see 9 : 2, F.).

²⁸ And Peter answered him and said, Lord, if it be thou, bid me come unto thee upon the waters.

A. And Peter, etc. This apostle entertained an ardent affection for the Saviour; the relief which he experienced when he heard the well-known voice of his Master, was indescribably great, and he could no longer control the impetuosity of his character (comp. 26 : 33, A.).—**B. Lord, if, etc.**—confirm all my delightful hopes that thou art near, by calling me to Thy side. Peter is rapid in his movements, but not foolishly adventurous.

²⁹ And he said, Come. And Peter went down from the boat, and walked upon the waters, to come to Jesus.

A. Come; the Lord's answer, which granted permission, implies that no unholy eagerness nor presumption governed Peter; still, its brevity may also indicate the sense to be: Peter, this trial of thy faith is thine own choice, not mine: if thou findest sufficient faith in thy heart, then *come.*—**B. Walked, etc.**—his faith temporarily prevailed (comp. Matt. 17 : 20). "If ye have faith —nothing shall be impossible to you."

³⁰ But when he saw the wind, he was afraid; and beginning to sink, he cried out, saying, Lord, save me.

A. Saw the wind. For a moment *he looked away from Jesus*, and dwelt more on the danger which threatened him than on the divine power which could control the "proud waves" (comp. Job 38 : 11). As soon as this thought took possession of his soul, and fear arose— a fear stronger than his faith—*he began to sink.*—**B. Save me.** The Lord had once before (Matt. 8 : 25, 26) heard the same cry, which betrayed indeed a *weak* faith, but still it was an appeal to the right source for help, and was not the language of actual unbelief.

³¹ And immediately Jesus stretched forth his hand, and took hold of him, and saith unto him, O thou of little faith, wherefore didst thou doubt?

A. Immediately . . . him=before the waves had entirely covered Peter. The latter might appropriately say: "Thy right hand hath holden me up" (Ps. 18 : 35).—**B. Of little faith** (see 8 : 26, B.).—**C. Wherefore, etc.**— why, after exercising faith and actually walking on the water, didst thou waver, or hesitate to proceed and trust to My power and grace? The expressive Greek word translated **doubt,** describes a conflict between two opposite emotions; here, faith in Christ struggles with the fear of perishing in the waters. The word again occurs in 28 : 17.

³² And when they were gone up into the boat, the wind ceased.

As in 8 : 26, the presence and power of the Saviour calm the raging winds. That divine presence alone can truly tranquillize the troubled conscience, and give peace to the soul.

³³ Then they that were in the boat worshipped him, saying, Of a truth thou art the Son of God.

A. They ... worshipped him—as one entitled to divine honor. For **worship** (see 2 : 2, D.). The rapid succession of the miraculous works—feeding 5000 men, walking on the sea, rescuing Peter, and coercing the storm —revealed a power over nature which none but God could wield. Some of the persons on the vessel, however, were amazed, but manifested a stupid astonishment rather than an enlightened faith (Mark 6 : 51, 52).—**B. Of a truth;** the one Greek word so translated here, is rendered *truly* in 27 : 54; *indeed*, in John 4 : 42; *verily*, in John 2 : 5. In all such cases it is an asseveration expressive of a strong conviction of the mind that the words convey truth (comp. 16 : 16, D.) for a still fuller confession of faith.—**C. Son of God** (see 3 : 17, B., and 8 : 29, C.).

³⁴ And when they had crossed over, they came to the land, unto Gennesaret.

Gennesaret was an unusually rich and fertile plain or

district of Lower Galilee, on the northwest or west side of the lake of that name, the region in which Bethsaida and Capernaum were situated (Joseph. War. 3, 10, 8). It is somewhat more than three miles in length and two in breath.

³⁵ And when the men of that place knew him, they sent into all that region round about, and brought unto him all that were sick.

The *men of that place* eagerly availed themselves of the opportunity to seek the blessings of Christ for themselves and others; they are evidently governed not by a mere selfish desire to receive benefits, but by that living faith in Christ which gives Him glory, and without which, according to 13 : 58, the present miracles would not have been wrought.

³⁶ And they besought him that they might only touch the border of his garment : and as many as touched were made whole.

A. **Besought him.** This expression does not imply that the Lord had manifested any unwillingness to relieve the sick, but indicates, as we learn from Mark 6 : 55, 56, that He declined at this time to remain long in one spot (comp. His own explanation in a similar case, Luke 4 : 42, 43).—C. **Made whole**—*healed*, as in Luke 7 : 3. The conduct of these people and the result show that they exercised faith ; the sower found here good ground, but the ultimate result of these labors of the Lord is not specially recorded.

CHAPTER XV.

¹ Then there came to Jesus from Jerusalem Pharisees and scribes, saying,

THE events which immediately followed those described in the foregoing chapter, appear to be recorded in John 6 : 21–71. Afterwards, while the Lord still remained in Galilee (John 7 : 1), the incidents occurred which are now related. The **Phrisees and scribes** here introduced as seeking Jesus in Galilee (evidently with an evil design), resided in the city of Jerusalem; any accusation made by them, as the most learned and eminent of the whole land, necessarily assumed a very grave character.

² Why do thy disciples transgress the tradition of the elders? for they wash not their hands when they eat bread.

A. Mark adds (ch. 7 : 2–4), various explanatory remarks.—B. **Tradition of the elders**—religious precepts derived from the earlier religious teachers, but not found in the word of God (see 5 : 21, D.).—**Eat bread**—the Hebrew phrase for taking an ordinary meal (Gen. 31 : 54; 37 : 25; 43 : 25; Mark 3 : 20). The laws of Moses contained numerous directions respecting the mode of cleansing those who had contracted any legal defilement (see Lev., ch. 11; ch. 15; Numb. ch. 19). But no command had been given that every Jew should wash his hands before each meal; the words in Exod. 29 : 4; 30 : 18–21; 40 : 12, referred only to officiating priests, and those in Lev. 15 : 11 to a special case. The practice had, however, become widely prevalent (even among the Persians,

Greeks and Romans), as it was customary for those at the table to "dip their hands" in the same dish (comp. Matt. 26:23; John 13:26), and convey food to the mouth with the fingers. The description in Mark 7:1-4, exhibits the Pharisaic mode of perverting by hypocritical acts a laudable practice, which, as far as the observance of personal cleanliness was concerned, our Lord naturally observed. So, too, according to Matt. 17:24 ff., He paid the tribute required in Exod. 30:13, and in ver. 3-6, below, He does not *forbid*, but desires only to *regulate* the religious custom of contributing to the temple. He distinguishes between obedience to God's laws and self-righteous practices of our own invention. The Lord knew that they ascribed to these human devices a higher sanctity than they did to the divine Law itself, and hence He refrained designedly from adopting them (comp. Luke 11:38 and Matt. 9:14, C.). His disciples imitated His example. The scribes and Pharisees who here introduce the subject, believe that they have now found an opportunity to present the Lord to the people as an irreligious person.

³ And he answered and said unto them, Why do ye also transgress the commandment of God because of your tradition?

Why, etc.—you charge My disciples and, indirectly, Me with transgressing mere human regulations which have no authority; but I, on the other hand, with better reason, accuse you of a real and very grievous sin—the transgression of the commandment of your Maker.—**Ye also**—*even* you, as the word here translated *also*, is often rendered (e. g. 8:27; 25:29). The Lord designs to show that their tradition (called their *doctrine*, 16:12), as a system, deserved no respect, and that, in some cases, they impiously set divine commands at naught (Mark 7:8).

⁴ For God said, Honour thy father and thy mother: and, He that speaketh evil of father or mother, let him die the death.

A. For God=who gave the law through Moses; the direct divine origin of the Mosaic law is thus demonstrated.—**B. Honor thy, etc.** (Exod. 20 : 12).—**He that speaketh evil of father, etc.** (Exod. 21 : 17; Lev. 20 : 9; Prov. 20 : 20; 28 : 24; 30 : 17).—**Die the death**—an English imitation of the Hebrew idiom, meaning, He shall *surely* (without any hope of escape) be put to death (see above, 13 : 14, C.). The Lord establishes the truth from the inspired writings, that positive divine commands exist respecting the duties of children to their parents, which no frivolous and hypocritical human rules can set aside without deep guilt.

⁵, ⁶ But ye say, Whosoever shall say to his father or his mother, That wherewith thou mightest have been profited by me is given to God; he shall not honour his father. And ye have made void the word of God because of your tradition.

A. Profited . . . to God=that, which ye, my parents, desire me to give to you for your personal benefit, I have consecrated to God, and therefore I cannot bestow it on you (Mark 7 : 11). The original Hebrew word is *Corban*, which repeatedly occurs in the O. T. (Lev. 1 : 2; 2 : 1; Numb. 5 : 15; Ezek. 20 : 28), and designates any *sacrifice* or *offering* brought to the temple; hence it was applied in its Greek form to the *treasury* (27 : 6). According to the tradition here quoted, when impoverished parents claimed aid or subsistence from their children, the latter were excused from the duty which nature and the revealed law imposed on them, if they vowed, or transferred to the priests, such things as the parents claimed.—**Honour**=requite (1 Tim. 5 : 4).—**B. Made void, etc.**—ye have, therefore, not only not obeyed an acknowledged divine command, but also presumed to

xv. 7-9.] CHAPTER XV. 363

disannul it, thus impiously, claiming for yourselves a higher authority than God Himself.

⁷ Ye hypocrites, well did Isaiah prophesy of you, saying,

A. Hypocrites (see 6 : 2, D.).—**B. Well**=justly, accurately (comp. Acts 28 : 25).—**C. Isaiah**—through whom God Himself spake (Isai. 29 : 13).—**D. Of you**=of the class of persons to which you belong (see 13 : 14, A.). The prophet, whose words, even when addressed to his contemporaries during the reign of Hezekiah, often referred to the times of the Messiah also, may have, in the Spirit, specially described both the men of his age and also those whom the Lord here addresses.

⁸ This people honoureth me with their lips; but their heart is far from me.

A. Me=God is the speaker; " the Lord said " (Isai. 29 : 13; comp. Hebr. 1 : 1). **B. This people**=of Jerusalem, called Ariel (Isai. 29 : 1).—**C. Honoreth . . . lips** =they employ, indeed, the language of religion, when they come to the temple (comp. James 4 : 8). The Hebrews often used the words *mouth, lips, tongue*, in the sense of *words, sayings*, etc. (e. g. Deut. 17 : 6).—**D. But their heart, etc.**—the feelings of their hearts, and their will, are turned away from me to the world and sin; hence their religious professions are insincere. Ye *profess* reverence before God, by calling your own inventions religious acts, but your spiritual pride, your want of love and faith, and your unholy sentiments prove that your worship of God is only a mockery (comp. Ezek. 33 : 31).

⁹ But in vain do they worship me, teaching as their doctrines the precepts of men.

A. But . . . Me=such a heartless worship I reject totally (comp. Isai. 1 : 10-15).—**B. Teaching, etc.**— when you substitute a formal worship and mere human inventions for the devout worship of the heart and holiness of the whole character. The sense of the words is the same as that of the original in Isai. 29 : 13, the language of which is somewhat modified. Both passages rebuke the sin of adopting a religion of human contrivances and forms, and then omitting " the weightier matters of the law, judgment, mercy and faith " (Matt. 23 : 23).—**Teaching as their doctrines,** lit. *teaching teachings*=exclusively teaching, not God's, but man's wisdom.

¹⁰ And he called to him the multitude, and said unto them, Hear, and understand.

Hearing, without understanding and without self-application, is of no avail (see 13 : 19). The Lord, turning away from the hardened scribes and Pharisees, who were overwhelmed and silenced by such an exposure, or, perhaps, after their departure, now teaches the people the true doctrine respecting uncleanness and sin in the eyes of God.

¹¹ Not that which entereth into the mouth defileth the man; but that which proceedeth out of the mouth, this defileth the man.

A. **Not . . . defileth the man.** The sense, according to ver. 20. is: It is no sin in the eyes of God to eat food without observing the Pharisaic ordinances respecting the washing of the hands. " There is nothing unclean of itself " (Rom. 14 : 14 ; 1 Tim. 4 : 4). But the other extreme of " surfeiting and drunkenness," which results from a depraved heart, *is* a sin to which the Lord refers in terms of solemn warning in Luke 21 : 34.—**Defileth.** The Greek word, which properly signifies *to make common*, as in Acts 2 : 44, is often used in the N. T. (corresponding to a Hebrew word signifying *to profane, stain, pollute* (Lev. 19 : 8; Isai. 23 : 9)), in a Levitical sense, namely, to render unclean or unholy ceremonially (see Acts 21 : 28; Hebr. 9 : 13; Rev. 21 : 27). In this Jewish sense the word *common* was applied to objects that were not ceremonially clean, holy, consecrated to God and His service (comp. Mark 7 : 2); where it is translated *defiled*. In Acts 10 : 14; 11 : 8 (where it is translated *common*) it is explained as meaning in the Jewish sense *unclean*, impure. **B. But that, etc.**—that, on the other hand, which renders man really unclean and offensive in the eyes of God, consists in the unholy and wicked feelings of the heart.

¹² Then came the disciples, and said unto him, Knoweth thou that the Pharisees were offended, when they heard this saying?

A. **Then . . . said**—after the Lord had entered the house (Mark 7 : 17). The Lord's answer (ver. 14) indicates that the disciples apprehended danger from the Pharisees.—B. **Offended . . . this saying**—in ver. 11. For the word **offended** see 5 : 29, C. Here, too, it signifies, not *were displeased*, but as in 13 : 57, doubtless *stumbled;* the sense is: They were led by that saying, which set aside the Jewish principles respecting clean and unclean things, to fall into the sin of reproaching the Lord as a despiser of religion. Or, it may mean here: They regarded the doctrine as offensive, scandalous.

¹³ But he answered and said, Every plant which my heavenly Father planted not, shall be rooted up.

Every plant—every human doctrine or device (which, namely, does not come from God), and, also, its adherents (comp. "branch" in John 15 : 2). The Lord doubtless refers to the words of the parable in 13, 30, 38, 40. The sense is: The doctrines are tares which will be destroyed. They themselves may temporarily prevail, but they are not "of God" (1 John 3 : 10), and therefore they and their unholy and soul-destroying doctrines shall ultimately be extirpated. The apostles subsequently taught that even when error does prevail, the believer has no real cause of alarm; there will be false teachers, who promulgate "doctrines of devils" (1 Tim. 4 : 1), but "the

Lord shall consume them with the spirit of His mouth " (2 Thess. 2 : 8).

[14] Let them alone: they are blind guides. And if the blind guide the blind, both shall fall into a pit.

A. **Let them alone**—do not regard them with apprehension; the same word in 13:30, in the same sense, is translated **Let.**—B. **Blind**—while they attempt to keep the pathway of religion, they are really ignorant of the truth, in consequence of the evil state of their heart, and thus they mislead all who are guided by them (comp. 23:16, ff.). The Lord, in allusion to Isai. 3:12; 9:16, declares that sin, while its influence is pernicious to others, reacts on itself, and proves to be its own destroyer. That the Lord refers, not to an inevitable blindness, but to one that results from obstinacy or wilful unbelief, appears from John 9: 39–41.—C. **Pit.** The sense of the proverb as here applied, is: They and their deluded adherents will destroy themselves.

[15] And Peter answered and said unto him, Declare unto us the parable.

Declare—the spiritual meaning, not of the words in ver. 14, but of the "saying" in ver. 11, as the Lord's answer in ver. 17–25 clearly shows. Peter, who had been educated as a Jew, does not appear to have obtained perfectly clear views of the subject until at a later period (Acts 10:14). He and his fellow-disciples were then taught by the Spirit that, in the Church, believers are not required to observe the ceremonial laws (Acts 15 : 5–11; Col. 2 : 16, 17; Hebr. 10:1); much less could inventions of men bind their conscience.

[16] And he said, Are ye also even yet without understanding?

Said, etc.—Are ye even yet (=at this point of time when ye have heard so many Gospel truths) unable to see the spiritual meaning of my words? Again was this rebuke needed in 16:9-12; comp. a similar reproach addressed to those who are "dull of hearing" (Hebr. 5:11, ff.).

¹⁷ Perceive ye not, that whatsoever goeth into the mouth passeth into the belly, and is cast out into the draught?

The sense is: Do ye not yet see my true meaning, namely, that the human *body* alone needs food, but that the living *soul* neither eats nor drinks? Can ye not see that the food of which ye partake, passes through the ordinary process of digestion, but cannot defile the inner man (=render your hearts unclean) since "it entereth not into the heart" (Mark 7:19=the mind or soul)?

¹⁸ But the things which proceed out of the mouth come forth out of the heart; and they defile the man.

A. But . . . heart—that which really renders man unclean in the eyes of God, is the evil in his "inward part" (Luke 11:39)—his heart, his moral nature as distinct from his bodily frame.—**B. They**=the sins of the heart defile man (Jerem. 17:9).

¹⁹ For out of the heart come forth evil thoughts, murders, adulteries, fornications, thefts, false witness, railings:

A. The heart—the soul, the seat both of the intellect and the affections; the term (13:19, B.), according to the Hebrew usage, includes the *understanding* (which, without divine grace is "darkness," Acts 26:18; 2 Cor. 4:4; Eph. 1:18), the *affections*, the *conscience* and the *will* (Gen. 6:5; 8:21; comp. Eph. 2:1-3; Ps. 52:5). The doctrine of Original Sin, or the entire corruption of human nature, is here plainly taught. The heart of the unrenewed man can produce naught but evil (comp. John 3:6; Rom. 5:12; Job 14:4).—**B. Evil thoughts, etc.,** comp. 9:4. The Lord specifies only a few of the many sins which men commit, as illustrations of the different forms of evil, some consisting in thoughts, others in words, others in feelings or emotions or desires, and others again in outward actions. All these are sins, and all originate in the corrupt heart or nature of man.

⁰ *These are the things which defile the man: but to eat with unwashen hands defileth not the man.*

A. These—*such* things; the *sins* of man, not articles of *food*, are offensive in the eyes of God.—**But to eat, etc.,** " Every creature of God, etc." (1 Tim. 4:4).—**Unwashen hands**=not ceremonially purified; the words obviously do not refer to merely soiled hands; the act of cleansing them in such a case, like that of putting suitable garments on the body was a matter of course; see ver. 2, B.

²¹ *And Jesus went out thence, and withdrew into the parts of Tyre and Sidon.*

A. Went out thence—being exposed to the persecutions of the Pharisees, which He desired to avoid for a season.—**B. Withdrew into**=retired, in a north-western direction, to the *vicinity* of Tyre, etc., but without actually entering the heathen territory from which the woman came before she addressed Him (ver. 22, and Mark 7:24). The **parts**—the portions of land where the boundary line between Galilee and Phenicia passed (see ver. 22, B.). For **Tyre** and **Sidon**, see 11:21, C.

²² *And, behold, a Canaanitish woman came out from those borders, and cried, saying, Have mercy on me, O Lord, thou Son of David; my daughter is grievously vexed with a devil.*

A. A Canaanitish woman; she was " a Greek, a Syrophenician by race " (Mark 7: 26). These various names are thus explained:—the ancient Phenicians, to whose country Tyre and Sidon belonged, were the descendants of Sidon, a son of Canaan (Gen. 10: 15, 19); the occupants of that portion of the coast of the Mediterranean Sea, long retained the common name of Canaanites which they bore in the age of Moses (Numb. 13: 29; Judges 1:

30, 31; Ps. 135 : 11). Phenicia itself was, in the course of time, attached to the Roman province of Syria (Acts 21 : 2, 3) and was called Syrophenicia, in order to distinguish it from the original Syrian territory, and also from that of the Libyophenicians in Africa, who occupied the territory of Carthage. At the Christian era, the Greek language and Greek manners, which had been generally introduced at the period of the conquests of Alexander the Great, predominated in the country. All these appellations indicate that the woman was emphatically a Gentile or *heathen.*—B. **Have mercy ... David** (comp. 9 : 27 and 1 : 1, C.). The woman was not a descendant of Abraham, and the terms in ver. 26 indicate that she was not even a proselyte (23 : 15, C.). Still, she had, like many others, heard of the gracious words and deeds of Jesus (Mark 7 : 25), and, as the issue reveals, already entertained a clear and earnest faith in Him (" faith cometh by hearing " Rom. 10 : 17) as the Messiah whom the Jews expected. " Have mercy on me." " She calls after Christ on the street, she follows Him into the house (Mark 7 : 24). Is she not a bold, presumptuous suppliant? Nay, all this is written for our own encouragement and consolation, and teaches us that it is precisely such boldness or earnestness in prayer, which gives, most pleasure to Christ "—LUTHER.—D. **Grievously, etc.**= miserably *possessed with a devil,* as the Greek word is elsewhere rendered, for instance (4 : 24; 8 : 16).

²³ **But he answered not a word. And his disciples came and besought him, saying, Send her away; for she crieth after us.**

A. **But he ... word**=neither consenting nor refusing, as, indeed, he appears to have done at first also in 9 : 27. In such cases the Lord's delay in answering doubtless proceeded not only from His desire to direct the attention of those around Him to such eminent faith as an

24

example for them, but also to exercise and deepen the individual's faith by such a trial (see above, 9 : 22).—**B. Disciples besought, etc.** The word *besought* (which occurs in the parallel passage, Mark 7 : 26), here seems to indicate the following as the sense of the words of the sympathizing disciples, who did not know the Lord's real motive :—Master, listen to her continued and earnest cries of distress; relieve and dismiss her graciously. There is no reason to think that, like the unjust Judge (Luke 18 : 5), they wished merely to be freed from importunate solicitations.

[24] But he answered and said, I was not sent but unto the lost sheep of the house of Israel.

If this answer of the Lord was directed primarily to the disciples, as indeed the tenor of the narrative indicates, it alludes to His words in 10 : 5, 6. He sometimes exercised and proved His disciples by such sayings (John 6 : 6), and here apparently intended to prepare them for the future extension of the blessings of the Gospel to the heathen world (Acts 10 : 34, 35). The present instance demonstrated to them in a most touching manner that, while the Jews were, after the flesh, the "children of the covenant" (Acts 3 : 25), nevertheless, the misery and helplessness of the Gentile world also appealed loudly to divine mercy : " for there is no difference between the Jew and the Greek, etc." (Rom. 10 : 12, and comp. Rom. 3 : 23 and 29; 1 Tim. 2 : 4; Ps. 145 : 9). The sense of the Lord's words is, not that the Gentiles were excluded from the enjoyment of His gifts (8 : 7, B.), but that His own personal labors were to be confined chiefly to the Holy Land (hence Paul calls him "a minister of the circumcision," Rom. 15 : 8), and that the blessings which resulted from these labors, were to be afterwards extended to the Gentile world. Comp. John

12 : 32 ; Rom. 15 : 8-12 ; see below, 18 : 11, B. for the word **lost**.

²⁵ But she came and worshipped him, saying, Lord, help me.

The woman knew well that she possessed no claims, and was only a poor, helpless heathen. Still, is *He* not as merciful as He is mighty? Has He not befriended others who were also helpless, miserable, sinful creatures? Her eagerness, her hopes, seem to urge her forward ; she kneels down before Him ("worshipped," see 2 : 2, D.), and faith inspires the simple but affecting prayer: Lord, help me.

²⁶ And he answered and said, It is not meet to take the children's bread, and cast it to the dogs.

Meet—good, proper, suitable (3 : 8, B.). There are cases in which divine *wisdom* exposes faith to trials that seem unusually harsh, but divine *love* has really chosen such a form of the trial. The actual death of Lazarus, and the deep affliction in which Martha and Mary were plunged by it, may seem to our erring sight to have been very rude trials, and yet all was designed "for the glory of God, etc." (John 11 : 4). The trial of this woman is also illustrated by the wrestling of Jacob with the angel (Gen. 32 : 24 ff.). In that awful contest the former was taught to feel his own insignificance when the latter touched his thigh. At that moment, when Jacob was deeply humbled, he resorted to the only weapons (2 Cor. 10 : 4 ; 1 Tim. 1 : 18, 19), which prevail with God, for we learn from Hosea 12 : 4, that he now abased himself before God ("wept") and prayed ("made supplication"). So, too, while this woman's faith had so far exhibited the essential features of earnestness, strength and perseverance, it was yet needful that her faith should manifest the attribute of profound humility ; and doubtless, as the angel's touch, thrilling in the whole frame of Jacob, prostrated his self-reliance and taught him to appeal to mercy alone, so the Saviour's words, thrilling in the woman's soul, expelled the last lingering feeling of carnal pride, and enabled her faith to shine forth in all its lustre. In the East the dog was not valued for his fidelity, but regarded only as a rapacious and unclean animal; hence his name was sometimes applied to man as a term of bitter reproach (1 Sam. 17:43; 2 Sam. 3:8; 2 Kings 8:13; Isai. 66:3; see above, 7:6, B.). In such a sense the Jews contemptuously compared heathens to dogs, and regarded themselves alone as "the household of God" or His "children." When a proverb is quoted, it is usual to employ the well-known words, even if the speaker would himself have chosen less harsh words (comp. 2 Peter 2:22). The Lord here, for wise and gracious purposes, quotes this proverbial language of the Jews, which was excessively offensive to heathens, and therefore adapted to subdue the woman's human pride and impatience. Its very harshness may have also led the Saviour to quote it, while He intended to act in opposition to it, in order to make the disciples feel how inappropriate it really was. But doubtless the tender tones of the Saviour's voice, the winning expression of His countenance, and the softened Greek word for **dogs** (here, a diminutive, equivalent to *little* dogs), all combined, like the colors of the rainbow while dark clouds still spread their gloom over portions of the sky, to teach the woman still longer to hope and to believe.

[27] But she said, Yea, Lord: for even the dogs eat of the crumbs which fall from their master's table.

This "saying" of the woman was a triumphant exhibition of faith, for, according to Mark 7:28, it instantly prevailed. The incident mentioned in Luke 16:21, combined with the woman's additional remark as recorded in

Mark 7 : 28 ("the children's crumbs") present the scene of children who have eaten abundantly, and now cheerfully feed little dogs. The sense of the woman's words then is: Yea, O Lord, *it is* meet to aid me! I do not presume to rob the Jews of their privileges; but then, even according to Thine own words, when the children have been fed, there are crumbs remaining, which no one refuses to the dogs. Thou art rich in power and mercy; even when Thou grantest all blessings to the Jews, Thou canst still help me.

²⁸ Then Jesus answered and said unto her, O woman, great is thy faith: be it done unto thee even as thou wilt. And her daughter was healed from that hour.

A. Then—when the fiery trial of her faith was "found unto praise and honor and glory" (1 Pet. 1 : 7; 4 : 12), and a brilliant example of faith and perseverance in prayer, or of "effectual fervent prayer" (James 5 : 16) had been given, not only to the spectators, but also to all succeeding generations.—**B. O woman . . . faith** (comp. Matt. 8 : 10), where a similar instance of faith in a heathen is described. The *greatness* of the woman's faith, whose "praise is of God" (Rom. 2 : 29) consisted in the happy combination of all the essential features of true faith, namely, clear views of Christ's character, or a certain amount of religious *knowledge* (respecting His power, grace, etc.), entire, unquestioning and humble *submission* to the Lord's will (thankful even for crumbs), and unshrinking *reliance* (she is never discouraged, but is confident that she will prevail). **C. Be it . . . wilt** (see 8 : 13, B.). The Christian can never "ask a hard thing" (2 Kings 2 : 10), that is, provided his faith be an enlightened and living faith; to such the Saviour declares that "nothing shall be impossible" (17 : 20). The unconditional offer made to Solomon, but which God desired him to receive with corresponding holy sentiments (1 Kings 3 : 5, 11), is now extended to all *believing* Christians (Matt. 7 : 7, C.; 21 : 22); for these are taught by the Spirit *how* to pray, and *what* they should pray for (Rom. 8 : 26).—D. **And her daughter, etc.** The Saviour's power, as in 8 : 13 and John 4 : 46–53, extended in all its fulness to the distant spot where the daughter was suffering from the unclean spirit (Mark 7 : 29). And even now, the believer's experience in the use of the means of grace, reveals to him the Saviour's invisible presence and power in "quenching all the fiery darts of the wicked."

²⁹ And Jesus departed thence, and came nigh unto the sea of Galilee; and he went up into the mountain, and sat there.

A. **Thence**=from the region of Tyre and Sidon.—B. **Sat**=waiting, and ready to confer His blessings on the people.

³⁰ And there came unto him great multitudes, having with them the lame, blind, dumb, maimed, and many others, and they cast them down at his feet; and he healed them.

Scenes like the present, in which the Saviour heals diseases and bodily infirmities of every form, often occur (see 4 : 23–25; 8 : 16; 14 : 34–36). The sick, whose bodily affections presented only a painful sight, are **cast down**—hastily deposited at Jesus' feet, implying the eagerness of their friends to secure the Lord's aid. Indeed, the only place where we ever can find health of the soul and salvation, is at the feet of Jesus, before whom every knee shall bow (Phil. 2 : 10).

³¹ Insomuch that the multitude wondered, when they saw the dumb speaking, the maimed whole, and the lame walking, and the blind seeing: and they glorified the God of Israel.

A. **Wondered . . . glorified.** Mere wonder at the mighty works of God, without serious reflection and self-examination, is not religion. Moses *wondered* when he saw the burning bush, but he also sought for further knowledge (Acts 7:31; Exod. 3:2, 3). Simon the sorcerer, on the other hand, wondered too when he beheld the miracles of Philip, but retained his vicious and unholy character (Acts 8:6, 13, 23). Here, as in Matt. 9:8, the spectators not only wonder, but they also **glorify** God, that is, ascribe honor and praise to Him.—B. **The God of Israel**—they rejoiced that the God whose people they were (Ps. 100:3) was so great and glorious. **Israel**, one of the names of the nation (see 8:10, C.), was derived from the patriarch Jacob called Israel, when his faith had prevailed (Gen. 32:28).

³² And Jesus called unto him his disciples, and said, I have compassion on the multitude, because they continue with me now three days and have nothing to eat: and I would not send them away fasting, lest haply they faint in the way.

A. **I have compassion** (18:27, A.). The sense is, that during the three days all the provisions had been gradually consumed, not that they had eaten nothing during three days (comp. Acts 27:33). If these people were returning home after the passover, the season of the year allowed them to pass two nights in the open air without serious inconvenience.—B. **They continue, etc.** The locality in which the following miracle was performed, was in the region of Decapolis (Mark 7:31), for which see 4:25, B. It was at a considerable distance from the scene of a miracle of a similar character (14:14, A.). There is a reference to both in 16:9, 10. While the Lord provided for the spiritual wants of His hearers, He mercifully considered those of the body also.

³³ And the disciples say unto him, Whence should we have so many loaves in a desert place, as to fill so great a multitude.

The Lord had not, in the course of the training of the

disciples, accustomed them to expect miracles on every occasion. Thus, in 12: 1, He did not appease their hunger by extraordinary means. The occurrence in 16:7 also teaches us that He desired them to observe the ordinary rules of human precaution, rather than continually and presumptuously to expect the miraculous interposition of God (comp. also Luke 8:3: John 13:29). Here, then, on the one hand, they refrain from asking for a repetition of the former miracle, as in 14:15, ff.; but on the other, they fail to manifest a ready comprehension of their Master's purpose as indicated in His words.

³⁴⁻³⁸ And Jesus saith unto them, How many loaves have ye? And they said, Seven, and a few small fishes. And he commanded the multitude to sit down on the ground. And he took the seven loaves and the fishes, and gave thanks, and brake, and gave to the disciples, and the disciples to the multitudes. And they did all eat, and were filled: and they took up that which remained over of the broken pieces seven baskets full. And they that did eat were four thousand men. beside women and children.

See 14:17-21. Some of the circumstances (a small supply of bread and fishes, the arrangement of the people on the ground, the giving of thanks, the distribution, the abundance of food, the preservation of the fragments) greatly resemble those which occurred on the former occasion. Others are different: the disciples themselves here produce their own provisions, the number of the males (4,000) is smaller, etc.; possibly the quantity of the fragments which remain after all are fed, is nearly the same. The **baskets** both here and in 16: 10 bear a Greek name different from that of those mentioned on the former occasion; the relative size, which their names do not indicate, is not known. As the *basket* mentioned in Acts 9:25, in which Paul was let down by the wall, was one of the kind here mentioned, these seven may possibly have been of a larger size than the twelve in 14:20. "What a mighty Lord He is! See how many trades He carries

on without human help! He ploughs, sows, harvests, threshes, grinds, bakes, and sets the table almost in the same moment! What a Lord we have in Christ!"— LUTHER.

⁹⁹ And he sent away the multitudes, and entered into the boat, and came into the borders of Magadan.

Magadan was situated on the western side of the sea. Dalmanutha (Mark 8 : 10), of which no trace is now known, was doubtless a village or town in the same region.

APPENDIX

EXCURSUS I.

KINGDOM, *of heaven—of God—of Christ—of the Father*. § 1. The word *kingdom* sometimes stands alone; Matthew generally introduces the phrase: *kingdom of heaven*, while Mark, Luke (both in his gospel and in the Acts), John in his gospel, and Paul in his epistles, employ that of *kingdom of God*. The fundamental idea expressed by all these terms, wherever they occur, is that of *the divine authority, as exclusively and cheerfully acknowledged by intelligent creatures;* such an acknowledgment establishes a state of security and of holy joy in consequence of the communion with the blessed God to which it conducts.

§ 2. The Jews had long been familiar with the conception of God as their king, in the sense of *Supreme Ruler* (1 Sam. 12 : 12), to which relation of God to the Jewish people the term *Theocracy* alludes=a government administered immediately or directly by God Himself; the term appears to have been introduced by Josephus, c. Ap. II. 16 (17). The prophets also represent God as the king or ruler of all the nations of the world: they then teach not only that He in reality possesses all dominion and power, but also that when his authority shall be generally understood and *recognized* at a future time (namely, after the Messiah has appeared), He will, in the fullest sense, be the king over all (Isai. 2 : 1-4); then will "the kingdoms of this world become the kingdoms of our Lord, and of His Christ" (Rev. 11 : 15). This point is distinctly stated in Dan. 2 : 44: "The God of heaven shall set up a kingdom which shall never be destroyed." Daniel proceeds to explain in ch. 7 : 14, 27, that this kingdom is that of the Messiah=of Christ. The same truth is elsewhere taught (Ps. 2 : 6; Jer. 23 : 5; Mic. ch. 4; Zech. 14 : 9; Ezek. 37 : 24).

§ 3. An earthly kingdom (as Lisco remarks in his work on the Parables, in his Introduction, § 6), presents four distinguishing features:—(1) A ruler or head; (2) Subjects, members of the state; (3) A leading policy or general system or spirit of government; (4) A distinctly defined and prescribed system of laws. These particulars, in such a combination, furnish an image of God's kingdom. (1) He is the Supreme Ruler; (2) His intelligent creatures, angels and men, viewed as subjects, constitute the noblest part of His kingdom; (3) That kingdom *comes* (Matt. 6: 10), or is erected and established in proportion as the divine authority becomes known and is acknowledged and duly obeyed; for its leading object or general purpose, namely, the glory of God revealed in the happiness of His creatures, is then manifested or realized. (4) Its great principle of law is love (Matt. 22: 37-40; Rom. 13: 8, 10) not only in this world, but also in the eternal world (1 Cor. 13: 8); and *that* law is set forth in the Holy Scriptures. Now this kingdom, in which love is the eternal law, is made perfect and complete, when the divine will meets with no further opposition, but is obeyed heartily, exclusively, completely, and forever, that is to say, when sin and death are completely overcome, and salvation and eternal blessedness constitute the portion or condition of the members of the kingdom.

§ 4. This kingdom is called, first, the kingdom *of God*, or, *of the Father*; the term indicates its general nature, its origin, etc; secondly, the kingdom *of Christ*, its immediate Head (Eph. 1: 20, 23), who is *one* with the Father (John 10: 30; Phil. 2: 9-11; Hebr. 1: 6); thirdly, the kingdom *of heaven*, in order to indicate its divine character, or its spiritual nature (John 18: 36, 37) as distinct from a perishable world, and also to express its purity, holiness, eternity, etc.; fourthly, *the kingdom*, to indicate that it alone exists legitimately, truly, and eternally.

§ 5. As God, the Creator, who is almighty and omnipresent, can enforce His will in all places, His kingdom, in the widest sense, "ruleth over all" (Ps. 103: 19), that is, over all space, over all creation, over heaven, earth, and hell. So, too, God is the Father of all (Mal. 2: 10), inasmuch as He gave life to all men; still He is called *Father* in a special sense, as when we say: "Our Father," in the Lord's Prayer, referring pre-eminently to our adoption through Christ as His children by faith (Rom. 8: 15). In the same restricted sense, "the kingdom of God" is a phrase not so much including the entire widely extended dominion of God, as rather, indicating *that* portion of it in which he is gladly recognized as the Lord, sincerely revered and worshipped, and ardently loved. In this sense the prophet Obadiah (ver. 21) says: "The kingdom shall be the Lord's." We may therefore say, that "the kingdom of God" is a phrase implying the existence of an intimate and happy communion between God's intelligent creatures and Himself, in whatever part of His empire those creatures may be found. The term can also designate, or be the name of, any institution which God may be pleased to devise and grant for the purpose of restoring that union between Himself and men, which sin had destroyed.

§ 6. The subjects or members of the kingdom of God are, first, the holy angels, who love, obey, and adore God; secondly, believers on earth, who, having received Christ in faith, are governed willingly and exclusively by the divine will, and in this sense, the kingdom of God is the Gospel kingdom (Matt. 6 : 33; 21 : 43; Acts 1 : 3); thirdly, "the spirits of just men made perfect" (Hebr. 12 : 23), that is, the redeemed in heaven, deceased "saints," who will accompany the Lord at His final coming to judgment (1 Thess. 3 : 13). For by all these the authority of God is recognized and truly revered, and they are happy in their communion with God.

§ 7. Now as the distinguishing features of the true subjects of the kingdom are, for instance, knowledge, love, obedience (see Rom. 14 : 17), this kingdom is not of a material, earthly character (John 18 : 36), but from its very nature belongs to the spiritual world; in this respect it is *invisible* (Luke 17 : 21; 1 Cor. 4 : 20). Nevertheless, in as far as true believers, while they are renewed and sanctified by the divine Spirit (CoL 1 : 13; Matt. 13 : 38), although no longer *of* the world, are still *in* the world, according to 1 John 4 : 5, 17, therefore the kingdom as an institution designed to bless and save men, is also in the world and among men, and is capable of being a *visible* kingdom.—The kingdom of God, if we may employ as an image, an earthly kingdom which has been enlarged by the recovery of a long-lost province, extended anew its borders when this world, long alienated from its God, was reclaimed by Christ, or will extend them when this world, by a renovating and sanctifying process, shall be fully annexed to those portions of the kingdom which remained faithful to the great King.

§ 8. Those who repent and believe are required to confess Christ before men (Matt. 10 : 32, 33), and by all possible means sustain the great instrumentality by which men are turned to God and maintained in the faith, namely, the preaching of the word (Mark 16 : 15; Acts 26 : 17, 18; Hebr. 10 : 25). Further, they are uniformly required to be baptized and to commemorate the Lord's death in the Holy Supper, of which the Acts and the Epistles furnish numerous illustrations. Their union on earth as disciples of Christ, constituting an organized society, resulted in the establishment of the visible kingdom of Christ on the day of Pentecost (see Acts 2 : 47; 8 : 1; 15 : 22; 1 Cor. 14 : 4). This *Church*, consisting of the true disciples of Christ, is termed the "body" of Christ, He being the head (Eph. 1 : 22, 23; 5 : 25-27; Col. 1 : 18, 24). Thus the Church "is the congregation of all believers, among whom the Gospel is preached in its purity, and the holy sacraments are administered according to the Gospel." Hence the Church of Christ is frequently called *the kingdom of God*, especially in the Parables (Matt. 5 : 19; 13 : 24, 31, 33, 47), since in it, through the means of grace (by which the Divine Spirit operates on the individual), the communion between God and man is restored; it is the divinely appointed medium through which men are conducted to heaven, wherefore it is called "the pillar and ground of the truth" (1 Tim. 3 : 15, 16). Now when the Church, thus viewed as the kingdom of God, is mentioned in reference to its purity, holiness, etc., the invisible Church is meant (see above, § 7); at other times, its visible organization, or its living members are specially the objects to which reference is made, and then the visible Church is meant.

§ 9. Now, this material world will come to an end (2 Pet. 3 : 10, 11), but the people of God will forever occupy the mansions in heaven which Christ has prepared for them (John 14 : 2). Then the kingdom of God, which at present counts human beings on earth among its members, will consist solely of inhabitants of heaven (as far as we have disclosures in the Scriptures), that is, the holy angels and the redeemed; all these will enjoy eternal bliss and glory in the presence of God. In this special sense the "kingdom" is sometimes mentioned in the N. T. (Matt. 25 : 34; Acts 14 : 22; 1 Cor. 15 : 50; 2 Tim. 4 : 18; Hebr. 12 : 28; James 2 : 5).

§ 10. The term: *Kingdom of*, etc. (while the fundamental idea of communion with God, flowing from a cheerful recognition of His authority is retained), is specially the kingdom of Christ, that is to say, it proclaims His atoning and redeeming work, commenced on earth and developed in its whole glorious extent in eternity. It may be defined, according to the connection in which it occurs, and the peculiar aspect in which it is viewed, in the following different modes, of which the parables of the Lord Jesus furnish many illustrations:—

(a) In its general sense, as shown above, it embraces angels and men, who love and obey God as their king, and it includes time and eternity (Luke 1 : 33).

(b) In a restricted sense, including human beings only, it designates living and departed saints, believers on earth and saints in heaven. All these form one kingdom, having one King whom they love and obey, or are governed by one Law—Love—which prompts to obedience. A distinction is sometimes made between the Messiah's kingdom of grace on earth (Matt. 19: 23), and the kingdom of glory in the eternal world (2 Tim. 4 : 18).

(c) Sometimes, in reference to earthly relations, the Church (16 : 18, D.) is meant in a special sense, viewed as the divinely appointed means for establishing a communion between men and God, including the old covenant which prepared the way for the new and better covenant (20 : 1, B.).—In some cases the visible Church in its whole extent is meant (Matt. 13 : 3, 19, 24, 31, 41, 47), consisting of all who confess Christ on earth, independently of their internal or spiritual state, and viewed only as Christians in distinction from Jews and Gentiles, infidels, etc. Thus, in Matt. 22 : 2-14, the "kingdom of heaven" (ver. 2) includes the man who had not on a wedding-garment (ver. 11; Col. 4 : 11). In other cases, the invisible Church, consisting of true believers alone, is specified; these alone constitute the true Church (Acts 1 : 3; 8 : 12), while many hypocrites and impenitent sinners are connected with the visible Church (comp. Matt

13 : 24 ff. with ver. 38, and see Matt. 5 : 20; 6 : 33; 11 : 11; 13 : 33; Luke 9 : 62; Col. 1 : 13; Rom. 14 : 17).

(d) The future state of the redeemed exclusively, as they exist in heaven, is sometimes meant. In such cases the Church is viewed in its eternal and heavenly fruits or results as the true realization, development, and completion of the kingdom of God. That kingdom, therefore, in this aspect, begins on earth, but is revealed in its bliss and glory only in the eternal world (Matt. 5 : 3, 10; 7 : 21; 8 : 11; 13 : 43; 25 : 1, 34; 26 : 29; Acts 14 : 22; 1 Cor. 6 : 9, 10; 15 : 50; Gal. 5 : 21; Eph. 5 : 5; 2 Tim. 4 : 18; James 2 : 5; 2 Pet. 1 : 11.)—The whole phrase, therefore, while the one fundamental conception stated above is always expressed by it, adapts itself to the various changes which necessarily occur in the spiritual state of a fallen creature like man, who must pass from spiritual death to spiritual life, and be transferred at last from this fleeting world to one that is eternal, before all the gracious purposes of God are fully attained.

EXCURSUS II.

DEMONIACS. The Greek word *demon* (*daimon, daimonion*, which the Greeks applied to any of their imaginary propitious or unpropitious gods or beings belonging to the invisible world) in the N. T. designates one of the evil spirits or fallen angels (Matt. 25 : 41; Eph. 6 : 11, 12; 2 Pet. 2 : 4) who, with their head, Satan (Mark 1 : 13), "the God of this world" (John 12 : 31; 2 Cor. 4 : 4; 1 Pet. 5 : 8), constitute a kingdom (Matt. 12 : 26), and produce all the moral and physical evils in the world (John 8 : 44; 1 John 3 : 8, 12). The fall of man (Gen. ch. 3; 2 Cor. 11 : 3; Rev. 12 : 9) was equivalent to his separation from God, the only source of bodily and spiritual life, health and happiness. Hence, not only was his moral nature thereby depraved, but his body became subject to sickness and death (Rom. 5 : 12 ff.). Even inanimate nature shared in the consequences of the curse of God which followed Adam's fall (Gen. 3 : 17; Rom. 8 : 20, 21). Thus man became exposed in his spiritual affairs to the assaults and dominion of Satan, and his bodily frame also shared in this awful result of sin. With regard to the *demoniacs*, that is, "persons possessed by demons"=by unclean or evil spirits, many points are not revealed to us; indeed, even in cases in which no direct agency of such beings occurs, as in dreams, madness, etc., the reciprocal action or the reaction of the body and the mind, and the peculiar movements of the soul and its faculties, present mysteries, which no one can, from the nature of the subject, fully unfold. Thus, among the demoniacs mentioned in the N. T., we find persons of both sexes, of various ages and conditions, etc. ;—for instance, a young female (Matt. 15 : 22), a boy or child (Matt. 17 : 18), two men (Matt. 8 : 28). Some, as in these last two cases, indicate extreme mental derangement : but the woman mentioned in Luke 13 : 11, 16, appears to have suffered from "the spirit of infirmity" or "Satan" only in her bodily organization. We cannot, for want of revealed facts, which we do not possess, decide whether such individuals had been more guilty of gross vice than others, or whether other causes produced such startling results. Neither can we explain all the incidents, the purposes of the demons, their immediate subsequent history, etc., to which the case in Matt. 8 : 28 ff. directs attention; nor can we always declare positively whether the words proceeding from the mouth of a demoniac were uttered with a consciousness of his personal identity (Matt. 8 : 29), or whether, while he himself was unconscious (as when persons speak in their sleep), the words and thoughts proceeded from the indwelling evil spirit (Mark 5:9; Luke 4 : 34; 9:39; Acts 16:16 ff.).—The following truths, on the other hand, are deduced with certainty from the N. T. The cases of the demoniacs were not simply those of ordinary diseases, epilepsy, etc., as the language and deportment of Christ and of the evangelists demonstrate (Matt. 9 : 32; 17 : 21; Mark 1 : 25; 9 : 25; Luke 4 : 35; and see Acts 10 : 38; 16 : 18). Satan and his angels do exercise a certain degree of power in the world over the souls of men when not shielded by divine grace (John 13 : 2, 27; Acts 5 : 3; 2 Cor. 4 : 4; Eph. 2 : 2; 2 Tim. 2 : 26) over their bodily nature (Matt. 17 : 15; Luke 13 : 16; Acts 5 : 16; 10 : 38; 1 Cor. 5 ; 5), and also over other objects; see ann. to 8 : 26, C.). Divine wisdom tolerates these and other evils for holy purposes; but this pernicious influence of Satan is already so greatly abridged (Luke 10 : 18; Acts 26 : 18; Rom. 16 : 20) that it ceases to be formidable to those who seek divine aid (James 4 : 7; Eph. 6 : 10 ff.; Col. 1 : 13; 1 Pet. 5 : 9). When the gracious plans of God shall have reached their consummation, Satan's whole power to harm God's creatures will be abolished entirely and forever (Hebr. 2 : 14; 1 John 3 : 8; 2 Thess. 2 : 8; Rev. 20 · 10, 14).

www.ingramcontent.com/pod-product-compliance
Lightning Source LLC
Chambersburg PA
CBHW022116290426
44112CB00008B/695